A/CN.4/SER.A/2008/Add.l (Part 1)

YEARBOOK OF THE INTERNATIONAL LAW COMMISSION

2008

Volume II
Part One

Documents of the sixtieth session

UNITED NATIONS
New York and Geneva, 2014

NOTE

Symbols of United Nations documents are composed of capital letters combined with figures. Mention of such a symbol indicates a reference to a United Nations document.

References to the *Yearbook of the International Law Commission* are abbreviated to *Yearbook* ..., followed by the year (for example, *Yearbook ... 2008*).

The *Yearbook* for each session of the International Law Commission comprises two volumes:

Volume I: summary records of the meetings of the session;

Volume II (Part One): reports of special rapporteurs and other documents considered during the session;

Volume II (Part Two): report of the Commission to the General Assembly.

All references to these works and quotations from them relate to the final printed texts of the volumes of the *Yearbook* issued as United Nations publications.

*

* *

The reports of the special rapporteurs and other documents considered by the Commission during its sixtieth session, which were originally issued in mimeographed form, are reproduced in the present volume, incorporating the corrigenda issued by the Secretariat and the editorial changes required for the presentation of the final text.

A/CN.4/SER.A/2008/Add.l (Part 1)

UNITED NATIONS PUBLICATION

Sales No.: E.13.V.3 (Part 1)
ISBN: 978-92-1-133809-6
e-ISBN: 978-92-1-055965-2

ISSN: 0082-8289

CONTENTS

ABBREVIATIONS

ASEAN	Association of Southeast Asian Nations
EBRD	European Bank for Reconstruction and Development
EC	European Community
EEC	European Economic Community
EU	European Union
FAO	Food and Agriculture Organization of the United Nations
GATS	General Agreement on Trade in Services
IAEA	International Atomic Energy Agency
IASC	Inter-Agency Standing Committee
ICAO	International Civil Aviation Organization
ICJ	International Court of Justice
ICPO–INTERPOL	International Criminal Police Organization
ICRC	International Committee of the Red Cross
IDRL	International Disaster Response Laws
IFRC	International Federation of Red Cross and Red Crescent Societies
ILC	International Law Commission
IMCO	Intergovernmental Maritime Consultative Organization (now IMO)
IMF	International Monetary Fund
IMO	International Maritime Organization
IOM	International Organization for Migration
NATO	North Atlantic Treaty Organization
NGO	non-governmental organization
OAS	Organization of American States
OAU	Organization of African Unity
OCHA	Office for the Coordination of Humanitarian Affairs
OECD	Organization for Economic Cooperation and Development
OPCW	Organization for the Prohibition of Chemical Weapons
PCIJ	Permanent Court of International Justice
TRIPS	Agreement on Trade-Related Aspects of Intellectual Property Rights
UNECE	United Nations Economic Commission for Europe
UNESCO	United Nations Educational, Scientific and Cultural Organization
UNHCR	Office of the United Nations High Commissioner for Refugees
UNITAR	United Nations Institute for Training and Research
UPU	Universal Postal Union
WHO	World Health Organization
WTO	World Trade Organization

*

* *

AC	Appeals Court
AFDI	*Annuaire français de droit international* (Paris)
AJIL	*American Journal of International Law* (Washington, D.C.)
BYBIL	*The British Year Book of International Law* (London)
ECHR	European Court of Human Rights
GC	Grand Chamber
I.C.J. Reports	ICJ, *Reports of Judgments, Advisory Opinions and Orders*
I.C.J. Pleadings	ICJ, *Pleadings, Oral Arguments, Documents*
ILM	*International Legal Materials* (Washington, D.C.)
P.C.I.J., Series A	PCIJ, *Collection of Judgments* (Nos. 1–24: up to and including 1930)
P.C.I.J., Series B	PCIJ, *Judgments, Orders and Advisory Opinions* (Nos. 1–18: up to and including 1930)
P.C.I.J., Series A/B	PCIJ, *Collection of Advisory Opinions* (Nos. 40–80: beginning in 1931)
SLR	*Sri Lanka Law Reports*

UKHL	United Kingdom House of Lords
UNRIAA	United Nations, *Reports of International Arbitral Awards*
U.S.C.	United States Code
WLR	*Weekly Law Reports*

*

* *

In the present volume, the "International Tribunal for the Former Yugoslavia" refers to the International Tribunal for the Prosecution of Persons Responsible for Serious Violations of International Humanitarian Law Committed in the Territory of the Former Yugoslavia since 1991.

*

* *

NOTE CONCERNING QUOTATIONS

In quotations, words or passages in italics followed by an asterisk were not italicized in the original text.

Unless otherwise indicated, quotations from works in languages other than English have been translated by the Secretariat.

*

* *

The Internet address of the International Law Commission is **www.un.org/law/ilc.**

FILLING OF CASUAL VACANCIES IN THE COMMISSION (ARTICLE 11 OF THE STATUTE)

[Agenda item 1]

DOCUMENT A/CN.4/602

Note by the Secretariat

[*Original: English*]
[*3 June 2008*]

1. Following the resignation of Mr. Ian Brownlie, effective 8 August 2008, one seat will become vacant on the International Law Commission.

2. In this case, article 11 of the Statute of the Commission is applicable. It prescribes that:

> In the case of a casual vacancy, the Commission itself shall fill the vacancy having due regard to the provisions contained in articles 2 and 8 above.

Article 2 reads:

> 1. The Commission shall consist of thirty-four members who shall be persons of recognized competence in international law.
>
> 2. No two members of the Commission shall be nationals of the same State.
>
> 3. In case of dual nationality a candidate shall be deemed to be a national of the State in which he ordinarily exercises civil and political rights.

Article 8 reads:

> At the election the electors shall bear in mind that the persons to be elected to the Commission should individually possess the qualifications required and that in the Commission as a whole representation of the main forms of civilization and of the principal legal systems of the world should be assured.

3. The term of the member to be elected by the Commission will expire at the end of 2011.

RESERVATIONS TO TREATIES

[Agenda item 2]

DOCUMENT A/CN.4/600

Thirteenth report on reservations to treaties, by Mr. Alain Pellet, Special Rapporteur*

[*Original: French*]
[*20 May 2008*]

CONTENTS

Multilateral instruments cited in the present report

	Source
Convention on the Political Rights of Women (New York, 31 March 1953)	United Nations, *Treaty Series*, vol. 193, No. 2613, p. 135.
European Convention on Extradition (Paris, 13 December 1957)	*Ibid.*, vol. 359, No. 5146, p. 273.
Convention on the Continental Shelf (Geneva 29 April 1958)	*Ibid.*, vol. 499, No. 7302, p. 311.
International Covenant on Economic, Social and Cultural Rights (New York, 16 December 1966)	*Ibid.*, vol. 993, No. 14531, p. 3.
Treaty for the Prohibition of Nuclear Weapons in Latin America (with annexed Additional Protocols I and II) (Mexico, Federal District, 14 February 1967)	*Ibid.*, vol. 634, No. 9068, p. 281.
Vienna Convention on the law of treaties (Vienna, 23 May 1969)	*Ibid.*, vol. 1155, No. 18232, p. 331.
International Convention for the prevention of pollution from ships, 1973 (MARPOL Convention) (London, 2 November 1973)	*Ibid.*, vol. 1340, No. 22484, p. 184.
Protocol of 1978 relating to the International Convention for the prevention of pollution from ships, 1973 (London, 17 February 1978)	*Ibid.*, p. 62.
Convention on the prevention and punishment of crimes against internationally protected persons, including diplomatic agents (New York, 14 December 1973)	*Ibid.*, vol. 1035, No. 15410, p. 167.
United Nations Convention on the Law of the Sea (Montego Bay, 10 December 1982)	*Ibid.*, vol. 1833, No. 31363, p. 3.

* The author gratefully acknowledges the major role played by Daniel Müller in the preparation of this report. Mr. Müller is the author of the commentary on articles 20 and 21, in Olivier Corten and Pierre Klein, eds., *Les Conventions de Vienne sur le droit des traités: commentaire article par article* (English edition to be published in 2011 by Oxford University Press).

	Source
Vienna Convention on the Law of Treaties between States and International Organizations or between International Organizations (Vienna, 21 March 1986)	A/CONF.129/15.
United Nations Convention against Illicit Traffic in Narcotic Drugs and Psychotropic Substances (Vienna, 20 December 1988)	United Nations, *Treaty Series*, vol. 1582, No. 27627, p. 95.
Basel Convention on the control of transboundary movements of hazardous wastes and their disposal (Basel, 22 March 1989)	*Ibid.*, vol. 1673, No. 28911, p. 57.
Convention on the rights of the child (New York, 20 November 1989)	*Ibid.*, vol. 1577, No. 27531, p. 3.
Framework Convention for the protection of national minorities (Strasbourg, 1 February 1995)	*Ibid.*, vol. 2151, No. 37548, p. 243.
International Convention for the Suppression of Terrorist Bombings (New York, 15 December 1997)	*Ibid.*, vol. 2149, No. 37517, p. 256.

Works cited in the present report

Buzzini, Gionata Piero

"Abstention, silence et droit international général", *Rivista di diritto internazionale*, vol. LXXXVIII, No. 2, 2005, pp. 342–382.

Drost, Heinrich

"Grundfragen der Lehre vom internationalen Rechtsgeschäft", *in* D. S. Constantopoulos and H. Wehberg, eds., *Gegenwartsprobleme des internationalen Rechtes und der Rechtsphilosophie: Festschrift für Rudolf Laun zu seinem siebzigsten Geburtstag.* Hamburg, Girardet, 1953, pp. 213–221.

Horn, Frank

Reservations and Interpretative Declarations to Multilateral Treaties. The Hague, T.M.C. Asser Instituut, 1988. 514 p. (Thesis, University of Uppsala, Sweden).

McNair, Lord

The Law of Treaties. Oxford, Clarendon Press, 1961. 789 p.

McRae, D. M.

"The legal effect of interpretative declarations", *BYBIL*, 1978, vol. 49, pp. 155–173.

Müller, Daniel

"Convention de Vienne de 1969: article 20" and "Convention de Vienne de 1969: article 21", *in* Olivier Corten and Pierre Klein, eds., *Les Conventions de Vienne sur le droit des traités: commentaire article par article.* Brussels, Bruylant, 2006, pp. 797–875 and pp. 883–929.

Rousseau, Charles

Droit international public. Vol. I. Introduction et Sources. Paris, Sirey, 1970. 464 p.

Salmon, Jean, ed.

Dictionnaire de droit international public. Brussels, Bruylant, 2001. 1198 p.

Sapienza, Rosario

Dichiarazioni interpretative unilaterali e trattati internazionali. Milan, Giuffrè, 1996. 291 p.

Reactions to interpretative declarations

1. The "provisional plan of the study"[1] does not mention the issue of States' and international organizations' reactions to interpretative declarations. This is because it was not originally intended that such reactions should be considered together with reservations; not until later did the desirability of a parallel study of reservations and interpretative declarations become clear.[2]

2. The Vienna Convention on the law of treaties (hereinafter the 1969 Vienna Convention) and the Vienna Convention on the Law of Treaties between States and International Organizations or between International Organizations (hereinafter the 1986 Vienna Convention) make no reference to interpretative declarations—which were touched upon only briefly in the *travaux préparatoires* for those texts[3]—and thus say nothing about reactions to interpretative declarations, the forms they may take, the procedure for formulating them or their effects. Accordingly, the scarcity or uncertainty of practice in this area makes it necessary to take an approach that differs from the one adopted in considering the issue of objection to and acceptance of reservations.[4] As the Commission has already noted in its work on interpretative declarations:

> In view of the lack of any provision on interpretative declarations in the 1969 and 1986 Vienna Conventions and the scarcity or relative uncertainty of practice with regard to such declarations, they cannot be considered in isolation. We can only proceed by analogy with (or in contrast

[1] Second report on reservations to treaties (*Yearbook ... 1996*, vol. II (Part One), document A/CN.4/477 and Add.1), p. 48, para. 37; see also the seventh report (*Yearbook ... 2002*, vol. II (Part One), document A/CN.4/526 and Add.1–3), p. 9, para. 18.

[2] See the fifth report on reservations to treaties (*Yearbook ... 2000*, vol. II (Part One), document A/CN.4/508 and Add.1–4), p. 181, paras. 217–218.

[3] See the third report on reservations to treaties (*Yearbook ... 1998*, vol. II (Part One), document A/CN.4/491 and Add.1–6), pp. 238–239, paras. 64–68.

[4] See the twelfth report on reservations to treaties (*Yearbook ... 2007*, vol. II (Part One), document A/CN.4/584), p. 35, para. 3.

to) reservations, taking great care, of course, to distinguish conditional interpretative declarations from those that are not conditional.[5]

3. In the light of these remarks, it is important not to overlook the differences between reservations and interpretative declarations, which are not intended to produce the same legal effects on the treaty: while a "reservation", by definition, purports "to exclude or to modify the legal effect of certain provisions of the treaty in their application to that State or to that international organization",[6] an interpretative declaration, according to draft guideline 1.2, "purports to specify or clarify the meaning or scope attributed by the declarant to a treaty or to certain of its provisions".[7]

4. The legal effects which reservations, on the one hand, and interpretative declarations, on the other, are meant to produce are thus different and do not, in fact, have the same impact on the treaty: whereas a reservation, by definition, purports to modify or to exclude completely the legal effects of either a provision of a treaty or the treaty as a whole with regard to certain aspects of its application to the reserving State or organization, an interpretative declaration does not (at least openly) purport to modify the treaty's legal effects with regard to the declarant, but merely to clarify its meaning. This essential difference[8] makes it justifiable, and indeed necessary, for the rules governing reactions to interpretative declarations to be more than a mere copy of the 1969 and 1986 Vienna Conventions' rules on acceptance of and objection to reservations (see section A below).

5. This is far less evident in the case of conditional interpretative declarations, which should be clearly distinguished from "simple" interpretative declarations.[9] Under draft guideline 1.2.1, a conditional interpretative declaration is a unilateral statement "whereby [the author] subjects its consent to be bound by the treaty to a specific interpretation of the treaty or of certain provisions thereof".[10] Thus, although a conditional interpretative declaration does not produce legal effects that differ from those of a "simple" interpretative declaration, it is characterized by the fact that its author "does not merely propose an interpretation, but makes its interpretation a condition of its consent to be bound by the treaty", so that the conditional interpretative declarations "come closer to being a reservation".[11] However, this does not in itself mean that the regime for reactions to interpretative declarations should be identical to the one for reactions to (acceptance of and objection to) reservations. This is only a working hypothesis that should be explored (see section B below).[12]

A. Interpretative declarations (general regime)

6. Owing to the exclusion of interpretative declarations from the 1969 and 1986 Vienna Conventions, articles 19–23 of those texts do not apply to reactions to interpretative declarations, according to the positions taken in the vast majority of cases in the literature, which stress the difference between the legal regimes applicable in this respect to reservations, on the one hand, and interpretative declarations, on the other.[13] This difference is clearly delineated in Ethiopia's objection to Yemen's declaration concerning the United Nations Convention on the Law of the Sea:

> [T]he declaration [of Yemen], not constituting a reservation as it is prohibited by article 309 of the Convention, is made under article 310 of same and as such is not governed by articles 19–23 of the Vienna Convention on the Law of Treaties providing for acceptance of and objections to reservations.[14]

7. Nonetheless, an interpretative declaration, like a reservation, may logically generate three types of reaction on the part of the States and international organizations concerned:

(*a*) A positive reaction whereby the author expresses, either explicitly or implicitly, agreement with the unilateral interpretation proposed by the State or organization that made the interpretative declaration (see paragraphs 8–12 below);

(*b*) A negative reaction whereby the author expresses disagreement with the interpretation proposed by the State or organization that made the interpretative declaration, or expresses opposition to its classification as an "interpretative declaration", usually on the ground that it is in reality a reservation (see paragraphs 13–23 below);

(*c*) Silence; i.e. the absence of any explicit manifestation of approval or opposition (see paragraphs 32–41 below).

Interpretative declarations or statements that are presented as such may also elicit a fourth type of reaction that does not specifically concern the substance of the declaration, but rather its classification (see paragraphs 24–31 below).

1. Positive reaction: approval

8. It appears that State practice with respect to positive reactions to interpretative declarations is virtually nonexistent. However, *Multilateral Treaties Deposited with the Secretary-General* ... includes a text submitted by Israel reacting positively to a declaration submitted by Egypt[15] concerning the United Nations Convention on the Law of the Sea:

---

[5] *Yearbook ... 2002*, vol. II (Part Two), commentary on section 2.4 (Procedure for interpretative declarations), p. 46. On the distinction, see draft guidelines 1.2 and 1.2.1 and the commentary pertaining to them, *Yearbook ... 1999*, vol. II (Part Two), pp. 97–106.

[6] *Yearbook ... 1998*, vol. II (Part Two), draft guideline 1.1, p. 99. See also draft guideline 1.1.1, *Yearbook ... 1999*, vol. II (Part Two), p. 93.

[7] *Yearbook ... 1999*, vol. II (Part Two), p. 97.

[8] *Ibid.*, p. 107, draft guideline 1.3 (Distinction between reservations and interpretative declarations).

[9] See paragraph 2 above.

[10] *Yearbook ... 1999*, vol. II (Part two), p. 103.

[11] *Ibid.*, para. (1) of the commentary to draft guideline 1.2.1.

[12] *Ibid.*, p. 105, para. (14) of the commentary to draft guideline 1.2.1.

[13] See, in particular, McRae, "The legal effect of interpretative declarations", especially p. 166; Horn, *Reservations and Interpretative Declarations to Multilateral Treaties*, p. 244; and Sapienza, *Dichiarazioni interpretative unilaterali e trattati internazionali*, p. 274.

[14] *Multilateral Treaties Deposited with the Secretary-General: Status as at 31 December 2006* (United Nations publication, Sales No. E.07.V.3), vol. II, chap. XXI.6.

[15] "The provisions of the 1979 Peace Treaty between Egypt and Israel concerning passage through the Strait of Tiran and the Gulf of Aqaba come within the framework of the general régime of waters forming straits referred to in part III of the Convention, wherein it is stipulated that the general régime shall not affect the legal status of waters forming straits and shall include certain obligations with regard to security and the maintenance of order in the State bordering the strait" (*ibid.*).

The concerns of the Government of Israel, with regard to the law of the sea, relate principally to ensuring maximum freedom of navigation and overflight everywhere and particularly through straits used for international navigation.

In this regard, the Government of Israel states that the regime of navigation and overflight, confirmed by the 1979 Treaty of Peace between Israel and Egypt, in which the Strait of Tiran and the Gulf of Aqaba are considered by the Parties to be international waterways open to all nations for unimpeded and non-suspendable freedom of navigation and overflight, is applicable to the said areas. Moreover, being fully compatible with the United Nations Convention on the Law of the Sea, the regime of the Peace Treaty will continue to prevail and to be applicable to the said areas.

It is the understanding of the Government of Israel that the declaration of the Arab Republic of Egypt in this regard, upon its ratification of the [said] Convention, is consonant with the above declaration.[16]

It appears from this declaration that the interpretation put forward by Egypt is regarded by Israel as correctly reflecting the meaning of chapter III of the Convention. The Egyptian interpretation is, in a manner of speaking, confirmed by the reasoned "approbatory declaration" made by Israel.

9. Another example that could be cited is the reaction of Norway to a declaration made by France concerning the Protocol of 1978 relating to the International Convention for the prevention of pollution from ships, 1973 (MARPOL Convention), published by the Secretary-General of IMO:

[T]he Government of Norway has taken due note of the communication, which is understood to be a declaration on the part of the Government of France and not a reservation to the provisions of the Convention with the legal consequence such a formal reservation would have had, if reservations to Annex I had been admissible.[17]

It appears that this statement can be interpreted to mean that Norway accepts the declaration by France insofar as it does not constitute a reservation.

10. These very rare examples show that a situation may arise in which a State or an international organization expresses agreement with a specific interpretation proposed by another State or international organization in an interpretative declaration. Such agreement between the respective interpretations of two or more parties is expressly envisaged in article 31, paragraph 3 (*a*), of the 1969 and 1986 Vienna Conventions, which provides that, for the interpretation of a treaty,

There shall be taken into account, together with the context:

(*a*) any subsequent agreement between the parties regarding the interpretation of the treaty or the application of its provisions.

11. However, it is not necessary at this stage of the study to specify the legal effect which the expression of such agreement with an interpretative declaration may produce. It suffices to note that such agreement should not be confused with the acceptance of a reservation, if only because, under article 20, paragraph 4, of the 1969 and 1986 Vienna Conventions, such acceptance entails the entry into force of the treaty for the reserving State—which is evidently not the case of a positive reaction to an interpretative declaration. To underscore the differences between the two, it would be wise to use different terms. The term "approval", which expresses the idea of agreement or acquiescence without prejudging the legal effect actually produced,[18] could be used to denote a positive reaction to an interpretative declaration.

12. In view of these considerations, a draft guideline 2.9.1 worded as follows could be placed at the beginning of section 2.9 (Formulation of reactions to interpretative declarations) to define the expression "approval of an interpretative declaration":

"**2.9** *Formulation of reactions to interpretative declarations*

"**2.9.1** *Approval of an interpretative declaration*

"'Approval' of an interpretative declaration means a unilateral statement made by a State or an international organization in response to an interpretative declaration in respect of a treaty formulated by another State or another international organization, whereby the former State or organization expresses agreement with the interpretation proposed in that declaration."

2. Negative reaction: opposition

13. Examples of negative reactions to an interpretative declaration, in other words, of a State or an international organization disagreeing with the interpretation given in an interpretative declaration, while not quite as exceptional, are nonetheless sporadic. The reaction of the United Kingdom of Great Britain and Northern Ireland to the interpretative declaration of the Syrian Arab Republic[19] in respect of article 52 of the 1969 Vienna Convention is an illustration of this:

The United Kingdom does not accept that the interpretation of Article 52 put forward by the Government of Syria correctly reflects the conclusions reached at the Conference of Vienna on the subject of coercion; the Conference dealt with this matter by adopting a Declaration on this subject which forms part of the Final Act.[20]

14. The various conventions on the law of the sea also generated negative reactions to the interpretative declarations made in connection with them. Upon ratification of the Convention on the Continental Shelf, Canada declared "that it does not find acceptable the declaration made by the Federal Republic of Germany with respect to article 5,

[16] *Ibid.* In fact, this statement expresses approval of both the classification and the substance of the declaration by Egypt; given the formulation of these declarations, it may be wondered whether they might have been made as a result of a diplomatic agreement.

[17] United Nations, *Treaty Series*, vol. 1341, No. 22484, p. 330. See also *Status of multilateral conventions and instruments in respect of which the International Maritime Organization or its Secretary-General performs depositary or other functions (as at 31 December 2007)*, p. 108, footnote 1.

[18] See Salmon, *Dictionnaire de droit international public*, pp. 74–75 ("Approbation").

[19] This declaration reads as follows:

"D—The Government of the Syrian Arab Republic interprets the provisions in article 52 as follows:

The expression "the threat or use of force" used in this article extends also to the employment of economic, political, military and psychological coercion and to all types of coercion constraining a State to conclude a treaty against its wishes or its interests."

(*Multilateral Treaties*... (see footnote 14 above), chap. XXIII.1)

[20] *Ibid.*

paragraph 1".[21] The United Nations Convention on the Law of the Sea, by virtue of its articles 309–310, which prohibit reservations but authorize interpretative declarations, gave rise to a considerable number of "interpretative declarations", which also prompted an onslaught of negative reactions by other contracting States. Tunisia, in its communication of 22 February 1994, made it known, for example, that:

In that declaration [of Malta], articles 74 and 83 of the Convention are interpreted to mean that, in the absence of any agreement on delimitation of the exclusive economic zone, the continental shelf or other maritime zones, the search for an equitable solution assumes that the boundary is the median line, in other words, a line every point of which is equidistant from the nearest points on the baselines from which the breadth of the territorial waters is measured.

The Tunisian Government believes that such an interpretation is not in the least consistent with the spirit and letter of the provisions of these articles, which do not provide for automatic application of the median line with regard to delimitation of the exclusive economic zone or the continental shelf.[22]

Another very clear-cut example can be found in the statement of Italy regarding the interpretative declaration of India in respect of the Convention:

Italy wishes to reiterate the declaration it made upon signature and confirmed upon ratification according to which "the rights of the coastal State in such zone do not include the right to obtain notification of military exercises or manoeuvres or to authorize them". According to the declaration made by Italy upon ratification this declaration applies as a reply to all past and future declarations by other States concerning the matters covered by it.[23]

15. Examples can also be found in the practice of States members of the Council of Europe. Thus, the Russian Federation, referring to numerous declarations by other States parties in respect of the Framework Convention for the protection of national minorities, in which they specified the meaning to be ascribed to the term "national minority", declared that it

considers that none is entitled to include unilaterally in reservations or declarations, made while signing or ratifying the Framework Convention for the Protection of National Minorities, a definition of the term "national minority", which is not contained in the Framework Convention. In the opinion of the Russian Federation, attempts to exclude from the scope of the Framework Convention the persons who permanently reside in the territory of States Parties to the Framework Convention and previously had a citizenship but have been arbitrarily deprived of it, contradict the purpose of the Framework Convention for the Protection of National Minorities.[24]

16. Furthermore, the example of the statement by Italy regarding the interpretative declaration of India (para. 14 above) shows that, in practice, States that react negatively to an interpretative declaration formulated by another State or another international organization often propose in the same breath another interpretation that they believe is "more accurate". This practice of "constructive" refusal was also followed by Italy in its statement in reaction to the interpretative declarations of several other States parties to the Basel Convention on the control of transboundary movements of hazardous wastes and their disposal:

The Government of Italy, in expressing its objection *vis-à-vis* the declarations made, upon signature, by the Governments of Colombia, Ecuador, Mexico, Uruguay and Venezuela, as well as other declarations of similar tenor that might be made in the future, considers that no provision of this Convention should be interpreted as restricting navigational rights recognized by international law. Consequently, a State party is not obliged to notify any other State or obtain authorization from it for simple passage through the territorial sea or the exercise of freedom of navigation in the exclusive economic zone by a vessel showing its flag and carrying a cargo of hazardous wastes.[25]

Other States which had made an interpretative declaration comparable to that of Italy did not feel it was necessary to react in the same way that Italy had, but merely remained silent.[26]

17. The practice also evoked reactions that, *prima facie*, were not outright rejections. In some cases, States seemed to accept the proposed interpretation on the condition that it was consistent with a supplementary interpretation. The conditions set by Austria, Germany and Turkey for consenting to Poland's interpretative declaration in respect of the European Convention on Extradition[27] are a good example of this. Hence, Germany considered

the placing of persons granted asylum in Poland on an equal standing with Polish nationals in Poland's declaration with respect to Article 6, paragraph 1 (*a*) of the Convention to be compatible with the object and purpose of the Convention only with the proviso that it does not exclude extradition of such persons to a state other than that in respect of which asylum has been granted.[28]

18. A number of Western States had a comparable reaction to the declaration made by Egypt upon ratification of the International Convention for the Suppression of Terrorist Bombings.[29] Considering that the declaration by Egypt "aims to broaden the scope of the Convention"[30] —which excludes assigning the status of "reservation"— Germany declared that it

[21] *Ibid.*, chap. XXI.4. The German interpretative declaration reads as follows: "[T]he Federal Republic of Germany declares with reference to article 5, paragraph 1 of the Convention on the Continental Shelf that in the opinion of the Federal Government article 5, paragraph 1 guarantees the exercise of fishing rights (*Fischerei*) in the waters above the continental shelf in the manner hitherto generally in practice" (*ibid.*).

[22] *Ibid.*, chap. XXI.6, note 19. The relevant part of the declaration by Malta reads as follows:

"The Government of Malta interprets article 74 and article 83 to the effect that in the absence of agreement on the delimitation of the exclusive economic zone or the continental shelf or other maritime zones, for an equitable solution to be achieved, the boundary shall be the median line, namely a line every point of which is equidistant from the nearest points of the baselines from which the breadth of the territorial waters of Malta and of such other States is measured."

(*Ibid.*)

[23] *Ibid.*

[24] United Nations, *Treaty Series*, vol. 2152, No. 37548, p. 297.

[25] *Multilateral Treaties* ... (see footnote 14 above), chap. XXVII.3.

[26] On the question of "silence", see paragraphs 32–41 below.

[27] Declaration by Poland of 15 June 1993:

"The Republic of Poland declares, in accordance with paragraph 1 (*a*) of Article 6, that it will under no circumstances extradite its own nationals.

"The Republic of Poland declares that, for the purposes of this Convention, in accordance with paragraph 1 (*b*) of Article 6, persons granted asylum in Poland will be treated as Polish nationals."

(United Nations, *Treaty Series*, vol. 1862, No. 5146, p. 469).

[28] *Ibid.*, p. 470. See also the identical reaction of Austria to the interpretative declaration of Romania (*ibid.*, vol. 2045, p. 202).

[29] The "reservation" by Egypt is formulated as follows:

"The Government of the Arab Republic of Egypt declares that it is bound by Article 19, paragraph 2, of the Convention insofar as the military forces of a State, in the exercise of their duties do not violate the rules and principles of international law."

(*Multilateral Treaties* ... (see footnote 14 above), chap. XVIII.9)

[30] *Ibid.*

is of the opinion that the Government of the Arab Republic of Egypt is only entitled to make such a declaration unilaterally for its own armed forces, and it interprets the declaration as having binding effect only on armed forces of the Arab Republic of Egypt. In the view of the Government of the Federal Republic of Germany, such a unilateral declaration cannot apply to the armed forces of other States Parties without their express consent. The Government of the Federal Republic of Germany therefore declares that it does not consent to the Egyptian declaration as so interpreted with regard to any armed forces other than those of the Arab Republic of Egypt, and in particular does not recognize any applicability of the Convention to the armed forces of the Federal Republic of Germany.[31]

19. In the context of the Protocol of 1978 relating to the International Convention for the prevention of pollution from ships, 1973 (MARPOL Convention), a declaration by Canada concerning Arctic waters also triggered conditional reactions. Belgium, Denmark, France, Germany, Greece, Italy, the Netherlands, Portugal, Spain and the United Kingdom declared that they

take note of this declaration by Canada and consider that it should be read in conformity with Articles 57, 234 and 236 of the United Nations Convention on the Law of the Sea. In particular, the ... Government recalls that Article 234 of that Convention applies within the limits of the exclusive economic zone or of a similar zone delimited in conformity with Article 57 of the Convention and that the laws and regulations contemplated in Article 234 shall have due regard to navigation and the protection and preservation of the marine environment based on the best available scientific evidence.[32]

20. The declaration by the Czech Republic made further to Germany's interpretative declaration[33] in respect of part X of the United Nations Convention on the Law of the Sea should be viewed from a slightly different perspective in that it is difficult to determine whether it is opposing the interpretation upheld by Germany or reclassifying the declaration as a reservation:

The Government of the Czech Republic having considered the declaration of the Federal Republic of Germany of 14 October 1994 pertaining to the interpretation of the provisions of Part X of the [said Convention], which deals with the right of access of land-locked States to and from the sea and freedom of transit, states that the [said] declaration of the Federal Republic of Germany cannot be interpreted with regard to the Czech Republic in contradiction with the provisions of Part X of the Convention.[34]

21. Such "conditional acceptances" do not constitute "approvals" within the meaning of draft guideline 2.9.1 and should be regarded as negative reactions. In fact, the authors of such declarations are not approving the proposed interpretation, but rather are putting forward another which, in their view, is the only one in conformity with the treaty.

22. All these examples show that a negative reaction to an interpretative declaration can take varying forms: it can be a refusal, purely and simply, of the interpretation formulated in the declaration, a counter-proposal of an interpretation of the contested provision(s), or an attempt to limit the scope of the initial declaration, which was, in turn, interpreted. In any case, reacting States or international organizations are seeking to prevent or limit the scope of the interpretative declaration or its legal effect on the treaty, its application or its interpretation. In this connection, a negative reaction is therefore comparable, to some extent, to an objection to a reservation without, however, producing the same effect. Thus, a State or an international organization cannot oppose the entry into force of a treaty between itself and the author of the interpretative declaration on the pretext that it disagrees with the interpretation contained in the declaration. The author views its negative reaction as a safeguard measure, a protest against establishing an interpretation of the treaty that it might consider opposable, which it does not find appropriate,[35] and about which it must speak out.

23. That is why "opposition"[36] might be an apt term for negative reactions to an interpretative declaration, rather than "objection", even though this word has sometimes been used in practice.[37] Based on the model adopted for the definition of objections,[38] draft guideline 2.9.2 could define such opposition to an interpretative declaration as the intention of, and effect anticipated by, its author, as follows:

"**2.9.2** *Opposition to an interpretative declaration*

"'Opposition' to an interpretative declaration means a unilateral statement made by a State or an international organization in response to an interpretative declaration in respect of a treaty formulated by another State or another international organization, whereby the former State or organization rejects the interpretation proposed in the interpretative declaration or proposes an interpretation other than that contained in the declaration with a view to excluding or limiting its effect."

3. Reclassification

24. As illustrated in the third report on reservations to treaties, naming or phrasing of a unilateral statement by its author as a "reservation" or an "interpretative

[31] *Ibid.* See also comparable declarations by Canada, the Netherlands, the United Kingdom and the United States of America (*ibid.*).

[32] *Status of multilateral conventions and instruments* ... (see footnote 17 above), p. 106, for the text of the declaration by Canada.

[33] The relevant part of the declaration by Germany reads as follows:

"As to the regulation of the freedom of transit enjoyed by land-locked States, transit through the territory of transit States must not interfere with the sovereignty of these States. In accordance with article 125, paragraph 3, the rights and facilities provided for in Part X in no way infringe upon the sovereignty and legitimate interests of transit States. The precise content of the freedom of transit has in each single case to be agreed upon by the transit State and the land-locked State concerned. In the absence of such agreement concerning the terms and modalities for exercising the right of access of persons and goods to transit through the territory of the Federal Republic of Germany is only regulated by national law, in particular, with regard to means and ways of transport and the use of traffic infrastructure."

(*Multilateral Treaties* ... (see footnote 14 above), chap. XXI.6)

[34] *Ibid.*, note 16.

[35] In this connection, see McNair, *The Law of Treaties*, pp. 430–431.

[36] In the *Dictionnaire de droit international public*, the term "protestation" is defined as follows: "Act by which one or more subjects of international law express their intention not to recognize the validity or opposability of acts, conduct or claims issuing from third parties" (Salmon, *op. cit.*, p. 907).

[37] See, for example, Italy's reaction to the interpretative declarations of Colombia, Ecuador, Mexico, Uruguay and Venezuela to the Basel Convention on the control of transboundary movements of hazardous wastes and their disposal (see footnote 25 above). The reaction of Canada to the interpretative declaration of Germany to the Convention on the Continental Shelf (see footnote 21 above) was also registered in the "objection" category by the Secretary-General.

[38] See draft guideline 2.6.1 and the commentary thereto, *Yearbook* ... *2005*, vol. II (Part Two), chap. X, sect. C.2, pp. 77–82, para. 438.

declaration" is not relevant for the purposes of classifying such a unilateral statement,[39] even if it provides a significant clue as to its nature.[40] This is conveyed by the phrase "however phrased or named" in draft guideline 1.1 (art. 2, para. 1 (*d*), of the 1969 and 1986 Vienna Conventions) and draft guideline 1.2 of the Guide to Practice.

25. What frequently occurs in practice is that interested States do not hesitate to react to unilateral statements which their authors call interpretative, and to expressly consider them as reservations.[41] These reactions, which might be called "reclassifications" to reflect their purpose, in no way resemble approval or opposition, since, of course, they do not refer to the actual content of the unilateral statement in question, but rather to its form and to the applicable legal regime.

26. There are numerous examples of this phenomenon:

(*a*) The reaction of the Netherlands to Algeria's interpretative declaration in respect of article 13, paragraphs 3–4, of the International Covenant on Economic, Social and Cultural Rights:

In the opinion of the Government of the Kingdom of the Netherlands, the interpretative declaration concerning article 13, paragraphs 3 and 4 of the International Covenant on Economic, Social and Cultural Rights must be regarded as a reservation to the Covenant. From the text and history of the Covenant it follows that the reservation with respect to article 13, paragraphs 3 and 4 made by the Government of Algeria is incompatible with the object and purpose of the Covenant. The Government of the Kingdom of the Netherlands therefore considers the reservation unacceptable and formally raises an objection to it;[42]

(*b*) The reactions of many States to the declaration made by Pakistan with respect to the same Covenant, which, after lengthy statements of reasons, conclude:

The Government of ... therefore regards the above-mentioned declarations as reservations and as incompatible with the object and purpose of the Covenant.

The Government of ... therefore objects to the above-mentioned reservations made by the Government of the Islamic Republic of Pakistan to the International Covenant on Economic, Social and Cultural Rights. This objection shall not preclude the entry into force of the Covenant between the Federal Republic of Germany and the Islamic Republic of Pakistan.[43]

(*c*) The reactions of many States to the declaration made by the Philippines with respect to the United Nations Convention on the Law of the Sea:

The ... considers that the statement which was made by the Government of the Philippines upon signing the United Nations Convention on the Law of the Sea and confirmed subsequently upon ratification of that Convention in essence contains reservations and exceptions to the said Convention, contrary to the provisions of article 309 thereof.[44]

(*d*) The reclassification formulated by Mexico, which considered that

the third declaration [formally classified as interpretative] submitted by the Government of the United States of America (...) constitutes a unilateral claim to justification, not envisaged in the Convention [the United Nations Convention against Illicit Traffic in Narcotic Drugs and Psychotropic Substances], for denying legal assistance to a State that requests it, which runs counter to the purposes of the Convention.[45]

(*e*) The reaction of Germany to a declaration whereby Tunisia indicated that it would not, in implementing the Convention on the rights of the child of, "adopt any legislative or statutory decision that conflicts with the Tunisian Constitution":

The Federal Republic of Germany considers the first of the declarations deposited by the Republic of Tunisia to be a reservation. It restricts the application of the first sentence of article 4.[46]

(*f*) The reactions of 19 States to the declaration made by Pakistan with respect to the International Convention for the Suppression of Terrorist Bombings, whereby Pakistan specified that "nothing in this Convention shall be applicable to struggles, including armed struggle, for the realization of right of self-determination launched against any alien or foreign occupation or domination":[47]

The Government of Austria considers that the declaration made by the Government of the Islamic Republic of Pakistan is in fact a reservation that seeks to limit the scope of the Convention on a unilateral basis and is therefore contrary to its objective and purpose.[48]

(*g*) The reactions of Germany and the Netherlands to the declaration made by Malaysia upon accession to the Convention on the prevention and punishment of crimes against internationally protected persons, including diplomatic agents, whereby Malaysia made the implementation of article 7 of the Convention subject to its domestic legislation:

The Government of the Federal Republic of Germany considers that in making the interpretation and application of Article 7 of the Convention subject to the national legislation of Malaysia, the Government of Malaysia introduces a general and indefinite reservation that makes it impossible to clearly identify in which way the Government of Malaysia intends to change the obligations arising from the Convention. Therefore the Government of the Federal Republic of

[39] *Yearbook ... 1998*, vol. II (Part One), document A/CN.4/491 and Add.1–6, p. 267, para. 275. See also draft guidelines 1.1 (Definition of reservations) and 1.2 (Definition of interpretative declarations), *Yearbook ... 1999*, vol. II (Part Two), pp. 91–92.

[40] In this connection, draft guideline 1.3.2 (Phrasing and name) provides that: "The phrasing or name given to a unilateral statement provides an indication of the purported legal effect. This is the case in particular when a State or international organization formulates several unilateral statements in respect of a single treaty and designates some of them as reservations and others as interpretative declarations" (*Yearbook ... 1999*, vol. II (Part Two), p. 92). See also the commentary on this provision, *ibid.*, pp. 109–111.

[41] Nor do the tribunals and treaty monitoring bodies hesitate to requalify an interpretative declaration as a reservation (see paragraphs (5)–(7) of the commentary to draft article 1.3.2, *ibid.*, pp. 109–111. This, however, does not touch on the *formulation* of these reactions; it is therefore not useful to revisit it here.

[42] *Multilateral Treaties* ... (see footnote 14 above), vol. I, chap. IV.3. See also the objection of Portugal (*ibid.*) and the objection of the Netherlands to the declaration of Kuwait (*ibid.*).

[43] *Ibid.* See also the objections registered by Denmark, Finland, France, Latvia, Norway, the Netherlands, Spain, Sweden and the United Kingdom (*ibid.*).

[44] *Ibid.*, vol. II, chap. XXI.6, objection by Belarus; see also the reactions similar in letter or in spirit from Australia, Bulgaria, the Russian Federation and Ukraine (*ibid.*).

[45] *Ibid.*, vol. I, chap. VI.19.

[46] *Ibid.*, chap. IV.11).

[47] *Ibid.*, vol. II, chap. XVIII.9.

[48] *Ibid.* See the reactions similar in letter or in spirit from Australia, Canada, Denmark, Finland, France, Germany, India, Israel, Italy, Japan, the Netherlands, New Zealand, Norway, Spain, Sweden, the United Kingdom and the United States (*ibid.*). See also the reactions of Germany and the Netherlands to the unilateral declaration made by Malaysia (*ibid.*).

Germany hereby objects to this declaration which is considered to be a reservation that is incompatible with the object and purpose of the Convention. This objection shall not preclude the entry into force of the Convention between the Federal Republic of Germany and Malaysia.[49]

(*h*) The reaction of Sweden to the declaration by Bangladesh indicating that article III of the Convention on the Political Rights of Women could only be implemented in accordance with the Constitution of Bangladesh:

In this context the Government of Sweden would like to recall, that under well-established international treaty law, the name assigned to a statement whereby the legal effect of certain provisions of a treaty is excluded or modified, does not determine its status as a reservation to the treaty. Thus, the Government of Sweden considers that the declarations made by the Government of Bangladesh, in the absence of further clarification, in substance constitute reservations to the Convention.

The Government of Sweden notes that the declaration relating to article III is of a general kind, stating that Bangladesh will apply the said article in consonance with the relevant provisions of its Constitution. The Government of Sweden is of the view that this declaration raises doubts as to the commitment of Bangladesh to the object and purpose of the Convention and would recall that, according to well-established international law, a reservation incompatible with the object and purpose of a treaty shall not be permitted.[50]

27. These examples show that reclassification consists of considering that a unilateral statement submitted as an "interpretative declaration" is in reality a "reservation", with all the legal effects that this entails. Thus, reclassification seeks to change the legal status of the unilateral statement in the relationship between the State or organization having submitted the statement and the "reclassifying" State or organization. As a general rule, such declarations, which are usually extensively reasoned,[51] are based essentially on the criteria for distinguishing between reservations and interpretative declarations.[52]

28. Draft guideline 2.9.3 is based on this State practice and defines "reclassification" accordingly:

"**2.9.3** *Reclassification of an interpretative declaration*

"1. 'Reclassification' means a unilateral statement made by a State or an international organization in response to a declaration in respect of a treaty formulated by another State or another international organization as an interpretative declaration, whereby the former State or organization purports to regard the declaration as a reservation and to treat it as such.

"2. [In formulating a reclassification, States and international organizations shall [take into account] [apply] draft guidelines 1.3 to 1.3.3.]."

29. The examples cited show that, in practice, States almost always combine the reclassification with an objection to the reservation. It should be borne in mind, however, that reclassifying an interpretative declaration as a reservation is one thing and objecting to the reservation thus "reclassified" is another. Nonetheless, it should be noted that even in the case of a reservation that is "disguised" (as an interpretative declaration)—which, from a legal standpoint, has always been a reservation—the rules of procedure and formulation as set out in the present Guide to Practice remain fully applicable. This clearly means that a State wishing to formulate a reclassification *and* an objection must abide by the procedural rules and time periods applicable to reclassification[53] *and* objection,[54] and that, in principle, the time period for formulating such a "combined statement" is accordingly shortened to the one provided for in article 20, paragraph 5, of the 1969 and 1986 Vienna Conventions and in draft guideline 2.6.13.[55] An objection submitted after that time period cannot produce all of its legal effects and the reclassified reservation must be regarded as having been accepted.[56]

30. This is why it is specified, at the end of draft guideline 2.9.3, paragraph 1, that the author State or organization must accordingly treat the reclassified reservation as such.

31. Paragraph 2, while following the usual practice, provides a logical corollary to the rules already adopted by the Commission with respect to the distinction between reservations and interpretative declarations. It seems desirable to place this provision here, for reasons more of convenience than of strict logic, as this stipulation concerns the substantive rules for making the distinction rather than the rules governing formulation as such. This is why the provision is in square brackets.

---

[49] *Ibid.*, chap. XVIII.7.

[50] *Ibid.*, chap. XVI.1. See also the identical declaration of Norway (*ibid.*).

[51] For a particularly striking example, see the reactions to Pakistan's interpretative declaration in relation to the International Covenant on Economic, Social and Cultural Rights (para. 26 (*b*) above and footnote 43 above).

[52] See draft guidelines 1.3–1.3.3, *Yearbook ... 1999*, vol. II (Part Two), p. 92:

"1.3 *Distinction between reservations and interpretative declarations*

"The character of a unilateral statement as a reservation or an interpretative declaration is determined by the legal effect it purports to produce.

"1.3.1 *Method of implementation of the distinction between reservations and interpretative declarations*

"To determine whether a unilateral statement formulated by a State or an international organization in respect of a treaty is a reservation or an interpretative declaration, it is appropriate to interpret the statement in good faith in accordance with the ordinary meaning to be given to its terms, in the light of the treaty to which it refers. Due regard shall be given to the intention of the State or the international organization concerned at the time the statement was formulated.

"1.3.2 *Phrasing and name*

"The phrasing or name given to a unilateral statement provides an indication of the purported legal effect. This is the case in particular when a State or an international organization formulates several unilateral statements in respect of a single treaty and designates some of them as reservations and others as interpretative declarations.

"1.3.3 *Formulation of a unilateral statement when a reservation is prohibited*

"When a treaty prohibits reservations to all or certain of its provisions, a unilateral statement formulated in respect thereof by a State or an international organization shall be presumed not to constitute a reservation except when it purports to exclude or modify the legal effect of certain provisions of the treaty or of the treaty as a whole with respect to certain specific aspects in their application to its author."

[53] See paragraphs 42–48 below.

[54] See the eleventh report on reservations to treaties, *Yearbook ... 2006*, vol. II (Part One), document A/CN.4/574, pp. 199–210, paras. 87–144.

[55] *Ibid.*, p. 207, para. 128, draft guideline 2.6.13.

[56] Ibid., p. 210, para. 143, draft guideline 2.6.15.

4. Silence

32. The practice surveyed above reveals that States make considerable use of silence in relation to interpretative declarations. Express positive and even express negative reactions are extremely rare. It should therefore be asked whether this pervasive silence can be taken to signify consent to the interpretation proposed by the State or the international organization that formulated the interpretative declaration.

33. In the case of reservations, silence, according to the presumption provided for in article 20, paragraph 5, of the 1969 and 1986 Vienna Conventions, means consent. ICJ, in its 1951 advisory opinion, noted the "very great allowance made for tacit assent to reservations",[57] and the work of the Commission has from the outset acknowledged the considerable part played by tacit acceptance.[58] Sir Humphrey Waldock justified the principle of tacit acceptance by pointing out that:

> It is ... true that, under the "flexible" system now proposed, the acceptance or rejection by a particular State of a reservation made by another primarily concerns their relations with each other, so that there may not be the same urgency to determine the status of a reservation as under the system of unanimous consent. Nevertheless, it seems very undesirable that a State, by refraining from making any comment upon a reservation, should be enabled more or less indefinitely to maintain an equivocal attitude as to the relations between itself and the reserving State.[59]

34. In the case of simple interpretative declarations (as opposed to conditional declarations), these concerns do not arise. By definition, an interpretative declaration purports only to "specify or clarify the meaning or scope attributed by the declarant to a treaty or to certain of its provisions" (para. 3 above), and in no way imposes conditions on its author's consent to be bound by the treaty.[60] Whether or not other States or international organizations consent to the interpretation put forward in the declaration has no effect on the author's legal status with respect to the treaty; the author becomes or remains a Contracting Party regardless. Continued silence on the part of the other parties has no effect on the status as a party of the State or organization that formulates an interpretative declaration: such silence cannot prevent the latter from becoming or remaining a party, in contrast to what could occur in the case of reservations under article 20, paragraph 4 (*c*), of the 1969 and 1986 Vienna Conventions were it not for the presumption provided for in paragraph 5 of that article.

35. Thus, since it is not possible to proceed by analogy with reservations, the issue of whether, in the absence of an express reaction, there is a presumption of approval of or opposition to interpretative declarations remains unresolved. In truth, however, this question can only be answered in the negative. It is indeed inconceivable that silence, in itself, could produce such a legal effect. The following comment by Buzzini in a study on silence in response to a violation of a rule of international law is fully applicable here: "Silence in itself says nothing because it is capable of 'saying' too many things at once."[61]

36. Silence can express either agreement or disagreement with the proposed interpretation. States may consider it unnecessary to respond to an interpretative declaration because it accurately reflects their own position, or they may feel that the interpretation is erroneous, but that there is no point in proclaiming as much because, in any event, the interpretation would not, in their view, be upheld by an impartial third party in case of a dispute. It is impossible to decide which of these two hypotheses is correct.

37. Moreover, this appears to be the position most widely supported in the literature. Horn states that:

> Interpretative declarations must be treated as unilaterally advanced interpretations and should therefore be governed only by the principles of interpretation. The general rule is that a unilateral interpretation cannot be opposed to any other party in the treaty. Inaction on behalf of the confronted states does not result in automatic construction of acceptance. It will only be one of many cumulative factors which together may evidence acquiescence. The institution of estoppel may become relevant, though this requires more explicit proof of the readiness of the confronted states to accept the interpretation.[62]

38. Thus, although silence cannot in itself be construed as either approval or opposition—neither of which can by any means be presumed—the position taken by Horn indicates that silence can, under certain conditions, be taken to signify acquiescence in accordance with the principles of good faith and, more particularly in the context of interpreting treaties, through the operation of article 31, paragraph 3 (*b*), of the 1969 and 1986 Vienna Conventions, which provides for the consideration, in interpreting a treaty, of "any subsequent practice in the application of the treaty which establishes the agreement of the parties regarding its interpretation". Further, the concept of acquiescence itself is not unknown in treaty law: article 45 of the 1969 Vienna Convention provides that:

> A State may no longer invoke a ground for invalidating, terminating, withdrawing from or suspending the operation of a treaty under articles 46 to 50 or articles 60 and 62 if, after becoming aware of the facts:
>
> [...]
>
> (*b*) it must by reason of its conduct be considered as having acquiesced in the validity of the treaty or in its maintenance in force or in operation, as the case may be.

Article 45 of the 1986 Vienna Convention reproduces this provision, adapting it to the specific case of international organizations.

39. But this provision does not define the "conduct" in question and it seems extremely difficult, if not impossible, to determine in advance the circumstances in which a State or an organization is bound to protest expressly in order to avoid being considered as having acquiesced to an interpretative declaration or to a practice that has been

---

[57] *Reservations to the Convention on the Prevention and Punishment of the Crime of Genocide, Advisory Opinion, I.C.J. Reports 1951*, p. 21.

[58] See Müller, "Convention de Vienne de 1969: article 20", pp. 814–815, paras. 31–32.

[59] First report on the law of treaties, *Yearbook ... 1962*, vol. II, document A/CN.4/144 and Add.1, p. 67, para. (15) of the commentary to article 18.

[60] The situation is evidently different with respect to conditional interpretative declarations (see paragraphs 49–55 below).

[61] Buzzini, "Abstention, silence et droit international général", p. 382.

[62] Horn, *op. cit.*, p. 244; see also McRae, *loc. cit.*, p. 168.

established on the basis of such a declaration.[63] In other words, it is particularly difficult to determine when and in what specific circumstances silence is tantamount to consent.[64] As the Eritrea Ethiopia Boundary Commission underscored:

The nature and extent of the conduct effective to produce a variation of the treaty is, of course, a matter of appreciation by the tribunal in each case. The decision of the International Court of Justice in the *Temple* case is generally pertinent in this connection. There, after identifying conduct by one party which it was reasonable to expect that the other party would expressly have rejected if it had disagreed with it, the Court concluded that the latter was stopped or precluded from challenging the validity and effect of the conduct of the first. This process has been variously described by such terms, amongst others, as estoppel, preclusion, acquiescence or implied or tacit agreement. But in each case the ingredients are the same: an act, course of conduct or omission by or under the authority of one party indicative of its view of the content of the applicable legal rule—whether of treaty or customary origin; the knowledge, actual or reasonably to be inferred, of the other party, of such conduct or omission; and a failure by the latter party within a reasonable time to reject, or dissociate itself from, the position taken by the first.[65]

40. It therefore seems impossible to provide, in the abstract, clear guidelines for determining when a silent State has, by its silence, created an effect of acquiescence or estoppel. This can only be determined on a case-by-case basis in the light of the circumstances in question.

41. Draft guidelines 2.9.8–2.9.9 reflect the principles inferred from State practice. The former unequivocally states that the presumption provided for in article 20, paragraph 5, of the 1969 and 1986 Vienna Conventions is not applicable with respect to silence on the part of a State or an international organization in response to an interpretative declaration and that silence cannot in itself be construed as either approval or opposition. The latter points out to users of the Guide to Practice that, although silence is not in principle equivalent to approval of or acquiescence to an interpretative declaration, in some circumstances the silent State may be considered as having acquiesced to the declaration by reason of its conduct or lack of conduct in relation to the interpretative declaration.

"**2.9.8** *Non-presumption of approval or opposition*

"Neither approval of nor opposition to an interpretative declaration shall be presumed.

"**2.9.9** *Silence in response to an interpretative declaration*

"1. "Consent to an interpretative declaration shall not be inferred from the mere silence of a State or an international organization in response to an interpretative declaration formulated by another State or another international organization in respect of a treaty.

"2. "In certain specific circumstances, however, a State or an international organization may be considered as having acquiesced to an interpretative declaration by reason of its silence or its conduct, as the case may be."

5. Rules applicable to the formulation of an approval, opposition or reclassification in respect of an interpretative declaration

42. While reactions to interpretative declarations differ considerably from acceptances of or objections to reservations, it seems appropriate to ensure, to the extent possible, that such reactions are publicized widely, on the understanding that States and international organizations have no legal obligation in this regard,[66] but that any legal effects which they may expect to arise from such reactions will depend in large part on how widely they disseminate those reactions. Although the legal effects of such reactions (combined with those of the initial declaration) on the interpretation and application of the treaty in question will not be discussed at this stage, it goes without saying that such unilateral statements are likely to play a role in the life of the treaty; this is their *raison d'être* and the purpose for which they are formulated by States and international organizations. ICJ has highlighted the importance of these statements in practice:

Interpretations placed upon legal instruments by the parties to them, though not conclusive as to their meaning, have considerable probative value when they contain recognition by a party of its own obligations under an instrument.[67]

43. In a study on unilateral statements, Sapienza also underlined the importance of reactions to interpretative declarations, which

contribute usefully to the settlement [of a dispute]. Statements will be still more useful to the interpreter when there is no dispute, but only a problem of interpretation.[68]

44. Notwithstanding the undeniable usefulness of reactions to interpretative declarations not only for the interpreter or judge, but also for enabling the other States and international organizations concerned to determine their own position with respect to the declaration, the 1969 Vienna Convention does not require that such reactions be communicated. As has already been indicated in the study on the form and communication of interpretative declarations themselves:

There seems to be no reason to transpose the rules governing the communication of reservations to simple interpretative declarations, which may be formulated orally; it would therefore be paradoxical to insist that they be formally communicated to other interested States or international organizations. By refraining from such communication, the author of the declaration runs the risk that the declaration may not have the intended effect, but this is a different problem altogether. It does not seem necessary, therefore, to include a clarification of this point in the Guide to Practice.[69]

[63] See, among others, Rousseau, *Droit international public*, p. 430, No. 347.

[64] In this connection, see Drost, "Grundfragen der Lehre vom internationalen Rechtsgeschäft", p. 218: "The question as to when silence can be construed as acceptance is a question of circumstances. The answer cannot be affirmative unless, given the factual circumstances—following prior notification, for example—silence cannot be understood simply as an objective situation, but as a conclusive expression of the underlying will."

[65] Decision regarding delimitation of the border between Eritrea and Ethiopia (13 April 2002), UNRIAA, vol. XXV (Sales No. E/F.05.V.5), p. 111, para. 3.9; see also the well-known separate opinion of Judge Alfaro in *Temple of Preah Vihear, Merits, Judgment, I.C.J. Reports 1962*, p. 40.

[66] See *Yearbook … 2001*, vol. II (Part One), A/CN.4/518 and Add.1–3, p. 157, para. 130.

[67] *International Status of South-West Africa, Advisory Opinion, I.C.J. Reports 1950*, pp. 135–136.

[68] Sapienza, *op. cit.*, p. 275.

[69] See footnote 66 above.

45. There is no reason to take a different approach with respect to reactions to such interpretative declarations and it would be inappropriate to impose more stringent formal requirements on them than on the interpretative declarations to which they respond. The same *caveat* applies, however: if States or international organizations do not adequately publicize their reactions to an interpretative declaration, they run the risk that the intended effects may not be produced. If the authors of such reactions want their position to be taken into account in the treaty's application, particularly when there is a dispute, it would probably be in their interest to:

(*a*) Formulate the reaction in writing to meet the requirements of legal security and to ensure notification of the reaction;

(*b*) State the reasons for the reaction; as shown by the practice described above.[70] States generally take care to explain, sometimes in great detail, the reasons for their approval, protest or reclassification. These reasons are useful not only for the interpreter: they can also alert the State or the international organization that submitted the interpretative declaration to the points found to be problematic in the declaration and, potentially, induce the author to revise or withdraw the declaration. This constitutes, with respect to interpretative declarations, the equivalent of the "reservations dialogue";

(*c*) Follow, in making such statements, the same communication and notification procedure applicable to the communication and notification of other declarations in respect of the treaty (reservations, objections or acceptances).

46. Although the Special Rapporteur is convinced of the soundness of these recommendations, he is hesitant to propose a draft guideline reflecting them because the Commission has not adopted equivalent guidelines with respect to interpretative declarations themselves. If, however, the Commission considers that it would be useful to include a draft guideline to this effect in the Guide to Practice, such a guideline could consist only of recommendations modelled on those adopted, for example, with respect to statements of reasons for reservations[71] and objections to reservations.[72] Such a provision, if included, could draw upon those concerning the procedure for other types of declarations in respect of a treaty—which is, in fact, quite uniform—as contained in draft guidelines 2.1.1–2.1.7 on reservations, 2.4.1 and 2.4.7 on interpretative declarations, 2.6.7, 2.6.9 and 2.6.10 on objections to reservations and 2.8.3–2.8.5 on express acceptance of reservations:[73]

"**2.9.5** *Written form of approval, opposition and reclassification*

"An approval, opposition or reclassification in respect of an interpretative declaration shall be formulated in writing.

"**2.9.6** *Statement of reasons for approval, opposition and reclassification*

"Whenever possible, an approval, opposition or reclassification in respect of an interpretative declaration should indicate the reasons why it is being made.

"**2.9.7** *Formulation and communication of an approval, opposition or reclassification*

"An approval, opposition or reclassification in respect of an interpretative declaration should, *mutatis mutandis*, be formulated and communicated in accordance with draft guidelines 2.1.3, 2.1.4, 2.1.5, 2.1.6 and 2.1.7."

47. With respect to time frames, reactions to interpretative declarations may in principle be formulated at any time. Interpretation occurs throughout the life of the treaty and there does not seem to be any reason why reactions to interpretative declarations should be confined to any specific time frame, when the declarations themselves are not, as a general rule (and in the absence of a provision to the contrary in the treaty), subject to any particular time frame.[74]

48. Moreover, and on this score reactions to interpretative declarations resemble acceptances of and objections to reservations, both contracting States and contracting international organizations and States and international organizations that are entitled to become parties to the treaty should be able to formulate an express reaction to an interpretative declaration at least from the time they become aware of it, on the understanding that the author of the declaration is responsible for disseminating it (or not)[75] and the reactions of non-contracting States or non-contracting international organizations will not necessarily produce the same legal effect as those formulated by Contracting Parties (and probably no effect at all, for as long as the author State or international organization has not expressed consent to be bound). It is thus perfectly logical that the Secretary-General should have accepted Ethiopia's opposition to the interpretative declaration formulated by Yemen with respect to the United Nations Convention on the Law of the Sea even though Ethiopia had not ratified the Convention.[76]

"**2.9.4** *Freedom to formulate an approval, protest or reclassification*

"An approval, opposition or reclassification in respect of an interpretative declaration may be formulated at any time by any contracting State or any contracting international organization and by any State or any international organization that is entitled to become a party to the treaty."

---

[70] See paragraphs 13–20 and 26 above.

[71] See *Yearbook ... 2007*, vol. II (Part One), document A/CN.4/586.

[72] See the eleventh report on reservations to treaties, *Yearbook ... 2006*, vol. II (Part One), document A/CN.4/574, p. 204, paras. 110–111.

[73] In the last two cases, the draft guidelines mentioned are numbered as shown in the eleventh and twelfth reports on reservations (*ibid.*, pp. 199–202, paras. 87–98 and pp. 203–204, paras. 105–111, and *Yearbook ... 2007*, vol. II (Part One), document A/CN.4/584, pp. 42–44, paras. 45–56); this numbering may be changed by the Drafting Committee.

[74] See *Yearbook ... 1999*, vol. II (Part Two), pp. 101–103, paras. (21)–(32) of the commentary to draft guideline 1.2.

[75] See footnote 66 above.

[76] See footnote 14 above.

B. Conditional interpretative declarations

49. Conditional interpretative declarations differ from "simple" interpretative declarations in their potential effect on the treaty's entry into force. The key feature of conditional interpretative declarations is that the author makes its consent to be bound by the treaty subject to the proposed interpretation. If this condition is not met, i.e. if the other States and international organizations parties to the treaty do not consent to this interpretation, the author of the interpretative declaration is considered not to be bound by the treaty, at least with regard to the parties to the treaty that contest the declaration. The declaration made by France upon signing[77] Additional Protocol II to the Treaty for the Prohibition of Nuclear Weapons in Latin America provides a particularly clear example of this:[78]

> In the event that the interpretative declaration thus made by the French Government should be contested wholly or in part by one or more Contracting Parties to the Treaty or to Protocol II, these instruments shall be null and void in relations between the French Republic and the contesting State or States.[79]

50. As recalled earlier,[80] this feature brings conditional interpretative declarations infinitely closer to reservations than "simple" interpretative declarations. The commentary on draft guideline 1.2.1 (Conditional interpretative declarations) states, in this connection:

> Consequently, it seems highly probable that the legal regime of conditional interpretative declarations would be infinitely closer to that of reservations, *especially with regard to the anticipated reactions of the other contracting parties to the treaty,** than would the rules applicable to simple interpretative declarations.[81]

51. Given the conditionality of such an interpretative declaration, the regime governing reactions to it must be more orderly and definite than the one applicable to "simple" interpretative declarations. There is a need to know with certainty and within a reasonable time period the position of the other States parties concerning the proposed interpretation so that the State or organization that submitted the conditional interpretative declaration will be able to take a decision on its legal status with respect to the treaty—is it or is it not a party to the treaty? These questions arise in the same conditions as those pertaining to reservations to treaties, the reactions to which (acceptance and objection) are governed by a very formal, rigid legal regime aimed principally at determining, as soon as possible, the legal status of the reserving State or organization. This aim is reflected not only by the relative formality of the rules, but also by the establishment of a presumption of acceptance after a certain period of time has elapsed in which another State or another international organization has not expressed disagreement with—i.e. objection to—the reservation.[82]

52. Thus, the procedure for reactions to conditional interpretative declarations should follow the same rules as those applicable to acceptance of and objection to reservations, including the rule on the presumption of acceptance. There may be doubts, however, about the 12-month time period set out in article 20, paragraph 5, of the 1969 and 1986 Vienna Conventions, which, as explained earlier, is probably not reflective of customary international law. Nonetheless, the reasons that led Sir Humphrey Waldock to propose this solution seem valid and transposable *mutatis mutandis* to the case of conditional interpretative declarations. As he explained:

> But there are, it is thought, good reasons for proposing the adoption of the longer period [of 12 months]. First, it is one thing to agree upon a short period [of three or six months] for the purposes of a particular treaty whose contents are known, and a somewhat different thing to agree upon it as a general rule applicable to every treaty which does not lay down a rule on the point. States may, therefore, find it easier to accept a general time limit for voicing objections, if a longer period is proposed.[83]

53. A problem of terminology arises, however. The relative parallelism noted up to this point between conditional interpretative declarations and reservations implies that reactions to such declarations could borrow the same vocabulary and be termed "acceptances" and "objections". However, the definition of objections to reservations does not seem to be at all suited to the case of a reaction expressing the disagreement of a State or an international organization with a conditional interpretative declaration made by another State or another international organization. Draft guideline 2.6.1 lays down a definition of objections to reservations that is based essentially on the effect intended by their author: according to this definition, an objection means a unilateral statement "whereby the ... State or organization purports to exclude or to modify the legal effects of the reservation, or to exclude the application of the treaty as a whole, in relations with the reserving State or organization".[84]

54. It is certainly difficult to state categorically, at the current stage of the work on the Guide to Practice and in the absence of a decision by the Commission on the legal effects of a conditional interpretative declaration on a treaty, whether an "objection" to such a declaration falls under this definition. However, there may be serious doubts about the wisdom of using the same terminology to denote both negative reactions to conditional interpretative declarations and objections to reservations. By definition, such a reaction can neither modify nor exclude the legal effect of the conditional interpretative declaration as such (regardless of what that legal effect may be); all it can do is to exclude the State or international organization from the circle of parties to the treaty. Refusal to accept the *conditional* interpretation proposed creates a situation in which the condition for consent to be bound is absent. What is more, it is

[77] The declaration was confirmed upon ratification, on 22 March 1974; see United Nations, *Treaty Series*, vol. 936, No. 9068, p. 419.

[78] See also *Yearbook ... 1999*, vol. II (Part Two), p. 103, para. (3) of the commentary to draft guideline 1.2.1.

[79] See footnote 77 above.

[80] See paragraph 5 above.

[81] *Yearbook ... 1999*, vol. II (Part Two), p. 105, para. (14) of the commentary to draft guideline 1.2.1.

[82] See *Yearbook ... 2003*, vol. II (Part Two), p. 69, draft guideline 2.4.8 (Late formulation of a conditional interpretative declaration): "A State or an international organization may not formulate a conditional interpretative declaration concerning a treaty after expressing its consent to be bound by the treaty except if none of the other Contracting Parties objects to the late formulation of the conditional interpretative declaration."

[83] *Yearbook ... 1962*, vol. II, document A/CN.4/144 and Add.1 (see footnote 59 above), p. 67, para. (16) of the commentary to article 18.

[84] *Yearbook ... 2005*, vol. II (Part Two), p. 76, para. 437.

not the author of the negative reaction, but the author of the conditional interpretative declaration, that has the responsibility to take the action that follows from the refusal.

55. The Special Rapporteur therefore considers that, for the moment, it is best to leave the terminology issue in abeyance until the Commission has taken a final decision on the effects of conditional interpretative declarations and on their possible assimilation to reservations.

"**2.9.10** *Reactions to conditional interpretative declarations*

"Guidelines 2.6 to 2.8.12 shall apply, *mutatis mutandis*, to reactions of States and international organizations to conditional interpretative declarations."

RESPONSIBILITY OF INTERNATIONAL ORGANIZATIONS

[Agenda item 3]

DOCUMENT A/CN.4/597

Sixth report on responsibility of international organizations,* by Mr. Giorgio Gaja, Special Rapporteur

[*Original: English*]
[*1 April 2008*]

CONTENTS

Multilateral instruments cited in the present report

	Source
Treaty establishing the European Economic Community (Treaty of Rome) (Rome, 25 March 1957)	United Nations, *Treaty Series*, vol. 298, No. 4300, p. 3.
Vienna Convention for the Protection of the Ozone Layer (Vienna, 22 March 1985)	*Ibid.*, vol. 1513, No. 26164, p. 293.

* The Special Rapporteur gratefully acknowledges the assistance given in the preparation of this report by Stefano Dorigo (PhD, University of Pisa, Italy), Paolo Palchetti (Associate Professor, University of Macerata, Italy) and Gerhard Thallinger (LLM, New York University).

Works cited in the present report

ALVAREZ, J. E.

"International organizations: accountability or responsibility?", *Canadian Council of International Law, 35th Annual Conference on Responsibility of Individuals, States and Organizations, Ottawa, 27 October 2006* (http://www.asil.org).

AMERASINGHE, C. F.

Principles of the Institutional Law of International Organizations. 2nd ed. Cambridge, Cambridge University Press, 2005. 535 p.

AMRALLAH, Borhan

"The international responsibility of the United Nations for activities carried out by U.N. peace-keeping forces", *Revue égyptienne de droit international*, vol. 32, 1976, pp. 57–82.

ARSANJANI, Mahnoush H.

"Claims against international organizations: *quis custodiet ipsos custodes*", *Yale Journal of World Public Order*, vol. 7, No. 2, spring 1981, pp. 131–176.

CANÇADO TRINDADE, A. A.

"Exhaustion of local remedies and the law of international organizations", *International Law Review*, vol. 57, 1979, pp. 81–123.

DAVÍ, Angelo

Comunità europee e sanzioni economiche internazionali. Naples, Jovene, 1993. 649 p.

DE VISSCHER, Paul

"Observations sur le fondement et la mise en oeuvre du principe de la responsabilité de l'Organisation des Nations Unies", *Revue de droit international et de droit comparé*, vol. XXXX, 1963, pp. 165–191.

EAGLETON, Clyde

"International organization and the law of responsibility", *Recueil des cours de l'Académie de droit international de La Haye, 1950–I.* Paris, Sirey. Vol. 76, pp. 319–425.

EHLERMANN, Claus-Dieter

"Communautés européennes et sanctions internationales: une réponse à J. Verhoeven", *Belgian Review of International Law*, vol. XVIII, 1984–1985, pp. 96–112.

GRAMLICH, Ludwig

"Diplomatic protection against acts of intergovernmental organs", *German Yearbook of International Law*, vol. 27, 1984, pp. 386–428.

HELISKOSKI, Joni

Mixed Agreements as a Technique for Organizing the International Relations of the European Community and its Member States. The Hague, Kluwer, 2001. 321 p.

INTERNATIONAL LAW ASSOCIATION

"Accountability of international organisations", *Report of the Seventy-First Conference held in Berlin, 16–21 August 2004.* London, 2004, pp. 164–234.

KLEIN, Eckart

"Sanctions by international organizations and economic communities", *Archiv des Völkerrechts*, vol. 30, 1992, pp. 101–113.

KLEIN, Pierre

La responsabilité des organisations internationales dans les ordres juridiques internes et en droit des gens. Brussels, Bruylant, 1998. 673 p.

MENG, Werner

"Internationale Organisationen im völkerrechtlichen Deliktsrecht, *Zeitschrift für ausländisches öffentliches Recht und Völkerrecht*, vol. 45, 1985, pp. 324–371, summary in English, pp. 355–357.

O'KEEFFE, David and Henry G. SCHERMERS, eds.

Mixed Agreements. Deventer, Kluwer, 1983. 248 p.

PALCHETTI, Paolo

"Reactions by the European Union to breaches of *erga omnes* obligations", *in* Enzo Cannizzaro, ed., *The European Union as an Actor in International Relations.* The Hague, Kluwer Law International, 2002, pp. 219–230.

PÉREZ GONZÁLEZ, Manuel

"Les organisations internationales et le droit de la responsabilité", *Revue générale de droit international public* (Paris), vol. XCII, 1988, pp. 63–102.

PITSCHAS, Christian

Die völkerrechtliche Verantwortlichkeit der Europäischen Gemeinschaft und ihrer Mitgliedstaaten. Berlin, Duncker & Humblot, 2001. 302 p.

REY ANEIROS, Adela

Una aproximación a la responsabilidad internacional de las organizaciones internacionales. Valencia, Tirant lo Blanch, 2006. 229 p.

RITTER, Jean-Pierre

"La protection diplomatique à l'égard d'une organisation internationale", *Annuaire français de droit international*, vol. 8, 1962, pp. 427–456.

RIVIER, Raphaële (and Philippe LAGRANGE)

"Travaux de la Commission du droit international (cinquante-huitième session) et de la Sixième Commission (soixante et unième session)", *Annuaire français de droit international*, vol. 52, 2006, pp. 305–350.

SCHERMERS, Henry G. and Niels M. BLOKKER

International Institutional Law: Unity within Diversity. 3rd rev. ed. The Hague, Martinus Nijhoff, 1995. 1305 p.

SIMMONDS, R.

Legal Problems Arising from the United Nations Military Operations in the Congo. The Hague, Martinus Nijhoff, 1968. 357 p.

STURMA, Pavel

"La participation de la Communauté européenne à des 'sanctions' internationales", *Revue du Marché commun et de l'Union européenne*, No. 366, March 1993, pp. 250–264.

TOMUSCHAT, Christian

"Kommentierung des Artikel 210", *in* Hans von der Groeben, Jochen Thiesing and Claus-Dieter Ehlermann, eds., *Kommentar zum EU-/EG-Vertrag.* 5th ed. Baden-Baden, Nomos, 1997. Vol. 5, pp. 17–60.

VACAS FERNÁNDEZ, Félix

La responsabilidad internacional de Naciones Unidas: fundamento y principales problemas de su puesta en práctica. Madrid, Dykinson, 2002. 167 p.

VERHOEVEN, Joe

"Protection diplomatique, épuisement des voies de recours et juridictions européennes", *Droit du pouvoir, pouvoir du droit: mélanges offerts à Jean Salmon.* Brussels, Bruylant, 2007, pp. 1511–1528.

"Communautés européennes et sanctions internationales", *Belgian Review of International Law*, vol. XVIII, 1984–1985, pp. 79–95.

WELLENS, Karel

Remedies against International Organisations. Cambridge, Cambridge University Press, 2002. 295 p.

Introduction

1. In its work on the responsibility of international organizations the International Law Commission has so far adopted 45 draft articles.[1] These build up Part One (arts. 1–30) and Part Two (arts. 31–45), respectively concerning "The internationally wrongful act of an international organization" and "Content of the international responsibility of an international organization".

2. Many of these articles have been the object of comments after their provisional adoption, especially in the debates held in the Sixth Committee on the report of the Commission and in written statements made by States and international organizations. Moreover, certain articles have been examined in judicial practice. Articles 3 and 5 were considered by the European Court of Human Rights in two recent decisions, first in *Behrami and Behrami* v. *France* and *Saramati* v. *France, Germany and Norway*[2] and then in *Berić and Others* v. *Bosnia and Herzegovina*.[3] Article 5 and the related commentary were referred to by the House of Lords in its judgement in *R (on the application of Al-Jedda)* v. *Secretary of State for Defence*.[4]

3. As was observed by the present writer in his fifth report and for the reasons there stated,[5] the Commission should be given an opportunity, before completing its first reading of the present draft, to review the texts that have been provisionally adopted in the light of all the available comments. The next report will contain a comprehensive survey of those comments and make some proposals for revising certain articles. The same report will also address all extant issues and propose a few general provisions to be included in part four. One of those remaining issues is the question of the existence of special rules which may take into account the peculiar features of certain organizations.

4. The present sixth report continues the examination of matters relating to the international responsibility of international organizations following the general pattern that the Commission adopted in the articles on responsibility of States for internationally wrongful acts.[6] Part three of those articles considers "The implementation of the international responsibility of a State";[7] the corresponding part in the present study discusses issues relating to the implementation of international responsibility of international organizations. After the introduction, it includes two chapters, respectively headed "Invocation of the responsibility of an international organization" and "Countermeasures".

5. Certain critics of the current draft articles have used as a mantra the refrain that the Commission is basically replacing the term "State" with "international organization" in the articles on responsibility of States for internationally wrongful acts.[8] It may therefore be useful to recall once again that neither the Special Rapporteur nor the Commission has started from a presumption that the solutions adopted with regard to States should also apply to international organizations: the Special Rapporteur had already said as much in his first report.[9] Any question was going to be, and has been, examined on its merits. Only when a question relating to the responsibility of international organizations appeared to be parallel to one that had already been examined with regard to States, and there was no reason for stating a different rule, was an identical solution adopted. Needless to say, some of the Commission's conclusions may seem questionable. There is no wish on the part of the Special Rapporteur to discourage informed criticism and suggestions for improvements on the part of any commentator. The present endeavour is a collective work, the purpose of which is to produce a text that could be of some use in international relations.

[1] The text of the draft articles so far adopted is reproduced in *Yearbook ... 2007*, vol. II (Part Two), para. 343, pp. 73 *et seq*.

[2] Decision of 2 May 2007 [GC], Nos. 71412/01 and 78166/01, paras. 29–33 and 121. This decision was referred to in the Sixth Committee by Denmark, intervening on behalf of the five Nordic countries (*Official Records of the General Assembly, Sixty-second Session, Sixth Committee*, 18th meeting (A/C.6/62/SR.18), para. 102), and Greece (*ibid.*, 19th meeting (A/C.6/62/SR.19), paras. 9–10). The Special Rapporteur had already recalled it during the debates in the Commission during the fifty-ninth session (*Yearbook ... 2001*, vol. I, 2932nd meeting).

[3] Decision of 16 October 2007, Nos. 36357/04 and others, paras. 8, 9 and 28, CEDH 2007-XII.

[4] Judgement of 12 December 2007 [2007] UKHL 58 (per Lord Bingham of Cornhill), reproduced in [2008] 2 WLR 31.

[5] *Yearbook ... 2007*, vol. II (Part One), document A/CN.4/583, pp. 6–7, paras. 3–6.

[6] *Yearbook ... 2001*, vol. II (Part Two), p. 26, para. 76.

[7] *Ibid.*, p. 29.

[8] The latest in time is a remark by Rivier, "Travaux de la Commission du droit international et de la Sixième Commission", p. 335. The author even assumed the existence of a decision by the Commission to align the new text on that on State responsibility.

[9] *Yearbook ... 2003*, vol. II (Part One), document A/CN.4/532, p. 109, para. 11.

CHAPTER I

Invocation of the responsibility of an international organization

6. Implementation of the responsibility of an international organization is here considered only insofar as responsibility may be invoked by a State or another international organization. Since, according to article 36 of the current draft, the international obligations set out in Part Two only concern the breach of an obligation under international law that an international organization owes to a State, another international organization or the international community as a whole,[10] it seems unnecessary to specify in part three that the scope of the articles on implementation of responsibility is similarly limited. The same approach was taken when drafting the articles on responsibility of States for internationally wrongful acts. These do not include in part three any provision

[10] *Yearbook ... 2007*, vol. II (Part Two), para. 343, p. 77.

stating that implementation of responsibility is covered only insofar as responsibility is invoked by another State. This limitation of the scope of part three could be taken as implied by article 33,[11] which corresponds to article 36 of the current draft.

7. In most cases, responsibility may be invoked only by an entity which could be considered as injured. Determining when a State may be regarded as injured could hardly vary according to whether the responsible entity is a State or an international organization. Thus, the definition of "injured State" in article 42 on responsibility of States for internationally wrongful acts[12] clearly applies also when a State invokes the responsibility of an international organization.

8. The possibility for an international organization to invoke, as an injured entity, the responsibility of a State was affirmed by ICJ in its advisory opinion on *Reparation for Injuries Suffered in the Service of the United Nations*, when the Court stated that it was "established that the Organization has capacity to bring claims on the international plane".[13] What the Court said with regard to a claim for reparation by the United Nations may be extended to all international organizations possessing legal personality, when an obligation owed to them has been breached, whether by a State or by another international organization.

9. The criteria for defining when an entity is injured by an internationally wrongful act of a State or an international organization do not appear to depend on the nature of that entity. Hence, an international organization would have to be considered as injured under the same conditions as a State. This would mean that an international organization may invoke the responsibility of another international organization in the three following cases: first, when the obligation breached is owed to the latter organization individually; secondly, when it is owed to several entities which include the latter organization, or to the international community as a whole, if the breach specially affects that organization; thirdly, when it is owed to several entities which include the latter organization, or to the international community as a whole, and the breach radically changes the position of all the entities to which the obligation is owed. While the second and third cases are generally rare, and it may be difficult to find pertinent examples concerning international organizations, the fact that international organizations may be injured under those conditions cannot be ruled out. It is therefore necessary to include also the second and third cases in the definition of injured international organizations.

10. The definition of the injured entity should therefore consist in an adaptation of the corresponding definition in article 42 on responsibility of States for internationally wrongful acts.[14] The following text is suggested:

"*Draft article 46. Invocation of responsibility by an injured State or international organization*

"A State or an international organization is entitled as an injured party to invoke the responsibility of another international organization if the obligation breached is owed to:

"(*a*) that State or the former international organization individually;

"(*b*) a group of parties including that State or that former international organization, or the international community as a whole, and the breach of the obligation:

"(i) specially affects that State or that international organization; or

"(ii) is of such a character as radically to change the position of all the parties to which the obligation is owed with respect to the further performance of the obligation."

11. While the rules of the internal law of a State will determine which is the State organ that is competent for bringing a claim, in the case of an international organization reference would have to be made to the rules of the organization.[15] These will also provide whether in certain cases there is an obligation for the competent organ to bring a claim.[16] The rules of the organization will further have to be applied in order to ascertain whether an organization waived a claim or acquiesced to the termination of a claim. Since the requirement that the conduct of the organization be appraised according to its pertinent rules is of general application, it seems preferable not to make a specific reference to the rules of the organization in part three. This would also be consistent with the fact that the articles on responsibility of States for internationally wrongful acts do not address the question of which State organ is to be regarded as competent for bringing or withdrawing a claim. It would be strange for the Commission to address the latter question for the first time in the present context.

12. Part three, chapter I, of the articles on responsibility of States for internationally wrongful acts includes some procedural rules of a general character. Two of them concern the modalities to be observed by a State when invoking the responsibility of another State with regard to notice of claims (art. 43) and the loss of the right to invoke responsibility (art. 45).[17] While those articles only consider claims that States may prefer against other States, there is nothing in the content of those articles that suggests that they would not also be applicable with regard to the invocation by a State of the responsibility of an international organization.

[11] *Yearbook ... 2001*, vol. II (Part Two), p. 94.

[12] *Ibid.*, p. 117.

[13] *Reparation for Injuries Suffered in the Service of the United Nations, Advisory Opinion, I.C.J. Reports 1949*, pp. 184–185.

[14] *Yearbook ... 2001*, vol. II (Part Two), p. 117.

[15] A definition of the "rules of the organization" is contained in article 4, paragraph 4, of the current draft (*Yearbook ... 2007*, vol. II (Part Two), para. 343, p. 74).

[16] Arsanjani, "Claims against international organizations: *quis custodiet ipsos custodes*", p. 147, raised the question whether "the U.N. is under an *obligation* to bring international claims on behalf of its injured staff".

[17] *Yearbook ... 2001*, vol. II (Part Two), p. 119 and p. 121, respectively.

13. The situation of international organizations does not differ from that of States in respect of notice of claims and the loss of the right to invoke responsibility. It seems therefore reasonable to extend to international organizations the same rules that are expressed with regard to States in the articles on responsibility of States for internationally wrongful acts.

14. The text of articles 43 and 45 on responsibility of States for internationally wrongful acts should be adapted, when considering the invocation of the responsibility of an international organization, in order to cover the case in which the claimant entity is either a State or another international organization. The draft articles would then read:

"*Draft article 47. Notice of claim by an injured State or international organization*

"1. An injured State which invokes the responsibility of an international organization shall give notice of its claim to that organization.

"2. An injured international organization which invokes the responsibility of another international organization shall give notice of its claim to the latter organization.

"3. The injured State or international organization may specify in particular:

"(*a*) the conduct that the responsible international organization should take in order to cease the wrongful act, if it is continuing;

"(*b*) what form reparation should take in accordance with the provisions of Part Two.

"*Draft article 48. Loss of the right to invoke responsibility*

"The responsibility of an international organization may not be invoked if:

"(*a*) the injured State or international organization has validly waived the claim;

"(*b*) the injured State or international organization is to be considered as having, by reason of its conduct, validly acquiesced in the lapse of the claim."

15. The articles on responsibility of States for internationally wrongful acts include, between the two articles which have been considered above, an article on admissibility of claims (art. 44)[18] which addresses questions relating to diplomatic protection.[19] The exercise by a State of diplomatic protection against an international organization is a rare occurrence. However, it is not inconceivable, in particular in relation to an organization that administers a territory or uses force.

16. Should a State exercise diplomatic protection against an international organization, nationality of the claim would be a first requirement. The more problematic question would be the need to exhaust local remedies. On this issue, a variety of views have been expressed in the literature, the prevailing opinion being that the local remedies rule applies when adequate and effective remedies are provided within the organization concerned.[20]

17. One can find some instances of practice in which the local remedies rule was invoked with regard to remedies existing within the European Union. Although this practice relates to claims that were addressed to the member States, one can infer that, had the responsibility of the Union been invoked, exhaustion of remedies existing within the Union would have been required. One of these instances of practice was a statement made on behalf of all the member States of the Union by the Director-General of the Legal Service of the European Commission before the ICAO Council in relation to a dispute between those States and the United States concerning measures taken for abating noise originating from aircraft. The member States of the Union contended that the claim by the United States was inadmissible because remedies relating to the controversial European Community regulation had not been exhausted, since the measure was at the time "subject to challenge before the

---

[18] *Ibid.*, p. 120.

[19] Diplomatic protection was defined by the Commission as "the invocation by a State, through diplomatic action or other means of peaceful settlement, of the responsibility of another State for an injury caused by an internationally wrongful act of that State to a natural or legal person that is a national of the former State with a view to the implementation of such responsibility" (*Ahmadou Sadio Diallo (Republic of Guinea* v. *Democratic Republic of the Congo), Preliminary Objections, Judgment, I.C.J. Reports 2007*, para. 39). In that case, ICJ considered that this definition—which is contained in article 1 of the draft articles on diplomatic protection, *Yearbook ... 2006*, vol. II (Part Two), p. 16—"reflected" customary international law.

[20] The applicability of the local remedies rule to claims addressed by States to international organizations was maintained by several authors: Ritter, "La protection diplomatique à l'égard d'une organisation internationale", pp. 454–455; De Visscher, "Observations sur le fondement et la mise en oeuvre du principe de la responsabilité de l'Organisation des Nations Unies", p. 174; Simmonds, *Legal Problems arising from the United Nations Military Operations in the Congo* , p. 238; Amrallah, "The international responsibility of the United Nations for activities carried out by U.N. peace-keeping forces", p. 67; Gramlich, "Diplomatic protection against acts of intergovernmental organs", p. 398 (more tentatively); Schermers and Blokker, *International Institutional Law: Unity within Diversity*, para. 1858; Pierre Klein, *La responsabilité des organisations internationales dans les ordres juridiques internes et en droit des gens*, pp. 534 *et seq.*; Pitschas, *Die völkerrechtliche Verantwortlichkeit der Europäischen Gemeinschaft und ihrer Mitgliedstaaten*, p. 250; and Wellens, *Remedies against International Organisations*, pp. 66–67. The same opinion was voiced by the International Law Association, in its "Final report on accountability of international organisations", p. 213. Eagleton, "International organization and the law of responsibility", p. 395, considered that the local remedies rule would not be applicable to a claim against the United Nations, but only because "the United Nations does not have a judicial system, or other means of '*local* redress' such as are regularly maintained by states". Cançado Trindade, "Exhaustion of local remedies and the law of international organizations", p. 108, noted that "when a claim for damages is lodged against an international organization, application of the rule is not excluded, but the law here may still develop in different directions". The view that the local remedies rule should be applied in a flexible manner was expressed by Pérez González, "Les organisations internationales et le droit de la responsabilité", p. 71. Amerasinghe, *Principles of the Institutional Law of International Organizations*, p. 486, considered that, since international organizations "do not have jurisdictional powers over individuals in general", it is "questionable whether they can provide suitable internal remedies. Thus, it is difficult to see how the rule of local remedies would be applicable". This view, which had already been expressed in the first edition of the same book, was shared by Vacas Fernández, *La responsabilidad internacional de Naciones Unidas: fundamento y principales problemas de su puesta in práctica*, pp. 139–140.

national courts of EU Member States and the European Court of Justice".[21]

18. Another example is provided by the judgement of the European Court of Human Rights in *Bosphorus Hava Yollari Turizm ve Ticaret Anonim Sirketi* v. *Ireland*.[22] The case concerned an alleged infringement of human rights owing to the implementation in Ireland of an European Community regulation. In finding that there were no remedies that the applicant had failed to exhaust, the Court included a consideration of the remedies available within the European Union.[23]

19. When an international organization addresses a claim on behalf of one of its agents, whether against a State or another international organization, the requirement of nationality clearly does not apply. The local remedies rule could be relevant only insofar as the claim by the organization also concerns damage caused to one of its agents as a private individual.[24] The entitlement of an organization to make such a claim was admitted by ICJ in its advisory opinion on *Reparation of Injuries Suffered in the Service of the United Nations*.[25] However, the eventuality of this type of claim being addressed by an international organization against another international organization is clearly remote.

20. The fact that issues of admissibility concerning nationality and local remedies may conceivably also arise with regard to claims addressed to international organizations does not entail that the present draft articles should include a provision on the lines of article 44 of the articles on responsibility of States for internationally wrongful acts.[26] That provision is essentially a reminder of the two main conditions for the exercise of diplomatic protection. It concerns a category of claims which is of considerable importance in the relations among States. Since the practical relevance of diplomatic protection with regard to State responsibility does not find a parallel in the present context, a provision on the admissibility of claims may well be omitted in the present draft. This would not imply that the requirements of nationality of claims and exhaustion of local remedies are always irrelevant when a claim is addressed against an international organization.

[21] "Oral statement and comments on the US response" (15 November 2000), *Yearbook ... 2004*, vol. II (Part One), document A/CN.4/545, annex, attachment No. 18.

[22] [GC], No. 45036/98 ECHR 2005–VI, p. 141, para. 105.

[23] Judgement of 30 June 2005, *ibid.*

[24] The local remedies rule does not apply with regard to claims concerning damage caused to agents insofar as it affects the respective State or international organization, because these matters lie outside the field of diplomatic protection. That point was stressed by Verhoeven, "Protection diplomatique, épuisement des voies de recours et juridictions européennes", p. 1517.

[25] *I.C.J. Reports 1949* (see footnote 13 above), p. 184.

[26] The text of article 44 (referred to in paragraph 15 above) runs as follows: "The responsibility of a State may not be invoked if:

"(*a*) the claim is not brought in accordance with any applicable rule relating to the nationality of claims;

"(*b*) the claim is one to which the rule of exhaustion of local remedies applies and any available and effective local remedy has not been exhausted."

(*Yearbook ... 2001*, vol. II (Part Two), p. 120)

21. Following the pattern of the articles on responsibility of States for internationally wrongful acts, the next question to be addressed concerns the case of a plurality of injured entities. With regard to a plurality of injured States, a provision contained in those articles (art. 46) says that: "Where several States are injured by the same internationally wrongful act, each injured State may separately invoke the responsibility of the State which has committed the internationally wrongful act."[27] What is said about a plurality of States being injured by another State may clearly be extended to the case that the responsible entity is an international organization instead of a State.

22. The same approach should be taken when the injured entities are international organizations. They may be injured on their own or together with certain States. These States would likely be members of an injured organization, but may conceivably be non-members. The existence of a plurality of injured entities would depend, first, on whether the obligation breached is owed to (*a*) two or more organizations or (*b*) to one or more organizations and to one or more States,[28] and, moreover, on whether the conditions that are laid down for determining whether an entity is injured by the breach of the obligation are fulfilled.

23. It follows that the content of the corresponding provision in the articles on responsibility of States for internationally wrongful acts may be used as a model, with the adaptations necessary for the present purposes. The following text is here proposed with the intention of covering a number of cases: that of two or more States being injured; that of two or more international organizations being injured; that of one or more States and one or more international organizations being injured.

"*Draft article 49. Plurality of injured entities*

"Where several entities are injured by the same internationally wrongful act of an international organization, each injured State or international organization may separately invoke the responsibility of the international organization which has committed the internationally wrongful act."

24. When an international organization is responsible for an internationally wrongful act, another entity may also be responsible for the same act. The possibility of a plurality of responsible States has been envisaged in article 47 on responsibility of States for internationally wrongful acts.[29] The possibility of a plurality of responsible entities is even more likely when one of them is an international organization, given the existence of a variety of cases in which this may occur. In particular, there are several instances in which both an organization and its members, or some of them, may incur responsibility

[27] *Ibid.*, p. 123.

[28] This may occur, for instance, with regard to certain mixed agreements concluded by the European Community and some of its member States (or all of them) with one or more non-member States, when the obligations owed to the Community and its members have not been separated (see O'Keeffe and Schermers, *Mixed Agreements* and Heliskoski, *Mixed Agreements as a Technique for Organizing the International Relations of the European Community and its Member States*).

[29] *Yearbook ... 2001*, vol. II (Part Two), p. 124.

for the same internationally wrongful act. Articles 28–29 of the present draft refer to some of those instances.[30] Another case is when both the organization and its members have jointly undertaken the same obligation towards a third party and the obligation is breached.[31]

25. With regard to a plurality of responsible States, the articles on responsibility of States for internationally wrongful acts make three points that are equally relevant when one of the responsible entities is an international organization. The first one is that the responsibility of each entity may be invoked in relation to the act. This point needs to be qualified, in view of the statement in article 29 of the present draft that when, under the conditions there provided, a member of an organization is responsible, that responsibility "is presumed to be subsidiary".[32] The concept of subsidiarity implies, in this context, that the responsibility of the member may be invoked only if the responsibility of the organization has been invoked first and to no avail or at any rate to little purpose.

26. The second and third points made in article 47 on responsibility of States for internationally wrongful acts are generally also applicable to the case that one of the responsible entities is an international organization: the injured party is not entitled "to recover, by way of compensation, more than the damage it has suffered" (art. 47, para. 2 (*a*)); the entity that provided reparation may have a right of recourse against the other responsible entities. With regard to these points it matters little who is the responsible entity.

27. While article 47 of the articles on responsibility of States for internationally wrongful acts provides a basis for the drafting of a text, a few adaptations seem necessary. One has to envisage the possibility that two or more organizations are responsible or that one or more organizations are responsible together with one or more States. Moreover, a proviso should cover the question of subsidiarity. Finally, the text may be slightly clearer if, unlike article 47, it specified which entity may have a right of recourse. The proposed text runs as follows:

"*Draft article 50. Plurality of responsible entities*

"1. Where an international organization and one or more States or other organizations are responsible for the same internationally wrongful act, the responsibility of each responsible entity may be invoked in relation to that act. However, if the responsibility of an entity is only subsidiary, it may be invoked only to the extent that the invocation of the primary responsibility has not led to reparation.

"2. Paragraph 1:

"(*a*) does not permit any injured State or international organization to recover, by way of compensation, more than the damage it has suffered;

"(*b*) is without prejudice to any right of recourse that the entity providing reparation may have against the other responsible entities."

28. Injured entities within the meaning of article 46 of the current draft are not the only ones that may invoke responsibility. According to article 48 on responsibility of States for internationally wrongful acts there are two cases in which a State other than "an injured" State may invoke responsibility.[33] The State in question would be entitled to request cessation of the internationally wrongful act and performance of the obligation of reparation "in the interest of the injured State or of the beneficiaries of the obligation breached" (art. 48, para. 2 (*b*)). The first case envisaged in article 48 is that "the obligation breached is owed to a group of States including that State, and is established for the protection of a collective interest of the group" (para. 1 (*a*)).

29. For the purposes of invoking responsibility in the circumstances so described, the fact that the obligation in question is breached by an international organization instead of a State appears to be immaterial. Nor does it appear relevant that the group of entities to which the obligation is owed includes an international organization. It seems reasonable that in the latter case international organizations may invoke responsibility under the same conditions applying to States.

30. One example from practice of a claim made by a non-injured State against an international organization is provided by the *European Communities: Regime for the Importation, Sale and Distribution of Bananas* case.[34] A WTO panel found that, although the United States had "no legal right or interest"[35] in the case, its potential interest in trade in goods and services and its "interest in a determination of whether the EC regime is inconsistent with the requirements of WTO rules" were "each sufficient to establish a right to pursue a WTO dispute settlement proceeding".[36] The panel referred in a footnote to a provision of the articles on responsibility of States for internationally wrongful acts adopted on first reading, which included in its definition of "injured State": "If the right infringed by the act of a State arises from a multilateral treaty, any other State party to the multilateral treaty, if it is established that the right has been expressly stipulated in that treaty for the protection of the collective interests of the States parties thereto."[37]

31. The second case in which, according to article 48 on responsibility of States for internationally wrongful acts, non-injured States may request cessation of the breach and performance of the obligation of reparation is that "the obligation breached is owed to the international community as a whole".[38] The fact that the breach

[30] *Yearbook ... 2007*, vol. II (Part Two), para. 343, p. 76.

[31] Mixed agreements referred to in footnote 28 above also provide an example for this purpose, when the obligations for the European Community and its members have not been separated.

[32] See footnote 30 above.

[33] *Yearbook ... 2001*, vol. II (Part Two), p. 126.

[34] WT/DS27/R/ECU, WT/DS27/R/MEX, WT/DS27/R/USA, WT/DS27/R/GTM and WT/DS27/R/HND (22 May 1997), chap. VII. Reproduced in WTO, *Dispute Settlement Reports 1997*, vols. II–III (Cambridge, Cambridge University Press).

[35] *Ibid.*, para. 7.47.

[36] *Ibid.*, para. 7.50.

[37] *Ibid.*, footnote 361. The quoted text is reproduced in *Yearbook ... 1996*, vol. II (Part Two), p. 62, art. 40, para. 2 (*f*).

[38] *Yearbook ... 2001*, vol. II (Part Two), p. 126, para. 1 (*b*).

is committed by an international organization instead of a State cannot make a difference in the entitlement of non-injured States to invoke responsibility. As was noted in that respect by OPCW, "there does not appear to be any reason why States—as distinct from other international organizations—may not also be able to invoke the responsibility of an international organization".[39]

32. A more difficult issue is whether an international organization would be entitled to invoke the responsibility of another international organization for the breach of an obligation owed to the international community as a whole.

33. Practice in that regard is not very indicative. This is not only because that practice relates to action taken by international organizations in respect of States. Organizations generally respond to breaches committed by their members and act on the basis of their respective rules. This does not imply the existence for international organizations of a more general entitlement to invoke responsibility in case of a breach of an obligation towards the international community as a whole. The most significant practice in this respect appears that of the European Union, which has often stated that non-members committed breaches of obligations which appear to be owed towards the international community as a whole. For instance, a Common Position of the Council of the European Union of 26 April 2000 referred to "severe and systematic violations of human rights in Burma".[40] In most cases this type of statement by the European Union led to the adoption of economic measures against the allegedly responsible State. Those measures will be discussed in the next chapter. For the present purposes, it is important to note that it is not altogether clear whether responsibility was jointly invoked by the member States of the European Union or by the European Union as a distinct organization.

34. There is only limited literature on the question whether an international organization would be entitled to invoke responsibility in the case of a breach of an obligation towards the international community as a whole. Writings generally focus on the European Union; the views expressed appear to be divided, although the majority of authors gives a favourable answer.[41]

35. In its 2007 report to the General Assembly, the Commission asked for comments on the following question:

> Article 48 on responsibility of States for internationally wrongful acts provides that, in case of a breach by a State of an obligation owed to the international community as a whole, States are entitled to claim from the responsible State cessation of the internationally wrongful act and performance of the obligation of reparation in the interest of the injured State or of the beneficiaries of the obligation breached. Should a breach of an obligation owed to the international community as a whole be committed by an international organization, would the other organizations or some of them be entitled to make a similar claim?[42]

36. In the Sixth Committee the views expressed were clearly in favour of a positive answer. While certain States gave an unqualified reply to this effect,[43] a higher number of States considered that only certain organizations would be entitled to invoke responsibility: those organizations that have the mandate to protect the general interests of the international community.[44] The latter view was shared by two international organizations in their written comments. OPCW wrote:

> In the case of international organizations, the ability to invoke responsibility for violations of obligations owed to the international community as a whole could depend on the scope of the activities of the organization as defined in its constituent document. Accordingly, every "concerned" international organization could be entitled to invoke responsibility and claim the cessation of the wrongful act to the extent that affects its mandate as set out in its constituent instrument.[45]

The European Commission voiced similar views:

> As the international community as a whole cannot act on its own lacking centralized institutions, it is for the individual members of that community to take action against the offender on behalf and in the interest of the community. It appears to the European Commission that this right pertains in principle to all members of the international community, including international organizations as subjects of international law. However, at the same time international organizations are entrusted by their statutes to carry out specific functions and to protect certain interests only. Where the breached obligation relates to subject matters that fall outside the organization's powers and functions, there would be no compelling reason why it should be allowed to take decentralized enforcement action. For example, it is hardly conceivable that a technical transport organization should be allowed to sanction a military alliance for a breach of a fundamental guarantee of international humanitarian law that may be owed to the international community as a whole.[46]

37. If this logic is followed, the possibility for an international organization of invoking responsibility for the breach of an obligation towards the international community would depend on the content of the obligation breached and on its relation to the mandate of that organization. This entitlement would not necessarily depend on the fact that the international organization is a member of the international community. It could be seen as delegated by the States that are members of the organization. The latter approach would seem in line with the following statement made by ICJ in its advisory opinion on the *Legality of the Use by a State of Nuclear Weapons in Armed Conflict*:

---

[39] A/CN.4/593 and Add.1, sect. F1 (reproduced in the present volume).

[40] *Official Journal of the European Communities*, No. L 122, vol. 43, p. 1 (24 May 2000).

[41] The opinion that at least certain international organizations could invoke responsibility in case of a breach of an obligation *erga omnes* was expressed by Ehlermann, "Communautés européennes et sanctions internationales: une réponse à J. Verhoeven", pp. 104–105; Eckart Klein, "Sanctions by international organizations and economic communities", p. 110; Davì, *Comunità europee e sanzioni economiche internazionali*, pp. 496 *et seq.*; Tomuschat, "Kommentierung des Artikel 210", pp. 28–29; Pierre Klein, *op. cit.*, pp. 401 *et seq.*; Rey Aneiros, *Una aproximación a la responsabilidad internacional de las organizaciones internacionales*, p. 166. The opposite view was maintained by Verhoeven, "Communautés européennes ...", pp. 89–90, and Sturma, "La participation de la Communauté européenne à des 'sanctions' internationales", p. 258. According to Palchetti, "Reactions by the European Union to breaches of *erga omnes* obligations", p. 226: "The role of the Community appears to be only that of implementing rights which are owed to its Member States."

[42] *Yearbook ... 2007*, vol. II (Part Two), p. 6, para. 30 (*a*).

[43] See the statements by Malaysia (*Official Records of the General Assembly, Sixty-second Session, Sixth Committee*, 19th meeting (A/C.6/62/SR.19), para. 75), Hungary (21st meeting (A/C.6/62/SR.21), para. 16), Cyprus (*ibid.*, para. 38) and Belgium (*ibid.*, para. 90).

[44] Thus the statements by Argentina (18th meeting (A/C.6/62/SR.18), para. 64), Denmark, on behalf of the five Nordic countries (*ibid.*, para. 100), Italy (19th meeting (A/C.6/62/SR.19), para. 40), Japan (*ibid.*, para. 100), the Netherlands (20th meeting (A/C.6/62/SR.20), para. 39), the Russian Federation (21st meeting (A/C.6/62/SR.21), para. 70) and Switzerland (*ibid.*, para. 85).

[45] A/CN.4/593 and Add.1, sect. F1 (reproduced in the present volume).

[46] *Ibid.*, sect. F2.

International organizations are subjects of international law which do not, unlike States, possess a general competence. International organizations are governed by the "principle of speciality", that is to say, they are invested by the States which create them with powers, the limits of which are a function of the common interests whose promotion those States entrust to them.[47]

38. In order to determine when a non-injured international organization would be entitled to invoke responsibility of another international organization for the breach of an obligation towards the international community, one could use wording similar to that used in article 22, paragraph 1 (*a*), for determining when an international organization may invoke necessity as a circumstance precluding wrongfulness.[48]

39. As a matter of drafting, while article 48 on responsibility of States for internationally wrongful acts may provide the basic model, various changes would have to be introduced in order to distinguish the entitlement that States have in invoking responsibility from the more limited entitlement of international organizations. In the last paragraph, given the absence in the proposed draft of a provision on admissibility of claims, an ambiguity in the text on State responsibility would be removed. For the present purposes, it is sufficient to extend to non-injured States or international organizations the applicability of the two provisions concerning notice of claims and the loss of the right to invoke responsibility.

40. The following text is therefore proposed:

"*Draft article 51. Invocation of responsibility by an entity other than an injured State or international organization*

"1. Any State or international organization other than an injured State or organization is entitled to invoke the responsibility of an international organization in accordance with paragraph 4 if the obligation breached is owed to a group of entities including the State or organization that invokes responsibility, and is established for the protection of a collective interest of the group.

"2. Any State other than an injured State is entitled to invoke the responsibility of an international organization in accordance with paragraph 4 if the obligation breached is owed to the international community as a whole.

"3. Any international organization that is not an injured organization is entitled to invoke the responsibility of another international organization in accordance with paragraph 4 if the obligation breached is owed to the international community as a whole and if the organization that invokes responsibility has been given the function to protect the interest of the international community underlying that obligation.

"4. Any State or international organization entitled to invoke responsibility under the preceding paragraphs may claim from the responsible international organization:

"(*a*) cessation of the internationally wrongful act, and assurances and guarantees of non-repetition in accordance with article 33;

"(*b*) performance of the obligation of reparation in accordance with Part Two, in the interest of the injured State or international organization or of the beneficiaries of the obligation breached.

"5. The requirements for the invocation of responsibility by an injured State or international organization under articles 47 and 48 apply to an invocation of responsibility by a State or international organization entitled to do so under the preceding paragraphs."

[47] *Legality of the Use by a State of Nuclear Weapons in Armed Conflict, Advisory Opinion, I.C.J. Reports 1996*, p. 78, para. 25.

[48] *Yearbook ... 2007*, vol. II (Part Two), para. 343, p. 75.

CHAPTER II

Countermeasures

41. In the context of the present part, countermeasures need to be examined insofar as they may be taken against an international organization which is responsible for an internationally wrongful act. Although the relevant practice is scarce, countermeasures are an important aspect of implementation of international responsibility which cannot be ignored in the present draft. Moreover, it would be hard to find a convincing reason for exempting international organizations from being possible targets of countermeasures.[49]

42. Practice relating to WTO offers some examples of countermeasures taken by certain States against the European Communities with the authorization of the Dispute Settlement Body: for instance by Canada in 1999 in response to the failure, on the part of the European Communities, to implement a decision concerning Canadian beef that was produced using growth hormones.[50] In another case, *United States: Import Measures on Certain Products from the European Communities*, a WTO panel considered that the suspension of concessions or other obligations that had been authorized by the Dispute Settlement Body was "essentially retaliatory in nature".[51]

[49] According to Alvarez, "International organizations: accountability or responsibility?", pp. 33–34. The whole work of the Commission on responsibility of international organizations would become "a train wreck—if, for example, the ILC's anticipated provision with respect to countermeasures directed at wrongful IO [international organization] action will provide new justifications for those who, such as certain members of the U.S. Congress, have long been inclined to 'sanction' the UN by, for example, withholding U.S. dues". It is not clear to which internationally wrongful act the author refers that was committed by the United Nations and injured the United States. Nor is it clear whether he suggests that, although countermeasures would have to be regarded as admissible against international organizations under international law, the Commission should refrain from saying so for tactical reasons.

[50] See http:// international.gc.ca.

[51] Report of the Panel (WT/DS165R of 17 July 2000), para. 6.23.

The panel did not make any distinction between countermeasures taken against a State and those taken against an international organization when it observed:

Under general international law, retaliation (also referred to as reprisals or countermeasures) has undergone major changes in the course of the XX century, specially, as a result of the prohibition of the use of force (*jus ad bellum*). Under international law, these types of countermeasures are now subject to requirements, such as those identified by the International Law Commission in its work on state responsibility (proportionality etc. ... see Article 43 of the Draft). However, in WTO, countermeasures, retaliations and reprisals are strictly regulated and can take place only within the framework of the WTO/DSU.[52]

43. These instances from practice confirm that injured States may generally take countermeasures against a responsible international organization under the same conditions applying to countermeasures against a responsible State. However, this conclusion needs to be qualified. Should an injured State intend to take countermeasures against a responsible organization of which that State is a member, the rules of the organization may impose some further restrictions or even forbid countermeasures in this case. For example, when two member States of the European Communities argued that their breaches of an obligation under the EEC Treaty were justified by the fact that the Council of that organization had previously committed a breach, the Court of Justice of the European Communities stated that

[E]xcept where otherwise expressly provided, the basic concept of the [EEC] Treaty requires that the Member States shall not take the law into their own hands. Therefore the fact that the Council failed to carry out its obligations cannot relieve the defendants from carrying out theirs.[53]

The fact that members are forbidden to take countermeasures finds in the European Communities a reason in the existing system of judicial remedies. However, restrictions may exist with regard to other international organizations even if similar remedies are not provided within the organization concerned.

44. Resort to countermeasures by an injured international organization against a responsible international organization is certainly a rare event. However, there are no reasons why an injured international organization should not have at its disposal such a significant instrument for inducing a responsible entity to comply with the obligations set out in Part Two. As was noted with regard to States, the rules of the responsible organization may restrict resort to countermeasures by an injured organization which is a member of the former organization. Moreover, the rules of the injured organization may also affect the possibility for that organization to take countermeasures against a responsible organization when the latter is a member of the former organization. Apart from these eventualities, one would have to consider whether the situation of an injured international organization is generally identical to that of an injured State or whether, as the Commission put it in a request for comments from States and international organizations, international organizations "encounter further restrictions than those that are listed in articles 49 to 53 of the articles on responsibility of States for internationally wrongful acts".[54]

45. In the Sixth Committee several States expressed the view that no distinction should be made between injured international organizations and injured States in this respect.[55] Some States, while admitting in principle that an international organization may take countermeasures like a State, stressed the need for the organization "to act within the limits of its mandate".[56] One State argued that there should exist, as an additional requirement for countermeasures to be taken by an international organization, "a close connection to the right protected by the obligation breached".[57] Another State remarked that when international organizations take countermeasures, they mainly resort to non-compliance of obligations under a treaty, but that State did not assume that there was a corresponding restriction to the possibility to resort to countermeasures.[58]

46. The rules of the organization will determine what sort of countermeasures may be taken and which organ of the organization is competent to take them. As already noted above (para. 11) with regard to the presentation and withdrawal of claims, it is not necessary to state in the draft presently under discussion that the conduct of an international organization is governed by its rules. It has to be expected that an international organization will act consistently with its own rules. However, should an organization fail to apply its own rules when taking countermeasures, the legal consequence is not necessarily that countermeasures would have to be regarded as unlawful. One would have to distinguish the position of the organization towards its members from that towards non-members. With regard to non-members, the fact that a countermeasure has been taken by the international organization in breach of its own rules does not *per se* make the countermeasure unlawful. On the contrary, in respect of members, since the rules of the organization are applicable in the relations between the organization and its members, those rules would set out the consequence of their breach on the lawfulness of countermeasures.

47. In the present context, there is little to change, apart from some of the wording, in article 49 of the articles on responsibility of States for internationally wrongful acts,[59] which describes the object and limits of countermeasures. For the purposes of the current draft, the text of

[52] *Ibid.*, footnote 100. The reference made by the panel to the work of the Commission concerns the articles on responsibility of States for internationally wrongful acts, adopted on first reading.

[53] Judgement of 13 November 1964, *Commission of the European Economic Community* v. *Grand Duchy of Luxembourg and Kingdom of Belgium*, joined cases 90 and 91/63, *European Court Reports 1964*, p. 631.

[54] *Yearbook ... 2007*, vol. II (Part Two), p. 6, para. 30 (*b*).

[55] See the statements of Denmark on behalf of the five Nordic countries (*Official Records of the General Assembly, Sixty-second Session, Sixth Committee*, 18th meeting (A/C.6/62/SR.18), para. 101), Japan (19th meeting (A/C.6/62/SR.19), para. 100), the Netherlands (20th meeting (A/C.6/62/SR.20), para. 40) and Belgium (21st meeting (A/C.6/62/SR.21), para. 91).

[56] Statement by the Russian Federation (21st meeting (A/C.6/62/SR.21), para. 71). Similarly, Switzerland (*ibid.*, para. 86) referred to the "mandate of the organization" and also to the "purpose" for which the organization was established. One may approach to these comments the suggestion by Malaysia (19th meeting (A/C.6/62/SR.19), para. 75) that "the Commission should consider whether additional restrictions should be imposed, taking into account the nature and legal capacity of international organizations".

[57] See the statement by Argentina (18th meeting (A/C.6/62/SR.18), para. 64).

[58] This remark was made by Italy (19th meeting (A/C.6/62/SR.19), para. 41).

[59] *Yearbook ... 2001*, vol. II (Part Two), p. 129.

paragraphs 1–2 has to be modified in order to cover countermeasures that an injured State or international organization may take against a responsible international organization. Paragraph 3 does not require any change. It seems useful to add two further paragraphs to this initial article, in order to stress the role that the rules of the organization may have in restricting or precluding countermeasures in the relations between an international organization and its members. One of the paragraphs would deal with the rules of the responsible organization and the other with the rules of the organization that invokes responsibility.

48. The following text is suggested:

"*Draft article 52. Object and limits of countermeasures*

"1. An injured State or international organization may only take countermeasures against an international organization which is responsible for an internationally wrongful act in order to induce that organization to comply with its obligations under Part Two.

"2. Countermeasures are limited to the non-performance for the time being of international obligations of the State or international organization taking the measures towards the responsible international organization.

"3. Countermeasures shall, as far as possible, be taken in such a way as to permit the resumption of performance of the obligations in question.

"4. Where an international organization is responsible for an internationally wrongful act, an injured member of that organization may take countermeasures against the organization only if this is not inconsistent with the rules of the same organization.

"5. Where an international organization which is responsible for an internationally wrongful act is a member of the injured international organization, the latter organization may take countermeasures against its member only if this is not inconsistent with the rules of the injured organization."

49. Countermeasures taken against an international organization involve by definition the non-performance by the injured State or international organization of one of its obligations, that is conduct which would, but for the previous breach, injure the responsible organization. Should the injured State or international organization not be under an obligation to take a certain conduct, that conduct would *per se* be lawful and therefore could not be considered a countermeasure.

50. Article 50 of the draft articles on responsibility of States for internationally wrongful acts[60] contains a list of obligations that a State may not lawfully breach when it takes countermeasures against another State. These are obligations that because of their importance have to be respected even when a State has been previously injured by a breach. The importance of the obligations concerned does not change according to the subject to whom they are owed; most of them can any way be characterized as obligations towards the international community as a whole. Thus, the list is also clearly relevant when an injured State intends to take countermeasures against an international organization.

51. Given the importance of the obligations that are listed, similar restrictions would also seem to apply to injured international organizations, even if some of the obligations that are mentioned in the list are of little relevance to most organizations. This is in particular the case of the obligation concerning "inviolability of diplomatic or consular agents, premises, archives and documents" (art. 50, para. 2 (*b*)). No doubt, international organizations have a more significant and parallel concern that should also be taken into account in the present context. The commentary concerning article 50 explains that the restriction in question seeks to protect diplomatic and consular agents from the risk of being "targeted by way of countermeasures"[61] to which they might otherwise be exposed. A similar risk exists for agents of international organizations. The same may be said of the premises, archives and documents of international organizations. These terms and the term "agents" are wide enough to include any mission that an international organization would send, permanently or temporarily, to another organization or a State. It seems therefore reasonable to reword the restriction in paragraph 2 (*b*) and refer to the inviolability of agents, premises, archives and documents of the responsible international organization.

52. The drafting of article 50, paragraph 2, on responsibility of States for internationally wrongful acts needs some adaptations. The text, which includes the change proposed in the previous paragraph, could run as follows:

"*Draft article 53. Obligations not affected by countermeasures*

"1. Countermeasures shall not affect:

"(*a*) the obligation to refrain from the threat or use of force as embodied in the Charter of the United Nations;

"(*b*) obligations for the protection of fundamental human rights;

"(*c*) obligations of a humanitarian character prohibiting reprisals;

"(*d*) other obligations under peremptory norms of general international law.

"2. A State or international organization taking countermeasures is not relieved from fulfilling its obligations:

"(*a*) under any dispute settlement procedure applicable between the injured State or international organization and the responsible international organization;

"(*b*) to respect the inviolability of the agents of the responsible international organization and of the premises, archives and documents of the same organization."

[60] *Ibid.*, p. 131.

[61] *Ibid.*, p. 134, para. (15).

53. When considering conditions and modalities of countermeasures that an injured State intends to take against a responsible State, articles 51–53 on responsibility of States for internationally wrongful acts[62] embody certain principles that have a general character. The first article states the requirement of proportionality; the following provision concerns the procedural conditions for resorting to countermeasures; in a rather self-evident statement, the third article considers termination of countermeasures. The principles embodied in these articles appear to be equally relevant when an injured State or international organization takes countermeasures against a responsible international organization. Moreover, a uniform regime of the questions dealt with in these articles, whether they are taken against a responsible State or a responsible international organization, would have a practical advantage. Thus, the arguably innovative elements that article 52 on State responsibility introduces with regard to the procedural conditions for resorting to countermeasures should also be extended to countermeasures that are taken against an international organization.

54. The requirement of proportionality was restated by ICJ in the *Gabčíkovo-Nagymaros Project* case. The Court was considering a measure taken by one State against another, but made a more general appraisal of proportionality, saying that "an important consideration is that the effects of a countermeasure must be commensurate with the injury suffered, taking account of the rights in question".[63] The requirement of proportionality may be of particular significance when countermeasures are taken by an international organization, given the potential involvement of all its members. As was noted by Belgium: "The transposition of that requirement to international organizations would … prevent countermeasures adopted by an international organization from exerting an excessively destructive impact."[64]

55. Article 51 on responsibility of States for internationally wrongful acts may be reproduced without change. Articles 52–53 require certain adaptations. The following texts are proposed:

"*Draft article 54. Proportionality*

"Countermeasures must be commensurate with the injury suffered, taking into account the gravity of the internationally wrongful act and the rights in question.

"*Draft article 55. Conditions relating to resort to countermeasures*

"1. Before taking countermeasures, an injured State or international organization shall:

"(*a*) call upon the responsible international organization, in accordance with article 47, to fulfil its obligations under Part Two;

"(*b*) notify the responsible international organization of any decision to take countermeasures and offer to negotiate with that organization.

"2. Notwithstanding paragraph 1 (*b*), the injured State or international organization may take such urgent countermeasures as are necessary to preserve its rights.

"3. Countermeasures may not be taken, and if already taken must be suspended without undue delay if:

"(*a*) the internationally wrongful act has ceased; and

"(*b*) the dispute is pending before a court or tribunal which has the authority to make decisions binding on the parties.

"4. Paragraph 3 does not apply if the responsible international organization fails to implement the dispute settlement procedures in good faith.

"*Draft article 56. Termination of countermeasures*

"Countermeasures shall be terminated as soon as the responsible international organization has complied with its obligations under Part Two in relation to the internationally wrongful act."

56. Two different questions arise with regard to measures that may be taken against a responsible international organization by a State or international organization which is not injured within the meaning of article 46. The question that will be examined first is parallel to the issue that was considered in article 54 on responsibility of States for internationally wrongful acts.[65] This provision states that the chapter on countermeasures does not prejudice the right that a State may have to take "lawful measures" when it is entitled to invoke international responsibility although it is not injured. This provision concerns the category of States which are referred to in article 51 of the present draft.

57. Since article 54 on responsibility of States for internationally wrongful acts is a "without prejudice" provision, one would clearly go beyond the purposes of the present study if one attempted to go any further when considering the measures that may be taken against a responsible international organization by a State which, although not injured, is entitled to invoke international responsibility. The only option in this respect is to restate what was said in the articles on State responsibility. However, it may be pointed out that, to the extent that these measures are *per se* lawful, there would not be any need to say that the right to take them is not prejudiced.

58. Article 51 of the current draft envisages the possibility that, under certain conditions, an international organization, although not injured within the meaning of article 46, may also invoke the responsibility of another international organization. Practice shows several examples of measures taken against a responsible State by an international organization which is not injured. This practice mostly originates from the European Union. For

[62] *Ibid.*, pp. 134–137.

[63] *Gabčíkovo-Nagymaros Project (Hungary/Slovakia), Judgment, I.C.J. Reports 1997*, p. 56, para. 85.

[64] *Official Records of the General Assembly, Sixty-second Session, Sixth Committee*, 21st meeting (A/C.6/62/SR.21), para. 92.

[65] *Yearbook … 2001*, vol. II (Part Two), p. 137.

instance, after the statement, referred to above (para. 33), concerning "severe and systematic violations of human rights in Burma", the Council of the European Union prohibited "the sale, supply and export to Burma/Myanmar of equipment which might be used for internal repression of terrorism".[66] In some cases, the measures that were adopted by the European Union were not consistent with its obligations towards the responsible State and thus were considered to be justified because of a previous breach of an international obligation by that State.[67]

59. It would be difficult to give an example of measures that an international organization has taken against another international organization in similar circumstances. This does not necessarily imply that the "without prejudice" provision should not include a reference to measures taken by international organizations that are not "injured" within the meaning of article 46 of the current draft. The possibility of an international organization taking countermeasures against another international organization cannot be excluded. Moreover, the European Union has recently asserted "the right of an international organization to take countermeasures against another international organization [in] situations where the former has the statutory function to protect the interest underlying the obligation that was breached by the latter".[68] This obligation was defined by the European Union as an "obligation owed to the international community as a whole". Thus, one cannot view as totally remote the eventuality of an international organization, which is not injured by a breach of one such obligation, taking measures against another international organization which is held responsible for the breach. This confirms that it would be preferable to include international organizations among the entities whose right to take "lawful measures" is not regarded as prejudiced by the chapter concerning countermeasures.

60. The second question to be discussed in the present context is of a different nature. It concerns the situation of those members of an international organization that have transferred to that organization competence over certain matters and may find themselves, as a consequence, unable to take effective countermeasures. This situation was described by the Court of Justice of the European Communities with regard to retaliations within the WTO system in the following manner:

> [I]n the absence of close cooperation, where a Member State, duly authorized within its sphere of competence to take cross-retaliation measures, considered that they would be ineffective if taken in the fields covered by GATS or TRIPS, it would not, under Community law, be empowered to retaliate in the field of trade in goods, since that is an area which on any view falls within the exclusive competence of the Community under Article 113 [now 133] of the [EC] Treaty. Conversely, if the Community were given the right to retaliate in the sector of goods but found itself incapable of exercising that right, it would, in the absence of close cooperation, find itself unable, in law, to retaliate in the areas covered by GATS or TRIPS, those being within the competence of the Member States.[69]

Since the European Community and its member States acquired under the WTO agreements separate rights and obligations reflecting their respective competences under Community law, the scenario envisaged by the Court of Justice has become real. It occurs also in the reverse situation of a State party to the WTO agreements intending to take countermeasures for a breach committed either by the Community or by one or more of its member States. The matter arose, although it was not discussed, in the *European Communities: Regime for the Importation, Sale and Distribution of Bananas* case, when Ecuador was authorized to suspend certain obligations towards the member States for a breach committed by the European Community.[70]

61. A similar question may arise when a State or international organization which is not injured, but which is entitled to invoke responsibility, intends to take measures against the responsible international organization. However, in view of the fact that the right to take measures in those circumstances is covered by a "without prejudice" provision, it is not necessary to enquire whether States or international organizations would then be in a position to request an international organization of which they are members to take measures against the responsible organization or whether an international organization may then request its members to take measures.

62. The possibility for an international organization to take countermeasures on behalf of its members that have been injured has been mainly discussed with regard to organizations implying a strong form of economic integration among their members, and in particular in respect of the European Union.[71] When the establishment of one such organization involves the transfer of an exclusive competence to the organization over economic matters, its members would find themselves in the position of no longer being able to resort to countermeasures, or at least to effective countermeasures, when they are injured. It is difficult to assume that, by transferring to an organization an exclusive competence over economic matters, States intend to renounce any possibility to resort to countermeasures affecting those matters. This would imply that an injured member may take measures through the organization, by requesting the organization to take measures on its behalf. The organization would then accede to this request or refuse to act in accordance with its own rules. With regard to measures that an organization may take under these circumstances, the requirement of proportionality, set out in article 54, would be of paramount importance.

---

[66] *Official Journal of the European Communities* (see footnote 40 above), p. 29.

[67] This was, for instance, the case of part of Council Regulation (EEC) suspending imports of all products originating in Argentina, *Official Journal of the European Communities*, No. L 102, vol. 25 (16 April 1982), p. 1. The view that international organizations may also take countermeasures when they are not "injured" in response to a breach of an obligation towards the international community as a whole was defended by Ehlermann, *loc. cit.*, pp. 104–105; Pierre Klein, *op. cit.*, p. 401; and Rey Aneiros, *op. cit.*, p. 166.

[68] A/CN.4/593, sect. F2 (reproduced in the present volume).

[69] Opinion 1/94, *European Court Reports 1994*, p. I–5421, para. 109.

[70] See paragraph 30 above. This case was analysed under the aspect discussed here by Heliskoski, *op. cit.*, pp. 220–221.

[71] Pierre Klein, *op. cit.*, pp. 400–401, considered that, in view of the degree of integration of an international organization, the transfer of powers would justify the organization in taking countermeasures when a member State has been injured. For similar views, see Ehlermann, *loc. cit.*, p. 106, and Meng, "Internationale Organisationen im völkerrechtlichen Deliktsrecht", pp. 350–354. According to Verhoeven, "Communautés européennes …", pp. 88–90, an international organization would then not be entitled to take measures, but could *implement* them.

63. For defining the international organizations which would be entitled to take countermeasures on behalf of their members, one could refer to the concept of regional economic integration organizations. This concept has been used in article 13 of the Vienna Convention for the Protection of the Ozone Layer[72] and in a number of later treaties. If the idea of referring to regional economic integration organizations is acceptable, one would have to include a definition in article 2, which concerns the use of terms.

64. While there are some reasons in favour of allowing an injured member of an international organization to take countermeasures through the organization, there would seem to be little justification for admitting the possibility that an organization may take countermeasures outside its field of competence through its members.

65. Also, in the reverse situation, it would be difficult to admit that an injured State may take measures against an international organization when the responsibility lies not with the organization, but with one of its members. Should one consider that the injured State may target the organization when only one of its members is responsible, the State taking countermeasures would be able, as a result of its free choice, to affect an international organization that has committed no breach. Similar considerations apply with regard to the case of an injured State intending to target a member of an international organization when only that organization is responsible.

66. The two questions considered here could be addressed in two different paragraphs in the following manner:

"*Draft article 57. Measures taken by an entity other than an injured State or international organization*

"1. This chapter does not prejudice the right of any State or international organization, entitled under article 51, paragraph 1, to invoke the responsibility of an international organization, to take lawful measures against the latter international organization to ensure cessation of the breach and reparation in the interest of the injured party or of the beneficiaries of the obligation breached.

"2. Where an injured State or international organization has transferred competence over certain matters to a regional economic integration organization of which it is a member, the organization, when so requested by the injured member, may take on its behalf countermeasures affecting those matters against a responsible international organization."

[72] Article 1, paragraph 6, contains the following definition: "'Regional economic integration organization' means an organization constituted by sovereign States of a given region which has competence in respect of matters governed by this Convention or its protocols and has been duly authorized, in accordance with its internal procedures, to sign, ratify, accept, approve or accede to the instruments concerned."

RESPONSIBILITY OF INTERNATIONAL ORGANIZATIONS

[Agenda item 3]

DOCUMENT A/CN.4/593 and Add.1

Comments and observations received from international organizations

[Original: English and French]
[31 March and 28 April 2008]

CONTENTS

Multilateral instruments cited in the present document

	Source
Convention on the Privileges and Immunities of the Specialized Agencies (New York, 21 November 1947)	United Nations, *Treaty Series*, vol. 33, No. 521, p. 261.
United Nations Convention on the Law of the Sea (Montego Bay, 10 December 1982)	*Ibid.*, vol. 1833, No. 31363, p. 3.
Marrakesh Agreement establishing the World Trade Organization (Marrakesh, 15 April 1994)	*Ibid.*, vol. 1867, No. 31874, p. 3.

Introduction

1. At its fifty-fifth session, in 2003, the International Law Commission asked the Secretariat to circulate, on an annual basis, the portions of its report relevant to the topic "Responsibility of international organizations" to international organizations for their comments.[1] Pursuant to that request, selected international organizations were invited to submit their comments on the relevant portions of the Commission's 2003, 2004, 2005, 2006 and 2007 reports.[2] Most recently, the Commission sought comments on chapter VIII of its 2007 report[3] and on the issues of particular interest to it noted in paragraphs 29 and 30 of that report.[4]

2. As at 15 April 2008, written comments had been received from the following six international organizations (dates of submission in parentheses): European Commission (18 February 2008); International Maritime Organization (14 December 2007); Organization for the Prohibition of Chemical Weapons (11 January 2008); World Health Organization (WHO) (28 March 2008); and World Trade Organization (18 February 2008); and the International Organization for Migration (15 April 2008). The comments from those six international organizations are reproduced below, in a topic-by-topic manner.

[1] *Yearbook ... 2003*, vol. II (Part Two), p. 18, para. 52.

[2] The written comments of international organizations received prior to 1 May 2007 are contained in *Yearbook ... 2004*, vol. II (Part One), document A/CN.4/545; *Yearbook ... 2005*, vol. II (Part One), document A/CN.4/556; *Yearbook ... 2006*, vol. II (Part One), document A/CN.4/568 and Add.1; and *Yearbook ... 2007*, vol. II (Part One), document A/CN.4/582.

[3] *Yearbook ... 2007*, vol. II (Part Two). The text of the draft articles on responsibility of international organizations provisionally adopted so far by the Commission appears in *ibid.*, para. 343. The text of draft articles and commentaries thereto adopted by the Commission at its fifty-ninth session appear in *ibid.*, para. 344.

[4] *Ibid.* Paragraphs 29 and 30 read as follows:

"29. The Commission would welcome comments and observations from Governments and international organizations on draft articles 31 to 45, in particular on draft article 43, relating to an obligation of members of a responsible international organization to take, in accordance with the rules of the organization, all appropriate measures in order to provide the organization with the means for effectively fulfilling its obligation to make reparation.

"30. The Commission would also welcome views from Governments and international organizations on the two following questions, due to be examined in the next report:

"(*a*) Article 48 on responsibility of States for internationally wrongful acts provides that, in case of a breach by a State of an obligation owed to the international community as whole, States are entitled to claim from the responsible State cessation of the internationally wrongful act and performance of the obligation of reparation in the interest of the injured State or of the beneficiaries of the obligation breached. Should a breach of an obligation owed to the international community as a whole be committed by an international organization, would the other organizations or some of them be entitled to make a similar claim?

"(*b*) If an injured international organization intends to resort to countermeasures, would it encounter further restrictions than those that are listed in articles 49 to 53 of the articles on responsibility of States for internationally wrongful acts?"

Comments and observations received from international organizations

A. General remarks

1. European Commission

As in previous years, the European Commission expresses some concerns as to the feasibility of subsuming all international organizations under the terms of this one draft in the light of the highly diverse nature of international organizations, of which the European Community is itself an example.

2. International Maritime Organization

As a general matter, it is unclear how the draft provisions would apply to the activities undertaken by this Organization (treaty making and technical cooperation). In the absence of scenarios which would indicate the application of the provisions, it is difficult to offer more specific comments on the implications for us as an international organization.

B. Content of the responsibility of an international organization—General principles

1. European Commission

1. The European Commission fully endorses the general principles on the content of international responsibility. Just as States, international organizations are under an obligation to cease the wrongful act and offer appropriate assurances of non-repetition, and to make full reparation for the injury caused by the internationally wrongful act. In particular, the dispute settlement practice of the European Community evidences the acknowledgment of international responsibility for breaches of its contractual obligations.

2. For example, the Community responds in a routine manner to decisions of the World Trade Organization Dispute Settlement Body to bring Community measures into conformity with its obligations arising from the covered agreements in compliance with the rules enshrined in the Dispute Settlement Understanding.[1] As a corollary, the European Community asks its World Trade Organization partners to cease applying retaliatory measures against it, once the internal legislation is brought in line with World Trade Organization requirements. Upon application from the European Community, a World Trade Organization Panel has recently issued two reports clarifying the relevant rules binding on all World Trade Organization members in that respect in the *Continued Suspension* cases.[2]

3. Moreover, the Community's consent to article 6 of Annex IX to the United Nations Convention on the Law of the Sea on "Responsibility and liability" shows the acceptance of the principle of full reparation. However, to date no case law on the interpretation of this provision can be reported. An application of Chile against the European Community in the *Swordfish* case[3] is currently suspended until 31 December 2008.[4]

[1] Marrakesh Agreement establishing the World Trade Organization, annex 2 (Understanding on Rules and Procedures governing the Settlement of Disputes).

[2] Panel Reports of 31 March 2008: *United States–Continued Suspension of Obligations in the EC–Hormones Dispute*, WT/DS 320R; *Canada–Continued Suspension of Obligations in the EC–Hormones Dispute*, WT/DS 321R.

[3] *Conservation and Sustainable Exploitation of Swordfish Stocks (Chile/European Community), Order of 20 December 2000, International Tribunal for the Law of the Sea (ITLOS) Reports 2000*, p. 148.

[4] *Ibid., Order of 30 November 2007, ITLOS Reports 2005–2007*, p. 128.

2. Organization for the Prohibition of Chemical Weapons

1. Articles 31 to 45 of the draft articles on responsibility of international organizations refer to the legal consequences arising from the commission of an internationally wrongful act by an international organization.

2. The text of the draft articles allows for the proposition that the international organization committing an internationally wrongful act would have three primary obligations: first, the duty to perform the obligation breached is not affected; secondly, the international organization must cease the commission of the wrongful act; and thirdly, it must take assurances and guarantees that there will be no repetition of such act.

3. With respect to draft articles 33 (*b*) and 40, in order to provide appropriate assurances and guarantees of non-repetition, the organization could be required to provide convincing evidence, as appropriate, of its commitment to ensure that the internationally wrongful act will not occur again. Reference may be made here to the *LaGrand* case,[1] in which the International Court of Justice stated, in the context of a State's non-compliance with its consular obligations, that "an apology is not sufficient".[2] The Court considered that "If a State, in proceedings before this Court, repeatedly refers to substantial activities which it is carrying out in order to achieve compliance with certain obligations under a treaty, then this expresses a commitment to follow through with the efforts in this regard".[3] This consideration should be relevant in the present context for assurances and guarantees of non-repetition by both international organizations and States.

[1] *LaGrand (Germany v. United States of America), Judgment, I.C.J. Reports 2001*, p. 466.

[2] *Ibid.*, p. 512, para. 123.

[3] *Ibid.*, pp. 512–513, para. 124.

3. World Health Organization

1. With regard to draft article 35, paragraph 2, it is noted that the rules of the organization could affect the content of the responsibility of an international organization *vis-à-vis* its member States and organizations. The World Health Organization agrees with that statement; however, besides the operation of the rules of the organization, we believe that there is a more general principle precluding by way of estoppel members of an organization who have voted in favour of a decision authorizing or requesting the organization to carry out certain activities from claiming that actions performed by the organization in response to that request constitute a breach of the organization's international obligations.

2. In the commentary to draft article 36, it is stated that an example of responsibility of an international organization towards entities other than States and other organizations is that of breaches of "rules of international law concerning employment". We find that statement rather undefined and overbroad. As already noted by the World Health Organization in a previous contribution as well as by other organizations, we cannot share the view that the rules governing employment of the officials of an organization are rules of international law. That statement is not supported by practice and is not consistent with the internal nature of those rules within the legal order of the organization as such.

C. Reparation for injury—General considerations

1. European Commission

1. When discussing draft article 34 on reparation, the Special Rapporteur points out that the fundamental principle of full reparation, as spelled out by the Permanent Court of International Justice in the *Factory at Chorzów* case,[1] should apply equally to international organizations. He argues that it would be absurd to exempt international organizations from facing reparation as the consequence of their internationally wrongful acts, as this would be tantamount to saying that international organizations would be entitled to ignore their obligations under international law (*Yearbook ... 2007*, vol. II (Part One) document A/CN.4/583, para. 22).

2. While the result is certainly obvious, one may wonder about the exact underlying reasoning. It seems that

[1] *Factory at Chorzów, Merits, Judgment No. 13, 1928, P.C.I.J., Series A, No. 17*, p. 47.

the duty of reparation also arises for an international organization for breaches of their obligations because of the fact that they were allowed to participate in the conduct of international relations as a subject of international law in the first place. In other words, the duty to make reparation for wrongful acts corresponds to the capacity to act under international law—no power, without responsibility. Viewed from this angle, it would indeed be absurd if one category of actors (States) would face more severe legal consequences for internationally wrongful acts than another category of actors (international organizations). Accordingly, the justification for the duty of reparation rests within the nature and function of international law as legal system designed to regulate the conduct of its subjects in a non-discriminatory way.

2. Organization for the Prohibition of Chemical Weapons

1. Articles 34 to 40 deal with the reparation of the injury. As provided in the articles on responsibility of States for internationally wrongful acts (see General Assembly resolution 56/83, annex), the draft articles on responsibility of international organizations also establish three forms of reparation for an internationally wrongful act: restitution, compensation and satisfaction.

2. The text of the draft articles allows for the proposition that the primary responsibility of the international organization committing the breach in question is to re-establish the situation as it was before the breach. However, when restitution is materially impossible or out of proportion the organization must provide compensation, whether moral or material. Draft article 40 (1) states that the international organization responsible for an internationally wrongful act is under the obligation to give satisfaction for the injury caused by that act "insofar as it cannot be made good by restitution or compensation". It would appear that there is an order of priority between the three forms of reparation provided for in the draft articles—restitution, compensation and satisfaction. Accordingly, when restitution is not possible, the organization in breach shall compensate, and if neither restitution nor compensation is possible then satisfaction will be the legal consequence for the breach.

3. World Health Organization

In the commentary to draft article 34, it is stated that international organizations sometimes grant compensation *ex gratia* due to a reluctance to admit their own international responsibility as a basis for reparations. While that statement may be correct in general, it should be noted that WHO has granted compensation on an *ex gratia* basis when there is no legal basis to pay compensation under the applicable rules of the Organization but it is felt that compensation is appropriate for humanitarian or equitable reasons. Such payments are thus not forms of settlement to avoid acknowledging responsibility, but on the contrary voluntary payments unrelated to the responsibility of the Organization. Examples that have occurred in this connection are payments for injuries or death of volunteers who participate in poliomyelitis vaccination campaigns coordinated by WHO. In such cases, there was no contractual obligation on WHO to compensate those injuries and payments were made on humanitarian grounds.

D. Draft article 43—Ensuring the effective performance of the obligation of reparation

Draft article 43, as provisionally adopted by the Commission at its fifty-ninth session, reads as follows:

Article 43. Ensuring the effective performance of the obligation of reparation

The members of a responsible international organization are required to take, in accordance with the rules of the organization, all appropriate measures in order to provide the organization with the means for effectively fulfilling its obligations under this chapter.

1. European Commission

While the principle is acceptable and the language appears satisfactory, the question arises whether the new draft article is well placed. Currently, as draft article 43, it is put at the end of chapter II on reparation for injury. That chapter mainly discusses the different forms of reparation, interest and mitigating circumstances. However, the additional duty of member States can also be seen as a general principle falling under chapter I. If that view was taken, a more appropriate place would be to insert the language of draft article 43 as a new paragraph 3 of draft article 34. As a consequence thereof, a slight modification in the wording would be warranted: the reference to "this chapter" in draft article 43 would have to be deleted, if the provision were to be moved to chapter I.

2. International Maritime Organization

The proposed articles would extend the terms of the draft articles on "Responsibility of States for internationally wrongful acts" (*Yearbook ... 2001*, vol. II (Part Two), p. 26, para. 76) to the "Responsibility of international organizations". The key provision on which comments are requested (draft article 43) concerns "ensuring the effective performance of the obligation of reparation" [...]. It is our understanding that this article would be effective in a case when the international organization concerned is found to be in breach of an international obligation (i.e. when an act—by an organ or agent of the organization—"is not in conformity with what is required of it by that obligation, regardless of its origin and character"). As threshold issues, we would wish to clarify (*a*) what process would be used for determining that a breach had occurred; (*b*) how the amount/form of reparation would be determined; and (*c*) what relationship this situation would have to the Convention on the Privileges and Immunities of the Specialized Agencies (which is mentioned in commentary under article 39 in the context of activities in the Congo in the 1960s, but not in an explanatory way relating to the proposed articles).

3. International Organization for Migration

While there is no question that inclusion of draft article 43 is justified, its precise placement should be reconsidered. Given the structure of the draft articles, it would be more logical to make it the second or third paragraph of article 34.

4. Organization for the Prohibition of Chemical Weapons

Regarding draft article 43, while desirable, it is our view that the inclusion in the draft articles of an obligation of member States to take all appropriate measures to provide the organization with the means for effectively fulfilling its obligations would amount to progressive development of international law. It may then also be useful to consider what such appropriate measures could consist of, especially if there is no reference thereto in the constituent documents of the organization. Such measures could conceivably include giving the organization the right to request contributions from member States when considered necessary, and explicit reference to an obligation on the part of member States to cooperate financially to enable the organization to make adequate reparation for wrongful acts committed by it.

5. World Health Organization

The World Health Organization supports the inclusion of draft article 43 with the language approved by the Drafting Committee. While members of an international organization do not have in principle a residual responsibility for the acts of that organization, international organizations may in practice find themselves without the necessary financial resources to pay reparation in case of a breach of their international obligations. That situation is largely dependent on the mode of financing of international organizations, through contributions assessed on members as well as through generally earmarked voluntary contributions. Consequently, an article of an expository nature reminding members of their commitment to enable their organization to fulfil its international obligations is certainly useful.

6. World Trade Organization

1. Regarding draft article 43, relating to an obligation of members of a responsible international organization to take, in accordance with the rules of that organization, all appropriate measures in order to provide the organization with the means for effectively fulfilling its obligation to make reparation, we have the following remarks, having regard to the comments enclosed in the Commission's report:

2. We are inclined to support the text currently in the draft, and not that proposed in footnote 441.[1] This has to do primarily with the "member driven" nature of our organization, pursuant to which our Director-General and the Secretariat have limited power to initiate any action of the World Trade Organization outside the limited implementation powers delegated by its members. In our opinion, an obligation—for instance—to pay financial compensation to a State or another international organization would require the prior consent of our members. An obligation directly binding our members would probably, in the case of a wrongful act committed by the World Trade Organization, better ensure that actions are taken to compensate for the consequences of the wrongful act. While we are mindful of the content of the commentary, particularly items 6 and 7, we are also concerned that the terms "in accordance with the rules of the organization" in draft article 43 could be invoked to limit the obligations of members if the obligation to repair consequences of wrongful acts is not expressly provided in the organization's internal rules.

E. Serious breaches of obligations under peremptory norms of general international law

European Commission

1. The Special Rapporteur puts forward the view that international organizations should also face the same consequences as States when their internationally wrongful act constitutes a serious breach of obligations under peremptory norms of general international law. Indeed, for the same reasons as those set out above, this parallelism is theoretically sound.

2. In this regard, the difficult question arises whether the draft articles should specifically emphasize the duty of member States of an international organization to bring the breach of the organization to an end. It would be hard to formulate a rule which equally applies to all members of an international organization, although only those sitting in a particular institution thereof could bring about the appropriate remedy if that institution had adopted the allegedly wrongful act. Thus, the Special Rapporteur has good reasons not to attempt to define a specific duty in the draft articles that members of the responsible organization would have (*Yearbook ... 2007*, vol. II (Part Two), document A/CN.4/583, para. 58), but to leave this issue to the applicable rules of the organization.

3. Finally, international organizations are also (like States) under an obligation not to recognize as lawful a situation created by a serious breach (draft article 45, para. 2). In this respect, the Special Rapporteur rightly mentions the declaration of the Community and its member States made in 1991. It should be pointed out that this is a joint statement of the international organization and its members (and not only of the member States as the Special Rapporteur erroneously writes (see *Yearbook ... 2007*, vol. II (Part One), document A/CN.4/583, para. 64) with respect to the particular facts at the time. It therefore also forms part of the practice of the European Community as an international organization.

F. Specific issues raised in chapter III.D of the report of the International Law Commission on the work of its fifty-ninth session

1. Invocation of responsibility by an international organization in case of a breach by another organization of an obligation owed to the international community as a whole

(a) *European Commission*

1. Should a breach of obligation owed to the international community as a whole be committed by an international organization, other organizations should, in principle, be entitled to claim from the responsible organization cessation of the internationally wrongful act and

[1] *Yearbook ... 2007*, vol. II (Part Two), p. 77, footnote 441. The text of the footnote reads as follows:

"The following text was proposed, discussed and supported by some members: 'The responsible international organization shall take all appropriate measures in accordance with its rules in order to ensure that its members provide the organization with the means for effectively fulfilling its obligations under this chapter.'"

performance of the obligation of reparation in the interested of the injured or of the beneficiary of the obligation breached.

2. See also observations regarding countermeasures.

(b) *International Organization for Migration*

Article 48 on responsibility of States for internationally wrongful acts (*Yearbook ... 2001*, vol. II (Part Two), p. 26, para. 76) could be transposed, a priori, to the draft articles on the responsibility of international organizations; however, it would be helpful if the Commission illustrated its point with a few specific examples.

(c) *Organization for the Prohibition of Chemical Weapons*

1. Pursuant to article 48 of the articles on responsibility of States for internationally wrongful acts (*Yearbook ... 2001*, vol. II (Part Two), p. 26, para. 76), only the "injured" State can claim the cessation of the internationally wrongful act and assurances and guarantees of non-repetition as well as performance of the obligation to make reparation. States other than the injured State, in contrast, cannot claim reparation in the form of restitution or compensation. In our view, the situation of international organizations is quite different, and their position is more restricted than that of States. In the case of international organizations, the ability to invoke responsibility for violations of obligations owed to the international community as a whole could depend on the scope of the activities of the organization as defined in its constituent document. Accordingly, every "concerned" international organization could be entitled to invoke responsibility and claim the cessation of the wrongful act to the extent that affects its mandate as set out in its constituent instrument. As for claiming reparation, the concerned organization would be able to claim for restitution or compensation only if it can be considered to be "injured".

2. In addition, the question only refers to the ability of other international organizations to invoke the responsibility of an international organization. However, there does not appear to be any reason why States—as distinct from other international organizations—may not also be able to invoke the responsibility of an international organization.

(d) *World Health Organization*

It is difficult, first of all, to imagine an international organization breaching an obligation owed to the international community as a whole within the terms of article 48 on responsibility of States (*Yearbook ... 2001*, vol. II (Part Two), p. 26, para. 76). Should that nonetheless occur, whether or not other international organizations could claim cessation of the act, non-repetition and performance of the obligation depends on the applicable rules of the organizations concerned. Unlike States, international organizations are functional entities established by their members to perform certain functions provided in their rules in the common interest. Whether or not they can take certain actions, even in response to breaches of international obligations such as those envisaged in article 48, will depend on the application of those rules, which of course include decisions taken by their competent governing bodies. The World Health Organization notes that other organizations have commented along similar lines with regard to draft article 45.

(e) *World Trade Organization*

1. Regarding the question raised in paragraph 30 (*a*) of the Commission's 2007 report, on whether, if a breach of an obligation owed to the international community as a whole is committed by an international organization (see para. 1 above), the other organizations or some of them would be entitled to claim cessation of the internationally wrongful act and reparation in the interest of the injured State or of the beneficiaries of the obligation breached, we have the following brief comments:

2. While, legally speaking, there is no specific reason in this context not to apply to international organizations the regime applicable to States, we are concerned with the consequences that an article similar to article 48 on responsibility of States (*Yearbook ... 2001*, vol. II (Part Two), p. 26, para. 76) could have on the performance of their tasks by international organizations and on their survival in case of breach of international law in the performance of those tasks. Indeed, there would be a risk of multiple claims for reparations, which could affect the willingness of such international organizations to initiate new actions in legally complex contexts, lest they be exposed to numerous legal claims. Moreover, multiple claims for reparations could divert the resources of international organizations from their original mandates.

3. We are generally of the view that, since international organizations are usually created to further common objectives, either the circumstances when they will be deemed liable or the conditions under which they may be subject to claims for reparation or countermeasures should be more limited than in the case of breach of international obligations by States. However, given the current degree of generality of the draft articles, this may not be easily done.

2. RESORT TO COUNTERMEASURES BY AN INTERNATIONAL ORGANIZATION

(a) *European Commission*

1. The right to take countermeasures against a breach of an international obligation that is owed to the international community as a whole is closely linked to the idea of decentralized enforcement of international law. As the international community as a whole cannot act on its own lacking centralized institutions, it is for individual members of that community to take action against the offender on behalf and in the interest of the community. It appears to the European Commission that this right pertains in principle to all members of the international community, including international organizations as subjects of international law. However, at the same time international organizations are entrusted by their statutes to carry out specific functions and to protect certain interests only. Where the breached obligation relates to subject matters that fall outside the organization's powers and functions, there would be no compelling reason why it should be allowed to take decentralized enforcement action. For

example, it is hardly conceivable that a technical transport organization should be allowed to sanction a military alliance for a breach of a fundamental guarantee of international humanitarian law that may be owed to the international community as a whole. Therefore, it seems advisable to restrict the right of an international organization to take countermeasures against another international organization to situations where the former has the statutory function to protect the interest underlying the obligation that was breached by the latter.

2. In conclusion, the European Community considers that

[…] (b) an injured international organization that intends to resort to countermeasures should encounter the further restriction than those listed in articles 49 to 53 of the articles on responsibility of States for internationally wrongful acts (*Yearbook … 2001*, vol. II (Part Two), p. 26, para. 76), namely that it can only resort to countermeasures where it has the statutory function to protect the interest underlying the obligation owed to the international community as a whole that was breached.

(b) *International Organization for Migration*

The possibility for an organization to resort to countermeasures should be subordinated to the existence of such a right in its constitutive instrument and other explicit norms adopted by its governing body. Resort to the concept of implicit powers to justify the application of countermeasures could lead to abuses, unless the existence of those particular countermeasures in international customary law is recognized and their invocation has been extended to international organizations.

(c) *Organization for the Prohibition of Chemical Weapons*

No comment at this time.

(d) *World Health Organization*

International organizations would in principle be subject to the same constraints as States, as illustrated in articles 49 to 53 of the articles on responsibility of States for internationally wrongful acts (*Yearbook … 2001*, vol. II (Part Two), p. 26, para. 76), in terms of their recourse to countermeasures. Having said that in general, certain provisions seem in practice to be scarcely relevant for international organizations, in particular those of article 50 on obligations that may not be affected by the adoption of countermeasures. International organizations hardly seem in a position to breach those obligations, in view of their particular status, the nature of their mandate, and the oversight mechanisms to which they are subject.

(e) *World Trade Organization*

Regarding the question raised in paragraph 30 (*b*) of the Commission's 2007 report, concerning countermeasures, we would simply note that, in some instances, the international organization itself will not be in a position to take countermeasures, but simply to allow its members to take such countermeasures. In some instances, such countermeasures may be in breach of the obligations of members under the rules of the international organization and may call for special derogations. Even when allowed under a particular treaty, countermeasures may breach other international obligations, thus potentially generating liabilities for the organization having authorized such countermeasures and the States having implemented them. We are also generally of the view that it is not the role of international organizations to take countermeasures against other international organizations, if this diverts their resources from their original mandates.

SHARED NATURAL RESOURCES

[Agenda item 4]

DOCUMENT A/CN.4/591

Fifth report on shared natural resources: transboundary aquifers, by Mr. Chusei Yamada, Special Rapporteur

[Original: English]
[21 February 2008]

CONTENTS

Multilateral instruments cited in the present report

	Source
United Nations Convention on the Law of the Sea (Montego Bay, 10 December 1982)	United Nations, *Treaty Series*, vol. 1833, No. 31363, p. 3.
Convention on the Protection and Use of Transboundary Watercourses and International Lakes (Helsinki, 17 March 1992)	*Ibid.*, vol. 1936, No. 33207, p. 269.
Convention on the Law of the Non-navigational Uses of International Watercourses (New York, 21 May 1997)	*Official Records of the General Assembly, Fifty-first Session, Supplement No. 49*, vol. III, resolution 51/229, annex.

Introduction

1. The International Law Commission, at its fifty-eighth session in 2006, adopted on first reading 19 draft articles on the law of transboundary aquifers and commentaries thereto and decided to transmit them, through the Secretary-General, to Governments for comments and observations, to be submitted to the Secretary-General by 1 January 2008. The Commission also solicited the views of Governments on the final form of the draft articles.[1]

2. During the debates on the reports of the Commission in the Sixth Committee of the General Assembly in 2006 and 2007, 45 Governments offered oral comments and observations. Twenty-three of them did so in both years. The Secretary-General has received written comments and observations from eight Governments, two of which had not made any previous oral submissions. Accordingly, the Commission now has comments and observations from a total of 47 Governments. The members of the Commission who were newly elected in 2006 also commented on the draft articles.[2] The Special Rapporteur is indeed grateful for all of the comments and observations.

3. In the view of the Special Rapporteur, the comments and observations made by Governments were favourable and supportive, in general, and encouraged the Commission to proceed to the second reading on the basis of the first-reading texts of the draft articles, while certain revisions, additions or deletions in the draft articles and also improvements in the commentaries were suggested. Accordingly, it is the intention of the Special Rapporteur to focus on the proposal of the revised draft articles for the second reading in the present report.

[1] *Yearbook ... 2006*, vol. II (Part Two), p. 21, para. 26 and p. 91, paras. 72–73.

[2] See *Yearbook ... 2007*, vol. I, 2930th and 2931st meetings.

Chapter I

Relationship between the work on transboundary aquifers and that on oil and natural gas

4. While awaiting the comments and observations from Governments on the first-reading draft articles and the commentaries thereto, the Commission, at its fifty-ninth session, in 2007, addressed the question of the relationship between the work on transboundary aquifers and that on oil and natural gas which had been raised often in the Commission, as well as in the Sixth Committee. In his fourth report to the Commission,[3] the Special Rapporteur concluded that, while there were some similarities between non-recharging aquifers and the natural conditions of oil and natural gas, the majority of regulations to be worked out for oil and natural gas would not be directly applicable to aquifers. Accordingly, he recommended that the Commission proceed with and complete the second reading of the law of transboundary aquifers independently from its possible future work on oil and natural gas. His recommendation received a positive reaction in the Commission.[4]

5. The oral and written comments and observations from Governments also dealt with this aspect. An overwhelming majority of the Governments making such comments and observations supported the suggestion that the law on transboundary aquifers be treated independently of any future work by the Commission on the issues related to oil and natural gas on a number of grounds.[5] These included the following points: the differences between aquifers and oil and natural gas are more significant than the similarities; aquifers provide more than half of humanity's freshwater needs and are a life-supporting resource of mankind; the challenges of managing aquifers, including the environmental impacts and effects, and the commercial considerations are quite different from those related to oil and natural gas; while oil and natural gas are strategically important to economic and social development, they do not constitute "a vital human need"; prospecting, exploration and exploitation of energy resources are a complex endeavour; gathering and assessing State practice on oil and natural gas would take a relatively long time; the draft articles on aquifers would not necessarily apply to oil and natural gas; and, finally, the work on aquifers would be helpful in determining the potential direction, substance and value of any work that might be carried out in the future by the Commission on oil and natural gas. However, one Government did not find the arguments for separation offered by the Commission persuasive.[6] Another suggested that a final decision on adopting separate texts of draft articles be deferred until a later stage.[7] Yet another, which supported the independent work on aquifers on second reading, stressed that it would be difficult to avoid in future the influence of work on a set of draft articles on one category of resources over another and that it was important not to reject *a priori* any possible links in the development of work in respect of various resources.[8]

[3] *Yearbook ... 2007*, vol. II (Part One), document A/CN.4/580.

[4] See *Yearbook ... 2007*, vol. II (Part Two), p. 51, para. 177.

[5] See *Official Records of the General Assembly, Sixty-second Session, Sixth Committee*, 22nd meeting, Sweden, on behalf of the Nordic countries (A/C.6/62/SR.22), para. 31; India, *ibid.*, para. 38; Argentina, *ibid.*, para. 57; Guatemala, *ibid.*, para. 72; United States of America, *ibid.*, para. 88; Malaysia, *ibid.*, 23rd meeting (A/C.6/62/SR.23), para. 8; Canada, *ibid.*, para. 18; Hungary, *ibid.*, para. 39; Romania, *ibid.*, 24th meeting (A/C.6/62/SR.24), para. 18; Mexico, *ibid.*, para. 10; Democratic Republic of the Congo, *ibid.*, para. 30; Greece, *ibid.*, para. 41; Cuba, *ibid.*, para. 68; Russian Federation, *ibid.*, para. 81; Japan, *ibid.*, para. 91; Syrian Arab Republic, *ibid.*, para. 93; Portugal, *ibid.*, para. 104; Israel, *ibid.*, para. 109; Brazil, *ibid.*, para. 110; New Zealand, *ibid.*, 25th meeting (A/C.6/62/SR.25), para. 14; Indonesia, *ibid.*, para. 33; Islamic Republic of Iran, *ibid.*, para. 44; Thailand, *ibid.*, para. 56; Venezuela (Bolivarian Republic of), *ibid.*, para. 62; Turkey, *ibid.*, para. 65; Poland, *ibid.*, 26th meeting (A/C.6/62/SR.26), para. 18.

[6] Netherlands, *ibid.*, 24th meeting (A/C.6/62/SR.24), para. 44, and written comment, A/CN.4/595 and Add.1 (reproduced in the present volume), sect. A.9.

[7] Uruguay, *Official Records of the General Assembly, Sixty-second Session, Sixth Committee*, 22nd meeting (A/C.6/62/SR.22), para. 68.

[8] Poland, *ibid.*, 26th meeting (A/C.6/62/SR.26), paras. 19–20.

6. While supporting the separation of the work on transboundary aquifers from that on oil and natural gas, many Governments expressed their views on the work on oil and natural gas. These views range from support for the initiation of work on oil and natural gas by the Commission on a priority basis to opposition to any such work. The Special Rapporteur does not intend to discuss the issue in the present report as it could be deferred until after the completion of the work on aquifers.

Chapter II

Final form of the draft articles

7. In response to the request by the Commission, many Governments also expressed their views on the final form of the draft articles. The views were divergent. Some Governments favoured a framework convention, which would be of greater benefit than a model convention, a non-binding resolution or simply a report by the Commission.[9] However, some Governments also pointed out that, in the event that a framework convention was preferred, care must be taken not to supersede existing bilateral or regional arrangements or to limit the flexibility of States to enter into such arrangements.[10] Other Governments favoured a non-binding declaration of the General Assembly, setting out general principles that would guide States in framing regional agreements; a set of recommendatory principles representing an authoritative statement of the international standards and best practice which should be followed and be given practical effect at the bilateral and regional levels; or a non-binding instrument in the form of guidelines or a set of model principles.[11] For several of them, the adoption of a convention, particularly if it was not ratified or not wholly supported, could paradoxically reduce the usefulness of the draft articles. Yet other Governments stated that a final decision on the form should not be made in a hurry and should be deferred until after the second reading.[12] Another Government suggested that the adoption of a non-legally binding instrument might merit consideration as a first step in the development of an adequate legal regime for the use of all shared natural resources.[13]

[9] Argentina, *ibid.*, 22nd meeting (A/C.6/62/SR.22), para. 57; Czech Republic, written comment, A/CN.4/595 and Add.1 (see footnote 6 above), sect. W.3, para. 1, and *Official Records of the General Assembly, Sixty-second Session, Sixth Committee*, 23rd meeting (A/C.6/62/SR.23), para. 57; Hungary, *ibid.*, para. 39; Portugal, *ibid.*, 24th meeting (A/C.6/62/SR.24), para. 104.

[10] United States, *ibid.*, 22nd meeting (A/C.6/62/SR.22), para. 88.

[11] China, *ibid.*, 22nd meeting (A/C.6/62/SR.22), para. 61; Uruguay, *ibid.*, para. 68; United States, *ibid.*, para. 88; Canada, *ibid.*, 23rd meeting (A/C.6/62/SR.23), para. 18; Israel, *ibid.*, 24th meeting (A/C.6/62/SR.24), para. 109; Brazil, *ibid.*, para. 110; New Zealand, *ibid.*, 25th meeting (A/C.6/62/SR.25), para. 15; Turkey, *ibid.*, para. 65.

[12] Guatemala, *ibid.*, 22nd meeting (A/C.6/62/SR.22), para. 71; Malaysia, *ibid.*, 23rd meeting (A/C.6/62/SR.23), para. 9; Poland, *ibid.*, 26th meeting (A/C.6/62/SR.26), para. 20.

[13] Netherlands, *ibid.*, 24th meeting (A/C.6/62/SR.24), para. 48, and written comment, A/CN.4/595 and Add.1 (see footnote 6 above), sect. W.6.

8. While the positions of Governments remain divided, the Special Rapporteur has noticed that some Governments have shifted from supporting a legally binding convention to a non-binding document. The Special Rapporteur believes that the ultimate goal of the Commission should be to aim at a legally binding convention because the law of transboundary aquifers is the follow-up to the Convention on the Law of the Non-navigational Uses of International Watercourses and the question of aquifers is as important, or even more important, for mankind as that of surface waters. However, it would not be realistic to expect that such a goal could be achieved in a reasonably short period in the absence of consensus in the international community. It is also recognized that the codification process of a convention now takes much longer than in the 1950s and 1960s even if there exists consensus. In the face of the global water crisis, urgent action is needed. It would be more practical to cope with the situation if the States concerned were to enter into bilateral or regional arrangements on the basis of the principles stipulated in the draft articles.

9. The Special Rapporteur therefore considers it best for the Commission to follow the two-step approach that was adopted in 2001 for the draft articles on responsibility of States for internationally wrongful acts.[14] Accordingly, the Special Rapporteur proposes that the following draft recommendation to the General Assembly be considered by the Commission:

The Commission decided, in accordance with article 23 of its Statute, to recommend that the General Assembly should:

(*a*) take note of the draft articles on the law of transboundary aquifers in a resolution and annex the draft articles to the resolution;

(*b*) recommend that States make appropriate arrangements bilaterally or regionally with the States concerned for proper management of their transboundary aquifers on the basis of the principles enunciated in the draft articles;

(*c*) also consider, at a later stage and in view of the importance of the topic, the possibility of convening a negotiating conference to examine the draft articles with a view to concluding a convention.

[14] *Yearbook ... 2001*, vol. II (Part Two), p. 25, paras. 72–73.

Chapter III

Revised draft articles for second reading

10. Taking into account the comments and observations from Governments, the Special Rapporteur proposes the revised draft articles contained in the annex to the present report for second reading by the Commission. In considering the comments and observations made by Governments, the Special Rapporteur placed more weight on those contained in their written and 2007 oral submissions than those expressed in the 2006 oral submissions of

the same Governments. The first-reading texts of the draft articles were formulated in such a manner as not to prejudge the final form. However, the revised texts are in the form of a convention, because the draft recommendation to the General Assembly in paragraph 9 above foresees the eventual possibility of a convention. The whole texts of the revised draft articles are reproduced in the annex to the present report. Substantial parts of the comments and observations from the Governments relate to the commentaries. Revised texts of the commentaries will be presented to the Commission as soon as the final texts of the draft articles have been adopted by the Commission.

A. Title

11. It was proposed that the title be changed to "Draft law on shared international aquifers".[15] It is recalled that the term "shared" was the subject of intense discussions, as some aquifer States thought that the term might implicate joint ownership of aquifers. The term "international" was also objected to as it might suggest internationalization of aquifers. The Commission adopted the term "transboundary" to allay these misgivings, as the term expresses solely physical factors. The use of the term "transboundary" in English is most appropriate and no revision of the title is required. However, the Special Rapporteur is aware of some difficulties in translating this term into other languages, in particular, Arabic. Efforts to find an appropriate translation are called for.

B. Article 1. Scope

12. The proposal was made that the chapeau of this article be amended to read "The goal of the present draft article is to regulate the following:".[16] This proposed version would result in ambiguity. The current chapeau which follows the standard formulation should be maintained. The view was expressed that the draft articles still did not adequately address the situation of an aquifer or aquifer system that crossed international boundaries, but had no hydraulic connection to surface water resources or had a hydraulic connection only to a river or lake located entirely within a single nation.[17] When articles 1 and 2 are read together, it should be clear that the draft articles apply to all aquifers and aquifer systems which are transboundary regardless of whether they are linked to any surface water or not. However, the Special Rapporteur intends to illustrate various cases in the commentaries.

13. Some Governments expressed concern about subparagraph (*b*). They feared that this formulation was overly broad and could impose unnecessary restrictions on activities in the area of aquifers. Suggestions were made that the Commission should limit the relevant activities to those likely to have "a major impact" or delete the subparagraph altogether if the identification of such activities was not feasible.[18] Subparagraph (*b*) is viewed as the essential element for the proper management of aquifers by groundwater scientists and administrators. It should not be deleted. However, the Special Rapporteur intends to identify the relevant activities in detail in the commentaries in order to allay the concerns of Governments. Another suggestion was made to include a reference to the activities of non-aquifer States which could have an impact on aquifers.[19] In the view of the Special Rapporteur, the authors of the activities should be clearly specified in the subsequent draft articles dealing with the rights and obligations of States.

14. A proposal was made to add a new subparagraph which reads:

"(*d*) Setting priorities in respect of the utilization of shared groundwaters and aquifer systems."[20]

The Special Rapporteur understands that the intention of the proposer was to have a provision on priority of utilization. It would be difficult to decide priority among the different kinds of utilization *a priori*. It should be decided in accordance with draft article 5. Another observation was made that the scope seemed to include only freshwater resources and it should be clearly stated that saltwater resources were excluded.[21] It is true that the Special Rapporteur has so far talked exclusively about freshwater resources. However, there are some cases of utilization of brine (salt water) aquifers in very limited instances where salt water is extracted and desalinized and water used for irrigation. This will be explained in the commentary. A suggestion was also made to repeat the adjective "transboundary" before "aquifer system" throughout the draft articles.[22] The Special Rapporteur believes that the intention to apply the adjective "transboundary" to both "aquifer" and "aquifer system" is clear.

C. Article 2. Use of terms

15. A proposal was made to modify subparagraph (*a*) to read: "'Aquifer' means a permeable underground geological formation bearing confined or unconfined water underlain or overlain by a less permeable layer and the water contained in the saturated zone of the formation."[23] The Special Rapporteur recognizes the importance of confined aquifers in the proposer's region which seems to have prompted the proposer to insert the terms "confined" and "overlain". The current definition of aquifer fully covers confined aquifers. It is also pointed out that a geological formation must always be underlain by a less

[15] Syrian Arab Republic, *Official Records of the General Assembly, Sixty-second Session, Sixth Committee*, 24th meeting (A/C.6/62/SR.24), para. 93.

[16] Saudi Arabia, written comment, A/CN.4/595 and Add.1 (see footnote 6 above), sect. C.4, para. 1.

[17] Indonesia, *Official Records of the General Assembly, Sixty-second Session, Sixth Committee*, 25th meeting (A/C.6/62/SR.25), para. 34.

[18] China, *Official Records of the General Assembly, Sixty-first Session, Sixth Committee*, 14th meeting (A/C.6/61/SR.14), para. 6, and Brazil, *ibid*., para. 85, and *Official Records of the General Assembly, Sixty-second Session, Sixth Committee*, 24th meeting (A/C.6/62/SR.24), para. 110.

[19] Mexico, *Official Records of the General Assembly, Sixty-first Session, Sixth Committee*, 14th meeting (A/C.6/61/SR.14), para. 34.

[20] Saudi Arabia, written comment, A/CN.4/595 and Add.1 (see footnote 6 above), sect. C.4, para. 2.

[21] Austria, *Official Records of the General Assembly, Sixty-first Session, Sixth Committee*, 13th meeting (A/C.6/61/SR.13), para. 41.

[22] Netherlands, written comment, A/CN.4/595 and Add.1 (see footnote 6 above), sect. D.6, para. 1.

[23] Saudi Arabia, written comment, A/CN.4/595 and Add.1 (see footnote 6 above), sect. D.8.

permeable layer in order to qualify as an aquifer. There are many ways to define an aquifer. In the view of the Special Rapporteur, the current formulation is scientifically and technically correct and also legally precise. Still on subparagraph (*a*), the Special Rapporteur proposes to delete the word "underground" before a "geological formation" because a "geological formation" by its nature exists only in the underground even if some part of it might be exposed to the surface of the Earth.

16. On subparagraph (*d*), one Government observed that it is understood that aquifers, especially in the form of confined groundwater, may also be found in areas under the jurisdiction or control of States outside their territories and that when the Commission considers the application of the draft articles to all shared natural resources during the second reading of the draft articles, it will become inevitable to revisit the definition of "aquifer State" and to address the application of the draft articles to shared natural resources that can be found under the continental shelves of States, notably oil and gas.[24] In the view of the Special Rapporteur, extending the scope of application to continental shelves would bring in complications and he is opposed to this suggestion. If a transboundary aquifer between State A and State B extends to the continental shelves of both States or of either State A or State B, then both States qualify as an aquifer State under the current definition of an aquifer State. If a domestic aquifer of State A extends to the continental shelf of State A and at the same time to that of State B or if an aquifer is located only within the continental shelves of both States, neither State qualifies as an aquifer State. Should the draft articles cover the aquifer in the latter case? First of all, aquifers are mostly located under land territories. Extension of such aquifers beyond the territorial seas is possible but rather rare. Rock reservoirs found exclusively on continental shelves usually hold oil and natural gas and in some cases brine. Therefore, if the Commission were to extend the scope of application to continental shelves, it would in fact be linking the work on transboundary aquifers with that on oil and natural gas.

17. The Special Rapporteur wishes to propose the following new subparagraph on the definition of the term "utilization", which appears often throughout the draft articles:

"(*d* bis) 'utilization of transboundary aquifers or aquifer systems' includes withdrawal of water, heat and minerals, storage and disposal;"

This new subparagraph lists only the most known and current uses and is not exhaustive. For storage and disposal, there is, for instance, a new technique to utilize an aquifer for carbon sequestration in the treatment of wastes. It leaves the responsibility to determine what constitutes acceptable "storage" and "disposal" to the aquifer States concerned. It is understood that regulations are in force in many States prohibiting the injection of toxic, radioactive or other hazardous wastes. The commentaries should elaborate on these aspects.

18. On subparagraphs (*f*) and (*g*), one Government proposed the addition of the expression "that part of" before "the catchment area" in subparagraph (*f*) and the addition of "or the upward flow system keeps the groundwater table permanently close to the surface" at the end of subparagraph (*g*).[25] The Special Rapporteur understands that the intention of the proposals was to clarify that the recharge zone is where infiltration through the soil is significant and/or where surface water contributed directly to aquifers and that the discharge zone could exist without any water being present on the surface. These are rather detailed technical clarifications and could be properly explained in the commentaries.

19. Similar terms such as "an impact", "environmental impact", "significant harm", "serious harm", "to affect", "significant adverse effect", and "detrimental effect" are used in various draft articles. These terms are carefully selected and should be construed in the context of the draft articles in which they are used. Their precise meaning will be elaborated in the commentaries.

D. Article 3. Sovereignty of aquifer States

20. Some Governments sought to strengthen the sovereignty aspects by a direct reference to General Assembly resolution 1803 (XVII) of 14 December 1962, by a new formulation ("Each aquifer State shall exercise its inherent sovereignty over the portion of a transboundary aquifer or aquifer system located within its territory for the purposes provided in article 1 in accordance with the present draft articles") or by deleting the last sentence of the article.[26] Others stated that sovereignty was also governed by the rules and generally accepted principles of international law and emphasized the principle of cooperation between States and the principle of mitigation in this connection.[27] The Special Rapporteur believes that the current formulation reflects the appropriate balance between these differing positions.

E. Article 4. Equitable and reasonable utilization

21. Some Governments emphasized the concept of sustainability, proposing to substitute "equitable and sustainable utilization" for "equitable and reasonable utilization".[28] It is not appropriate to apply the concept

[24] Netherlands, written comment, A/CN.4/595 and Add.1 (see footnote 6 above), sect. D.6, para. 2.

[25] Hungary, *Official Records of the General Assembly, Sixty-first Session, Sixth Committee*, 14th meeting (A/C.6/61/SR.14), para. 12.

[26] Brazil, *Official Records of the General Assembly, Sixty-second Session, Sixth Committee*, 24th meeting (A/C.6/62/SR.24), para. 110; China, *Official Records of the General Assembly, Sixty-first Session, Sixth Committee*, 14th meeting (A/C.6/61/SR.14), para. 5; Cuba, *Official Records of the General Assembly, Sixty-second Session, Sixth Committee*, 24th meeting (A/C.6/62/SR.24), para. 65; Venezuela (Bolivarian Republic of), *ibid.*, 25th meeting (A/C.6/62/SR.25), para. 63; and Turkey, written comment, A/CN.4/595 and Add.1 (see footnote 6 above), sect. E.6.

[27] Portugal, written comment, A/CN.4/595 and Add.1 (see footnote 6 above), sect. E.5, and *Official Records of the General Assembly, Sixty-first Session, Sixth Committee*, 14th meeting (A/C.6/61/SR.14), para. 69; Russian Federation, *ibid.*, 18th meeting (A/C.6/61/SR.18), para. 69.

[28] Cuba, *Official Records of the General Assembly, Sixty-second Session, Sixth Committee*, 24th meeting (A/C.6/62/SR.24), para. 64; Syrian Arab Republic, *ibid.*, para. 95; Mexico, *Official Records of the General Assembly, Sixty-first Session, Sixth Committee*, 14th meeting (A/C.6/61/SR.14), para. 35.

of sustainability to aquifers because the waters in non-recharging aquifers are not renewable resources and even the waters in recharging aquifers receive only a fraction of recharge in comparison with the total amount of water stored in such aquifers. On subparagraph (*c*), the proposal was made to change the expression "present and future needs" to "the needs of present and future generations".[29] This change might make the timespan unduly long. Also on subparagraph (*c*), the proposal was made to delete the expression "alternative water resources" because neither groundwater resources nor surface water resources could be treated as alternatives to one another and they are already a part of the utilization plan.[30] The Special Rapporteur understands that this argument is correct when a State establishes the overall utilization plan for the whole of its water resources. However, it should be pointed out that the utilization plan in subparagraph (*c*) is the one which relates only to a transboundary aquifer, excluding domestic aquifers and international rivers and other water resources which are not linked to that transboundary aquifer. Accordingly, the need to take into account alternative water resources arises in establishing such a plan. There was a suggestion for a new subparagraph (*e*) which would read "no State may assign, lease or sell, in whole or in part, to any other State, whether an aquifer State or a non-aquifer State, its right to utilize aquifers".[31] The Special Rapporteur feels that this must be left to States to decide.

F. Article 5. Factors relevant to equitable and reasonable utilization

22. Suggestions were made to change subparagraph 1 (*c*) to read "the compatibility of a given mode of utilization with the natural characteristics of the aquifer or aquifer system within each State" and to have a new subparagraph which takes into consideration the area, extent, thickness and characteristics of the aquifer and the direction in which groundwaters flow.[32] The proposed new version of subparagraph 1 (*c*) relates more to the question of priority among the different kinds of utilization and is not what the current subparagraph (*c*) aims at but is more relevant to paragraph 2. Such priority could not be given to a particular kind of utilization *a priori*. The latter proposal could be elaborated in the commentaries to subparagraph 1 (*c*). A suggestion was made to delete subparagraph 1 (*g*) on the same rationale as the one underpinning the suggestion to delete "alternative water resources" from article 4 (*c*).[33] The observation made by the Special Rapporteur regarding that suggestion in paragraph 21 above also applies here. There was also a suggestion to add another factor—any existing and planned other activities and their effects—in view of the fact that the draft articles would cover activities other than the utilization of aquifers.[34] Other activities are regulated in draft articles 6, 10 and 14. The Special Rapporteur finds it rather difficult to see the direct relevance of such activities in determining equitable and reasonable utilization of aquifers. However, if they have relevance, subparagraph 1 (*b*) may cover the case. Textual modifications were suggested to clarify subparagraph 1 (*d*) and "vital human needs" in paragraph 2.[35] The Special Rapporteur feels that they would be better clarified in the commentaries.

G. Article 6. Obligation not to cause significant harm to other aquifer States

23. Some Governments repeated their objections to the high threshold of "significant" harm. Others stated that the scope of the obligation, "significant harm", "impact", "appropriate measures" and the authority which should decide the measures to be taken must be clarified.[36] These should be elaborated in the commentaries. Another Government proposed the following alternative text for article 6:

> 1. Aquifer States shall, in utilizing a transboundary aquifer or aquifer system in their territories, pay due diligence to prevent the causing of significant harm to other aquifer States.
>
> 2. Aquifer States shall, in undertaking activities other than utilization of a transboundary aquifer or aquifer system that have, or are likely to have, an impact on that transboundary aquifer or aquifer system, refrain from causing significant harm through that aquifer or aquifer system to other aquifer States.
>
> 3. Where significant harm nevertheless is caused to another aquifer State, the aquifer States whose activities cause such harm shall try, in consultation with the affected State, to eliminate or mitigate such harm, having due regard for the provisions of draft articles 4 and 5.[37]

The Special Rapporteur feels that this new text would weaken the obligations to be prescribed in this article.

24. One Government suggested that the subject of draft article 6, paragraph 2, should be all States rather than aquifer States.[38] The Special Rapporteur considers that the case in which a non-aquifer State may cause harm to aquifer States through a transboundary aquifer would be limited to the case where a recharge or discharge zone is located in such a non-aquifer State. That case is already governed by draft article 10.

25. Some Governments regretted the omission of a provision on compensation from draft article 6, paragraph 3.[39] One Government wished to have an explicit

[29] Cuba, *Official Records of the General Assembly, Sixty-second Session, Sixth Committee*, 24th meeting (A/C.6/62/SR.24), para. 66.

[30] Turkey, written comment, A/CN.4/595 and Add.1 (see footnote 6 above), sect. F.9.

[31] Saudi Arabia, *ibid.*, F.7, para. 2.

[32] *Ibid.*, sect. G.8, para. 1.

[33] Turkey, written comment, A/CN.4/595 and Add.1 (see footnote 6 above), sect. G.10.

[34] Netherlands, *ibid.*, sect. G.6.

[35] Greece, *Official Records of the General Assembly, Sixty-first Session, Sixth Committee*, 15th meeting (A/C.6/61/SR.15), para. 34, and Malaysia, *ibid.*, para. 48.

[36] Portugal, written comment, A/CN.4/595 and Add.1 (see footnote 6 above), sect. D.7, para. 1; Sweden, on behalf of the Nordic countries, *Official Records of the General Assembly, Sixty-second Session, Sixth Committee*, 22nd meeting (A/C.6/62/SR.22), para. 31; Uruguay, *Official Records of the General Assembly, Sixty-first Session, Sixth Committee* 14th meeting (A/C.6/61/SR.14), para. 80; Greece, *ibid.*, 15th meeting (A/C.6/61/SR.15), para. 35; Romania, *ibid.*, 19th meeting (A/C.6/61/SR.19), para. 59.

[37] Turkey, written comment, A/CN.4/595 and Add.1 (see footnote 6 above), sect. H.9, para. 1.

[38] Netherlands, *ibid.*, sect. H.7, para. 2.

[39] *Ibid.*, para. 139; Hungary, *Official Records of the General Assembly, Sixty-first Session, Sixth Committee*, 14th meeting (A/C.6/61/SR.14), para. 10; Cuba, *ibid.*, 16th meeting (A/C.6/61/SR.16), para. 11.

provision on irreversible harm, the compensatory obligation of the State causing the harm, the method of compensation and the designation of the competent authority for it.[40] Since the views of Governments are divided on this issue, the Special Rapporteur intends to elaborate the legal framework relevant to the issue in the commentaries.

H. Article 7. General obligation to cooperate

26. One Government suggested the deletion of "good faith" from paragraph 1 as the term "good faith" raises fears that States may, in good faith, take measures that were not negotiated with the other party and that could have adverse effects on the needs of the other party.[41] "Good faith" is incorporated here not as an element of excuse for evading the obligation of cooperation and it is found in an equivalent article 8, paragraph 1, of the Convention on the Law of the Non-navigational Uses of International Watercourses. On draft article 7, paragraph 2, there were opposing suggestions to replace "should" by "shall" and to change the paragraph to read "aquifer States should give positive consideration to establishing joint mechanism of cooperation".[42] The Special Rapporteur's suggestion is to keep the text as it is.

I. Article 8. Regular exchange of data and information

27. There were no comments or observations which called for modification of this draft article.

J. Article 9. Protection and preservation of ecosystems

28. There was a suggestion to broaden the scope of this draft article from aquifer States to all States.[43] This article is intended to protect ecosystems not only within aquifers but also ecosystems located outside aquifers. The Special Rapporteur intends to submit the clarification on the scope of the latter ecosystems so that the decision could be made whether non-aquifer States should be required to protect such ecosystems. Another suggestion was to add at the end of the article "whilst giving special regard to basic human needs".[44] The Special Rapporteur feels that the derogation from the obligations in this article should be governed by the general rules of international law, namely circumstances precluding wrongfulness, which in a particular case might include the basic human water need.

K. Article 10. Recharge and discharge zones

29. There were no comments or observations which called for modification of this draft article.

L. Article 11. Prevention, reduction and control of pollution

30. The comment that the threshold of "significant harm" was too high (see paragraph 23 above) was repeated here.[45] One Government suggested that there must be a reference to the procedures which States should adopt in the event of problems of the quality of water and proposed to insert "adopt all the measures to" before "prevent, reduce and ...".[46] The Special Rapporteur feels that the current formulation is clearer in prescribing the obligation to prevent, reduce and control pollution and that the procedural measures would be more appropriately explained in the commentaries. Another Government suggested broadening the scope of this draft article from aquifer States to all States.[47] The Special Rapporteur wonders whether non-aquifer States, in whose territory there exists neither a recharge nor a discharge zone of a transboundary aquifer of other States, have any role to play in preventing, reducing or controlling pollution of that aquifer.

31. Regarding the second sentence of this draft article, suggestions were made to replace "precautionary approach" by "precautionary principle"[48] and to broaden the application of "precautionary principle" to utilization by revising the text to read "aquifer States shall apply the precautionary principle to the utilization of transboundary aquifers and transboundary aquifer systems".[49] The Special Rapporteur intends to cite instances where "precautionary approach" and "precautionary principle" are used in various conventions and to define what is meant by the terms. The Special Rapporteur considers that the utilization of aquifers *per se* is not hazardous and should not necessarily involve resort to a precautionary approach.

32. In order to put more focus on "precautionary approach", the Special Rapporteur proposes to alter the word order of the second sentence of this article to read:

"Aquifer States shall take a precautionary approach in view of uncertainty about the nature and extent of transboundary aquifers or aquifer systems ..."

M. Article 12. Monitoring

33. There was a proposal to modify the first two sentences to read: "Aquifer States shall monitor their transboundary aquifer or aquifer system. They shall carry out these monitoring activities, where appropriate, jointly with other aquifer States concerned and in collaboration with the competent international organizations".[50] The Special Rapporteur does not see a rationale behind this proposal. There was another suggestion for an additional clause indicating that the aquifer States, following consultation among themselves, would formulate the objectives

[40] Saudi Arabia, written comment, A/CN.4/595 and Add.1 (see footnote 6 above), sect. H.8.

[41] Czech Republic, *ibid.*, sect. I.3, para. 1.

[42] *Ibid.*, para. 2, and China, *Official Records of the General Assembly, Sixty-first Session, Sixth Committee*, 14th meeting (A/C.6/61/SR.14), para. 6.

[43] Netherlands, written comment, A/CN.4/595 and Add.1 (see footnote 6 above), sect. K.2.

[44] Turkey, *ibid.*, sect. K.3.

[45] Sweden, on behalf of the Nordic countries, *Official Records of the General Assembly, Sixty-second Session, Sixth Committee*, 22nd meeting (A/C.6/62/SR.22), para. 31.

[46] Portugal, written comment, A/CN.4/595 and Add.1 (see footnote 6 above), sect. M.6.

[47] Netherlands, *ibid.*, sect. M.5, para. 1.

[48] See footnote 45 above.

[49] Netherlands, written comment, A/CN.4/595 and Add.1 (see footnote 6 above), sect. M.5, para. 2.

[50] Turkey, written comment, A/CN.4/595 and Add.1 (see footnote 6 above), sect. N.2.

of monitoring, on the basis of which the monitoring system and parameters to be monitored would be decided.[51] The Special Rapporteur feels that this could be elaborated in the commentaries.

N. Article 13. Management

34. There were no comments or observations which called for modification of this draft article.

O. Article 14. Planned activities

35. A suggestion was made to align paragraph 2 with paragraph 1 by making an explicit reference to "environmental effects" in the first paragraph.[52] It was pointed out that the assessment which is required in the first paragraph is limited to the possible effects upon another State and could be narrower than an environmental impact assessment. The notification to be provided in accordance with the second paragraph must be accompanied by such an assessment as well as an environmental impact assessment if the latter is also available. The same Government proposed to provide for the obligation to refrain from implementing planned activities during the consultation and negotiations between the States concerned.[53] It is recalled that the general preference was to have simpler procedural requirements than those set out in the Convention on the Law of the Non-navigational Uses of International Watercourses. The introduction of a time period for refraining from implementation of planned activities would not be fair unless it were accompanied by the time limits of other actions and omissions, such as reply to notification, consultation and negotiations, and also by other procedural requirements. Related also to this aspect, another Government proposed the addition of the phrase: "Should no agreement be reached within a reasonable period, notifying State could exercise its sovereign rights to implement its planned activity with best efforts to reduce its adverse effects".[54] Still related to this aspect, the views were expressed that the provision would allow affected States to veto planned activities in other States; that the affected States should have the right to consult with the States of planned activities even if they were not notified of the plans; and that a legal regime for activities covered here could only be established with the consent of the State of planned activities.[55] The Special Rapporteur is of the view that in the absence of established rules in this respect *vis-à-vis* aquifers, these procedural requirements must be left to the best judgment of the States concerned. The definition of "significant adverse effect" sought by some Governments[56] will be discussed in the commentaries.

[51] Thailand, *Official Records of the General Assembly, Sixty-second Session, Sixth Committee,* 25th meeting (A/C.6/62/SR.25), para. 55.

[52] Netherlands, written comment, A/CN.4/595 and Add.1 (see footnote 6 above), sect. P.6.

[53] *Ibid.*

[54] Turkey, *ibid.*, sect. P.7.

[55] Ethiopia, *Official Records of the General Assembly, Sixty-first Session, Sixth Committee,* 14th meeting (A/C.6/61/SR.14), para. 90; Jordan, *ibid.*, 15th meeting (A/C.6/61/SR.15), para. 14; and Russian Federation, *ibid.*, 18th meeting (A/C.6/61/SR.18), para. 69.

[56] Portugal, written comment, A/CN.4/595 and Add.1 (see footnote 6 above), sect. D.7, para. 1.

P. Article 15. Scientific and technical cooperation with developing States

36. A suggestion was made to replace "shall" by "could" in the second sentence of the chapeau of this article as "shall" implies obligation.[57] The sentence in question provides a non-exhaustive list of various kinds of cooperation. It could be modified to read: "Such cooperation includes, *inter alia* ...".

Q. Articles 16. Emergency situations, 17. Protection in time of armed conflict, 18. Data and information concerning national defence or security and 19. Bilateral and regional agreements and arrangements

37. There were no comments or observations which called for modification of these four draft articles.

R. Additional articles

38. If the draft articles are eventually to become a convention as foreseen in the draft recommendation to the General Assembly in paragraph 9 above, they should include an article on the relationship with other agreements. The Special Rapporteur proposes the following draft article on the relation to other conventions for the consideration by the Commission:

"*Article 20. Relation to other conventions and international agreements*

"1. The present draft articles shall not alter the rights and obligations of the States parties which arise from other conventions and international agreements compatible with the present draft articles and which do not affect the enjoyment by other States parties of their rights or the performance of their obligations under the present draft articles.

"2. Notwithstanding the provisions of paragraph 1, when the States parties to the present draft articles are parties also to the Convention on the Law of the Non-navigational Uses of International Watercourses, the provisions of the latter concerning transboundary aquifers or aquifer systems apply only to the extent that they are compatible with those of the present draft articles."

39. Paragraph 1 is intended to define the relationship between the present draft articles and other conventions and international agreements that regulate transboundary aquifers as well as those that regulate mainly matters other than transboundary aquifers but have some limited application to transboundary aquifers. An example of the latter case is the Convention on the Protection and Use of Transboundary Watercourses and International Lakes, concluded under the auspices of the ECE. Another example is article 194 of the United Nations Convention on the Law of the Sea (Measures to prevent, reduce and control pollution of the marine environment) and, in particular, its paragraph 3 (*a*), concerning pollution from land-based sources. Many environmental agreements may also be relevant. If the provisions of the

[57] Turkey, written comment, A/CN.4/595 and Add.1 (see footnote 6 above), sect. Q.6.

present draft articles and those of other conventions and international agreements are compatible, there would be no problem in parallel application. If, however, there exists conflict, it would not be appropriate to stipulate a general rule of priority. A decision on such priority would be possible only after the contents of the relevant provisions are fully examined. Accordingly, the Special Rapporteur formulated this draft article on the basis of article 311, paragraph 2 of the United Nations Convention on the Law of the Sea. Bilateral and regional agreements regulated by draft article 12 are also covered by this paragraph. Many Governments stated that the draft articles should not affect the existing agreements. The Special Rapporteur intends to state in the commentaries that the State parties to those agreements should consider harmonizing such agreements with the basic principles of the present draft articles and where those parties consider that adjustment in application of the provisions of the present draft articles is required because of the special characteristics and utilization of a particular transboundary aquifer or aquifer system, they should consult among themselves with a view to negotiating in good faith for the purpose of concluding an agreement beneficial to all the parties.

40. Paragraph 2 relates to transboundary aquifers and aquifer systems that are hydraulically linked to international watercourses which are subject to the scope of both the present draft articles and the Convention on the Law of the Non-navigational Uses of International Watercourses. The present draft articles focus exclusively on aquifers while the convention focuses on surface waters; its relevance to aquifers is peripheral. Should a conflict arise, the present draft articles should prevail as they are formulated to govern exclusively transboundary aquifers and are the follow-up to the convention.

41. It was suggested to include a dispute-settlement mechanism if the text should take the form of a convention.[58] The Special Rapporteur suggests to leave the matter of dispute settlement to the negotiating conference. While the setting up of a mechanism to settle disputes concerning aquifers is of utmost importance, the disputes which are likely to arise in real life would mainly relate to the interpretation and application of the provisions of a bilateral or regional agreement concerning a specific aquifer. The provision on the settlement of disputes for the draft articles could be a rather brief statement of principles. The preamble and final clauses are also left to the negotiating conference.

[58] Republic of Korea, written comment, A/CN.4/595 and Add.1 (see footnote 6 above), sect. W.5, para. 1.

Chapter IV

Acknowledgements

42. In addition to the valuable assistance and support from the Codification Division of the Office of Legal Affairs, the Special Rapporteur continues to receive scientific and technical advice from UNESCO, in particular the group of experts it sent to Tokyo in January 2008;[59] legal and administrative assistance from the Ministry of Foreign Affairs of Japan; and support from the academic members and legal experts of the study group established by the Ministry on the topic of shared natural resources.[60] UNESCO invited the Special Rapporteur to two of its regional seminars, one for European States in Paris in May 2007 and the other, cosponsored with the Government of Canada, for American States in Montreal in September 2007, where the Special Rapporteur had the privilege to meet with experts from the regions and to take part in a field trip to observe the management of transboundary aquifers. The Special Rapporteur wishes to takes this opportunity to express his sincere gratitude for their most valuable contributions.

[59] Alice Aureli and Raya Stephan of UNESCO, Gabriel Eckstein of the Texas Tech University School of Law, Shammy Puri of the International Association of Hydrogeologists, Lloyd Woosley of the United States Geological Survey and Stefano Burchi of FAO.

[60] Kazuhiro Nakatani of the University of Tokyo, Mariko Kawano of Waseda University, Itsuko Nakai of Konan University, Mari Koyano of Hokkaido University, Hiroyuki Banzai of Surugadai University, Tadashi Mori of Metropolitan University Tokyo, Yasuhiro Shigeta of the University of Kyoto, Jun Tsuruta of the Maritime Safety Academy, Naoki Iwatsuki of Rikkyo University and Junko Iwaishi of Sophia University.

Annex

THE LAW OF TRANSBOUNDARY AQUIFERS

Part I

INTRODUCTION

Article 1. Scope

The present draft articles apply to:

(*a*) utilization of transboundary aquifers and aquifer systems;

(*b*) other activities that have or are likely to have an impact upon those aquifers and aquifer systems; and

(*c*) measures for the protection, preservation and management of those aquifers and aquifer systems.

Article 2. Use of terms

For the purposes of the present draft articles:

(*a*) "aquifer" means a permeable water-bearing geological formation underlain by a less permeable layer and the water contained in the saturated zone of the formation;

(*b*) "aquifer system" means a series of two or more aquifers that are hydraulically connected;

(*c*) "transboundary aquifer" or "transboundary aquifer system" means respectively, an aquifer or aquifer system, parts of which are situated in different States;

(*d*) "aquifer State" means a State in whose territory any part of a transboundary aquifer or aquifer system is situated;

(*d* bis) "utilization of transboundary aquifers and aquifer systems" includes withdrawal of water, heat and minerals, storage and disposal;

(*e*) "recharging aquifer" means an aquifer that receives a non-negligible amount of contemporary water recharge;

(*f*) "recharge zone" means the zone which contributes water to an aquifer, consisting of the catchment area of rainfall water and the area where such water flows to an aquifer by runoff on the ground and infiltration through soil;

(*g*) "discharge zone" means the zone where water originating from an aquifer flows to its outlets, such as a watercourse, a lake, an oasis, a wetland or an ocean.

Part II

GENERAL PRINCIPLES

Article 3. Sovereignty of aquifer States

Each aquifer State has sovereignty over the portion of a transboundary aquifer or aquifer system located within its territory. It shall exercise its sovereignty in accordance with the present draft articles.

Article 4. Equitable and reasonable utilization

Aquifer States shall utilize a transboundary aquifer or aquifer system according to the principle of equitable and reasonable utilization, as follows:

(*a*) they shall utilize the transboundary aquifer or aquifer system in a manner that is consistent with the equitable and reasonable accrual of benefits therefrom to the aquifer States concerned;

(*b*) they shall aim at maximizing the long-term benefits derived from the use of water contained therein;

(*c*) they shall establish individually or jointly an overall utilization plan, taking into account present and future needs of, and alternative water resources for, the aquifer States; and

(*d*) they shall not utilize a recharging transboundary aquifer or aquifer system at a level that would prevent continuance of its effective functioning.

Article 5. Factors relevant to equitable and reasonable utilization

1. Utilization of a transboundary aquifer or aquifer system in an equitable and reasonable manner within the meaning of draft article 4 requires taking into account all relevant factors, including:

(*a*) the population dependent on the aquifer or aquifer system in each aquifer State;

(*b*) the social, economic and other needs, present and future, of the aquifer States concerned;

(*c*) the natural characteristics of the aquifer or aquifer system;

(*d*) the contribution to the formation and recharge of the aquifer or aquifer system;

(*e*) the existing and potential utilization of the aquifer or aquifer system;

(*f*) the effects of the utilization of the aquifer or aquifer system in one aquifer State on other aquifer States concerned;

(*g*) the availability of alternatives to a particular existing and planned utilization of the aquifer or aquifer system;

(*h*) the development, protection and conservation of the aquifer or aquifer system and the costs of measures to be taken to that effect;

(*i*) the role of the aquifer or aquifer system in the related ecosystem.

2. The weight to be given to each factor is to be determined by its importance with regard to a specific transboundary aquifer or aquifer system in comparison with that of other relevant factors. In determining what is equitable and reasonable utilization, all relevant factors are to be considered together and a conclusion reached on the basis of all the factors. However, in weighing different utilizations of a transboundary aquifer or aquifer system, special regard shall be given to vital human needs.

Article 6. Obligation not to cause significant harm to other aquifer States

1. Aquifer States shall, in utilizing a transboundary aquifer or aquifer system in their territories, take all appropriate measures to prevent the causing of significant harm to other aquifer States.

2. Aquifer States shall, in undertaking activities other than utilization of a transboundary aquifer or aquifer system that have, or are likely to have, an impact on that transboundary aquifer or aquifer system, take all appropriate measures to prevent the causing of significant harm through that aquifer or aquifer system to other aquifer States.

3. Where significant harm nevertheless is caused to another aquifer State, the aquifer States whose activities cause such harm shall take, in consultation with the affected State, all appropriate measures to eliminate or mitigate such harm, having due regard for the provisions of draft articles 4 and 5.

Article 7. General obligation to cooperate

1. Aquifer States shall cooperate on the basis of sovereign equality, territorial integrity, sustainable development, mutual benefit and good faith in order to attain equitable and reasonable utilization and appropriate protection of their transboundary aquifer or aquifer system.

2. For the purpose of paragraph 1, aquifer States should establish joint mechanisms of cooperation.

Article 8. Regular exchange of data and information

1. Pursuant to draft article 7, aquifer States shall, on a regular basis, exchange readily available data and information on the condition of the transboundary aquifer or aquifer system, in particular of a geological, hydrogeological, hydrological, meteorological and ecological nature and related to the hydrochemistry of the aquifer or aquifer system, as well as related forecasts.

2. Where knowledge about the nature and extent of some transboundary aquifer or aquifer systems is inadequate, aquifer States concerned shall employ their best efforts to collect and generate more complete data and information relating to such aquifer or aquifer systems, taking into account current practices and standards. They shall take such action individually or jointly and, where appropriate, together with or through international organizations.

3. If an aquifer State is requested by another aquifer State to provide data and information relating to the aquifer or aquifer systems that are not readily available, it shall employ its best efforts to comply with the request. The requested State may condition its compliance upon payment by the requesting State of the reasonable costs of collecting and, where appropriate, processing such data or information.

4. Aquifer States shall, where appropriate, employ their best efforts to collect and process data and information in a manner that facilitates their utilization by the other aquifer States to which such data and information are communicated.

PART III

PROTECTION, PRESERVATION AND MANAGEMENT

Article 9. Protection and preservation of ecosystems

Aquifer States shall take all appropriate measures to protect and preserve ecosystems within, or dependent upon, their transboundary aquifers or aquifer systems, including measures to ensure that the quality and quantity of water retained in the aquifer or aquifer system, as well as that released in its discharge zones, are sufficient to protect and preserve such ecosystems.

Article 10. Recharge and discharge zones

1. Aquifer States shall identify recharge and discharge zones of their transboundary aquifer or aquifer system and, within these zones, shall take special measures to minimize detrimental impacts on the recharge and discharge processes.

2. All States in whose territory a recharge or discharge zone is located, in whole or in part, and which are not aquifer States with regard to that aquifer or aquifer system, shall cooperate with the aquifer States to protect the aquifer or aquifer system.

Article 11. Prevention, reduction and control of pollution

Aquifer States shall, individually and, where appropriate, jointly, prevent, reduce and control pollution of their transboundary aquifer or aquifer system, including through the recharge process, that may cause significant harm to other aquifer States. Aquifer States shall take a precautionary approach in view of uncertainty about the nature and extent of transboundary aquifers or aquifer systems and of their vulnerability to pollution.

Article 12. Monitoring

1. Aquifer States shall monitor their transboundary aquifer or aquifer system. They shall, wherever possible, carry out these monitoring activities jointly with other aquifer States concerned and, where appropriate, in collaboration with the competent international organizations. Where, however, monitoring activities are not carried out jointly, the aquifer States shall exchange the monitored data among themselves.

2. Aquifer States shall use agreed or harmonized standards and methodology for monitoring their transboundary aquifer or aquifer system. They should identify key parameters that they will monitor based on an agreed conceptual model of the aquifer or aquifer system. These parameters should include parameters on the condition of the aquifer or aquifer system as listed in draft article 8, paragraph 1, and also on the utilization of the aquifer and aquifer system.

Article 13. Management

Aquifer States shall establish and implement plans for the proper management of their transboundary aquifer or aquifer system in accordance with the provisions of the present draft articles. They shall, at the request by any of them, enter into consultations concerning the management of the transboundary aquifer or aquifer system. A joint management mechanism shall be established, wherever appropriate.

PART IV

ACTIVITIES AFFECTING OTHER STATES

Article 14. Planned activities

1. When a State has reasonable grounds for believing that a particular planned activity in its territory may affect a transboundary aquifer or aquifer system and thereby may have a significant adverse effect upon another State, it shall, as far as practicable, assess the possible effects of such activity.

2. Before a State implements or permits the implementation of planned activities which may affect a transboundary aquifer or aquifer system and thereby may have a significant adverse effect upon another State, it shall provide that State with timely notification thereof. Such notification shall be accompanied by available technical data and information, including any environmental impact assessment, in order to enable the notified State to evaluate the possible effects of the planned activities.

3. If the notifying and the notified States disagree on the possible effect of the planned activities, they shall enter into consultations and, if necessary, negotiations with a view to arriving at an equitable resolution of the situation. They may utilize an independent fact-finding body to make an impartial assessment of the effect of the planned activities.

PART V

MISCELLANEOUS PROVISIONS

Article 15. Scientific and technical cooperation with developing States

States shall, directly or through competent international organizations, promote scientific, educational, technical and other cooperation with developing States for the protection and management of transboundary aquifers or aquifer systems. Such cooperation shall include, *inter alia*:

(*a*) Training of their scientific and technical personnel;

(*b*) Facilitating their participation in relevant international programmes;

(*c*) Supplying them with necessary equipment and facilities;

(*d*) Enhancing their capacity to manufacture such equipment;

(*e*) Providing advice on and developing facilities for research, monitoring, educational and other programmes;

(*f*) Providing advice on and developing facilities for minimizing the detrimental effects of major activities affecting transboundary aquifers or aquifer systems;

(*g*) Preparing environmental impact assessments.

Article 16. Emergency situations

1. For the purpose of the present draft article, "emergency" means a situation, resulting suddenly from natural causes or from human conduct, that poses an imminent threat of causing serious harm to aquifer States or other States.

2. Where an emergency affects a transboundary aquifer or aquifer system and thereby poses an imminent threat to States, the following shall apply:

(*a*) The State within whose territory the emergency originates shall:

(i) without delay and by the most expeditious means available, notify other potentially affected States and competent international organizations of the emergency;

(ii) in cooperation with potentially affected States and, where appropriate, competent international organizations, immediately take all practicable measures necessitated by the circumstances to prevent, mitigate and eliminate any harmful effect of the emergency;

(*b*) States shall provide scientific, technical, logistical and other cooperation to other States experiencing an emergency. Cooperation may include coordination of international emergency actions and communications, making available trained emergency response personnel, emergency response equipments and supplies, scientific and technical expertise and humanitarian assistance.

3. Where an emergency poses a threat to vital human needs, aquifer States, notwithstanding draft articles 4 and 6, may take measures that are strictly necessary to meet such needs.

Article 17. Protection in time of armed conflict

Transboundary aquifers or aquifer systems and related installations, facilities and other works shall enjoy the protection accorded by the principles and rules of international law applicable in international and non-international armed conflicts and shall not be used in violation of those principles and rules.

Article 18. Data and information concerning national defence or security

Nothing in the present draft articles obliges a State to provide data or information the confidentiality of which is essential to its national defence or security. Nevertheless, that State shall cooperate in good faith with other States with a view to providing as much information as possible under the circumstances.

Article 19. Bilateral and regional agreements and arrangements

For the purpose of managing a particular transboundary aquifer or aquifer system, aquifer States are encouraged to enter into a bilateral or regional agreement or arrangement among themselves. Such agreement or arrangement may be entered into with respect to an entire aquifer or aquifer system or any part thereof or a particular project, programme or utilization except insofar as the agreement or arrangement adversely affects, to a significant extent, the utilization, by one or more other aquifer States of the water in that aquifer or aquifer system, without their express consent.

Article 20. Relation to other conventions and international agreements

1. The present draft articles shall not alter the rights and obligations of the States parties which arise from other conventions and international agreements compatible with the present draft articles and which do not affect the enjoyment by other States parties of their rights or the performance of their obligations under the present draft articles.

2. Notwithstanding the provisions of paragraph 1, when the States parties to the present draft articles are parties also to the Convention on the Law of the Non-navigational Uses of International Watercourses, the provisions of the latter concerning transboundary aquifers or aquifer systems apply only to the extent that they are compatible with those of the present draft articles.

SHARED NATURAL RESOURCES

[Agenda item 4]

DOCUMENT A/CN.4/595 and Add.1

Comments and observations by Governments on the draft articles on the law of transboundary aquifers

[Original: Arabic/Spanish/French/English]
[26 March and 7 May 2008]

CONTENTS

Multilateral instruments cited in the present document

	Source
Vienna Convention on the Law of Treaties (Vienna, 23 May 1969)	United Nations, *Treaty Series*, vol. 1155, No. 18232, p. 331.
United Nations Convention on the Law of the Sea (Montego Bay, 10 December 1982)	*Ibid.*, vol. 1833, No. 31363, p. 3.
Convention on the Protection and Use of Transboundary Watercourses and International Lakes (Helsinki, 17 March 1992)	*Ibid.*, vol. 1936, No. 33207, p. 269.
Convention on Biological Diversity (Rio de Janeiro, 5 June 1992)	*Ibid.*, vol. 1760, No. 30619, p. 79.
Convention on the Law of the Non-navigational Uses of International Watercourses (New York, 21 May 1997)	*Official Records of the General Assembly, Fifty-first Session, Supplement No. 49*, vol. III, resolution 51/229, annex.

Introduction

1. At its fifty-eighth session (2006), the International Law Commission adopted, on first reading, draft articles on the law of transboundary aquifers.[1] In paragraph 73 of its report, the Commission decided, in accordance with articles 16 and 21 of its statute, to request the Secretary-General to transmit the draft articles to Governments for comments and observations, requesting also that such comments and observations be submitted to the Secretary-General by 1 January 2008. In paragraph 26 of the report, the Commission noted that it would welcome comments and observations from Governments on all aspects of the draft articles, the commentaries to the draft articles and on the final form. The Secretary-General circulated a note dated 27 November 2006 transmitting the draft articles to Governments. In paragraph 5 of its resolution 61/34 and paragraph 6 of its resolution 62/66, the General Assembly drew the attention of Governments to the importance, for the Commission, of having their views on the draft articles.

2. As at 7 May 2008, replies had been received from the following States: Austria, Brazil, Canada, Colombia, Cuba, the Czech Republic, Finland, Germany, Hungary, Iraq, Israel, The Netherlands, Poland, Portugal, Saudi Arabia, Republic of Korea, Serbia, Turkey and the United States of America. The replies have been organized thematically, starting with general comments and continuing on an article-by-article basis.

[1] The text of the draft articles appears in *Yearbook ... 2006*, vol. II (Part Two), para.75 and the text of the draft articles with their commentaries in *ibid.*, para.76.

Comments and observations received from Governments

A. General comments

1. Brazil

1. Brazil expresses its appreciation for the work done by the Commission in the consideration of such a complex and relevant issue. Brazil also wishes to thank the Special Rapporteur, Mr. Chusei Yamada, and the Working Group chaired by Mr. Enrique Candioti for their efficient work and contribution, which made it possible to conclude the first reading in a relatively short time.

2. The main contribution to be made by the Commission, whose draft articles should guide the future work of the United Nations General Assembly on that matter, should be the establishment of a set of generic principles. These principles should be sufficiently flexible and balanced in order to allow for States where the transboundary aquifers are located to base their cooperation with a view to taking the best advantage of the aquifers in an equitable manner and according to the specific characteristics of each aquifer. It is up to the States themselves to develop, as appropriate, their own instruments and mechanisms, taking into consideration particular situations and different regional realities. Due to multiple situations and regional realities, the draft articles should recognize the primacy of regional agreements as the most appropriate to regulate cooperation as regards transboundary aquifers.

3. The work of the Commission and the General Assembly should be directed towards the establishment of generic principles which could guide States in the negotiation of regional agreements of a more specific nature. By doing so, the Commission and the General Assembly will avoid the risks of elaborating a text that will not gather broad consensus among States for being too ambitious and with too many technical and legal details. Furthermore, a text which is more flexible and open could contribute to raising awareness about the subject and heightening the priority of the issue in the agendas of States, encouraging them to negotiate regional agreements. In the view of Brazil, the draft articles reflect a careful balance between the principle of sovereignty of States over the natural resources located under their jurisdiction and the obligation of not causing significant harm to such resources. It is imperative to maintain such a balance and avoid excessive restrictions to legitimate activities carried out by States.

2. Canada

Canada appreciates the valuable work of the Commission in its examination of possible options for international law that may be applicable to transboundary aquifers. In some aspects, notably in its application of the *sic utere tuo ut alienum non laedas* principle as the basis for an obligation not to cause transboundary harm, the Commission reinforces that principle as a bedrock of customary international law.

3. Colombia

1. The draft articles submitted by the Commission address the substantive issues relating to transboundary underground water resources, as well as the rights and responsibilities of States with regard to conserving and preserving such resources. They provide a regulatory framework designed to ensure the comprehensive and harmonious management of water resources with a view to the conservation, management and utilization of transboundary aquifers.

2. The outcomes of the activities set out in the draft articles will be extremely important and useful for States with shared aquifers and natural resources, since they will generate the data needed to prioritize activities and to ensure that those resources are managed in an environmentally sensitive manner.

3. Nevertheless, the following points should be borne in mind for Colombia: a comprehensive legal review should be undertaken in order to determine the compatibility of the draft articles with current provisions of national legislation on the same subject, such as Act No. 191 of 1995 (Border Act)[1] and the National Code on Natural Resources and Environmental Protection,[2] the relevant regulatory decrees and the multilateral and bilateral agreements governing Colombia's relationships involving those resources.

4. In order to comply with the provisions of draft articles 4, 5, 8, 9, 11, 12, 13 and 14, each State will initially be required to undertake to identify, delimit and assess the condition, capacity (supply) and usability (feasibility of utilization) of the aquifers located within its borders. In this connection, it is important to consider whether it would be possible to establish financial machinery or a mechanism for international cooperation to assist States to carry out that task.

5. In order to implement, in a consistent manner, the provisions of draft articles 1 and 14 relating to other activities, it will be necessary to begin harmonizing the requirements, conditions and terms of reference for works or activities involving aquifers or groundwater recharge zones that require licences or environmental permits.

6. With regard to the proposal concerning the regular exchange of data and information between States with jurisdiction over a transboundary aquifer, it will first be necessary to develop data-collection protocols and formats so as to ensure that the data and information collected are complementary and add value, thus providing the necessary inputs for the joint development by the countries concerned of planning and management activities.

7. It is noticeable that the draft articles, when referring to the harm or eventual harm caused to aquifers, employ qualifiers such as "significant" ("*sensible*" or "*significativo*" in Spanish) or "serious" ("*grave*" in Spanish). In this regard, the meaning and scope of those terms should be clarified, the draft articles should therefore define the scope of that concept so as to provide a basis for determining the cases in which the legal effects provided for by the draft articles will be produced.

4. Cuba

1. It is not sufficient to use the phrase "equitable and reasonable utilization" in various places throughout the text, given the increasingly strong preference in environmental law to employ the term "sustainable", as reflected in the Convention on Biological Diversity. Cuba therefore believes that the phrase "equitable and sustainable utilization" would be more appropriate.

2. Cuba also wishes to express its gratitude to the Special Rapporteur for his efforts in preparing the four reports considered by the Commission and, in particular, for his proposal to take a step-by-step approach to the topic, beginning with transboundary groundwaters. It also extends its thanks to Mr. Enrique Candioti, Chairman of the Working Group on Shared Natural Resources, for his efforts in preparing the draft articles.

5. Czech Republic

1. The Czech Republic appreciates the result of the discussions of the Commission held to date, namely the draft articles on the law of transboundary aquifers. It is of the opinion that this text can serve in the future as the basis for the negotiation of detailed bilateral or multilateral agreements on transboundary aquifers. The draft articles on transboundary aquifers constitute a balance between the principles of sovereignty of States over natural resources, their reasonable and equitable utilization, their preservation and protection and the obligation not to cause significant harm.

2. Nevertheless, the Czech Republic would like to make several comments on the draft articles on the law of transboundary aquifers, in particular on draft articles 7 and 14 (see below).

6. Finland

1. It should be noted that the draft articles are burdened with an overly timid approach. For example, the environmental protection obligations laid down in the draft articles remain modest as compared with the Economic Commission for Europe Convention on the Protection and Use of Transboundary Watercourses and International Lakes concluded in 1992. While the Convention has not been used as a reference document in the preparation of

[1] "Por medio de la cual se dictan disposiciones sobre Zonas de Frontera". *Diario Oficial* No. 41.903, of 23 June 1995.

[2] *Ibid.*, No. 34.243, of 27 January 1975. "Código Nacional de Recursos Naturales Renovables y de Protección al Medio Ambiente".

the draft articles, it is one of the very few international regional instruments where the framework for cooperation in the case of groundwaters has been properly developed and which could serve as a model for the further preparation of the Commission draft.

2. The 1997 Convention on the Law of the Non-navigational Uses of International Watercourses also sets an example, although one that is not entirely encouraging. At the time of the negotiations on that Convention, the Commission draft articles relating to that Convention could be strengthened only in certain respects, and regarding many conflicting issues, the Commission text was referred to as a compromise. It was striking that States were not willing to become bound, through a legally binding instrument, by the principles adopted by them for instance at the United Nations Conference on Environment and Development held in Rio de Janeiro in 1992. The 1997 Convention has attracted only a small number of ratifications.

3. The draft articles on the law of transboundary aquifers are largely based on the principles adopted in the 1997 Convention, essentially designed to regulate surface waters. In the United Nations Economic Commission for Europe Convention, the term "transboundary waters" means both surface and ground waters which mark, cross or are located on boundaries between two or more States. There is nevertheless reason to consider any specific features of groundwaters independently, instead of leaning too much on the 1997 Convention. It is also worth noting that environmental issues relating to groundwaters are completely different in nature from those connected to gas and oil, so the same principles do not apply. This should be taken into account by the Commission if it decides to commence the consideration of gas and oil in the future.

4. Today, many international conventions regarding the environment are drafted as framework conventions. Cooperation regarding them is governed and developed through meetings of the parties and subsidiary bodies. Different types of conventional regimes have resulted from this kind of cooperation. For example, detailed protocols have been adopted under a number of conventions with a view to specifying general provisions laid down in them. It is worth noting that the Commission draft articles do not contain elements of such regime thinking. Instead, the document is meant as a general instrument intended to create a framework for regional or bilateral cooperation. Even if this starting point has its justification, it also has its risks. States are not necessarily motivated to ratify a general convention standing for a collection of principles; nor is such a convention bound to generate significant added value. Furthermore, in the absence of a dynamic regime element, an eventual general convention would not be more than a dormant list of principles. It would be important to encourage States to engage in mutual, bilateral cooperation, emphasizing the importance of mutual agreements, plans and other forms of cooperation between neighbouring States with a view to making more specific agreements on the details relating to the use and protection of water resources.

5. In the interests of clarity, consideration should be given to harmonizing the relevant terms throughout the draft articles. It should be pointed out that in draft article 6, the term "significant harm" is introduced to establish the threshold for the negative impact resulting, *inter alia*, from the utilization of a transboundary aquifer on other States. In draft article 14 related to the planned activities, however, an aquifer State would be obliged to notify other States in case the planned activities would have "a significant adverse effect" upon them. Furthermore, in draft article 16 concerning the measures to be taken in emergency situations, an aquifer State would be obliged to notify other potentially affected States of any emergency situation that may cause them "serious harm".

6. The different formulations used in the draft articles also reveal that the Commission has not drawn up the text along the lines of the prevailing approach of sustainable development. As a further example, paragraph 1 of draft article 5(*b*) refers to the social, economic and other needs with no mention of the environmental dimension. It would be appropriate to replace the term "reasonable" in draft article 4 by "sustainable" to reflect the approach of sustainable development.

7. In future work, the impacts of different types of environmental threats on the quality and quantity of groundwaters will have to be a key consideration. In this respect, the Commission should consider any impacts of climate change in particular. In further work done for the preparation of the draft articles, in addition to the abstraction and protection of groundwater, any new uses of aquifers, i.e. formations storing groundwater, such as carbon dioxide storage or resources of geothermal heat, should also be taken into consideration.

8. In conclusion, Finland would like to focus attention on the 1992 ECE Convention on the Protection and Use of Transboundary Watercourses and International Lakes, the contents of which are much more comprehensive and detailed than the present draft international instrument under preparation. The Convention in question, ratified, so far, by 36 States including the Russian Federation, took effect in 1996. The parties adopted the supplement to the Water Convention in 2003, enabling States outside the ECE area to accede to the Convention too.

7. Germany

1. Germany is pleased that the Commission has taken up the issue of transboundary aquifers because the use of groundwater can often trigger conflicts, particularly beyond Europe's borders. This is true in relation to both the quantity and the composition of groundwater. Given the conflict potential, an international convention or a declaration of principles seems to be a useful step. In particular, the general principles as laid down in draft articles 3 to 8 are a clear improvement on the manner of resource utilization to date, anchoring the principles of cooperation and coordinated utilization.

2. As regards the utilization of groundwater in Germany and of transboundary groundwater between Germany and its neighbouring countries, Germany even today meets the requirements outlined in the Commission draft articles since it is bound by the European Union Water

Framework Directive (Directive 2000/60/EC)[1] and the Groundwater Daughter Directive (Directive 2006/118/EC)[2] on the protection of groundwater and these have been implemented in Federal and Land law.

3. For Germany, it is important to ensure that work caused by any future reporting requirements linked to the implementation and application of the United Nations regulations does not duplicate that created by the obligations laid down in the Water Framework Directive and/or the Groundwater Daughter Directive.

4. As a matter of principle, groundwater should be considered separately, in a different way from oil and gas deposits, even if some geological factors would suggest dealing with them together. However, the geological approach completely ignores social and economic implications which play an important role when it comes to groundwater. Oil and gas deposits are usually found much deeper than groundwater deposits and this makes comparisons problematic.

5. Germany would be pleased to see its proposals reflected in the forthcoming second reading. As the Special Rapporteur recommended, this reading should be conducted regardless of any possible future work on oil and gas.

[1] *Official Journal of the European Communities*, No. L 327/1 (22 December 2000).

[2] *Official Journal of the European Union*, No. L 372/19 (27 December 2006).

8. Israel

1. Israel does not see a reason to divide the draft articles into two separate parts. Israel suggests combining Parts II and III in order to avoid the implication that a hierarchy exists between the different articles. As reflected in its comments below, Israel notes that cooperation between all States in all relevant matters regarding transboundary aquifers, as discussed in the draft articles, is of great importance and is vital for the preservation and management of the aquifers, as well for the well-being of the populations concerned.

2. Israel would like to reiterate its support, which was already voiced in its address to the Sixth Committee on 2 November 2007,[1] for the conclusions of the Special Rapporteur in his fourth report[2], in which he expressed the view that the Commission should deal with the matter of transboundary aquifers independent of its future work regarding oil and natural gas.

[1] See *Official Records of the General Assembly, Sixty-second Session, Sixth Committee*, 24th meeting (A/C.6/62/SR.24), p. 19, para. 109.

[2] *Yearbook ... 2007*, vol. II (Part One), document A/CN.4/580, para.15.

9. The Netherlands

The Netherlands follows with great interest the work of the Commission on shared natural resources. The Netherlands is a country where many natural resources can be found that it shares with other States or are in areas beyond the limits of national jurisdiction. These include groundwater, mineral deposits, such as oil and gas, and migratory species on land, in the air, and in the sea. The international regulation of the uses of and impacts on shared natural resources is therefore evidently of the highest significance to the Netherlands. Only aquifers are covered by the present draft articles. Further work on other shared natural resources is anticipated following the completion of the work on aquifers. It would therefore seem that one or more additional sets of rules are envisaged for those other shared natural resources. The present approach would seem to forego the opportunity to develop an overarching set of rules for all shared natural resources. In particular, it has not been sufficiently clarified why the draft articles could not also apply to gaseous substances and liquid substances other than groundwater. It is noted in paragraph (2) of the General Commentary to the draft articles that the Special Rapporteur is aware that there are many similarities with oil and gas, and that it would be necessary to give due attention to the relationship before completing the second reading. The Netherlands supports this view and would like to call upon the Commission to give due attention to this aspect during the second reading of the draft articles. It would appear that the majority of the draft articles, notably the underlying obligation of equitable and reasonable utilization and the obligation not to cause significant harm to other States, equally apply to other shared natural resources, such as gaseous substances and liquid substances other than groundwater. The Netherlands is therefore not yet convinced that a separate approach is required for other shared natural resources.

10. Poland

1. Poland welcomes the completion of the first reading of the draft articles on the law of transboundary aquifers. The topic represents an urgently needed further development of international law on water resources.

2. Since water resources are essential for human existence, the international regulations on the utilization and protection of transboundary aquifers and aquifer systems are very topical and of the highest significance.

3. In the opinion of Poland, the draft articles provide generally useful guidance for States on the principles and rules concerning transboundary aquifers and aquifer systems, creating a proper balance between the need to utilize aquifers and the need to protect them in the long term. However, it might also be useful to include in the draft articles provisions on general duties applicable to all States as well as a reference to the activities of non-aquifer States, which could have an impact on transboundary aquifers and aquifer systems.

4. In order to avoid possible overlap, it seems also essential to identify the relationship between the draft articles and the 1997 United Nations Convention on the Law of the Non-navigational Uses of International Watercourses, because transboundary aquifers which are hydraulically connected with international watercourses will be subject to both instruments.

5. Taking into account the great diversity of transboundary aquifers and aquifer systems, the Commission has to be

commended for taking a framework approach in elaborating the draft articles, which could be adapted to the needs of specific transboundary aquifers through bilateral or regional agreements between States that share a particular aquifer or aquifer system.

6. As to the general principles referred to in Part II of the draft articles, it seems that the nature of the topic in question fully justifies stressing the aspect of sustainability. Thus, the principle of sustainable development fully deserved to be included in this part.

7. Moreover, it is proposed that two other principles of international environmental law, namely the principle of obligatory education, as well as the precautionary principle be also added to this part.

8. The principle of obligatory education in such a highly vulnerable area as underground water resources has special importance for the public and, particularly, Government and municipal authorities, i.e. those directly responsible for water utilization and management.

9. As to the precautionary approach principle (the term needs further clarification), it should be treated as a general principle applicable throughout the draft articles to issues such as overexploitation, the lowering of water tables, surface subsidence, and not just to the prevention, reduction and control of pollution (see draft article 11).

11. Portugal

1. Portugal would like to commend the Special Rapporteur for his commitment to the development of this topic, in view of its complex multidisciplinary character, and for his exhaustive work in producing a very good set of draft articles, taking into account the importance of aquifers for the future of mankind. Portugal continues to have the highest expectations of his work. A word of appreciation is also due to the Working Group on Shared Natural Resources and to the experts on groundwaters that cooperated with the Commission.

2. The solutions presented so far are well balanced and one can detect some similarities between the draft articles and some articles of the 1997 Convention on the Law of the Non-navigational Uses of International Watercourses, as well as the United Nations Convention on the Law of the Sea, which demonstrates that these solutions are in line with the progression of contemporary international law.

3. Additionally, this being a major concern to Portugal, the draft articles are compatible with the European Law on the matter already binding Portugal, namely the Directive 2000/60/EC of the European Parliament and of the Council of 23 October 2000 establishing a framework for Community action in the field of water policy[1] and the Directive 2006/118/EC of the European Parliament and of the Council of 12 December 2006 on the protection of groundwater against pollution and deterioration.[2] Nevertheless, Portugal considers that even though there is specific European law applicable to this subject matter, it should not hamper the European Union's Member States in contributing to the development and universal codification of the law of transboundary aquifers.

4. In a general perspective, Portugal notes that the draft articles reflect a greater concern with the qualitative aspects rather than with the quantitative aspects. Portugal believes that the quantitative aspects and the qualitative aspects should not be dissociated and that the draft articles should reflect both aspects in a more balanced way. In what concerns the quality of the groundwaters, the draft articles refer the question of prevention and control of pollution, which is an aspect of fundamental concern. However, there is no reference to the procedure that States should adopt in the event of present or future problems related to the quality of water in transnational aquifers. It is very important that the States affected or otherwise involved with the pollution problem adopt similar and simultaneous measures to minimize it.

5. Portugal would like also to state that it finds commendable the inclusion in the draft articles of provisions concerning the human right to water and the principles of international environmental law.

12. Republic of Korea

1. The Republic of Korea considers that the valuable work on shared natural resources by the Commission represents a timely contribution to the progress development through codification in this field of law.

2. The Republic of Korea notes that some provisions in the draft articles codify existing customary rules, thus reflecting current practice and obligations of States, doctrine and jurisprudence. However, there appear to be other provisions which go beyond the current practice and obligations of States, which means that the draft articles are more than a declaration of customary law or a reasonable progressive development of that law. It is emphasized that more careful consideration and discussion will thus be needed.

3. It might be the case that if there are no real incentives for non-aquifer States, then only aquifer States would become parties to such an instrument.

4. Regarding non-party States, State Parties would be reluctant to assume potentially significant obligations for the benefit of non-Party States that have not themselves accepted the obligations of the convention.

5. An important decision is before the Commission as to whether it needs to move beyond transboundary aquifers and then to deal also with other shared natural resources. It is advisable that the Commission exercise caution in this matter. States and industries have immense economic and political stakes in the allocation and regulation of oil and gas resources, and any proposal by the Commission is likely to be highly controversial. States in the international community already have considerable experience and practice in dealing with transboundary oil and gas reservoir. It is doubtful whether the Commission should go beyond the issue of transboundary aquifers.

---

[1] *Official Journal of the European Communities*, No. L 327/1 (22 December 2000).

[2] *Official Journal of the European Union*, No. L 372/19 (27 December 2006).

13. Saudi Arabia

1. The draft articles do not address: (*a*) the banning of directional, slant and horizontal drilling in aquifers; (*b*) the non-provision to parties that are not aquifer or aquifer system States; (*c*) how to take into account differences in the area, extent, thickness, and other characteristics of an aquifer, the direction of the flow of the groundwaters, or variations in population from State to State; (*d*) the use of pollution-causing substances and their effect on aquifers or aquifer systems; (*e*) non-renewable aquifers, aquifers in desert regions and aquifers in regions with abundant rainfall.

2. The draft articles deal with hidden groundwater sources, a subject fraught with dangers because of the lack of precise information and data, and the many underground geological formations, such as fissures and folds, which might impede the flow of such groundwaters. Those factors were not taken into account.

3. The draft articles do not distinguish between dry desert areas that receive little rain and areas that are rich in groundwaters. This is why utilization of transboundary aquifers in desert areas must be prioritized for specific purposes, such as for provision of drinking water.

4. It would be preferable to have a mechanism for the exchange of successful experiences in the management of transboundary aquifers in order for other countries to benefit from that experience.

5. The general concept underlying the draft articles encompasses both aquifers and aquifer systems. However, some of the articles refer only to aquifers, not aquifer systems, including draft article 6 (2), draft article 7 (1), and draft article 8, *inter alia.*

6. In paragraph (4) of the general commentary, the Commission considered the question of whether it would be necessary to structure the draft articles in such a way as to have obligations that will apply to all States generally, obligations of aquifer States *vis-à-vis* other aquifer States and obligations of aquifer States *vis-à-vis* non-aquifer States. It was decided that, in order to be effective, some draft articles would have to impose obligations on States which do not share the transboundary aquifer in question and in certain cases give rights to the latter States towards the States of that aquifer. In reaching these conclusions, the Commission stressed the need to protect the transboundary aquifer or aquifer system.

7. The wording of this paragraph requires clarification as it suggests that it is possible that some non-aquifer States may be given rights towards the States of an aquifer, despite the fact that they are not States of that aquifer and are not parties to that project. This item should be reconsidered. The text also speaks of obligations that will apply to all States generally and obligations of aquifer States vis-à-vis other aquifer States. Those obligations, however, were not specified.

14. Serbia

Following consultations with relevant institutions and institutes in Serbia, Serbia has considered all aspects of the draft articles and the commentaries thereto and does not have any supplemental comments to add.

15. Switzerland

1. As is well known, groundwater is suffering a silent but continuous depletion worldwide, both in quantity and quality. The Commission draft articles are a step forward towards an integrated water resources management. They underpin the decision taken by Member States at the World Summit on Sustainable Development in 2002 with a view to:

> Develop integrated water resources management and water efficiency plans by 2005, with support to developing countries, through actions at all levels to:
>
> (*a*) Develop and implement national/regional strategies, plans and programs with regard to integrated river basin, watershed and groundwater management and introduce measures to improve the efficiency of water infrastructure to reduce losses and increase recycling of water.[1]

2. Switzerland is party to the 1992 ECE Convention on the Protection and Use of Transboundary Watercourses and International Lakes. Swiss legislation on the subject includes the Federal Law of 24 January 1991 on Water Protection (SR 814.20), the Federal Law of 21 June 1991 on Flood Protection (SR 721.100) and the Federal Law of 7 October 1983 relating to the Protection of the Environment (SR 814.01).

3. The Commission draft articles are in line with Swiss legislation. Not all of the draft articles are equally relevant to the situation in Switzerland, however. Some address hydro-geological conditions rarely encountered in Switzerland, such as management of fossil groundwater or weakly provisioned aquifers under precarious conditions in terms of aquifer recharge. In Switzerland, the aspects of quality of transboundary water are also very important (draft article 11). In addition, large aquifers are closely connected with the surface water of rivers such as the Rhine or the Arve.[2] This aspect is relatively little developed in the draft articles.

---

[1] *Report of the World Summit on Sustainable Development Johannesburg, South Africa, 26 August–4 September 2002* (A/CONF.199/20, Sales No. E.03.II.A.1), Plan of Implementation of the World Summit on Sustainable Development, annex, para. 26.

[2] Transboundary aquifers of Switzerland include: the alluvial aquifer of the Rhine in the upstream part of Lake Constance between Switzerland, Liechtenstein and Austria; the alluvial aquifer in the downstream part of the Lake Constance between Switzerland and Germany; the alluvial aquifer of the Arve between Switzerland and France. The first agreement to regulate the use of the small transboundary aquifer between Switzerland and France dates back to 1978 (*Arrangement relatif à la protection, à l'utilisation et à la réalimentation de la nappe souterraine franco-suisse du Genevois*, 1 January 1978). The exploitation of pumping stations on both sides and the functioning of an artificial recharge station using water from the river Arve were regulated in order to counter its overexploitation in the 1970s. This aquifer supplies about 20 per cent of the drinking water of the Canton of Geneva (estimated reserve of 17 million m^3). Since 1 January 2008, the agreement has been replaced by a convention between the Canton of Geneva and the relevant French cities (*Convention relative à la protection, à l'utilisation, à la réalimentation et au suivi de la nappe souterraine franco–suisse du Genevois*).

16. United States of America

1. The United States of America believes that the work of the International Law Commission on transboundary aquifers constitutes an important advance in providing guidance for the reasonable use and protection of underground aquifers, which are playing an increasingly important role as water sources for human populations. The current absence of guidance to States struggling to cope with pressures on transboundary aquifers should be addressed and the Commission's efforts to develop a set of flexible tools for using and protecting these aquifers can be a very useful contribution for such States. In its work to date, the Commission has struck a reasonable balance between the scope of coverage and extent of proposed obligations. Namely, the draft encompasses a wide scope—addressing activities, wherever located, that have or are likely to have an impact on transboundary aquifers—in order to protect aquifer systems, but is careful not to overstate the proposed obligations of parties to protect aquifers to the detriment of other important activities. In short, the Commission has made very good progress on a complex and important matter.

2. The United States continues to strongly prefer context-specific, regional and local arrangements as the best way to address pressures on transboundary groundwaters, rather than a global framework treaty. Although the draft articles may have been drafted with a framework convention in mind, the United States supports recasting such articles as recommendatory, non-binding principles—as was done in the case of liability for transboundary harm. There is still much to learn about transboundary aquifers in general, and specific aquifer conditions and State practice vary widely. Numerous factors might appropriately be taken into account in any specific negotiation, such as hydrological characteristics of the aquifer at issue; present uses and expectations regarding future uses; climate conditions and expectations; and economic, social and cultural considerations. Thus, groundwater arrangements are best handled by regional or local action taking into account the political, social, economic and other factors affecting each unique situation. In addition, the current draft articles go beyond current law and practice. They contain a set of obligations—including procedures for data exchange, monitoring, resource management and technical cooperation—that clearly go well beyond the current obligations of States, and so would not be suitable as a declaration of what customary law is or even a reasonable progressive development of that law. Recasting such articles as recommendatory, non-binding principles, therefore, would be consistent with the general character of much of the substance of the text, but it would require that the language should be revised to remove mandatory language and statements of obligation.

3. While the United States is not convinced that a global treaty will garner sufficient support, it is recognized that many States have expressed an interest in such a convention. If the Commission continues in this direction, despite United States reservations, there are a number of important issues that it believes would need to be addressed. Such issues include: (*a*) the relationship between a framework convention and other bilateral or regional arrangements, and (*b*) the role of non-aquifer States parties.

4. The first set of issues deals with the relationship between a convention and other agreements that affect the management and protection of transboundary aquifers. A number of other agreements have already been concluded, such as the agreements between the United States and its neighbours for the management of their boundary waters. As the Commission considers these articles further, it should ensure that parties to a framework convention have the option to conclude agreements with other aquifer States that may diverge in substance from a framework convention. Aquifer States are in the best position to judge their local situation, to weigh competing considerations and needs with respect to particular aquifers, and to manage their common aquifers as they deem best, and they should not be inhibited from doing so. Thus, the Commission should be careful not to adopt provisions that would appear to supersede existing bilateral or regional arrangements or to limit the flexibility of States in entering into such arrangements.

5. In addition, although article 19 encourages aquifer States to enter bilateral and regional agreements and arrangements to manage common aquifers, it also prohibits aquifer States from entering into an agreement or arrangement regarding a particular aquifer or aquifer system that would adversely affect, to a significant extent, the utilization, by one or more other aquifer States, of the water in that aquifer or aquifer system without their express consent. While the commentary states that this prohibition is not meant to give such other aquifer States a veto over contracting States, the effect of its plain language arguably empowers a non-participating aquifer State to thwart the conclusion of an agreement or to exact unreasonable concessions from negotiating States by withholding its express consent.

6. The United States recognizes the importance of involving all relevant aquifer States in any agreement affecting a particular transboundary aquifer. Nevertheless, the obligation to seek the express consent of the aquifer States that would be significantly adversely affected, but that are not participating in the negotiation of that agreement, may impose unnecessary and unreasonable constraints on negotiating aquifer States. States parties, whether acting alone or in concert, still would be bound to utilize the relevant transboundary aquifer in an equitable and reasonable manner (draft article 4), and avoid causing significant harm to other aquifer States (draft article 6), among other obligations. Making the conclusion of such an agreement also dependent upon the express consent of other aquifer States, therefore, seems unnecessary, as any effort to conclude an agreement would be circumscribed by the above-mentioned provisions, and may be unreasonable to the extent it gives such other States undue influence over the separate negotiations. Rather, the United States recommends that States should be required to consult other interested aquifer States and invite such States, where appropriate, to participate in the agreement or arrangement. Such an obligation ensures that all aquifer States are made aware of the agreement and have a reasonable opportunity to participate in its development, without placing unduly burdensome restrictions on a subset of aquifer States interested in concluding a particular agreement or arrangement.

7. A second set of issues concerns States parties that do not share transboundary aquifers. The current draft articles contemplate that non-aquifer States will become parties and will have obligations with respect to activities that might affect aquifer States. Certain articles impose obligations on non-aquifer States parties, including: draft article 10 concerning States in which recharge or discharge zones are located; draft article 14 concerning activities of States that may affect transboundary aquifers; draft article 15 concerning technical cooperation with developing States; and draft article 16 concerning emergency situations that might affect a transboundary aquifer. These articles recognize that aquifers are vulnerable to pollution and other damage from sources outside the immediate circle of aquifer States. However, the articles on cooperation, information exchange, protection of ecosystems, pollution control and management do not apply to non-aquifer States. The United States recommends further consideration as to whether non-aquifer States parties should be integrated in some way in these latter provisions. For instance, draft article 11 requires aquifer States parties, where appropriate, to prevent, reduce and control pollution of their transboundary aquifer or aquifer system that may cause significant harm to aquifer States parties. However, it may be worth considering whether this obligation should be expanded to require protection against pollution that may cause significant harm to non-aquifer States parties as well, given that non-aquifer States parties would already be obligated pursuant to draft article 10 to cooperate with aquifer States parties to protect the aquifer or aquifer system.

8. Finally, if the Commission were to develop a framework convention, it would be necessary to add final clauses and ensure appropriate terminology throughout the text. In particular, the current draft articles only use the terms "aquifer State" or "State" throughout the text. However, a convention should use terms such as "aquifer Party" or "State Party" instead in order to avoid any confusion as to the breadth of the obligations set out in the convention.

B. Title

Iraq

The word "shared" should be added to the title of the draft articles, which would then read "Draft articles on the law of shared transboundary aquifers". The same should apply throughout the draft articles.

C. Draft article 1. Scope

1. Brazil

1. Brazil has reservations regarding draft article 1 (*b*). The rather broad wording could end up imposing unnecessary limitations on activities conducted in the surroundings of an aquifer. The current wording may encompass in the scope of the draft articles issues like agriculture and the use of pesticides, urban draining systems and waste deposits, for instance, which would go far beyond the initial scope of the draft articles. The aforementioned provision may also be problematic as regards the activities of less likely impact, since there is no guarantee of direct link between the activity and the impact. Also problematic is the use of the word "impact" (without the qualifier "significant") instead of the word "harm", which has a more specific meaning and is used in different provisions in Parts II and III. The use of the expression "significant harm" instead of "impact" would be a way to address somehow Brazil's concern on this point. However, Brazil would prefer the outright exclusion of this clause, as provisions (*a*) and (*c*) already define appropriately the scope of the draft articles.

2. In respect of the commentary to draft article 1, Brazil expresses its strong reservation to the reference made in paragraph (2) to the Convention on the Law of the Non-navigational Uses of International Watercourses (1997) as regards the application of the articles of that Convention to transboundary aquifers connected to international watercourses. Brazil is not a party to the 1997 Convention, which has not entered into force due to lack of consensus in relation to many of its provisions. Furthermore, Brazil cannot accept the use of the expression "international waters" to refer to transboundary waters, as it might put into question the State sovereignty over water resources located in its territory.

2. Israel

1. Israel supports the use of the word "utilization" in draft article 1 (*a*). Israel believes that the use of the term "other activities" in draft article 1 (*b*) is overly broad and could lead to misinterpretation.

2. Israel recommends that it be explored whether certain provisions of draft article 1 (*c*) are already covered by the 1997 Convention on the Law of the Non-Navigational Uses of International Watercourses, as well as the nature of the relationship between the draft articles and the Convention.

3. The Netherlands

The Commission notes in paragraph (2) of the commentary to draft article 1 that the dual application of the provisions of the 1997 Convention on the Law of the Non-navigational Uses of International Watercourses and the draft articles to aquifers and aquifer systems that are hydraulically connected to international watercourses would not in principle cause any problem, as these legal regimes are not expected to be in conflict with each other. However, the Netherlands would like to note that the principle of equitable and reasonable utilization has been redefined in order to apply it to non-renewable resources. The Netherlands agrees with the application of the principle of maximalization of long-term benefits in the case of the use of non-renewable resources as opposed to the application of the principle of sustainable utilization in the case of the use of renewable resources. Yet, it is in this regard that the Netherlands discerns a possible tension between the two legal regimes. It believes that further clarification is required to explain how the application of two different definitions of the same principle to aquifers that are hydraulically connected to international watercourses can be reconciled.

4. Saudi Arabia

1. Saudi Arabia proposes that the chapeau of this draft article be modified to read: "The goal of the present draft articles is to regulate the following:"

2. It is also proposed that the draft article should include provisions regarding priority with regard to the utilization of transboundary groundwaters. Accordingly, a new subparagraph (*d*) should be added and should read:

"Setting priorities in respect of the utilization of shared groundwaters and aquifer systems."

D. Draft article 2. Use of terms

1. Brazil

The concept of aquifers should be improved in order to address the possibility of extraction, as there are rocks containing water which cannot be extracted and thus do not constitute an aquifer in the technical sense. An aquifer is not necessarily supported by a less permeable formation (for instance, a fractured aquifer supported by a porous one is also an aquifer). Thus, Brazil suggests the following wording for draft article 2 (*a*):

"'Aquifer' means an underground permeable geological formation, which contains water and from which it is possible to extract significant quantities of water."

2. Colombia

In view of the frequent use of the phrase "equitable and reasonable use" of resources in various international contexts, Colombia takes the view that the phrase should be defined and its definition incorporated into the draft articles.

3. Germany

1. The phrase "underlain by a less permeable layer" in subparagraph (*a*) could be deleted as it is unnecessary and a source of potential confusion.

2. The following should be added to subparagraph (*f*):

"[...] by runoff on the ground and infiltration or direct percolation through soil."

3. It would be better to use "quantity or quality" than "quantity and quality" in paragraph (4) of the commentary to draft article 2 (third last sentence). Even the transfer of small quantities of water can have a significant effect on the receiving aquifer depending on the chemical composition, so the term aquifer system would have to be used.

4. Hungary

1. The expression "catchment area" in the definition of recharge zone in subparagraph (*f*) is more commonly used in connection with surface waters. Furthermore, not only the groundwater recharge zone can be underneath, but the surface of a discharge zone also belongs to the catchment area of rainfall. In other words, the recharge zone is only that part of a catchment area, where infiltration through the soil is significant and/or surface water contributes directly to the groundwater.

Hungary therefore proposes the following wording for subparagraph (*f*):

"'Recharge zone' means the zone which contributes water to an aquifer, including [consisting of] that part of the catchment area of rainfall where water flows to an aquifer by runoff on the ground and/or infiltration through soil."

2. The definition of discharge zone in subparagraph (*g*) covers only situations where there is actually some form of surface water. In the understanding of Hungary, a discharge zone can exist without water present on the surface. In many areas the upward flow system keeps the groundwater table permanently close to the surface and they are definitely considered discharge zones. Considering draft article 10 on recharge and discharge zones definitions should aim at the particular characteristics which help to make distinct certain areas within the total area above the transboundary aquifer.

Hungary therefore proposes the following wording for subparagraph (*g*):

"'Discharge zone' means the zone where water originating from an aquifer flows to its outlets, such as watercourse, lake, oasis, wetland and ocean, or the upward flow system keeps the groundwater table permanently close to the surface."

5. Iraq

In subparagraph (*f*), the phrase "and other water sources" should be added. The subparagraph would then read as follows:

"'Recharge zone' means the zone which contributes water to an aquifer, consisting of the catchment area of rainfall water and other water sources and the area where such water flows to an aquifer by runoff on the ground and infiltration through soil."

6. The Netherlands

1. Although the intention to apply the adjective "transboundary" to both "aquifer" and "aquifer system" in the definition of "aquifer State" in subparagraph (*d*) may be clear for some, it would avoid confusion for others if the adjective is repeated before "aquifer system" in this paragraph, as well as other parts of the draft articles.

2. It is the understanding of the Netherlands that aquifers, especially in the form of confined ground waters, may also be found in areas under the jurisdiction or control of States outside their territory. When the Commission considers the application of the draft articles to all shared natural resources during the second reading of the draft articles, it will, in the view of the Netherlands, become inevitable to revisit the definition of "aquifer State" and to address the application of the draft articles to shared natural resources that can be found under the continental shelves of States, notably oil and gas.

7. Portugal

1. Portugal views with some concern the lack of definition of "significant harm" (draft article 6) and of "significant adverse effect" (draft article 14). There is a danger in leaving such subjective terms to be interpreted by States

on a case-by-case basis, in accordance with their own interests of the moment. In fact, it may create an unjustified disadvantage to weaker States. It makes it harder to make a distinction, as well, between the two terms.

2. Furthermore, one should also ponder on the benefit of defining the term "ecosystem" (draft article 9) as done in the draft principles on the allocation of loss in case transboundary harm arising out of hazardous activities.[1]

3. The term "adversely affects, to a significant extent" (draft article 19) suffers an equal problem of lack of clarity, raising doubts as how one must assess the extent of such effects.

4. Being part of fundamental provisions of the draft articles, the lack of a uniform and clear understanding of those terms may lead to diverse interpretations and even to non-compliance of the obligations of the States on this matter. This being so, it may be a good option to define them in draft article 2 regarding the use of terms.

[1] *Yearbook ... 2006*, vol. II (Part One), document A/CN.4/566.

8. Saudi Arabia

Subparagraph (*a*) should be modified to read:

"'Aquifer' means a permeable underground geological formation bearing confined or unconfined water underlain or overlain by a less permeable layer and the water contained in the saturated zone of the formation."

9. Switzerland

1. In draft article 2 and in subsequent draft articles, the word "recharge" in English has been translated into "*réalimentation*" in French. Switzerland believes it would be appropriate to keep the word "*recharge*" also in the French version, as this has a closer connotation to human activities (artificial recharge).

2. In draft article 2 and in subsequent draft articles, the term "*zone de déversement*" (in English: "discharge zone") might more appropriately be called "*zone d'exutoire*" in French.

E. Draft article 3. Sovereignty of aquifer States

1. Austria

Austria had once suggested moving the reference to sovereignty to the preamble. However, in light of the present draft articles it seems preferable to keep the text of draft article 3 in order to establish a certain balance of the rights and obligations, emphasizing that sovereignty is the fundamental rule on which the entirety of the draft articles is based so that the latter have to be interpreted accordingly.

2. Brazil

It is fundamental to keep the language in draft article 3 that reaffirms the sovereignty of the State over the aquifers located in its territory. Notwithstanding, the last part of the draft article should be modified in order to affirm that sovereignty shall be exercised in conformity with international law and not "in accordance with the present draft articles". It is important to add, after the reference to international law, the following words: "as referred to, *inter alia*, by United Nations General Assembly resolution 1803 (XVII) of 14 December 1962".

3. Cuba

The last sentence of draft article 3 should be deleted, taking into account that a State would have sovereignty over aquifers within its territory and would therefore be free to set policy in respect of any given aquifer.

4. Israel

Israel welcomes the emphasis the draft articles give to the issue of sovereignty over transboundary aquifers. However, Israel does not support the making of exceptions to accepted customary international law on this issue. Therefore, Israel suggests adding the words "international law and" after the word "with" to draft article 3.

5. Portugal

Portugal believes that it is pertinent to reflect upon whether or not to shift towards a more actual and mitigated doctrine of sovereignty. Without putting in doubt the State's sovereignty over the portion of a transboundary aquifer or aquifer system located within its territory, it may be worthwhile to consider emphasizing, as a general rule, the principle of cooperation between States.

6. Turkey

An explicit reference to the sovereignty of States over the natural resources within their territories is preferred. This reference is particularly important in case that dialogue or cooperation among the riparian States of the transboundary aquifer is not at the level which enables joint equitable and reasonable utilization. Therefore, States should be able to exercise full sovereign rights to exploit, develop and manage the water resources located within their land territories according to the present draft articles. In this context, the proposed version of the article 3 is as follows.

"Each aquifer State shall exercise its inherent sovereignty over the portion of a transboundary aquifer or aquifer system located within its territory for the purposes provided in article 3 in accordance with the present draft articles."

F. Draft article 4. Equitable and reasonable utilization

1. Austria

1. Draft article 4 has to be seen in close context with draft article 5 on "factors relevant to equitable and reasonable utilization". However, certain concepts used in these draft articles need to be clarified:

2. The concept of "accrued benefits" introduced in subparagraph (*a*) raises certain doubts. First, the enumeration of the factors relevant to equitable and reasonable utilization in draft article 5 that elaborates draft article 4 does not respect the fundamental rule embodied in draft article 3 as it refers only, *inter alia*, to the contribution to the formation and recharge of the aquifer or aquifer system.

In the light of draft article 3, this element must be inserted in the draft article so that draft article 4, subparagraph (*a*) should read:

"They shall utilize the transboundary aquifer or aquifer system in a manner that is consistent with their share of the aquifer and its recharge."

Secondly, as the commentary indicates, no convincing reason is provided why "utilization" should be replaced by "accrued benefits", in particular as the criteria set in draft article 5 refer to "utilization". Although the commentary to subparagraphs (*b*) to (*d*) explains in a very clear and sophisticated manner the difficulties faced when determining "equitable and reasonable utilization" of transboundary aquifers, in particular when dealing with recharging and non-recharging aquifers, it could be accepted that a reference to such kind of use is made so that the full text of draft article 4 subparagraph (*a*) should read:

"They shall utilize the transboundary aquifer or aquifer system in a manner that is consistent with their share of the aquifer and its recharge as well as with the equitable and reasonable utilization."

3. The concept of "maximizing the long-term benefits" would need to be further explored if the draft articles were to be transformed into an international legally binding instrument as it includes many vague issues such as "wasteful utilization". In the case of a transboundary aquifer, it is in particular unclear who should determine the meaning of "maximizing the long-term benefits" in a particular case. It must be taken into account that it is extremely difficult to apply the concept of "maximizing benefit" to a transboundary context as free transfer of benefits would be required for this purpose, which is difficult to achieve in a transboundary context. In addition, it cannot be excluded that the various aquifer States would come to different conclusions regarding the evaluation of the benefits since these benefits are often evaluated rather by political than by purely economic and ecological criteria.

2. Cuba

Cuba proposes adding the word "generations" in subparagraph (*c*). The text would then read:

"They shall establish individually or jointly an overall utilization plan, taking into account the needs of present and future generations, and alternative water sources for the aquifer States."

3. Germany

The following should be added to paragraph (1) of the commentary to draft article 4:

"The use of an aquifer's geological formation might be more important in the future, especially regarding the sequestration of carbon dioxide in deep aquifers. Other examples for the utilization of the geological formation include the disposal of brines from mining activities or the disposal of nuclear waste which might lead to deteriorating water quality."

4. Iraq

1. Subparagraph (*b*) should be merged with subparagraph (*a*), and should read as follows:

"They shall utilize the shared transboundary aquifer or aquifer system in an equitable and reasonable manner that maximizes the long-term benefits derived from the use of water contained therein."

2. In subparagraph (*c*), the words "and alternative water sources for" should be omitted.

3. In subparagraph (*d*), the word "unrecharged" should be added. The subparagraph would then read:

"They shall not utilize a recharging or unrecharged transboundary aquifer, or a recharging or unrecharged transboundary aquifer system, at a level that would prevent continuance of its effective functioning."

5. Israel

1. Israel believes that the draft articles 4 to 6 have successfully identified some important general principles that have gained the recognition of States, namely the principle of equitable and reasonable utilization of aquifers and the obligation not to cause significant harm to other aquifer States. Having said that, Israel suggests adopting an approach that would treat these principles on equal footing, with no one principle prevailing over the other.

2. In light of the foregoing, Israel would like to propose adding in the chapeau of draft article 4 after the word "utilization", the following words: "with due regard to the avoidance of significant harm to other aquifer States".

3. Israel believes that the obligation to develop an "overall utilization plan", as stipulated in subparagraph (*c*), requires further consideration, as, in its opinion, the proposed subparagraph sets forth an undue burden on States. Moreover, by allowing individual establishment of utilization plans, rather than calling for collaborative efforts only, the obligation to cooperate is subverted. Therefore the words "individually or" should be deleted from subparagraph (*c*).

4. Israel wishes to voice its support for the principle of sustainability and welcomes its endorsement in subparagraph (*d*). Nevertheless, Israel recommends that the term "optimal and sustainable use" be used instead, as such term is similarly used in article 5 of the 1997 Convention on the Law of the Non-navigational Uses of International Watercourses.

6. Poland

Following the suggestion to add the principle of sustainable development to Part II (see general comments above), an appropriate reference should be made in draft article 4.

7. Saudi Arabia

1. A specific definition for equitable and reasonable utilization should be set forth. Subparagraph (*c*) leaves the door open to change and unpredictability because the needs of States vary. It would be advisable to have firm rules in this regard. Subparagraph (*d*) is unclear and may require some clarification or redrafting.

2. A new subparagraph (*e*) should be added and should read:

"No State may assign, lease or sell, in whole or in part, to any other State, whether an aquifer State or a non-aquifer State, its right to utilize a transboundary aquifer."

8. SWITZERLAND

1. Subparagraph (*c*) provides that aquifer States shall establish "*individually* or jointly" an overall utilization plan. Switzerland believes that a utilization plan for a transboundary aquifer should not be established *individually*. As it is rightly said in draft article 13, a "*joint* management" of aquifers is needed. This would be difficult to achieve if there were two (or more) contradictory utilization plans.

2. In subparagraph (*d*), the expression "effective functioning" is not clear. The idea that would need to be conveyed is that, over time, the net output should not be higher than the input.

9. TURKEY

With regard to subparagraph (*c*), integrated water resources management is the basic concept for the utilization of surface and groundwater resources. It takes into account hydrological, social, economic and environmental aspects and looks for what is useful, sustainable, feasible, equitable and environmentally friendly. However, it does not consider the exploitation of water resources in a basin. Moreover, neither groundwater resources nor surface water resources could be treated as alternative to each other. They are rather complementary. Therefore, in establishing overall utilization plans, "alternative water resources" should not be an element to be taken into account as they are already a part of the plan. So, the phrase "alternative water resources" ought to be deleted.

G. Draft article 5. Factors relevant to equitable and reasonable utilization

1. BRAZIL

1. In paragraph 1, Brazil suggests the inclusion of an additional item related to the use of the geothermal potential. Such a potential is still underused by the majority of the developing and least developed countries. The new item could have the following wording: "The utilization of geothermal potential, whenever available."

2. Draft article 5 establishes relevant factors for the determination of the concept of "equitable and reasonable utilization". Brazil particularly appreciates the general principle contained in the last sentence of paragraph 2: "However, in weighing different utilizations of a transboundary aquifer or aquifer system, special regard shall be given to vital human needs."

2. CUBA

With respect to the reference that "special regard shall be given to vital human needs" in paragraph 2, Cuba wishes to draw attention to the possibility that efforts to meet human needs could jeopardize the natural functioning of the ecosystem in the area of the aquifer to be tapped, even where such utilization is justified on the basis of equity.

3. GERMANY

1. Paragraph (2) of the commentary to draft article 5 reads:

> System variables relate to aquifer conductivity (permeability) and storability.

Here, "hydraulic conductivity" should be listed after "aquifer conductivity (permeability)" and "storability" replaced by "storativity".

2. The sentence in the same paragraph (2) reading: "They are groundwater level distribution and water characteristics such as temperature, hardness..." should be amended to read: "such as thickness of the aquifer, temperature, hardness".

3. Paragraph (5) of the commentary to draft article 5 reads:

> In determining "vital human needs", special attention is to be paid to providing sufficient water to sustain human life, including both drinking water and water required for production of food in order to prevent starvation.

In many arid and semi-arid countries, groundwater-based agriculture is the main reason for the massive over-use of groundwater reserves. With the definition used, too much scope is given for over-use under the pretext of food security. Most agriculture in these countries is today for export purposes, not for food security. Food autarky is unrealistic in almost all arid and semi-arid countries. Therefore Germany recommends deleting this definition and using the narrower definition provided by the International Law Association:

> Vital human needs means waters used for immediate human survival, including drinking, cooking, and sanitary needs, as well as water needed for the immediate sustenance of a household. [1]

[1] Art. 3 (20) of the Berlin Rules on Water Resources of the International Law Association (2004), International Law Association, *Report of the Seventy-First Conference held in Berlin, 16–21 August 2004.*

4. IRAQ

1. The phrase "through bilateral or multilateral agreements" should be added to the chapeau, which would then read:

"Utilization of a transboundary aquifer or aquifer system in an equitable and reasonable manner within the meaning of draft article 4, through bilateral or multilateral agreements, requires taking into account all relevant factors, including [...]."

2. In subparagraph (*g*), the word "other" should be added in order to make the text more comprehensive where it refers to alternatives to a particular utilization. The subparagraph would then read:

"The availability of alternatives to a particular existing or planned utilization of the aquifer or other aquifer system."

5. ISRAEL

It is important to avoid deviating from the content of the 1997 Convention on the Law of the Non-navigational

Uses of International Watercourses insofar as the formulation of the factors relevant to determining what constitutes equitable and reasonable utilization are concerned, in order to preserve a regime of legal uniformity and consistency, as recommended by Israel in its remarks delivered to the Sixth Committee on 2 November 2007.[1] In this context, Israel would like to emphasize two such deviations found in the draft articles:

(*a*) Subparagraph (*d*) introduces a new factor of "the contribution to the formation and recharge of the aquifer or aquifer system". It is the view of Israel that in applying the principle of equitable and reasonable utilization, the needs of the neighbouring communities are what matter most. There is no evidence to support the contrary proposition that waters be allocated, for example, according to the amount of rain that falls on the respective feeding areas in the territory of each party. Having said that, in light of the currently available technology, which allows the artificial injection of water into aquifers, there may be some merit in advancing the contention that a State which artificially contributes water to an aquifer should be rewarded for its efforts with a greater apportionment of the water from that aquifer. Such a rule would serve to provide an incentive to States to actively recharge their aquifers. This, of course, should be conditioned upon the fact that the artificially injected water be of accepted quality, so as to avoid pollution. In short, Israel believes that subparagraph (*d*) in its present form gives the impression that natural contributions are a relevant factor in determining equitable and reasonable utilization, in contradiction to customary international law. Hence, this subparagraph should be deleted or corrected so as to refer to artificial contributions of clean water to aquifers only.

(*b*) Subparagraph (*g*) lists "the availability of alternatives to a particular existing and planned utilization of the aquifer or aquifer system". While alternative sources of water are no doubt a relevant factor, Israel believes that their mere availability is not enough, and that their feasibility must be taken into account as well. Israel suggests returning to the original formulation in article 6(*g*) of the 1997 Convention on Non-navigational Uses of International Water Courses by adding the words "of comparable value" after "the availability of alternatives".

[1] See *Official Records of the General Assembly, Sixty-second Session, Sixth Committee*, 24th meeting (A/C.6/62/SR.24), para. 109.

6. The Netherlands

Pursuant to draft article 1, the present draft articles cover, in addition to the utilization of transboundary aquifers and transboundary aquifer systems, other activities that have or are likely to have an impact upon those aquifers or aquifer systems. In paragraph (6) of the commentary to draft article 1, it is noted that it is necessary to regulate such other activities in order to properly manage aquifers. The Netherlands agrees that such activities should be subject to the present draft articles and would have expected that this would have implications for the identification of factors relevant to the equitable and reasonable utilization of aquifers and aquifer systems. Accordingly, the Netherlands would like to suggest that any existing and planned other such activities as well as their effects should be added to subparagraph (*d*) of draft article 5 as an additional factor relevant to the equitable and reasonable utilization of aquifers and aquifer systems.

7. Poland

1. It is proposed that in subparagraph (*f*) the words "actual and potential" be inserted at the beginning of this provision.

2. Following the suggestion to add the principle of sustainable development to Part II (see general comments above), an appropriate reference should be made in draft article 5.

8. Saudi Arabia

1. Subparagraph (*c*) should be amended to read:

"The compatibility of a given mode of utilization with the natural characteristics of the aquifer or aquifer system within each State."

A new subparagraph (*e*) *bis* should be added that takes into consideration the area, extent, thickness and characteristics of the aquifer and the direction in which groundwaters flow.

2. Paragraph (3) of the commentary to draft article 5 provides, *inter alia*, "[b]eside feasibility and sustainability, the viability of alternatives plays an important role in the analysis. For example, a sustainable alternative could be considered as preferable in terms of aquifer recharge and discharge ratio, but less viable than a controlled depletion alternative." The first two lines of this paragraph are unclear.

3. The sentence beginning with "For instance ..." in paragraph (4) of the commentary to draft article 5 should read:

"There are various manners in which lakes receive groundwater inflow. Some receive groundwater inflow throughout their entire bed. Some receive groundwater inflow through seepage throughout their entire bed. Some receive groundwater inflow through part of their bed, while the rest of the channel receives inflows through seepage."

9. Switzerland

1. Subparagraph (*d*) on the "contribution to the formation" of the aquifer (in French "*contribution à la formation*") does not seem to be a relevant factor to equitable and reasonable utilization of the aquifer or aquifer system, as the aquifer was formed some million years ago. The term "transformation" instead of "formation" in both the French and the English versions may be more suitable.

2. In subparagraph (*i*), the reference to the "related ecosystem" is unclear. It would be advisable to repeat the formulation used in draft article 9 ("ecosystems within, or dependent upon their transboundary aquifers or aquifer systems"/"*écosystèmes qui sont situés à l'interieur, ou sont tributaries, de leurs aquifères ou systèmes aquifères transfrontières*").

10. Turkey

The rationale with regard to subparagraph (*c*) of draft article 4 applies to subparagraph (*g*) which should be deleted.

H. Draft article 6. Obligation not to cause significant harm to other aquifer States

1. Brazil

1. Brazil supports the use of the term "significant harm". "Significant harm", as referred to in paragraphs 1 and 2, must be understood as the harm caused through the aquifer. Brazil underlines the importance of the understanding already expressed by the Commission that the obligation to take appropriate measures in order to avoid significant harm constitutes an obligation of "conduct" and not one of "result".

2. With regard to the utilization of the term "activities that have or are likely to have an impact", its context is different from the one observed in draft article 1 (*b*). For this reason, the expression could be maintained in the text if the word "impact" is replaced by "significant impact". The Commission should find proper language to make it clearer that the obligation to take all measures to prevent significant harm is applicable only to activities of which it is reasonable to believe that States are aware or with respect to activities of which States are aware to have real or potential impact on the aquifers.

2. Colombia

The commentary deals with the use of the term "significant", since the reference to significant harm gives rise to the presumption that there may also be insignificant harm. Taking the view that neither of those adjectives is suitable to describe harm, Colombia proposes that only the word "harm" should be used, without any qualification. Colombia proposes amending all the draft articles in order to delete the term "significant".

3. Cuba

Cuba believes that the phrase "prevent the causing of [...] harm" used in paragraph 2 should be replaced by "avoid the causing of [...] harm", as the object in environmental matters is not to prevent, but rather to avoid, causing harm in all its forms.

4. Finland

The environmental perspectives should be given more weight in the draft articles. Article 6 introduces the threshold of "significant harm" which is, considering the vulnerability of groundwaters, rather high.

5. Hungary

The Commission decided to eliminate the provision concerning compensation when significant harm is caused even though all appropriate measures were taken to prevent that from happening. Hungary believes that in view of the recent development in the field of international environmental law, in every case when significant harm is caused by an aquifer State to another aquifer State, adequate compensation should be provided in accordance with "the polluter pays" principle. Hungary would like to point out that under this principle, States have an objective responsibility, that is to say, if they cause significant harm, they have to pay compensation regardless whether they have taken all appropriate measures to prevent the harm or not. This principle and the obligation deriving from it are both well established in other instruments of international law. Hungary is of the view that a reference to this principle and to the obligation should have been included in the draft in order to give a clear indication to the specific regime of international law that shall apply. In the commentary of this article, it is mentioned that this issue is covered by other rules of international law, including the draft principles on liability. This reasoning might not be appropriate, since international liability in general is based on imputability, however in the field of international environmental law, there are exceptions, liability may be established on the pure basis of causing harm.

6. Israel

1. Israel recommends introducing a threshold higher than that of taking "all appropriate measures" and eliminating the word "significant" in paragraph 1. Such recommendation is consistent with Israel's comments above, as well as the remarks Israel made in its address to the Sixth Committee on 2 November 2007,[1] and takes into account the susceptibility of aquifers.

2. Furthermore, Israel would like to suggest the addition of concrete provisions that would elaborate upon the obligation set forth in draft article 6. For example, it might be worth considering the adoption of a more detailed list of obligations, such as those listed in article 41 of the Berlin Rules of 2004.[2] Furthermore, Israel suggests that the precautionary principle, which many now consider to be a customary rule of international environmental law, be noted as well.

[1] See *Official Records of the General Assembly, Sixty-second Session, Sixth Committee*, 24th meeting (A/C.6/62/SR.24), para. 109.

[2] International Law Association, *Report of the Seventy-First Conference held in Berlin, 16–21 August 2004*, London, 2004.

7. The Netherlands

1. Paragraph 1 addresses aspects concerning prevention which, in case of non-compliance, could entail State responsibility. This has, in the view of the Netherlands, correctly been presented as a duty of due diligence. Paragraph 3 deals with the eventuality where significant harm is caused in spite of compliance with the duty of due diligence and, hence, with paragraph 1. The Netherlands is not convinced by the arguments advanced in paragraph (6) of the commentary to delete in this paragraph the obligation to discuss the question of compensation if significant harm is caused in spite of compliance with the duty of diligence. Although international law on international liability for the injurious consequences arising out of acts not prohibited by international law has further developed in recent years, including through the elaboration of the draft principles on the allocation of loss in the case of transboundary harm arising out of hazardous activities,[1] the Netherlands believes that these developments do not justify the deletion

[1] *Yearbook....2006*, vol II (Part One), document A/CN.4/566.

in this paragraph of the obligation to discuss the question of compensation if significant harm is caused in spite of compliance with the duty of due diligence. In particular, the draft principles on the allocation of loss in the case of transboundary harm arising out of hazardous activities only apply to hazardous activities relating to use of aquifers and aquifer systems and do not cover non-hazardous activities. Furthermore, the cross reference in the draft article on the obligation not to cause significant harm to the draft article on equitable and reasonable utilization links the question of compensation to the interplay of these two draft articles. In specific circumstances, the result may be that it is not equitable or reasonable to require the payment of compensation for significant harm if the duty of due diligence is complied with.

2. In paragraph 4 of the general commentary, it is noted that some draft articles would have to impose obligations on States which do not share the transboundary aquifer in question in order for the draft articles to be effective. The Netherlands agrees with this approach and notes that this is particularly relevant as a result of the application of the present draft articles to activities other than the utilization of transboundary aquifers. Accordingly, the Netherlands believes that the subject of paragraph 2 of draft article 6 should be all States rather than aquifer States. Activities carried out in a non-aquifer State may have an impact on a transboundary aquifer situated in other States and, hence, cause significant harm. Such broadening of the scope of this draft article would, furthermore, be in line with draft article 14 on planned activities which applies to all States and not only to aquifer States. The arguments in paragraph (1) of the commentary to draft article 14 to broaden the scope of that draft article to all States apply, in the view of the Netherlands, *mutatis mutandis*, to paragraph 2 of draft article 6 and, furthermore, to draft articles 9 and 11.

8. Saudi Arabia

Draft article 6 should include an explicit provision on irreversible harm, the compensatory obligation of the State causing the harm and the method of compensation, and should designate the competent authority therefore.

9. Turkey

1. The debate on the interpretation of "significant harm" and the definition of appropriate thresholds of significant harm continues. Although the concept "to prevent causing significant harm" is used in most international codes, it is vague, relative and difficult to apply. Furthermore, "appropriate measures to prevent causing significant harm" are hard to set without certain thresholds.

2. On the other hand, in groundwater resources, even exploitation or small amount of contamination could be interpreted as significant harm. Therefore, this draft article in general is ambitious and should be modified. The proposed text is as follows:

"1. Aquifer States shall, in utilizing a transboundary aquifer or aquifer system in their territories, pay due diligence to prevent the causing of significant harm to other aquifer States."

"2. Aquifer States shall, in undertaking activities other than utilization of a transboundary aquifer or aquifer system that have or likely to have, an impact on that transboundary aquifer or aquifer system shall refrain from causing significant harm through that aquifer or aquifer system to other aquifer States."

"3. Where significant harm nevertheless is caused to another aquifer State, the aquifer States whose activities cause such harm shall try, in consultation with the affected State, to eliminate or mitigate such harm, having due regard for the provisions of draft articles 4 and 5."

I. Draft article 7. General obligation to cooperate

1. Austria

Austria supports the concept of a general obligation of aquifer States to cooperate. However, as currently drafted, the inclusion of the words "mutual benefit" is unclear. "Mutual benefit" is a goal to be achieved through cooperation, but it remains doubtful whether it is to be listed as a basic principle.

2. Brazil

Brazil supports the wording of draft article 7 and the principles contained therein, taking them as a good basis for cooperation. These principles, including the ones related to sovereign equality and territorial integrity, establish along with other principles a balanced approach in order to facilitate cooperation among aquifer States, based on good faith and mutual respect.

3. Czech Republic

1. The term "good faith" in draft article 7 raises fears that States may, in good faith, take measures that were not negotiated with the other party and that could have adverse effects on the needs of the other party.

2. Pursuant to paragraph 2, aquifer States should establish joint mechanisms of cooperation. In the opinion of the Czech Republic, it would be better to use "shall" instead of "should" as this would make the States to establish joint mechanisms in all cases.

4. Germany

The following should be added to paragraph 2:

"Aquifer States shall integrate cooperation on groundwater into existing mechanisms of cooperation on surface water where appropriate."

The establishment of new independent cooperation mechanisms exclusively for groundwater is unrealistic in many regions in the medium term. Where aquifers are not in hydraulic contact with surface water, separate cooperation on groundwater is desirable. It should always be examined therefore whether existing institutional structures for transboundary water cooperation can be extended to incorporate groundwater before creating new structures.

5. Israel

Israel would like to express its support for paragraph (2) of draft article 7 and proposes strengthening the obligation to establish joint mechanisms of cooperation by changing the word "should" to "shall". It might be further strengthened by detailing which issues shall be subject to the joint mechanisms of cooperation, and referencing the appropriate draft articles, such as exchange of data and information (draft article 8), monitoring (draft article 12) and management (draft article 13).

6. POLAND

In view of the importance of cooperation for the protection, preservation and management of aquifers and aquifers systems, the forms of cooperation should be elaborated in more detail. Paragraph 2 of this draft article might then read as follows:

"2. For the purpose of paragraph 1 aquifer States should establish joint mechanisms of cooperation concerning, *inter alia*:

"(*a*) management;

"(*b*) monitoring and assessment;

"(*c*) databases;

"(*d*) coordinated communication, warning, and alarm systems;

"(*e*) research and development; and

"(*f*) mutual assistance."

7. SAUDI ARABIA

More detail is needed in respect of "sovereign equality" and "territorial integrity" because groundwaters are different from surface waters (e.g. rivers) inasmuch as it is difficult to apply such concepts to groundwaters.

J. Draft article 8. Regular exchange of data and information

1. AUSTRIA

Similar provisions on "regular exchange of data and information" as contained in draft article 8 are found in many treaties. Austria supports the inclusion of such a provision, as international practice underlines the importance of a regular exchange of data and information. As regards the current text, Austria would like to point out two issues:

(*a*) The last sentence of paragraph 2 should read:

"They shall take such action individually or, where appropriate, jointly and together with or through international organizations."

(*b*) As regards the term "best efforts" in paragraph 4, Austria understands this as a provision expressing that a State should endeavour to provide the data and information, but not as a strict obligation to provide them.

2. BRAZIL

Draft articles 8 and 12 make references to measures to be taken by one or more States with the assistance of international organizations "where appropriate". Draft article 8 does not specify who shall determine which situations are considered "appropriate" for the assistance of international organizations. In the view of Brazil, it is important to clarify in the draft articles that only States are entitled to such a right. The main practical difficulty with regard to the exchange of data and information is the lack of standardization of databases, parameters and information systems. For that reason, it would be useful to add in draft article 8 a specific reference to the importance of a "collective effort to integrate and make compatible, whenever possible, the existing databases, taking into consideration regional contexts and experiences". In South America, for instance, the Brazilian Geological Service has entered into agreements with many countries in order to make available an Information System of Groundwaters (SIAGAS).

3. COLOMBIA

With a view to ensuring that States with shared aquifers establish a monitoring and control network, it is proposed that paragraph 4 should be worded as follows:

"States sharing aquifers shall, where appropriate, employ their best efforts to collect and process data and information in a manner that facilitates their utilization by the other States to which such data and information are communicated, with a view to establishing a joint network for environmental monitoring and control of aquifers."

4. SWITZERLAND

Draft article 8 should encourage States more clearly to establish inventories of aquifers. Many States are still unaware of the extent, quality and quantity of their aquifers. In addition, draft article 8 should refer back to the draft article 4 (*c*). Indeed, the quality of any utilization plan depends on the availability of the relevant data.

K. Draft article 9. Protection and preservation of ecosystems

1. ISRAEL

Due to the increasing concerns of Israel and many other countries about the environmental effects of misusing aquifers and aquifer systems, Israel would like to commend the Commission for drafting articles 9 and 11, which oblige States to protect and preserve aquifers and the respective ecosystems in which they function.

2. THE NETHERLANDS

In paragraph (4) of the commentary to draft article 9, the Commission notes that the obligation of States enshrined in this draft article is limited to the protection of "relevant ecosystems". The wording of the draft article suggests that the relevant ecosystems are: (*a*) ecosystems within transboundary aquifers; and (*b*) ecosystems dependent upon transboundary aquifers. The Netherlands wonders whether the relevant ecosystems have been identified correctly. In particular, the Netherlands does not believe that the draft articles should aim at the protection and preservation of ecosystems dependent upon transboundary aquifers (category (*b*)) as the protection and preservation of these ecosystems will not have an impact on transboundary aquifers. It would rather seem that the reverse situation needs to be addressed. Accordingly, the draft articles should aim at the protection and preservation of ecosystems upon which transboundary aquifers are dependent, such as the ecosystems of recharge zones. Furthermore, it may be useful to explain in the commentary that the obligation enshrined in this draft article is an obligation of due diligence as is noted in the paragraph (2) of commentary to draft article 11. Finally, the Netherlands believes that the scope of this draft article should be broadened from aquifer States to all States.

3. TURKEY

Even though protection and preservation of ecosystems are highly important in management of transboundary groundwater resources, special regard should be given to basic human water needs. Accordingly, the phrase "whilst giving special regard to basic human needs" should be added to the end of this draft article.

L. Draft article 10. Recharge and discharge zones

1. AUSTRIA

Draft article 10 is an evolution of international law in the field of groundwater law. The commentary explains the necessity to involve also the States in whose territory a recharge or discharge zone is located. Austria agrees with this intention. As regards the establishment of an obligation for those States to cooperate, it remains doubtful whether this is feasible, taking into account the complexity of transboundary aquifers and aquifer systems. In Austria's view, the obligation should be reversed so that it should be an obligation for the aquifer States to seek cooperation with States in whose territory a recharge or discharge zone is located.

2. BRAZIL

Part III of the draft articles sets forth important obligations to aquifer States. Paragraph 2 of draft article 10 may also establish an obligation to non-aquifer States. Brazil supports, in general terms, the content and the balanced structure of the present Part, which is based on previously adopted universal and regional legal instruments. However, it is necessary to be more precise on certain aspects of draft article 10, as there is a debate about what really constitutes a recharge zone. Attempts should be made to avoid the risk of getting lost in the identification and treatment of far too large areas. The identification of the "most significant" recharge and discharge areas, an expression that should be added to draft article 10, would already demand a considerable effort, but it would contribute to the sustainable management of groundwaters.

3. ISRAEL

1. Israel recommends strengthening the obligation this draft article places on States. Therefore, Israel suggests that the Commission consider adopting stronger language than is currently proposed in paragraph 1, by replacing the words, "minimize detrimental impacts" with language that would serve to ensure the protection of aquifers and aquifer systems.

2. Israel believes that paragraph 2 does not afford adequate protection to aquifer States from the potential abuse of recharge zones located in non-aquifer States. Instead of providing a general obligation of cooperation to protect the aquifer or aquifer system, non-aquifer States in which a recharge zone is located should be responsible for all of the specific obligations related to protecting aquifers set forth in draft articles 6 and 11.

4. POLAND

It is proposed that draft article 10 also refers to eliminating any detrimental impacts on the recharge and discharge processes, to the extent practicable. It would read:

"1. Aquifer States shall identify recharge and discharge zones of their transboundary aquifer or aquifer systems and, within these zones, shall take special measures to prevent, minimize, control and, to the extent practicable, eliminate detrimental impacts on the recharge and discharge processes."

M. Draft article 11. Prevention, reduction and control of pollution

1. AUSTRIA

Austria firmly supports the inclusion of the "precautionary approach", but would like to see the second sentence redrafted as follows:

"Aquifer States shall take a precautionary approach."

Although Austria does not oppose the ideas expressed in the second sentence, it thinks the explanation given should be part of the commentary.

2. BRAZIL

1. Draft article 11 sets forth the obligation of aquifer States to prevent, reduce and control pollution that may cause significant harm to other aquifer States. According to the provision, in view of the uncertainty about the nature and extent of transboundary aquifers and aquifer systems and of their vulnerability to pollution, aquifer States shall take a "precautionary approach". As the Commission is aware, while some transboundary aquifers are already polluted to varying degrees, others are not. The obligation to "prevent" relates to new pollution, while the obligation to "reduce" and "control" relates to existing pollution. Paragraph (2) of the commentary to this draft article provides that the obligation to reduce and control pollution reflects the current practice of States. It also notes that an occasional obligation of abating immediately existing pollution could result in "undue hardship" on the State of origin of the pollution that is disproportionate to the benefit that would accrue to an aquifer State experiencing the harm. Brazil agrees with this interpretation.

2. Brazil supports the decision of the Commission to make reference to a "precautionary approach" instead of a reference to a "precautionary principle". Brazil agrees that "precautionary approach" is an expression less susceptible to controversy in view of scientific uncertainties and aquifer vulnerabilities. It is preferable to keep the term "precautionary approach" in the draft articles.

3. FINLAND

The environmental perspectives should be given more weight in the draft articles. The widely accepted precautionary principle should be fostered with the goal of reducing the risk of spoiling groundwater that could result from an accident.

4. Hungary

Hungary belongs to the group of countries which considers that the precautionary principle is already included in international environmental law. However, Hungary is aware of the fact that some countries state the opposite. Hungary believes that including the notion of "precautionary principle" into the text of the draft articles would largely contribute to the general acceptance of this principle in international law.

5. The Netherlands

1. The Commission observes in paragraph (1) of the commentary that this draft article is a specific application of the general principles contained in draft article 4 (equitable and reasonable utilization) and draft article 6 (obligation not to cause significant harm to other aquifer States). The Netherlands would like to draw the attention of the Commission to the academic debate on the interpretation of the corresponding articles of the 1997 Convention on the Law of Non-navigational Uses of International Watercourses, in particular to the question whether the special rules in the chapter of protection, preservation and management prevail over the chapter on general principles with respect to the quality of water. It would be useful to further clarify the relationship between these draft articles, in particular the application of the draft article on the equitable and reasonable utilization of aquifers in relation to the protection and preservation of the quality of water contained in an aquifer. Furthermore, the Netherlands believes that the scope of this draft article should be broadened from aquifer States to all States.

2. In paragraph (6) of the commentary, the Commission further notes that there are differing views whether or not the precautionary principle has been established as customary international law and it has therefore used the less-disputed expression "precautionary approach". The Netherlands firmly believes that the precautionary principle is part and parcel of customary international law and, irrespective of this consideration, prefers the use of the term "precautionary principle" in the draft articles. The Netherlands, furthermore, believes that it is necessary to clarify in what respect aquifer States must apply the precautionary principle. It would appear from the present formulation and context that the precautionary principle must be applied in connection with the prevention, reduction and control of pollution of transboundary aquifers. The Netherlands believes, however, that the precautionary principle must be applied in connection with any utilization of transboundary aquifers. This could be formulated as follows in a separate article to be included in Part III:

"Aquifer States shall apply the precautionary principle to the utilization of transboundary aquifers and transboundary aquifer systems."

6. Poland

The following redrafting of this provision with regard to the elimination of pollution is proposed:

"Aquifer States shall, individually and, where appropriate, jointly, prevent, minimize, control and, to the extent practicable, eliminate pollution of their aquifer or aquifer system, including through the recharge process that may cause significant harm to other aquifer States."

7. Portugal

In order to address matters concerning the quality of groundwaters, Portugal is of the view that in draft article 11 it would be relevant to adopt the following drafting:

"Aquifer States shall, individually and, were appropriate, jointly, *adopt all the measures* to prevent, reduce and control pollution of their transboundary aquifer or aquifer system ..."

8. Saudi Arabia

More detail is needed in respect of defining what is meant by "precautionary approach"; the obligations of States also need to be clarified.

9. Switzerland

In the view of Switzerland, this provision should be strengthened. Sufficient quality is a precondition for the use of any aquifer or aquifer system.

N. Draft article 12. Monitoring

1. Brazil

1. Draft article 12 contains rules regarding monitoring and some concepts, such as the convenience of seeking harmonized standards and parameters with a view to monitoring the management of a transboundary aquifer. The draft article recommends aquifer States to carry out such activities together, where possible. The obligation exists, independently from the joint monitoring and is applicable to the exchange of information. The term "as appropriate" should be added to the end of paragraph 1, as the exchange of information is not possible sometimes for technical or other reasons.

2. Paragraph 2 establishes the use of standards and methodology for monitoring transboundary aquifers as key elements of the obligations of aquifer States. Brazil suggests the inclusion of the expression "where possible" in paragraph 2 with relation to the obligation to use agreed and harmonized standards, so that it can be more realistic.

2. Turkey

It would be more appropriate to have a moderate phrase:

"Aquifer States shall monitor their transboundary aquifer or aquifer system. They shall carry out these monitoring activities, where appropriate, jointly with other aquifer States concerned and in collaboration with the competent international organizations."

O. Draft article 13. Management

1. Austria

Draft article 13 follows examples of existing treaties. The commentary explains that aquifer States should establish management plans on the domestic level and enter into consultations if requested. In Austria's view, the first sentence should be redrafted to clearly reflect the obligation to establish management plans on the domestic level.

2. Brazil

The first part of draft article 13 poses difficulties to Brazil, as it regulates the establishment and implementation of management plans for aquifers based exclusively on the Commission draft articles. These plans must be developed at the regional level not only in accordance with the principles foreseen in the draft articles, but mainly according to regional and subregional agreements. The second obligation established in the draft article, which is to enter into consultations concerning the joint management of the transboundary aquifer or aquifer system, at the request of any of the aquifer States, tends to encourage a unilateral view of the matter. The wording of the second part of article 13 must be reformulated in order to indicate in a more positive manner that the States "should obtain consensus on the ways and methods of consultations" as regards the management of aquifers. The last part of the draft article introduces the notion of "joint management mechanism", which might not be realistic, as the Commission seems to suggest in its commentary. In the view of Brazil, it would be better to refer to the harmonization of management criteria to make it more complementary and cooperative. Notwithstanding, each State must manage the portion of the aquifer located in its own territory. Thus it would be inappropriate to use expressions like "joint management" or "joint management mechanism".

3. Germany

1. A paragraph should be added to the draft article to emphasize the importance of exchanging basic socio-economic information:

"Within this joint management mechanism, aquifer States shall exchange data and information on the socio-economic situation and development within their aquifer territory. The aquifer States shall employ their best efforts to collect and create individually or jointly such data and information as they consider a basis for management plans."

2. As a result, the following should be added to the commentary:

"Paragraph 2 relates to data and information on the current socio-economic situation of inhabitants in the aquifer territory or of people relying on the aquifer for their well-being. It relates furthermore to data and information on socio-economic developments among these people. Socio-economic data and information include detailed information about (*a*) all economic activities that utilize the aquifer or water from the aquifer; (*b*) all utilization of water from the aquifer for water supply; (*c*) the number of the people relying on the aquifer for economic or domestic purposes; and (*d*) changes in the utilization, e.g. through growth of population, migration etc."

P. Draft article 14. Planned activities

1. Brazil

In respect of Part IV, draft article 14, Brazil supports the balanced approach adopted by the Commission in the elaboration of such a sensitive provision. It is important to highlight that the draft article does not set forth an obligation to establish an independent fact-finding body, thus differently from the Convention on the Law of the Non-navigational Uses of International Watercourses of 1997. Brazil supports the current wording and would not be in a position to accept the introduction of a provision concerning a "suspensive effect" on planned activities.

2. Colombia

The term "significant" should not be used to describe the effect; the words "adverse effect" should be used rather than the phrase "significant adverse effect". Similarly, Colombia proposes that the notification of activities that may affect an aquifer, referred to in paragraph 2 should be accompanied by technical and scientific data.

3. Cuba

Cuba believes that, with a view to ensuring its proper implementation, draft article 14 should specify the meaning of "significant adverse effect".

4. Czech Republic

Under draft article 14, when a State has reasonable grounds for believing that a particular planned activity in its territory may affect a transboundary aquifer or aquifer system and thereby may have a significant adverse effect upon another State, it shall, as far as practicable, assess the possible effects of such activity. In the opinion of the Czech Republic, such assessment can in no way be left to only one party; all States concerned must participate in such assessment.

5. Israel

The word "equitable", as used in draft article 14, appears to have a different meaning than as used previously in the text. Israel believes that the meaning used for this term should be consistent throughout the text of the draft articles and, therefore, Israel recommends the use of an alternative term in draft article 14 in order to avoid confusion.

6. The Netherlands

Pursuant to paragraph 1, a prior assessment of the possible "effects" of a planned activity should be undertaken which would thus include an assessment of the "environmental effects". However, the use of the word "any" in paragraph 2 suggests that "environmental impact assessments" only have to be notified in case such environmental impacts assessment are available. The formulation of this paragraph, which is based on article 12 of the 1997 Convention on the Law of the Non-navigational Uses of International Watercourses, does not seem to have been aligned with paragraph 1. In any case, the Netherlands believes that the notification must be accompanied by available technical data and information, including the assessment undertaken pursuant to paragraph 1. An explicit reference to "environmental effects" could and, in the view of the Netherlands, should be maintained in this draft article, for example by making an explicit reference to environmental effects in paragraph 1. Although the Netherlands understands, as reflected in paragraph (1) of the commentary to draft article 14, the reasons of the Commission to provide for simpler procedural requirements in these draft articles than those contained in the 1997 Convention, one essential procedural element would seem to be missing in the draft articles. This element is the obligation to refrain upon request from implementing or permitting the implementation of the planned activity during the course of consultations and negotiations. This is not only a safeguard for the potentially affected State during the consultations and negotiations, but also for the planning State after those consultations and negotiations have ended, be it successfully or unsuccessfully.

7. TURKEY

Paragraph 3 of this draft article does not give a clear idea about the future of a planned activity, which might have adverse effects on the other aquifer States, if no reasonable resolution of the situation is reached at the end of consultation and negotiation processes. Hence, the following phrase could be added at the end of the said paragraph in order to eliminate this ambiguity:

"Should no agreement be reached within a reasonable period, notifying State could exercise its sovereign rights to implement its planned activity with best efforts to reduce its adverse effects."

Q. Draft article 15. Scientific and technical cooperation with developing States

1. BRAZIL

In Part V, draft article 15 sets forth rules regarding scientific and technical cooperation with developing States. Brazil agrees with this provision, but suggests the inclusion of two additional subparagraphs. The items would read:

"Data collection and joint conduct of technical studies and projects;"

and

"Promotion of technical knowledge and experience exchange among aquifer States with a view to improving their capacity and strengthening cooperation among them as regards groundwater management."

2. COLOMBIA

Re-emphasizing the importance of a system for the monitoring and control of aquifers, Colombia proposes inserting an additional subparagraph, which would read:

"Supporting the establishment of a network for the monitoring and control of transboundary aquifers."

3. ISRAEL

Israel would like to emphasize its support of cooperation with developing States in the field of water technology.

4. POLAND

Since compliance with the obligations set forth in the draft articles by developing States depends predominantly on their material resources and capacity this draft article rightly attempts to ensure that developing States have appropriate material resources and capacity. However, in Poland's opinion, the cooperation in question should be broadened to also address financial and legal matters. It is thus suggested that this provision read as follows:

"*Article 15. Scientific, technical, educational, financial and legal cooperation with developing States*

"States shall, directly or through competent international organizations, promote scientific, educational, technical, legal and other cooperation with developing States for the protection and management of transboundary aquifers or aquifer systems. Such cooperation shall include, *inter alia*:

"(*a*) training scientific, technical, and legal personnel;

"(*b*) facilitating participation in relevant international programmes;

"(*c*) supplying them with necessary equipment and facilities;

"(*d*) enhancing their capacity to manufacture such equipment;

"(*e*) providing advice on and developing facilities for research, monitoring, educational and other programmes;

"(*f*) providing advice on and developing facilities for minimizing any detrimental effects of major activities affecting transboundary aquifers or aquifer systems;

"(*g*) preparing environmental impact assessments; and

"(*h*) mobilizing financial resources and establishing appropriate mechanisms in order to help them carry out relevant projects and facilitate their capacity building."

5. SAUDI ARABIA

1. The first line of this draft article includes the phrase "States shall ... promote". It is necessary to define what is meant by the word "States". Does the word mean all States of the world? It would be necessary to provide clarification.

2. Saudi Arabia suggests that this draft article should urge developed States, in view of their methodological and practical experience, to share their experience in the joint management of transboundary aquifers.

6. TURKEY

The first sentence of draft article 15 promotes scientific, educational, technical and other cooperation with developing States. However, the second sentence, which is "Such cooperation shall include, *inter alia*" implies obligations. Therefore, it would be appropriate to replace "shall" with "could" in the second sentence.

R. Draft article 16. Emergency situations

1. Austria

Austria agrees with draft articles 16 and 17, although they raise questions regarding their relationship. It should be clarified whether draft article 16 applies to situations falling under draft article 17.

2. Brazil

With respect to draft article 16, it would be preferable to use the word "risk" instead of "threat". Even though it is relatively clear that the word "threat" in the draft article does not have the meaning it has in the realm of international security, it would be important to avoid, as much as possible, the use of expressions that may lead to an international action. If the word "threat" mentioned in the provision is associated to the idea of harm, the word "risk" should be used as it has a neutral meaning.

3. Cuba

With regard to paragraph 1 of draft article 16, Cuba believes that what is meant by "causing serious harm" should be specified, as the wording is imprecise.

4. Israel

1. Israel would like to propose the removal of the word "suddenly" from paragraph 1 of the draft article. In this regard, Israel would like to point out that its understanding of the draft article is that it essentially refers to cases in which there arises a "state of necessity", as such term is defined under general international law. In the *Gabčíkovo–Nagymaros Project* case,[1] the International Court of Justice dealt with the rules concerning what constitutes a "state of necessity". Its decision is particularly poignant, since the state of necessity that was considered in the ruling was of an ecological nature, related to water management. In that decision, the Court determined that one of the component elements of a state of necessity is the existence of "imminent peril". The Court decided in paragraph 54 that:

> A "peril" appearing in the long term might be held to be "imminent" as soon as it is established, at the relevant point in time, that the realization of that peril, however far off it might be, is not hereby any less certain and inevitable. [2]

2. Israel believes that this finding is particularly relevant to aquifers, which are characterized by the gradual nature in which they are harmed. Israel therefore believes that emergency situations should be deemed to arise as soon as the impending peril is discovered, however far off it might be.

3. Regarding paragraph 2 it is necessary to be cautious about advancing a general rule that requires States to aid another State that is experiencing an emergency. Such a blanket obligation, however desirable it may be, is not yet a part of customary international law. Moreover, the importance of this principle notwithstanding, Israel questions its practicability.

[1] *Gabčíkovo-Nagymaros Project (Hungary/Slovakia), Judgment, I.C.J. Reports 1997*, p. 7.

[2] *Ibid.*, p. 42, para. 54.

5. The Netherlands

Although the Netherlands sympathizes with the objective of the obligation imposed on States to provide scientific, technical, logistical and other cooperation to other States experiencing an emergency, it doubts whether this provision reflects customary international law. The Netherlands believes that a State experiencing an emergency may request other States for "assistance" and that such other States are obliged to consider and decide upon such request, but this does not mean that an obligation is incumbent on such other States to actually render any assistance. The word "cooperation" would seem to have been used to make this provision more acceptable, but in fact obscures the contemporary state of international law on this point. If the Commission wishes to incorporate this provision as a progressive development of international law, this should be clearly stated in the commentary on this draft article. Similarly, the Netherlands sympathizes with the objective of the special derogation provision of paragraph 3 pursuant to which aquifer States may disregard two basic obligations, namely the principle of equitable and reasonable utilization and the obligation not to cause significant harm to other aquifer States, in order to protect vital human needs. The Netherlands is, however, not yet convinced that a special temporary derogation provision is needed in addition to a State's right to invoke circumstances precluding wrongfulness under the law of State responsibility to justify non-compliance with a particular obligation incumbent on it. The invocation of circumstances precluding wrongfulness is subject to safeguards and it merits further consideration whether or not to forego these safeguards to protect vital human needs. If the Commission wishes to do so, these implications should be addressed in the commentary on the draft article.

6. Poland

The question arises of why this provision should be limited to "sudden" emergencies. Some emergencies could emerge over a significant period of time and be nonetheless exigent. Accordingly, it is proposed to redraft its paragraph 1:

"1. For the purpose of the present article, "emergency" means a situation, whether resulting from natural causes or from human conduct, and whether arising suddenly or from the accumulation of prior events or activities the significance of which was unrecognized at the time, that poses an imminent threat of causing serious harm to aquifer States or other States."

7. Saudi Arabia

Subparagraph (*b*) includes the word "States". It is necessary to define and provide clarification as to the meaning of that word.

S. Draft article 17. Protection in time of armed conflict

1. Austria

It could be required to adjust draft article 17 to the result of the work of the Commission on the "Effect of Armed Conflict on Treaties".

2. Brazil

Brazil endorses the current wording of draft article 17.

T. Draft article 18. Data and information concerning national defence or security

1. Brazil

Brazil endorses the current wording of draft article 18. Brazil would not accept any amendments that may impose a limit on the right of States to decide about data or information they wish to share. The obligation to cooperate in good faith makes the article adequately balanced, as it does not interfere with the right of States in respect of information considered sensitive to national security.

2. Finland

Exchanging information concerning transboundary aquifers at regular intervals and with sufficient coverage is particularly important. The data to be shared should include contact information regarding authorities involved in the protection of the environment both at the State and regional levels. For any emergency, easy access to the authorities should be ensured. Under draft article 18, the sharing of key information should not be expressly prevented or hampered, and all activities should be carried out in good faith.

3. Israel

The exception to the obligation to exchange data and information set forth in draft article 18 allows for States to refrain from conveying data and information only in cases in which national defence or security would be affected, and does not relate to other important national interests found in article 56(5) of the Berlin Rules of 2004,[1] such as intellectual property rights, the right to privacy, or important cultural or natural treasures, all which could be endangered by a requirement to share information. Thus, it is worth considering the expansion of the list of exceptions to the obligation to exchange data and information in order to protect these important interests as well.

[1] International Law Association, *Report of the Seventy-First Conference held in Berlin, 16–21 August 2004*, London, 2004.

U. Draft article 19. Bilateral and regional agreements and arrangements

1. Austria

1. Draft article 19 still raises certain problems: (*a*) it is unclear whether it intends to define the draft articles, if converted into a convention, as the basis only of a framework agreement that requires further agreements for the individual transboundary aquifers or whether such a convention should be applicable without such agreements; (*b*) a clarification is also needed regarding the relationship with draft article 13, in particular its last sentence concerning the establishment of "joint management mechanisms". Such mechanisms will obviously constitute bilateral and regional agreements and arrangements as envisaged in draft article 19; (*c*) it fails to indicate the extent up to which such implementing agreements may deviate from the present draft articles. In particular, it is not clear whether this provision is designed to deviate from the rule on *inter-se* treaties as embodied in the 1969 Vienna Convention on the Law of Treaties. Although the commentary on this provision explicitly refers to article 4 of the 1997 Convention on International Watercourses, the former is far less elaborated than the latter; (*d*) it further lacks any indication of the relation to existing or future agreements.

2. The formulation of the draft articles must also take into account the particular position of member States of regional economic integration organizations the competences of which comprise issues addressed by such a convention.

2. Brazil

Draft article 19 deals with bilateral and regional agreements and arrangements. This provision contains recommendatory language and encourages aquifer States to enter into such agreements and arrangements. Brazil agrees with paragraph (2) of the commentary by the Commission that the second sentence of draft article 19 cannot be understood as conferring to the other aquifer States a veto power on the projects or programmes mentioned in the provision. However, in order to avoid any interpretation contrary to the spirit of the draft article, the Commission should try to find, in its second reading of the draft articles, some additional language to make it very clear that there is no such veto power.

3. The Netherlands

The draft articles have not been presented in the form of a framework for cooperation. The Netherlands agrees with the Commission as reflected in paragraph (1) of the commentary to draft article 19 that, in the case of groundwater, as well as other liquid substances and gaseous substances, the development of bilateral and regional agreements is still in an embryonic stage and that the framework for cooperation remains to be properly developed. The drafting and placement of the draft article relating to bilateral and regional agreements and arrangements reflects this approach, and is fully endorsed by the Netherlands.

4. Saudi Arabia

1. Bilateral utilization has positive and negative aspects. Among its positive aspects is that it leads to a greater, more fruitful cooperation among peoples in border areas, thus encouraging peaceful relations. Among its negative aspects is that it might come, however partially, at the expense of another State. The draft article addressed this problem by stating that "except insofar as the agreement or arrangement adversely affects, to a significant extent, the utilization, by one or more other aquifer States of the water in that aquifer or aquifer system, without their express consent".

2. However, the statement "adversely affects, to a significant extent" is broad and requires some specification and definition so that it cannot be misinterpreted or wrongly used by another aquifer State or States. Unless the adverse affect is specified or clearly defined, one or more States could end up having "veto" power.

3. Paragraph (2) of the commentary to draft article 19 includes the phrase "except for some rare cases". It would be advisable to clarify what those rare cases are so that they cannot be used as a justification for numerous interpretations.

5. Switzerland

In the third line of the French version of article 19 there is a small oversight in the words "*tout ou partie*".

V. Additional draft articles and rearrangement of draft articles

1. Iraq

1. Certain articles should be rearranged and reordered in a more appropriate manner, as follows: article 9: Administration; article 10: Monitoring; article 11: Protection and preservation of ecosystems.

2. Add a new article in Part V entitled: "Cooperation between aquifer or aquifer system States and relevant international organizations" in order to include cooperation with such organizations in the content of the proposed draft articles.

3. Add another article entitled "Compulsory arbitration clause" involving recourse to international tribunals in the event of any international dispute concerning the interpretation or application of the law.

2. Switzerland

1. Federal clause: in federal States, groundwater management often lies within the competence of regional entities. In Switzerland, for example, agreements on transboundary water have been concluded by the cantons with the neighbouring States with whom they share the water.

2. The interrelationship between surface and groundwater should be developed.

3. Provisions for dispute settlement should be developed (beyond article 14 (3), which is restricted to the situation of planned activities).

W. Final form

1. Brazil

During the second reading the draft articles, the Commission shall decide on the final format of the instrument the Commission will submit to the General Assembly, either a draft convention, or draft articles for its approval and adoption. Brazil reiterates its preference for a non-binding instrument. The technical specificity and incipient knowledge of aquifers, as well as the diverse conditions of the aquifers, require the adoption of flexible guidelines at this stage. These guidelines shall constitute a framework for the development of cooperation among States, especially through bilateral and regional arrangements and agreements. The 1997 Convention on the Law of the Non-navigational Uses of International Watercourses sets a precedent that needs to be observed. The Convention contains controversial provisions, *inter alia*, with respect to the settlement of disputes and, as a result of that, has not been able to gather a sufficient number of ratifications to enter into force. This precedent demonstrates that an incremental approach may be the best way to advance international law in this matter. The negotiation of a binding instrument may give the impression that it is possible to jump stages and accelerate the process, but experience has shown that with regard to new subjects based on diverse realities the best way is frequently to adopt non-binding instruments that provide general, flexible and adaptable parameters. It is the view of Brazil that the best way to move forward with the issue of transboundary aquifers is to transform the draft articles into a non-binding declaration, which would encourage States to negotiate regional and subregional legal instruments of a more specific nature and, if necessary, in a binding format. The adoption of a declaration at this stage does not prejudice the future adoption of a universal binding framework convention, as the law of transboundary aquifers advances on a regional level and aquifer States strengthen their cooperation mechanisms. However, this important step depends on a process that has not yet been concluded. Finally, in case the Commission decides to propose a non-binding instrument, the Commission should adapt the language used in the draft articles accordingly, in particular by excluding from the text the term "shall", which bears a clear mandatory meaning.

2. Canada

As Canada has noted in its comments in the Sixth Committee, it can support this work, as a set of model principles, for possible use by Governments, especially in a regional context where several States may share a groundwater resource. However, there is a need for the draft articles to reflect the utility of alternative mechanisms and to necessarily defer to those that already exist at the bilateral or multilateral level (certainly so in the case of Canada). Indeed, given Canada's existing effective mechanisms, it is not possible for Canada at this point to actively support the draft articles forming the basis for a multilateral convention.

3. Czech Republic

1. The Czech Republic has been considering the question of the best final form of the draft articles on the law of transboundary aquifers. It has been stressed several times during the work of the Commission that the project of transboundary aquifers shows many features identical or similar to the draft articles that resulted in the adoption of the 1997 Convention on the Law of the Non-navigational Uses of International Watercourses, as well as to the 2001 draft articles on the prevention of transboundary harm from hazardous activities.[1] It would therefore be only logical that the draft articles on the law of transboundary aquifers be finalized in the form of a framework convention.

2. On the other hand, one can argue that the 1997 Convention has not yet entered into force owing to insufficient interest of States in its ratification, and express concerns that the draft articles on transboundary aquifers could have the same fate.

3. Yet, in this concrete case, it appears that the form of a convention would have more advantages than a non-binding resolution or even a mere report of the Commission. The point is that this concrete case is a case of the progressive development of international law. While the failure of a convention codifying customary rules of international law could lead to the questioning of the generally binding nature of these customary rules, there would be no such risk in considering the progressive development of law through a framework convention. Although the entry of such a convention into force may take a relatively longer time and would be binding only on a smaller number of States, a binding convention would be a more appropriate instrument of development of international law in the given area.

4. It remains a question for the Commission whether the draft articles on transboundary aquifers and the future draft articles on oil and natural gas should or should not be incorporated into one convention. Despite the existence of many similarities between groundwaters and oil and natural gas issues, the Czech Republic rather sees differences. That is why it is of the opinion that the reading of the draft articles can be completed regardless of the results achieved in the Commission's discussion on legal questions relating to oil and natural gas. The Czech Republic actually perceives the shared natural resources issues as a very broad subject and is therefore of the opinion that the Commission would achieve more outputs if working on such broad subject.

5. According to the Czech Republic, it is necessary to find out the practice of States regarding international legal issues relating to oil and natural gas. The Czech Republic would like to point out that gathering such information and its subsequent assessment can take a relatively long time. This is also a reason why the Czech Republic believes that it would be useful to complete work on transboundary aquifers regardless of the progress made in the work on oil and natural gas issues.

[1] *Yearbook ... 2001*, vol. II (Part Two), pp. 146–148, para.97.

4. Finland

The draft articles have been presented in the form of a convention. It should yet to be considered how much added value such a convention would potentially generate. It is uncertain whether such a convention would enter into force soon. Moreover, eventual negotiations would also run the risk of watering down the draft articles.

5. Republic of Korea

1. It seems better if the draft articles could be incorporated in the form of a declaration on the subject. As an alternative, the draft articles could be a set of recommendations, as is the case with the issue of liability for transboundary harm. If the text should take the form of a convention, it would be more advisable to include a dispute-settlement mechanism for the current draft articles.

2. It is to be recommended that parties to a framework convention, if so adopted, should have the option to join with other aquifer States to conclude agreements and thus opt out from the convention in some substance. The opt-out option would be meaningful because particular aquifer States are in the position to best judge their particular situations weighing competing considerations peculiar to their situation regarding their own common aquifers. It is suggested that the addition of such phrases as "unless otherwise agreed" could be considered, as an opt-out clause.

6. The Netherlands

In paragraph (3) of the general commentary, the Commission has taken the view that it is still premature to reach a conclusion on the question of the final form in light of the differing views expressed by States in the Sixth Committee of the General Assembly. The Netherlands appreciates the cautious approach of the Commission and suggests to revisit this question only after due consideration has been given to the application of the draft articles to shared natural resources other than groundwater. In the view of the Netherlands, it is in any case not desirable to consider the development of a convention before the completion of the work on those other shared natural resources. Pending the completion of the work on all shared natural resources, the adoption of a non-legally binding instrument on the law of transboundary aquifers may merit consideration as a first step in the development of an adequate legal regime for the use of shared natural resources.

7. Poland

It seems in the light of the diverse views expressed by States and the fact that international practice is still evolving that it would be premature at this stage to reach a decision on this issue.

8. Portugal

Portugal supports the intention of the Commission to proceed with a second reading of the draft articles. Portugal would like to reaffirm its conviction that the final form of the draft articles should be an international framework convention.

9. Switzerland

The text represents a sound general framework, mostly reflecting norms recognized as customary international law. Switzerland could imagine its provisions either being used as a legally binding instrument on a global, regional or bilateral level, or serving as a model for a specific agreement between neighbouring countries on a specific aquifer.

EFFECTS OF ARMED CONFLICTS ON TREATIES

[Agenda item 5]

DOCUMENT A/CN.4/589

Fourth report on the effects of armed conflicts on treaties: procedure for suspension and termination, by Mr. Ian Brownlie, Special Rapporteur

[*Original: English*]
[*14 November 2007*]

CONTENTS

Multilateral instruments cited in the present report

	Source
Geneva Conventions on the Law of the Sea (Geneva, 29 April 1958)	
Convention on the Continental Shelf	United Nations, *Treaty Series*, vol. 499, No. 7302, p. 311.
Convention on the Territorial Sea and the Contiguous Zone	*Ibid.*, vol. 516, No. 7477, p. 205.
Convention on the High Seas	*Ibid.*, vol. 450, No. 6465, p. 11.
Convention on Fishing and Conservation of the Living Resources of the High Seas	*Ibid.*, vol. 559, No. 8164, p. 285.
Vienna Convention on Diplomatic Relations (Vienna, 18 April 1961)	*Ibid.*, vol. 500, No. 7310, p. 95.
Vienna Convention on Consular Relations (Vienna, 24 April 1963)	*Ibid.*, vol. 596, No. 8638, p. 261.
Vienna Convention on the law of treaties (Vienna, 23 May 1969)	*Ibid.*, vol. 1155, No. 18232, p. 331.

Introduction

1. In the third report on the effects of armed conflicts on treaties,[1] the mode of suspension or termination was treated in draft article 8 by analogy with articles 42–45 of the Vienna Convention on the law of treaties (hereinafter the 1969 Vienna Convention). Both in the debate in plenary and in the Working Group on the Effects of Armed Conflicts on Treaties, it was pointed out that this question required further examination.

2. During the proceedings in the Working Group, it was agreed that the Special Rapporteur should be requested to carry out a more developed examination of the question of procedure, with particular reference to article 65 of the 1969 Vienna Convention. In order to expedite this examination, the Secretariat has prepared an informal memorandum on the legislative history of article 65 of the Convention, excerpts of which are included in the present report.

[1] *Yearbook ... 2007*, vol. II (Part One), document A/CN.4/578.

Chapter I

The provisions of the 1969 Vienna Convention

3. By way of preface it is necessary to indicate the limited relevance of the provisions of the 1969 Vienna Convention.

4. Part V of the 1969 Vienna Convention deals with "Invalidity, termination and suspension of the operation of treaties" and consists of five sections as follows:

Section 1: General provisions (arts. 42–45)

Section 2: Invalidity of treaties (arts. 46–53)

Section 3: Termination and suspension of the operation of treaties (arts. 54–64)

Section 4: Procedure (arts. 65–68)

Section 5: Consequences of the invalidity, termination or suspension of the operation of a treaty (arts. 69–72).

5. In the result, the provisions which directly concern the issue of procedure are as follows:

Section 4. Procedure

Article 65. Procedure to be followed with respect to invalidity, termination, withdrawal from or suspension of the operation of a treaty

1. A party which, under the provisions of the present Convention, invokes either a defect in its consent to be bound by a treaty or a ground for impeaching the validity of a treaty, terminating it, withdrawing from it or suspending its operation, must notify the other parties of its claim. The notification shall indicate the measure proposed to be taken with respect to the treaty and the reasons therefor.

2. If, after the expiry of a period which, except in cases of special urgency, shall not be less than three months after the receipt of the notification, no party has raised any objection, the party making the notification may carry out in the manner provided in article 67 the measure which it has proposed.

3. If, however, objection has been raised by any other party, the parties shall seek a solution through the means indicated in Article 33 of the Charter of the United Nations.

4. Nothing in the foregoing paragraphs shall affect the rights or obligations of the parties under any provisions in force binding the parties with regard to the settlement of disputes.

5. Without prejudice to article 45, the fact that a State has not previously made the notification prescribed in paragraph 1 shall not prevent it from making such notification in answer to another party claiming performance of the treaty or alleging its violation.

Article 66. Procedures for judicial settlement, arbitration and conciliation

If, under paragraph 3 of article 65, no solution has been reached within a period of 12 months following the date on which the objection was raised, the following procedures shall be followed:

(*a*) any one of the parties to a dispute concerning the application or the interpretation of article 53 or 64 may, by a written application, submit it to the International Court of Justice for a decision unless the parties by common consent agree to submit the dispute to arbitration;

(*b*) any one of the parties to a dispute concerning the application or the interpretation of any of the other articles in Part V of the present Convention may set in motion the procedure specified in the Annex to the Convention by submitting a request to that effect to the Secretary-General of the United Nations.

Article 67. Instruments for declaring invalid, terminating, withdrawing from or suspending the operation of a treaty

1. The notification provided for under article 65, paragraph 1, must be made in writing.

2. Any act of declaring invalid, terminating, withdrawing from or suspending the operation of a treaty pursuant to the provisions of the treaty or of paragraphs 2 or 3 of article 65 shall be carried out through an instrument communicated to the other parties. If the instrument is not signed by the Head of State, Head of Government or Minister for Foreign Affairs, the representative of the State communicating it may be called upon to produce full powers.

Article 68. Revocation of notifications and instruments provided for in article 65 and 67

A notification or instrument provided for in article 65 or 67 may be revoked at any time before it takes effect.

6. The difficulty which has to be faced is that these provisions on procedure in cases of termination or suspension do not apply to "any question that may arise in regard to a treaty ... from the outbreak of hostilities between States". This is stipulated in article 73, which applies to the provisions of the 1969 Vienna Convention as a whole.

Chapter II

The legislative history of article 65 of the 1969 Vienna Convention

7. The presence of article 73 has the consequence that the Commission will be at liberty, and have the necessity, to design a solution for the particular case of the effect of armed conflict on treaties.

A. Relevance of the legislative history

8. The irrelevance of article 65 as a matter of formal application of the provisions does not have the implication that the legislative history is redundant. The relevance of the policy considerations taken into account in formulating article 65 to the procedure applicable in the case of the effects of armed conflicts cannot be ruled out *ab initio*. At the same time, there remains the possibility, to be examined in due course, that the case of armed conflict is qualitatively different from the cases of termination or suspension presently encompassed by the 1969 Vienna Convention, and that in consequence the policy considerations are also different.

B. The legislative history of article 65 summarized (as in the Commission)

9. The original of article 65 was draft article 62 of the draft articles on the law of treaties considered by the Commission in 1966.[2] The sources are analysed in some detail in the 2007 memorandum prepared by the Secretariat on the legislative history of article 65 of the 1969 Vienna Convention. The key stages in the process were as follows:

First reading—draft article 51 (1963–1964)

10. The Secretariat analysis is as follows:

1963–In his second report (A/CN.4/156 and Add.1–3),[3] Special Rapporteur Waldock included a Section IV containing four draft articles (23–26) on the "Procedure for annulling, denouncing, terminating, withdrawing from or suspending a treaty and the severance of treaty provisions".

- The Commission's discussion of the Special Rapporteur's proposals for the procedure for annulment, denunciation, termination etc. were held at the 698th to 700th, and 705th to 707th (art. 26—severance) meetings.[4]

- The Drafting Committee subsequently proposed a revised drafting for draft article 25, which was discussed at the 714th meeting.[5]

1963–That year the Commission adopted a further set of draft articles ..., including former draft articles 24 and 25, which have been renumbered as draft articles 50 (procedure under a right provided for in the treaty) and 51 (procedure in other cases), with commentaries. **Draft article 51 was the first time the formulation, later adopted by the Commission as draft article 62, appeared in the proposals for draft articles.**

1964–The first reading of the entire set of draft articles (including draft article 51) was subsequently concluded in 1964, following which the Commission transmitted the draft articles to Governments for comments.

- Draft article 51 was only raised twice in the debate in 1964 (by Mr. Rosenne at the 743rd meeting[6] and Mr. Briggs at the 754th meeting).

The text of draft article 51, as adopted on first reading, was as follows:

Article 51. Procedure in other cases

1. A party alleging the nullity of a treaty, or a ground for terminating, withdrawing from or suspending the operation of a treaty otherwise than under a provision of the treaty, shall be bound to notify the other party or parties of its claim. The notification must:

(*a*) Indicate the measure proposed to be taken with respect to the treaty and the grounds upon which the claim is based;

(*b*) Specify a reasonable period for the reply of the other party or parties, which period shall not be less than three months except in cases of special urgency.

2. If no party makes any objection, or if no reply is received before the expiry of the period specified, the party making the notification may take the measure proposed. In that event it shall so inform the other party or parties.

3. If, however, objection has been raised by any other party, the parties shall seek a solution of the question through the means indicated in Article 33 of the Charter of the United Nations.

4. Nothing in the foregoing paragraphs shall affect the rights or obligations of the parties under any provisions in force binding the parties with regard to the settlement of disputes.

5. Subject to article 47, the fact that a State may not have made any previous notification to the other party or parties shall not prevent it from invoking the nullity of or a ground for terminating a treaty in answer to a demand for the performance of the treaty or to a complaint alleging a violation of the treaty.[7]

Second reading—draft article 62 (1965–1966)

11. The Secretariat analysis is as follows:

1965–Several Governments submitted comments on, *inter alia*, draft article 51 as adopted by the Commission on first reading (A/CN.4/182 et al).[8]

1965–The Commission did not consider draft article 51, as it was only able to consider the first 29 draft articles. The only reference in the debate that year to draft article 51 was in a statement by Mr. Rosenne at the 797th meeting.[9]

1966–In his fifth report (A/CN.4/183 and Add.1–4), Special Rapporteur Waldock included a section on article 51 reviewing the comments made by Governments and making suggestions.[10]

1966–While the Commission was unable to discuss art. 51 at its Monaco session early in 1966, several passing references to it were made in the debate.1966 The Special Rapporteur's proposals for article 51 were considered by the Commission at its 845th meeting,[11] following which the draft article was referred to the Drafting Committee. Passing reference to the provision was subsequently made at the 849th, 861st and 863rd meetings.[12] The report of the Drafting Committee

[2] *Yearbook ... 1966*, vol. II, document A/6309/Rev.1, p. 185.

[3] *Yearbook ... 1963*, vol. II, p. 36.

[4] *Ibid.*, vol. I, pp. 163–182 and 209–232.

[5] *Ibid.*, pp. 278–280.

[6] *Yearbook ... 1964*, vol. I, pp. 129–130.

[7] *Yearbook ... 1963*, vol. II, document A/5509, p. 214.

[8] *Yearbook ... 1966*, vol. II, document A/6309/Rev.1, annex, p. 279.

[9] *Yearbook ... 1965*, vol. I, p. 148, para. 7.

[10] *Yearbook ... 1966*, vol. II, p. 46.

[11] *Ibid.*, vol. I (Part Two), p. 3.

[12] *Ibid.*, pp. 32, 129 and 142.

on draft article 51 was presented to the plenary and considered at the 864th meeting,[13] and was referred back to the Drafting Committee. The Commission considered a revised proposal for draft article 51, presented by the Drafting Committee, at its 865th meeting, following which **article 51 was adopted**, on second reading, by a vote.[14] Reference to draft article 51, as adopted, was subsequently made at the 868th, 876th and 887th meetings.[15]

1966–Draft article 51 was subsequently renumbered as draft article 62 and adopted on second reading, together with a commentary.

The text of draft article 62, as adopted on second reading, was as follows:

Article 62. Procedure to be followed in cases of invalidity, termination, withdrawal from or suspension of the operation of a treaty

1. A party which claims that a treaty is invalid or which alleges a ground for terminating, withdrawing from or suspending the operation of a treaty under the provisions of the present articles must notify the other parties of its claim. The notification shall indicate the measure proposed to be taken with respect to the treaty and the grounds therefor.

2. If, after the expiry of a period which, except in cases of special urgency, shall not be less than three months after the receipt of the notification, no party has raised any objection, the party making the notification may carry out in the manner provided in article 63 the measure which it has proposed.

3. If, however, objection has been raised by any other party, the parties shall seek a solution through the means indicated in Article 33 of the Charter of the United Nations.

4. Nothing in the foregoing paragraphs shall affect the rights or obligations of the parties under any provisions in force binding the parties with regard to the settlement of disputes.

5. Without prejudice to article 42, the fact that a State has not previously made the notification prescribed in paragraph 1 shall not prevent it from making such notification in answer to another party claiming performance of the treaty or alleging its violation.

12. For present purposes the results of this analysis are inevitably limited, but the legislative history provides some useful indications of certain basic policy questions.

C. The policy considerations emerging from the work of the Commission

13. The work of the Commission in the period from 1963 to 1966 reveals the policy considerations lying behind draft article 51 (and, subsequently, draft article 62), as presented in the report of the Commission to the General Assembly in 1966.[16]

14. At the outset it should be emphasized that the question of procedure which is formally the subject of draft article 62 was closely related to the issues of substance. Indeed, the "procedural" elements provided the safeguards against the arbitrary assertion of grounds upon which treaties may be determined to be invalid, or terminated, or suspended. This consideration of legal security was indicated in a series of studies by different Special Rapporteurs.[17]

15. The policy elements were summarized in the commentary of the Commission attached to draft article 62 in the report of the Commission to the General Assembly in 1966, as follows:

(1) Many members of the Commission regarded the present article as a key article for the application of the provisions of the present part dealing with the invalidity, termination or suspension of the operation of treaties. They thought that some of the grounds upon which treaties may be considered invalid or terminated or suspended under those sections, if allowed to be arbitrarily asserted in face of objection from the other party, would involve real dangers for the security of treaties. These dangers, were, they felt, particularly serious in regard to claims to denounce or withdraw from a treaty by reason of an alleged breach by the other party or by reason of a fundamental change of circumstances. In order to minimize these dangers the Commission has sought to define as precisely and as objectively as possible the conditions under which the various grounds may be invoked. But whenever a party to a treaty invokes one of these grounds, the question whether or not its claim is justified will nearly always turn upon facts the determination or appreciation of which may be controversial. Accordingly, the Commission considered it essential that the present articles should contain procedural safeguards against the possibility that the nullity, termination or suspension of the operation of a treaty may be arbitrarily asserted as a mere pretext for getting rid of an inconvenient obligation.[18]

16. In case of objections to a claim to terminate or suspend treaty provisions, some members of the Commission insisted that the resulting disputes should be subject to the compulsory jurisdiction of ICJ. The majority in the Commission were unable to accept such a procedural check, and were satisfied with the seeking of a solution through the means indicated in Article 33 of the Charter of the United Nations. This solution was justified in the commentary in the following passages:

(5) *Paragraph 1* provides that a party claiming the nullity of the treaty or alleging a ground for terminating it or withdrawing from it or suspending its operation shall put in motion a regular procedure under which it must first notify the other parties of its claim. In doing so it must indicate the measure which it proposes to take with respect to the treaty, i.e. denunciation, termination, suspension, etc. and its grounds for taking that measure. Then by *paragraph 2* it must give the other parties a reasonable period within which to reply. Except in cases of special urgency, the period must not be less than three months. The second stage of the procedure depends on whether or not objection is raised by any party. If there is none or there is no reply before the expiry of the period, the party may take the measure proposed in the manner provided in article 63, i.e. by an instrument duly executed and communicated to other parties. If, on the other hand, objection is raised, the parties are required by *paragraph 3*, to seek a solution to the question through the means indicated in Article 33 of the Charter. The Commission did not find it possible to carry the procedural provisions beyond this point without becoming involved in some measure and in one form or another in compulsory solution to the question at issue between the parties. If after recourse to the means indicated in Article 33 the parties should reach a deadlock, it would be for each Government to appreciate the situation and to act as good faith demands. There would also remain the right of every State, whether or not a Member of the United Nations, under certain conditions, to refer the dispute to the competent organ of the United Nations.

(6) Even if, for the reasons previously mentioned in this commentary, the Commission felt obliged not to go beyond Article 33 of the Charter in providing for procedural checks upon arbitrary action, it considered that the establishment of the procedural provisions of the present article as an integral part of the law relating to the invalidity, termination and suspension of the operation of treaties would be a valuable step forward. The express subordination of the substantive rights arising under the provisions of the various articles to the procedure prescribed in the present article and the checks on unilateral action

[13] *Ibid.*, p. 148.

[14] *Ibid.*, p. 159, para. 51.

[15] *Ibid.*, pp. 171, 219 and 287.

[16] *Ibid.*, vol. II, p. 169, document A/6309/Rev.1.

[17] In this respect the following materials are of particular relevance: second report on the law of treaties by G. Fitzmaurice, *Yearbook ... 1957*, vol. II, document A/CN.4/107, pp. 20–70; second report by Sir Humphrey Waldock, *Yearbook ... 1963*, vol. II, document A/CN.4/156 and Add. 1–3, pp. 35–93; and fifth report by Sir Humphrey Waldock, *Yearbook ... 1966*, vol. II, document A/CN.4/183 and Add.1–4, pp. 46–50.

[18] *Yearbook ... 1966*, vol. II, document A/6309/Rev.1, p. 262.

which the procedure contains would, it was thought, give a substantial measure of protection against purely arbitrary assertions of the nullity, termination or suspension of the operation of a treaty.[19]

17. The limitations upon the procedural checks were explained by Sir Humphrey Waldock during the 864th meeting of the Commission in 1966:

13. Sir Humphrey WALDOCK, Special Rapporteur, said that articles 51 and 50 must be viewed in the light of the earlier articles, particularly article 30. The order of the two articles had been deliberately reversed by the Drafting Committee, so as to make it clear that article 50, which dealt with the final act of termination of a treaty, presupposed that the act was performed in the circumstances in which termination was legitimate.

14. The difficulty in article 51 was that despite its safeguards, its provisions on negotiations and its reference to Article 33 of the Charter, it did not deal with the possibility of a deadlock. Clearly, ... under article 51, the parties would be left to act on their own responsibility. That looseness was inherent in the rules of contemporary international law on the adjudication of disputes.

15. He sympathized with Mr. Jiménez de Aréchaga's wish to see the provisions of article 51 made as clear as possible *but it should be remembered that the Commission had not covered all the factual causes of termination in its draft articles; obsolescence, for example, had not been dealt with specifically. As far as State responsibility and State succession were concerned, however, he himself believed that they were governed by different principles.* *[20]

18. These observations involve a frank estimation of the limitations presented by the provisions of draft article 51, which was the predecessor of article 65 of the 1969 Vienna Convention. Two elements are especially significant. In the first place, Sir Humphrey Waldock emphasizes the looseness "inherent in the rules of contemporary international law on the adjudication of disputes". And it must be clear that the picture has not changed very much since 1966. Secondly, the references by Sir Humphrey to other factual causes of termination, such as State succession, is of interest. In the context of the work of the Commission, it is clear that the outbreak of an armed conflict was such another factual cause. And it is equally clear that the Commission also regarded the incidence of armed conflict to be "governed by different principles".

D. The legislative history of article 65 summarized (United Nations Conference on the Law of Treaties)

19. The Secretariat analysis is as follows:

Introduction

8. The following changes were made during the Vienna Conference to draft article 62 as adopted by the Commission in 1966, resulting in the text of what is now article 65 of the Vienna Convention:

Article 65

Procedure to be followed with respect to invalidity, termination, withdrawal from or suspension of the operation of a treaty

1. A party which, under the provisions of the present Convention, invokes either a defect in its consent to be bound by a treaty or a ground for impeaching the validity of a treaty, terminating it, withdrawing from it or suspending its operation, must notify other parties of its claim. The notification shall indicate the measure proposed to be taken with respect to the treaty and the reasons therefor.

2. If, after the expiry of a period which, in cases of special urgency, shall not be less than three months after the receipt of the notification, no party has raised any objection, the party making the notification may carry out in the manner provided in article 67 the measure which it has proposed.

3. If, however, objection has been raised by any other party, the parties shall seek a solution through the means indicated in Article 33 of the Charter of the United Nations.

4. Nothing in the foregoing paragraphs shall affect the rights or obligations of the parties under any provisions in force binding the parties with regard to the settlement of disputes.

5. Without prejudice to article 45, the fact that a State has not previously made the notification prescribed in paragraph 1 shall not prevent it from making such notification in answer to another party claiming performance of the treaty or alleging its violation.

9. As can be seen from the comparison, other than changes in cross-references, the only substantive changes made to the article, during the Vienna Conference, were to the title and to paragraph 1. Paragraphs 2 to 5 were adopted with the formulation proposed in the Commission's draft.

10. What follows is a synopsis of the consideration of the provision at the Vienna Conference, resulting in the adoption of article 65 with the above amendments.

Summary of the consideration of article 65 [62] at the Vienna Conference

11. Draft article 62, as proposed by the International Law Commission, was considered by the Committee of the Whole of the Vienna Conference at its 1968 session, and a revised text as proposed by the Drafting Committee (containing only an amendment proposed by France) was adopted by the Committee of the Whole that year. The draft article was subsequently adopted by the Plenary of the Conference in 1969.

Detailed chronology of consideration of article 65 [62] at the Vienna Conference

12. Two sessions of the Vienna Conference were held, in 1968 and 1969 respectively. The following is a description of the consideration of draft article 65 [62] during those sessions.

a. *Discussion and action in the Committee of the Whole at the 1968 session*

13. Draft article 62, as proposed by the International Law Commission, was considered by the Committee of the Whole at the 1968 session. Although several Governments submitted drafting proposals, only a proposal by France amending paragraph 1, was adopted. The draft article was then transmitted to the Drafting Committee, which simply incorporated the French amendment into paragraph 1. The Committee of the Whole considered and adopted the text for draft article 62, as proposed by the Drafting Committee, at the 83rd meeting (paras. 14–16).

1968
- Report of the Committee of the Whole (see paras. 573–581)
- Summary records of the 68th to 74th and 80th meetings of the Committee of the Whole containing discussion of draft article 62, as proposed by the International Law Commission
- Summary record of the 83rd meeting of the Committee of the Whole

b. *Discussion and action in the Plenary of the Conference at the 1969 session*

14. Draft article 62, as approved by the Committee of the Whole, was adopted by the Plenary of the Conference at its 25th meeting, held on 15 May 1969. The article was subsequently renumbered as article 65 of the Vienna Convention on the Law of Treaties. Note that some delegations conditioned their support for the provision on the inclusion of draft article 62 *bis*, which became article 66 of the Vienna Convention.

[19] *Ibid.*, p. 263.

[20] *Ibid.*, vol. I (Part Two), p. 149.

20. The French amendment, adopted by the Committee of the Whole at the 83rd meeting, is of particular significance. The purpose of the amendment was explained at the sixty-eighth meeting by Mr. de Bresson:

> Mr. de BRESSON (France), introducing his delegation's amendment to paragraph 1 (A/CONF.39/C.1/L.342), said that a study of Part V showed that the International Law Commission had drawn a distinction between cases where the validity of a treaty might be contested in accordance with the provisions of articles 43 to 47, and those, covered by articles 48 to 50 and 61, where a treaty was void *ab initio*. Although that difference was not expressly stated anywhere in the draft convention, the difference of terminology used in the two groups of articles was evident, and the Committee must consider whether that difference affected the obligation to notify other parties of a claim of invalidity or an allegation of a ground for termination, withdrawal or suspension. In its comments on article 39, the French delegation had pointed out that the actual text of article 62 gave no clear answer to that important question.
>
> A *prima facie* examination of article 39, paragraph 1, gave the impression that the second sentence was complementary to the first, and that the paragraph as a whole established no distinction between "relative" invalidity and invalidity *ab initio*; that interpretation also led to the assumption that article 62, paragraph 1, covered cases under articles 43 to 50 and article 61. A closer study of Part V showed, however, that that interpretation was unduly simple and that article 39, paragraph 1, might be held to refer to two distinct but parallel means of contesting validity.
>
> In that event, it could be argued that article 62, paragraph 1, only covered claims of invalidity on the grounds referred to in articles 43 to 47. But the second sentence of article 39, paragraph 1, provided for no recourse to article 62 in the cases of invalidity *ab initio* covered by articles 48 to 50 and article 61, and the grounds of invalidity in such cases could be invoked without reference to article 62, paragraph 1, and even without the intervention of the parties. That interpretation was further corroborated by the difference in the terms used in paragraphs 4 and 5 of article 41 for States invoking "relative" invalidity and those claiming invalidity *ab initio*, and also by the absence of any reference to the provisions in question in article 42.
>
> The possible consequences of that anomaly would be to enable any party to a treaty unilaterally to claim invalidity on the very grounds which were most difficult to establish, and to open the way to States other than the parties to benefit by the invalidity provided for by those articles.
>
> It had been claimed that the International Law Commission had meant article 62 to apply to all the provisions of Part V, but the French delegation considered that no ambiguity should be allowed to remain on such a fundamental point, and it had introduced its amendment with the sole purpose of clarifying the text in accordance with the generally recognized meaning.[21]

[21] *Official Records of the United Nations Conference on the Law of Treaties, First Session, Vienna, 26 March–24 May 1968, Summary records of the plenary meetings and of the meetings of the Committee of the Whole*, 68th meeting of the Committee of the Whole, p. 403, paras. 9–13.

21. This amendment, which was adopted by the Committee of the Whole, provides reinforcement to the view that the issues of substance (invalidity), and the question of the procedure to be followed, were seen to be closely related.

22. Article 62 (as it then was) was adopted by the plenary by 106 votes to none with two abstentions.[22]

E. The legislative history of article 65 (the phrase "except in cases of special urgency")

23. This phrase forms part of the text of article 65 as finally adopted at the United Nations Conference on the Law of Treaties. The formulation first appears in draft article 51 (the predecessor of article 65) on first reading in 1964 (see paragraph 10 above). The records contain no precise explanation of its provenance and it failed to provoke discussion in the plenary. It did, however, lead to discussion in the Drafting Committee, and this is referred to by Sir Humphrey Waldock in his fifth report on the law of treaties. There, in examining the proposals of Governments, Sir Humphrey observed:

> The Finnish Government also suggests that in paragraph 1(*b*) a time-limit should be fixed within which the other party's reply would have to be given in cases of "special urgency"; and it suggests a limit of two weeks or one month. This question, if the Special Rapporteur's memory is correct, was considered in the Drafting Committee which, however, thought it difficult to fix in advance a rigid time-limit to apply to all cases of "special urgency". In practice, cases of special urgency are likely to be cases arising from a sudden and serious violation of the treaty by the other party; and it seems possible to conceive of cases where even a time-limit of two weeks might be too long in the particular circumstances of the violation.[23]

24. In evaluating this element in the records it must be borne in mind that the reference to "cases of special urgency" can have no necessary relation to cases of armed conflict, given the explicit provisions of article 73 of the 1969 Vienna Convention. At the same time, it is helpful to have the indication that the concept of "special urgency" was regarded as fact-based and related to "the particular circumstances of the violation".

[22] *Ibid., Second Session, Vienna, 9 April–22 May 1969, Summary records of the plenary meetings and of the meetings of the Committee of the Whole*, 25th plenary meeting, pp. 136–137, para. 43.

[23] *Yearbook ... 1966*, vol. II, document A/CN.4/183 and Add.1–4, pp. 49–50, para. 7.

Chapter III

The special character of the "effects of armed conflicts on treaties" as a basis of termination or suspension

25. The Commission, during its work on the law of treaties in the years 1963 to 1966, held the opinion that it was not convenient to include "the case of an outbreak of hostilities between parties to a treaty".[24] This response has been examined in the first report on the effects of armed conflicts on treaties.[25] Thus, in the commentary to draft article 69 of the 1966 report to the General Assembly (art. 73 of the 1969 Vienna Convention), the Commission observed (in relation to the cases of State succession and State responsibility):

> Both these matters may have an impact on the operation of certain parts of the law of treaties in conditions of entirely normal international relations, and the Commission felt that considerations of logic and of the completeness of the draft articles indicated the desirability of inserting a general reservation covering cases of succession and cases of State responsibility.

[24] *Ibid.*, document A/6309/Rev.1, p. 267, para. (2) of the commentary to article 69.

[25] *Yearbook ... 2005*, vol. II (Part One), document A/CN.4/552, paras. 7–9.

(2) Different considerations appeared to the Commission to apply to the case of an outbreak of hostilities between parties to a treaty. It recognized that the state of facts resulting from an outbreak of hostilities may have the practical effect of preventing the application of the treaty in the circumstances prevailing. It also recognized that questions may arise as to the legal consequences of an outbreak of hostilities with respect to obligations arising from treaties. But it considered that in the international law of to-day the outbreak of hostilities between States must be considered as an entirely abnormal condition, and that the rules governing its legal consequences should not be regarded as forming part of the general rules of international law applicable in the normal relations between States. Thus, the Geneva conventions codifying the law of the sea contain no reservation in regard to the case of an outbreak of hostilities notwithstanding the obvious impact which such an event may have on the application of many provisions of those Conventions; nor do they purport in any way to regulate the consequences of such an event. It is true that one article in the Vienna Convention on Diplomatic Relations (article 44) and a similar article in the Convention on Consular Relations (article 26) contain a reference to cases of "armed conflict". Very special considerations, however, dictated the mention of cases of armed conflict in those articles and then only to underline that the rules laid down in the articles hold good even in such cases. The Vienna Conventions do not otherwise purport to regulate the consequences of an outbreak of hostilities; nor do they contain any general reservation with regard to the effect of that event on the application of their provisions. Accordingly, the Commission concluded that it was justified in considering the case of an outbreak of hostilities between parties to a treaty to be wholly outside the scope of the general law of treaties to be codified in the present articles; and that no account should be taken of that case or any mention made of it in the draft articles.[26]

[26] *Yearbook ... 1966*, vol. II, document A/6309/Rev.1, pp. 267–268, paras. (1)–(2).

26. In the event, the case of the outbreak of hostilities between States was included in article 73 of the 1969 Vienna Convention. As will be recalled, article 73 provides simply that: "The provisions of the present Convention *shall not prejudge** any question that may arise in regard to a treaty ... from the outbreak of hostilities between States."

27. With due respect, the policy considerations invoked by the Commission in 1966 (see paragraph 25 above) have a generality which limits their reference. It is necessary to produce a more realistic analysis and one which is related directly to the modalities of termination and suspension.

28. The analysis now presented rests upon the general assumption that article 65 of the 1969 Vienna Convention does not provide helpful analogies for present purposes and that the case of armed conflict (or the outbreak of hostilities) is essentially different from what may be called the standard cases of invalidity, termination or suspension represented in part V of the Convention, and to which article 65 refers. The French amendment to article 62 (as it then was) at the United Nations Conference on the Law of Treaties was intended to clarify that the procedure of notification applied to the provisions of part V *as a whole*.

Chapter IV

The special character of the "effects of armed conflicts on treaties": distinguishing elements

29. The distinguishing elements are presented in order of significance:

(*a*) In the standard cases of termination or suspension the precipitating factor is the breach of the treaty or the revelation of invalidity as such. In the case of an armed conflict or military occupation, the precipitating factor is normally independent of the breach of treaty or the element of invalidity concerned. In other words, the dominant element (in the sense of causation) is extraneous to the breach of the treaty provisions;

(*b*) A further and equally significant factor is that the *cause* of the termination or suspension is not the breach of the treaty concerned but the considerations of security and necessity dictated by the circumstances of the armed conflict. It is in this respect particularly clear that the case of armed conflict is not a paradigm of the other cases of termination or suspension recognized in the 1969 Vienna Convention. It is also reasonably clear that the policy choice between termination and suspension is driven by elements of security and proportionate response. In other words, the policy elements include elements of necessity;

(*c*) The special character of the case of armed conflict can be illustrated by reference to the polarity between the Commission debates leading to article 65 and the practical consequences of an armed conflict. The focus of attention in the Commission was the appearance of the elements of a legal dispute, and the consequential need for provision for peaceful settlement and, in particular, the creation of an obligation concerning dispute settlement. The provisions of article 65 directly reflect those concerns;

(*d*) In the circumstances of an armed conflict, the significance of peaceful settlement as a procedural safeguard is reduced if not eliminated. Indeed, the peaceful settlement scenario will be transformed by the incidence of an armed conflict. Moreover, identification of the legal dispute or disputes will be complex. The factors involved would result in a sequence of related disputes, as follows:

(i) The original act of termination of a treaty and the resulting notification, coupled with an objection;

(ii) A dispute as to the implementation of the provisions of article 67 of the 1969 Vienna Convention;

(iii) The legality of the armed conflict, both as to the progenitor, and the responsive measures of the target State, as additional sources of dispute;

(iv) The issues concerning the legality of countermeasures taken by the State party which objects in face of a notification of termination or suspension;

(v) Also to be taken into account would be special legal factors conditioning the application of the provisions concerning notification and objection, stemming from the legal duty not to terminate or suspend the operation of a treaty if the effect would be to benefit an aggressor State.

Chapter V

The modalities of notification in cases of armed conflict

30. In the light of the considerations set forth above, it may be asked whether the duty of notification can realistically feature in a set of provisions relating to the incidence of an armed conflict. After careful consideration, the Special Rapporteur has concluded that the role of notification cannot be ruled out *ab initio*.

31. The reasons for this conclusion are as follows. In the first place, notification, even in cases of armed conflict, constitutes a part of the procedural safeguards militating against unilateral action, and creating inducements to resort to a process of dispute settlement.

32. In addition, notification will remain feasible in the situations in which normal relations are maintained to a certain extent, in spite of the existence of an armed conflict. It is clear that the circumstances of armed conflict are very varied.

33. A further, and very significant, legal factor is the effect of draft article 3 in the third report on the effects of armed conflicts on treaties,[27] according to which the outbreak of an armed conflict "does not necessarily terminate or suspend the operation of treaties". The process of notification is congruent with this regime of stability.

34. In the light of these considerations there is a certain case for maintaining a set of provisions concerning the modalities of termination and suspension. An efficient version of such provisions is to be found in draft article 26 as proposed by Mr. G. Fitzmaurice in his second report on the law of treaties[28] as follows:

The process of termination or withdrawal by notice (modalities)

1. In order to be valid and effective, notice of termination or withdrawal must, whether given under a treaty or other special agreement of the parties, or in consequence of a ground arising by operation of law, comply with the conditions specified in paragraphs 2 to 9 below, it being understood that any reference to a treaty includes any separate agreement of the parties providing for termination in relation to the treaty.

2. Any notice given under a treaty must comply with the conditions specified in the treaty, and must be given in the circumstances and manner therein indicated. Where the notice is not given under the treaty but in the exercise of a faculty conferred by operation of law, it must state the date on which it purports to take effect, and the period of notice specified must be a reasonable one having regard to the character of the treaty and the surrounding circumstances. Except as provided in the remaining paragraphs of the present article, any failure or irregularity in the foregoing respects will render the notice inoperative, unless, either expressly or tacitly (by conduct or non-objection), all the other parties accept it as good.

3. All notices must be formally communicated to the appropriate quarter in accordance with paragraph 2 of article 25 above. It is not sufficient to announce termination or withdrawal or give notice of it publicly, or publish it [in] the press. In the case of bilateral treaties, notice is given to the other party. In the case of plurilateral or multilateral treaties it must be given to each of the other parties individually, unless the treaty enables notice to be given to a "headquarters" government, international organization or other specified authority.

4. Notices take effect on the date of their deposit with the appropriate authority, and any period to which the notice is subject runs from then. In the case of notices given to several governments in respect of the same treaty, a uniform date must be indicated in the notices, and the moment of their communication must, so far as possible, be synchronized.

5. Where the treaty requires a specified period of notice, or only permits of notice to take effect at the end of certain periods, and a notice is given purporting to take effect immediately, or after a shorter period than the one specified, the notice will not be void, but (if it is a notice given under the treaty) will take effect only on the expiry of the correct period as indicated in the treaty. If, however, and whether or not the treaty allows notice to be given under certain conditions, the notice in question does not purport to be given under the treaty, but in the exercise of a faculty conferred by law, the question of the period of notice will be governed by the relevant provisions of paragraph 2 above, and the notice will not take effect before the expiry of a reasonable period.

6. Unless the treaty expressly so permits, notices of termination or withdrawal must be unconditional. Except as so provided, an intimation, public declaration or announcement that a party will terminate or withdraw from a treaty in certain events, or unless certain conditions are fulfilled, does not constitute an actual notice of termination or withdrawal, and will require to be completed by an unconditional notice in due course.

7. Except where the treaty expressly provides for the separate termination or denunciation of, or withdrawal from, some particular part of, or certain individual clauses of the treaty, any notice of termination or withdrawal must relate to the treaty as a whole. In the absence of such express provision, a partial notice is invalid and inoperative.

8. Equally, unless the contrary is both stated in the notice, and permitted by the treaty, a notice of termination or withdrawal applies automatically to all annexes, protocols, notes, letters and declarations attached to the treaty and forming an integral part of it, in the sense that they are without significant meaning or effect apart from, or in the absence of, the treaty.

9. Unless the treaty otherwise provides, any notice of termination or withdrawal may be cancelled or revoked at any time before it takes effect or before the expiry of the period of notice to which it is subject; provided that such cancellation or revocation receives the assent of any other party which, in consequence of the original notification of termination or withdrawal, has itself given such a notification or has otherwise changed its position.[29]

35. This set of provisions is to be preferred to the content of article 65 of the 1969 Vienna Convention for the following reasons. In the first place, the drafts presented by the subsequent Special Rapporteur, Sir Humphrey Waldock, were not successors to the Fitzmaurice draft (as in paragraph 34 above), but were antecedents of what became article 65 of the Convention.[30] The advantage of the Fitzmaurice draft is that it provides detailed provisions directly related to the procedure of termination and suspension. The disadvantage of the Waldock draft (and its successors) is the inclusion of machinery for the compulsory settlement of disputes.

36. It is reasonably clear that the prominence of the question of dispute settlement in the Waldock draft is hardly suited to the context of an armed conflict.

---

[27] *Yearbook ... 2007*, vol. II (Part One), document A/CN.4/578, para. 15.

[28] *Yearbook ... 1957*, vol. II, p. 16, document A/CN.4/107.

[29] *Ibid.*, p. 34.

[30] See *Yearbook ... 1963*, vol. II, document A/CN.4/156 and Add.1–3, second report on the law of treaties, by Sir Humphrey Waldock, pp. 86–90, art. 25 and commentary.

Chapter VI

The absence of notice of termination or suspension in relation to an armed conflict

37. The provisions of article 65 of the 1969 Vienna Convention do not relate to the case of an armed conflict as dictated by article 73, and this appears to be true. The key question is what the result is in the following situations:

- First: The existence of armed conflict impedes the giving of notice of termination or suspension within a reasonable period

- Second: The existence of an armed conflict is the *legal cause* of the termination or suspension, but no notice is given at any stage.

38. At this stage in the analysis it must be assumed that, in certain conditions, the incidence of armed conflict may justify termination or suspension between the parties and third States. The conditions of susceptibility are set forth in the 2007 revised formulation of the Working Group on the Effects of Armed Conflicts on Treaties for draft article 4, as follows (A/CN.4/L.718, p. 4 (mimeographed)):

In order to ascertain whether a treaty is susceptible to termination or suspension in the event of armed conflict, resort shall be had to:

(*a*) Articles 31 and 32 of the Vienna Convention on the Law of Treaties; and

(*b*) The nature and extent of the armed conflict, the effect of the armed conflict on the treaty, the subject matter of the treaty and the number of parties to the treaty."

39. Two questions can now be confronted. The first is whether the regime of notice as presented by various Special Rapporteurs, and in the provisions of article 65 of the 1969 Vienna Convention, is feasible at all in relation to cases of armed conflict. The second question is this: if the regime of notice is regarded as inapplicable, what legal regime remains in place?

40. It is helpful to deal with these two questions together. There are two possible answers to the first question:

(*a*) That the regime of notice is simply not feasible;

(*b*) The application of a doctrine of waiver of the requirement of notice if the following conditions are present:

(i) Conduct of the other party constituting waiver of the requirement of notice;

(ii) Conduct of the other party indicating knowledge of the termination or suspension;

(iii) Express agreement to have recourse to recognized procedures of peaceful settlement, after the end of the armed conflict.

41. In case the principle of notice were to be ruled out as a matter of principle, as being infeasible, what legal regime would remain in place? The answer would appear to be: a legal regime broadly similar to the regime established by the provisions of the 1969 Vienna Convention. This was recognized by the Special Rapporteur, Sir Humphrey Waldock, in 1966. In his words:

The difficulty in article 51 was that despite its safeguards, its provisions on negotiations and its reference to Article 33 of the Charter, it did not deal with the possibility of a deadlock. Clearly, under article 50, if no settlement was reached after exhausting the procedures specified in article 51, the parties would be left to act on their own responsibility. That looseness was inherent in the rules of contemporary international law on the adjudication of disputes.[31]

42. At the end of the day, the procedure of notification in article 65 of the 1969 Vienna Convention, aside from its function as a safeguard of the stability of treaties, has the role of providing evidence of the existence of a dispute. However, in most circumstances it will be possible to prove the existence of a dispute by other means. It is also to be recalled that no duty of notification exists in general international law.

[31] *Yearbook ... 1966*, vol. I (Part Two), 864th meeting, p. 149, para. 14.

Chapter VII

Some conclusions

43. It is not intended to summarize the views advanced above. The purpose of this report has been to promote the formation of collective opinion within the Commission. There are certain choices to be made.

Option 1

44. The first possibility is to decide that there is no sufficient justification for a regime of notification similar to the content of article 65 of the 1969 Vienna Convention.

Option 2

45. The second option is to maintain a regime of notification which would reflect the considerations set forth in paragraphs 30–34 above. Such a regime could be based upon the drafts produced by Mr. G. Fitzmaurice in his second report. The relevant drafts are as follows:

Draft article 8 bis. *The act of termination of withdrawal*

1. The act and process of terminating or withdrawing from a treaty by any party is an executive one, and, on the international plane, the

function of the executive authority of the State. This applies whether the act consists of (i) a notice given under the treaty itself, or under a separate agreement of the parties, or in consequence of a ground of termination or suspension arising by operation of law; (ii) entering into a direct terminating agreement, or a replacing, revising or modifying treaty; or (iii) an acceptance of an invalid or irregular notice of termination, or of a repudiation. Consequently, the provisions of article 9 (The exercise of the treaty-making power) in the introduction to the present Code (A/CN.4/101) apply mutatis mutandis to the process of termination and withdrawal in the same way as they do to that of the making and conclusion of treaties.

2. A notice of termination or withdrawal consists, on the international plane, of a formal instrument or notification emanating from the competent executive authority of the State, and communicated through the diplomatic or other accredited channel to the other party or parties to the treaty, or to such "headquarters" government or authority as the treaty may specify, signifying the intention of the party concerned to terminate the treaty, or withdraw from participation in it, on the expiry of the required or appropriate period of notice.[32]

Draft article 8 ter. *The process of termination or withdrawal by notice*[33]

46. For the reasons given in paragraphs 35–36 above, this set of provisions is to be preferred to the content of article 65 of the 1969 Vienna Convention.

[32] *Yearbook ... 1957* (see footnote 28 above), p. 34, art. 25.

[33] The text of this draft article (art. 26 in the Fitzmaurice report, *ibid.*) is set forth in paragraph 34 above.

Option 3

47. There is some justification for a principle of waiver of the requirement of notice as follows:

"*Draft article 9. Loss of a right to invoke a ground for invalidating, terminating, withdrawing from or suspending the operation of a treaty*

"A State may no longer invoke a ground for invalidating, terminating, withdrawing from or suspending the operation of a treaty under articles 46 to 50 or articles 60 and 62 if, after becoming aware of the facts:

"(*a*) it shall have expressly agreed that the treaty is valid or remains in force or continues in operation, as the case may be; or

"(*b*) it must by reason of its conduct be considered as having acquiesced in the validity of the treaty or in its maintenance in force or in operation, as the case may be."

This text replicates the provisions of article 45 of the 1969 Vienna Convention.

48. The question of the separability of treaty provisions has been left aside and is the subject of a separate study.[34]

[34] A/CN.4/L.721 (reproduced in the present volume).

EFFECTS OF ARMED CONFLICTS ON TREATIES

[Agenda item 5]

DOCUMENT A/CN.4/592 and Add.1

Comments and observations received from international organizations

[Original: English]
[27 February and 21 April 2008]

CONTENTS

Multilateral instruments cited in the present report

	Source
Articles of Agreement of the International Monetary Fund (Washington, D.C., 27 December 1945)	United Nations, *Treaty Series*, vol. 2, No. 20, p. 39.
Convention on the International Maritime Organization (Geneva, 6 March 1948)	*Ibid.*, vol. 289, No. 4214, p. 3.
Consolidated version of the Treaty establishing the European Community (Rome, 25 March 1957)	*Official Journal of the European Union*, No. C 321, vol. 49 (29 December 2006), p. 174.
Vienna Convention on the Law of Treaties (Vienna, 23 May 1969)	United Nations, *Treaty Series*, vol. 1155, No. 18232, p. 331.
International Convention for the Safety of Life at Sea (London, 1 November 1974)	*Ibid.*, vol. 1184 , No. 18961, p. 2.
First ACP–EEC Convention (Lomé, 28 February 1975)	ILM, vol. 14 (1975), p. 604.
Second ACP–EEC Convention (Lomé, 31 October 1979)	United Nations, *Treaty Series*, vol. 1277, No. 21071, p. 3.
Third ACP–EEC Convention (Lomé, 8 December 1984)	*Ibid.*, vol. 1922, No. 32846, p. 3.
Fourth ACP–EEC Convention (Lomé, 15 December 1989)	*Ibid.*, vol. 1924, No. 32847, p. 3.

	Source
Agreement Amending the Fourth ACP–EC Convention of Lomé (Mauritius, 4 November 1995)	*Official Journal of the European Communities*, No. L 156, vol. 41 (29 May 1998), p. 3.
International Convention for the Prevention of Pollution from Ships, 1973 (MARPOL Convention) (London, 2 November 1973), as amended by the Protocol of 1978 (London, 17 February 1978)	*Ibid.*, vol. 1340, No. 22484, pp. 61.
International Convention on Liability and Compensation for Damage in Connection with the Carriage of Hazardous and Noxious Substances by Sea, 1996 (London, 9 May 1996) (HNS Convention)	*HNS Convention* (IMO publication, Sales No. IMO–479E). See also ILM, vol. XXXV (1996), p. 1415.
Partnership agreement between the members of the African, Caribbean and Pacific Group of States and the European Community and its member States (Cotonou, 23 June 2000)	*Official Journal of the European Communities*, No. L 317, vol. 43 (15 December 2000), p. 3.
Agreement amending the Partnership Agreement between the members of the African, Caribbean and Pacific Group of States, of the one part, and the European Community and its Member States, of the other part, signed in Cotonou on 23 June 2000 (Luxembourg, 25 June 2005)	*Official Journal of the European Union*, No. L 209 (11 August 2005), p. 27.

Works cited in the present report

BRANDTNER, Barbara and Allan ROSAS

"Human rights and the external relations of the European Community: an analysis of doctrine and practice", *European Journal of International Law*, vol. 9, 1998, pp. 468–490.

GIANVITI, François

"Some Specific Legal Features of the International Monetary Fund", *in* Robert C. Effros, ed., *Current Legal Issues Affecting Central Banks*, vol. 4. Washington, D.C., International Monetary Fund, 1997, pp. 1–15.

GOLD, Joseph

Membership and Nonmembership in the International Monetary Fund: A Study in International Law and Organization. Washington, D.C., International Monetary Fund, 1974. 683 p.

HOFFMEISTER, Frank

"Les politiques de coopération au développement et d'assistance économique, technique et financière et les droits de l'homme"", *in* Mercedes Candela Soriano, ed., *Les droits de l'homme dans les politiques de l'Union européenne.* Brussels, Larcier, 2006, pp. 255–268.

KOKOTT, Julianne

"Kommentar zu artikel 297", *in* R. Streinz, ed., *EUV/EGV: Vertrag über die Europäische Union und Vertrag zur Gründung der Europäischen Gemeinschaft.* Munich, C. H. Beck, 2003, pp. 2449–2459.

MUNDKUR, Ramanand

"Recognition of Governments in International Organizations, Including at the International Monetary Fund", *Current Developments in Monetary and Financial Law*, vol. 4, 2005, pp. 77–97.

PAASIVIRTA, Esa

"Human Rights, Diplomacy and Sanctions: Aspects to 'Human Rights Clauses' in the External Agreements of the European Union", *in* Jarna Petman and Jan Klabbers, eds., *Nordic Cosmopolitanism: Essays in International Law for Martti Koskenniemi.* Leiden, Nijhoff, 2003, pp. 155–180.

Introduction

1. At its fifty-ninth session, the International Law Commission requested the Secretariat to circulate a note to international organizations requesting information about their practice with regard to the effects of armed conflicts on treaties involving them.[1] Pursuant to that request, a letter was transmitted to selected international organizations bringing to their attention the fact that the Working Group of the International Law Commission on the effects of armed conflicts on treaties had, in 2007, recommended that the question of the inclusion (within the scope of the topic) of treaties involving intergovernmental organizations be left in abeyance until a later stage of the Commission's work on the overall topic (see A/CN.4/L.718, para. 4 (1)(*a*)(ii)). The organizations were invited to submit their comments and observations, including information on their respective practice, regarding the effects of armed conflicts on treaties involving them.

[1] *Yearbook ... 2007*, vol. II (Part Two), para. 272.

2. As at 21 April 2008, communications had been received from the following five international organizations (dates of submission in parentheses): European Bank for Reconstruction and Development (10 January 2008); European Commission (6 February 2008); International Atomic Energy Agency (26 November 2007); International Maritime Organization (9 January 2008): and the IMF (21 April 2008). While the European Bank for Reconstruction and Development and the International Atomic Energy Agency indicated that they had no comments, the written submissions of the European Commission,[2] the International Maritime Organization and IMF are reproduced below.

[2] The European Commission further forwarded to the International Law Commission a study commissioned in 1985, entitled "Protection of the Environment in Times of Armed Conflict", which, *inter alia*, considered the applicability of environmental treaties during armed conflict. In doing so, the European Commission noted that while the study did not embody its official view, it was nonetheless helpful for the work of the International Law Commission. A copy of the study is available on the website maintained by the Secretariat for the International Law Commission, located at www.un.org/law/ilc.

Comments and observations received from international organizations

A. European Commission[1]

1. The effect of armed conflict on the Treaty establishing the European Community

1. Under article 297 of the Treaty establishing the European Community, the member States shall consult each other with a view to taking together the steps needed to prevent the functioning of the common market being affected by measures which a member State may be called upon to take in the event of serious internal disturbances affecting the maintenance of law and order, in the event of war, serious international tension constituting a threat of war, or in order to carry out obligations it has accepted for the purpose of maintaining peace and international security. If such national measures have the effect of distorting the conditions of competition in the common market, the Commission shall, together with the State concerned, examine how these measures can be adjusted to the rules laid down in the Treaty (article 298 (1)). If the Commission considers that a member State is making improper use of the powers provided in article 297, it may bring the matter directly before the Court of Justice (article 298 (2)).

2. Absent an armed conflict between the member States since the foundation of the Community, these provisions only played a practical role so far when an armed conflict occurred outside the territories where the Treaty is applicable as such. In the Falkland war between the United Kingdom and Argentina, article 297 of the Treaty served as a legal basis for the United Kingdom to maintain stricter sanctions towards Argentina than those decided by the Community itself.[2] Article 297 was also invoked by Greece to justify its trade embargo against the former Yugoslav Republic of Macedonia in the early 1990s. Since the European Commission did not accept that the name dispute between the two countries fell within the scope of article 297, the European Court of Justice was seized under article 298. The latter did not take provisional measures.[3] After a resolution of the dispute in September 1995, Greece abolished the embargo and the case before the Court was discontinued.

2. The effect of armed conflict on treaties to which the European Community is a party

3. Questions on the effect of armed conflict on treaties to which the European Community is a party occur occasionally in practice. [Reference may be made to the practice of the European Commission] with respect to the conflict in the former Yugoslavia in 1991 and with respect to certain other conflicts.

(a) *The conflict in the former Yugoslavia*

4. In 1980, the European Economic Community and its member States concluded a Cooperation Agreement with the Socialist Federal Republic of Yugoslavia. The Council of the European Community approved that agreement by adopting regulation No. 314/83 of 24 January 1983.[4]

5. On 11 November 1991, the Council and the representatives of the Governments of the member States, meeting within the Council, suspended the application of the Cooperation Agreement.[5] As laid down in its preamble, the decision was motivated by several factors. First, the European Community and its member States took note of the crisis in Yugoslavia and the concern expressed by the Security Council, in resolution 713 (1991), that the prolongation of the situation constituted a threat to international peace and security. Second, it was considered that the pursuit of hostilities and their consequences on economic and trade relations constituted a radical change in the conditions under which the Cooperation Agreement was concluded; these consequences would call into question the application of the Agreement. Third, it was noted that the appeal launched by the European Community and its member States on 6 October 1991 calling for compliance with the ceasefire agreement of 4 October 1991 had not been heeded. Fourth, the European Community and its member States had announced on 6 October 1991 their decision to terminate the Cooperation Agreement, should the agreement of 4 October 1991 reached between the parties to the conflict not be observed. Transposing the decision into Community law, the Council adopted regulation No. 3300/91 suspending the trade concessions provided for by the Cooperation Agreement.[6]

6. As suspension of the application of the Agreement had direct consequences for private importers of goods from the Socialist Federal Republic of Yugoslavia to the European Community, a German court referred several preliminary questions to the European Court of Justice. In its judgment of 16 June 1998, the Court affirmed the validity of Council regulation 3300/91.[7] Holding that customary international law forms part of Community law, it scrutinized whether the Community legislator had conformed itself with the fundamental principle of *pacta sunt servanda* under article 26 of the Vienna Convention on the Law of Treaties. In that context, the Court made the following observations:

---

[1] The present submission has been reproduced as received. The designations employed and the presentation of the material in this submission do not imply the expression of any opinion whatsoever on the part of the Secretariat of the United Nations concerning the legal status of any country, territory, city or area or of its authorities, or concerning the delimitation of its frontiers or boundaries.

[2] Kokott, "Kommentar zu artikel 297", p. 2455.

[3] European Court of Justice, case C-120/94 R, *Commission of the European Communities v. Hellenic Republic*, 1994, ECR I-3037.

[4] *Official Journal of the European Communities*, No. L 41, vol. 26 (14 February 1983), p. 1.

[5] *Ibid.*, No. L 315, vol. 34 (15 November 1991), p. 47.

[6] *Ibid.*, p. 1. Council regulation (EEC) No. 3300/91 of 11 November 1991 suspending the trade concessions provided for by the Cooperation Agreement between the European Economic Community and the Socialist Federal Republic of Yugoslavia.

[7] European Court of Justice, Case C-162/96, *A. Racke GmbH & Co. v. Hauptzollamt Mainz*, [1998] ECR I-3655.

53. For it to be possible to contemplate the termination or suspension of an agreement by reason of a fundamental change of circumstances, customary international law, as codified in article 62(1) of the Vienna Convention, lays down two conditions. First, the existence of those circumstances must have constituted an essential basis of the consent of the parties to be bound by the treaty; secondly, that change must have had the effect of radically transforming the extent of the obligations still to be performed under the treaty.

54. Concerning the first condition, the preamble to the Cooperation Agreement states that the contracting parties are resolved 'to promote the development and diversification of economic, financial and trade cooperation in order to foster a better balance and an improvement in the structure of their trade and expand its volume and to improve the welfare of their populations' and that they are conscious 'of the need to take into account the significance of the new situation created by the enlargement of the Community for the organization of more harmonious economic and trade relations between the Community and the Socialist Federal Republic of Yugoslavia'. Pursuant to those considerations, article 1 of the Agreement provides that its object 'is to promote overall cooperation between the contracting parties with a view to contributing to the economic and social development of the Socialist Federal Republic of Yugoslavia and helping to strengthen relations between the parties'.

55. In view of such a wide-ranging objective, the maintenance of a situation of peace in Yugoslavia, indispensable for neighbourly relations, and the existence of institutions capable of ensuring implementation of the cooperation envisaged by the Agreement throughout the territory of Yugoslavia constituted an essential condition for initiating and pursuing that cooperation.

56. Regarding the second condition, it does not appear that, by holding in the second recital in the preamble to the disputed regulation that 'the pursuit of hostilities and their consequences on economic and trade relations, both between the republics of Yugoslavia and with the Community, constitute a radical change in the conditions under which the Cooperation Agreement between the European Economic Community and the Socialist Federal Republic of Yugoslavia and its Protocols ... were concluded' and that 'they call into question the application of such Agreements and Protocols', the Council made a manifest error of assessment.

57. While it is true, as Racke argues, that a certain volume of trade had to continue with Yugoslavia and that the Community could have continued to grant tariff concessions, the fact remains, as the Advocate General has pointed out in paragraph 93 of his Opinion, that application of the customary international law rules in question does not require an impossibility to perform obligations, and that there was no point in continuing to grant preferences, with a view to stimulating trade, in circumstances where Yugoslavia was breaking up.

58. As for the question raised in the order for reference whether, having regard to article 65 of the Vienna Convention, it was permissible to proceed with the suspension of the Cooperation Agreement with no prior notification or waiting period, this Court observes that, in the joint statements of 5, 6 and 28 October 1991, the Community and the member States announced that they would adopt restrictive measures against those parties which did not observe the ceasefire agreement of 4 October 1991 which they had signed in the presence of the President of the Council and the President of the Conference on Yugoslavia; moreover, the Community had made known during the conclusion of that agreement that it would bring the Cooperation Agreement to an end in the event of the ceasefire not being observed (*Bulletin of the European Communities* 10-1991, paragraphs 1.4.6, 1.4.7 and 1.4.16).

59. Even if such declarations do not satisfy the formal requirements laid down by article 65 of the Vienna Convention, it should be noted that the specific procedural requirements there laid down do not form part of customary international law.

60. Examination of the first question has thus disclosed no factor of such a kind as to affect the validity of the suspending regulation.

7. On 25 November 1991, the Council terminated the Cooperation Agreement[8] with a six-month notice according to article 60 (2) of the Agreement.

[8] Council decision 91/602/EEC of 25 November 1991, *Official Journal of the European Communities*, No. L 325, vol. 34 (27 November 1991), p. 23.

(b) *Certain conflicts in or between African, Caribbean and Pacific countries*

8. Over decades, the European Community and its member States have entered into contractual relations with a number of African, Caribbean and Pacific States. Following on the so-called "Lomé I–IV" agreements, the current contractual relationship is laid down in the "African, Caribbean and Pacific–European Union Partnership Agreement" signed in Cotonou on 23 June 2000 and revised in Luxembourg on 25 June 2005. According to article 9 (2) of the Agreement, fourth subparagraph, respect for human rights, democratic principles and the rule of law shall underpin the domestic and international policies of the parties and constitute the essential elements of the Agreement. Under article 11 (4) of the Agreement, "in situations of violent conflict the parties shall take all suitable action to prevent intensification of violence, to limit its territorial spread, and to facilitate a peaceful settlement of the existing disputes". Article 96 of the agreement provides for a specific consultation mechanism between the parties before either party can take appropriate measures if it considers that the other party has failed to fulfil an obligation stemming from the respect for human rights, democratic principles and the rule of law referred to in article 9 (2) of the Agreement. Such measures must be taken in accordance with international law and be proportional to the violation (article 96 (2)(*c*) of the Agreement).

9. While it is not the purpose of this communication to provide detailed comments on individual cases, it should be noted that the European Community and its member States may resort to the mechanism provided for under article 96 of the Agreement in order to suspend parts of the Agreement, as appropriate, also in reaction to the outbreak of non-international armed conflict in a partner country if and insofar as large-scale violations of human rights law occur as a consequence of that conflict.[9] The same is true if the army of a partner country commits serious human rights violations during an armed conflict with another country.[10] More details on Community practice in this area can be drawn from academic literature.[11]

[9] Commission of the European Communities, "Communication from the Commission to the Council and the European Parliament—Co-operation with ACP Countries Involved in Armed Conflicts", Brussels, 19 May 1999, COM (1999) 240 final, p. 4, annex 1. The communication refers to article 366a of the Lomé IV Convention, which is the predecessor of article 96 of the Cotonou Agreements, as the legal basis for suspending the agreement "in case of serious violations of human rights or of other essential elements referred to in article 5 of the Lomé Convention as a consequence of armed conflicts, the European Community shall request consultations under the procedure referred to in article 366a, and may decide to suspend development cooperation or other aspects of the Convention with a given country".

[10] *Ibid.*, p. 11.

[11] See, *inter alia*, Brandtner and Rosas, "Human rights and the external relations of the European Community: an analysis of doctrine and practice"; Paasivirta, "Human rights and diplomacy: aspects to human rights clauses in the European Union's external agreements"; Hoffmeister, "Les politiques de coopération au développement et d'assistance économique, technique et financière et les droits de l'homme", especially pp. 265–267.

3. Relationship of Community practice to the International Law Commission project

10. The European Commission would wish to relate the above limited practice to the draft articles of the International Law Commission project as proposed in the third report of the Special Rapporteur, Ian Brownlie.[12]

11. First, the constituent instrument of the European Community could theoretically fall within the scope of the present study as a treaty concluded between member States (article 5 of the Vienna Convention on the Law of Treaties). However, as it contains specific provisions on the effect of armed conflict on the internal market, and given the specific legal nature of the Community, member States would apply these Community rules rather than general international law rules, as codified in the project.

12. Second, with regard to treaties to which the Community is a party, the Yugoslav and the African, Caribbean and Pacific cases seem to confirm the rule in draft article 3 (*b*) on non-automatic termination or suspension. The outbreak of armed conflict in the countries concerned did not automatically have an effect on the Community treaty. Rather, such events constituted a ground for taking a decision to (partially) suspend or terminate the treaty.

13. Third, the Yugoslav case shows that both the Community legislator and the European Court of Justice regarded the outbreak of armed conflict as a fundamental change of circumstance within the meaning of article 62 of the Vienna Convention on the Law of Treaties. In that respect, Community practice would demonstrate the utility of draft article 13 (*d*).

14. Fourth, the African, Caribbean and Pacific cases evidence that the Community has a specific mechanism at its disposal to resort to the suspension of its treaty obligations facing armed conflict, if and insofar as large-scale violations of human rights occur during this conflict. This ground may fall under draft article 13 (*a*)—Suspension by common agreement of the parties—because the grounds and procedures for such suspension are previously agreed between the parties at the time when the treaty is concluded.

15. In the light of these points, it appears that there is little need to broaden the scope of the study and to adapt the present draft to the specific situation of the European Community. Rather, as it does with respect to the Vienna Convention on the Law of Treaties of 1969, the Community would possibly be in a position to have recourse to the articles, even if their scope were not formally extended to international treaties concluded by international organizations.

[12] *Yearbook ... 2007*, vol. II (Part One), document A/CN.4/578.

B. International Maritime Organization

1. The International Maritime Organization (IMO) notes the recommendation contained in paragraph 4(l)(*a*)(ii) of the report of the Working Group of the International Law Commission (A/CN.4/L.718), to the effect that the question of the inclusion of treaties involving intergovernmental organizations be left in abeyance until a later stage of the Commission's work on the overall topic.

2. At this point in time, IMO would like to offer the following comments and observations. First, IMO is the United Nations specialized agency charged with the competency to regulate the safety and security of navigation, the protection of the marine environment from shipping activities and the legal issues relating thereto. To this end, article 3(*b*) of the Convention on the International Maritime Organization, 1948, simply provides that the Organization shall "provide for the drafting of conventions, agreements, or other suitable instruments, and recommend these to Governments and to intergovernmental organizations, and convene such conferences as may be necessary". The IMO Convention does not contain any provisions about its operation or the activities of IMO in times of war, nor does it specify whether the conventions (now numbering 51) and other numerous instruments of less than treaty status adopted under the auspices of IMO should continue to operate during times of war.

3. Secondly, in general, the treaty instruments adopted under the auspices of IMO, including those relating to the protection of the environment, apply to ships engaged in international commercial navigation. They do not, as a rule, apply to warships or other Government vessels operating, for the time being, for other non-commercial purposes, even in times of peace. This position is sometimes, but not always, reflected in the conventions adopted by IMO. For example, the International Convention for the Safety of Life at Sea, 1974, which is the main IMO convention dealing with the safety and security of ships, and which is adhered to by ships comprising over 98 per cent of the world's tonnage, contains no provisions at all relating either to its application to warships, or to the effects of armed conflicts. The presumption is that the Convention is not applicable to warships at all. The further question, i.e. whether this Convention would continue to apply to commercial vessels during periods of armed conflicts, and if so to what extent, would appear to depend therefore upon general principles of treaty law.

4. By comparison, article 3(3) of the International Convention for the Prevention of Pollution from Ships as (MARPOL Convention), modified by the Protocol of 1978 relating thereto, provides:

> The present Convention shall not apply to any warship, naval auxiliary or other ship owned or operated by a State and used, for the time being, only on Government non-commercial service. However, each Party shall ensure by the adoption of appropriate measures not impairing the operations or operational capabilities of such ships owned or operated by it, that such ships act in a manner consistent, so far as is reasonable and practicable, with the present Convention.

5. Another variation on this theme is the formulation contained in paragraphs 4 and 5 of article 4 of the International Convention on Liability and Compensation for Damage in Connection with the Carriage of Hazardous and Noxious Substances by Sea, 1996 (HNS Convention), which provide as follows:

> 4. Except as provided in paragraph 5, the provisions of this Convention shall not apply to warships, naval auxiliary or other ships owned or operated by a State and used, for the time being, only on Government non-commercial service.

5. A State Party may decide to apply this Convention to its warships or other vessels described in paragraph 4, in which case it shall notify the Secretary-General thereof specifying the terms and conditions of such application.

6. While the provisions contained in the MARPOL and HNS Conventions clearly apply to Governments during times of peace, again the Conventions are silent as to their continued operation during periods of armed conflict, even for commercial vessels.

7. It could be assumed that a situation of peace between the States party thereto is essential for their good operation, however, to our knowledge, the matter has never been raised or discussed at IMO. Given the multinational character of all of these treaties, it is difficult to see how they could continue to operate fully in times of armed conflict, if they continue to operate at all.

8. There are several other treaties involving IMO, perhaps the most important of which are the Agreement between the International Maritime Organization and the Government of the United Kingdom of Great Britain and Northern Ireland Regarding the Headquarters of the Organization, 1968[1] and the Agreement between the International Maritime Organization and the Government of Sweden Regarding the World Maritime University, 1983.[2] Other notable agreements are those with the United Nations and some of its bodies, as well as various agreements of cooperation with other international organizations. None of them deal with the effects of armed conflicts on their operation. While some of their provisions might be capable of application during periods of armed conflict, other provisions, if not the treaties in their entirety, would doubtless be suspended for the duration.

[1] Agreement regarding the Headquarters of the Organization (London, 28 November 1968), United Nations, *Treaty Series*, vol. 677, No. 9632, p. 3.

[2] Agreement regarding the World Maritime University (London, 9 February 1983), *Ibid.*, vol. 1409, No. 23595, p. 233.

C. International Monetary Fund

1. In the context of its study of draft articles regarding the effects of armed conflicts on treaties, the International Law Commission has requested information from international organizations about their practices with regard to the effects of armed conflicts on treaties involving them. Currently, the definition of "treaty" under draft article 2 excludes treaties between States and international organizations and between international organizations, and the question of the inclusion of treaties involving international organizations has been left in abeyance until a later stage of the Commission's work on the overall topic.

2. The International Monetary Fund (IMF) has no experience with respect to the effects of armed conflicts on treaties between IMF and States or international organizations. However, IMF has ample experience with respect to the effects of armed conflicts on IMF members under its Articles of Agreement. For purposes of analysing and distilling this experience, it is important to recognize two general principles.

3. First, armed conflicts do not affect an IMF member's membership status unless, as a result of the conflict, the international community no longer recognizes the member as a "country" within the meaning of the Articles of Agreement (e.g. due to dissolution or annexation).

4. Second, even if the armed conflict does not change the status of a member as a country, it may have an impact on the member's Government and, thereby, the ability of the member to exercise its rights and obligations under the Articles.

1. Armed conflicts and International Monetary Fund membership

5. Unless an armed conflict affects a member's status as a country within the meaning of the Articles of Agreement, the country will remain a Fund member. Thus, an IMF member under military occupation by another country retains its membership in IMF. For instance, when Iraq was occupied in 2003, it retained its IMF membership. Similarly, when Iraq occupied Kuwait in 1990–1991, Kuwait retained its IMF membership. Moreover, when, because of an armed conflict, a part of an IMF member secedes from an IMF member and that secession is recognized by the international community, the IMF member retains its IMF membership and the seceding country would need to apply for IMF membership (as an independent country)[1] if interested in IMF membership. For instance, in 1971, following an internal armed conflict, Bangladesh seceded from Pakistan, applied for IMF membership and subsequently became an IMF member in 1972. Pakistan retained its IMF membership.

6. However, if as a result of an armed conflict, the international community has formed a view that a country no longer exists, membership is terminated. Thus, IMF membership would terminate if the IMF member ceased to exist as a result of either annexation or dissolution. With respect to dissolution, a recent example is the dissolution of the Socialist Federal Republic of Yugoslavia. Upon the Fund's determination of the dissolution of that country in 1992 (which took into account the views of the international community), its membership in the Fund terminated. The Fund also determined (again taking into account the views of the international community) that there were five successor countries to the Socialist Federal Republic of Yugoslavia, all of which were eligible to succeed to its membership in the Fund.[2]

[1] The country would need to apply for IMF membership under article II, section 2, of the Articles of Agreement and to meet the IMF membership criteria, which in IMF practice have been: (*a*) the applicant is a "country", (*b*) the country is in formal control of its external relations, (*c*) the country is willing to perform the obligations of membership as set out in the Articles and (*d*) the country is able to perform the obligations of membership as set out in the Articles (see Gold, *Membership and Nonmembership in the International Monetary Fund: A Study in International Law and Organization* pp. 41–42).

[2] Croatia (on 15 January 1993), Slovenia (on 15 January 1993), the former Yugoslav Republic of Macedonia (on 21 April 1993), Bosnia and Herzegovina (on 20 December 1995), and the Federal Republic of Yugoslavia (on 20 December 2000) succeeded to the membership in the Fund of the former Socialist Federal Republic of Yugoslavia, in each case, effective 14 December 1992. See Francois Gianviti, "Some specific legal features of the International Monetary Fund", pp. 1–15.

2. Effects of armed conflicts on the Government of a member of the International Monetary Fund

7. IMF members exercise their membership rights through their Governments, and armed conflicts may affect such Governments. While countries—not Governments—are IMF members (see article II of the Articles of Agreement), a member's relations with IMF are exercised through its Government. Accordingly, only the Government of a member with which IMF can carry on its activities may exercise its membership rights (e.g. use of Fund resources). As a result of an armed conflict, there may be situations where a determination is made that there is no Government that can exercise the rights of a member. This situation existed for a period following the occupation of Iraq in 2003. Moreover, since October 1992, IMF has concluded that there is no effective Government in Somalia with which IMF could carry on its activities with Somalia. In some cases, the Fund may determine that, as a result of the conflict, a Government continues to exist, but that it exists in exile. Following a coup in 1991 in Haiti, the IMF Board of Governors decided (again, reflecting the views of the international community) to deal with the authority in exile, rather than the authority in effective control, as the member country's Government. Where an armed conflict leads to an occupation of a member and, as a result, there is no longer an internationally recognized Government, the occupying Power is responsible for the performance of the occupied member's obligations under the Articles of Agreement.[3] Consistent with the approach that it takes with respect to the status of a member as a "country", the above determinations by IMF as to whether to recognize a Government is largely informed by the views of the international community. If there is no clear guidance from the international community, IMF staff will determine whether a majority of IMF members (in terms of voting power) recognize or deal with the authority as a Government in their bilateral relations.[4]

[3] See Article XXXI, section 2 (*g*), of the Articles of Agreement.

[4] See Mundkur, "Recognition of Governments in international organizations, including at the International Monetary Fund", pp. 77–97.

EFFECTS OF ARMED CONFLICTS ON TREATIES

[Agenda item 5]

DOCUMENT A/CN.4/L.721

Note by the Chairperson of the Working Group on effects of armed conflicts on treaties: Draft article 8

[*Original: English*]
[*5 May 2008*]

CONTENTS

Introduction

1. The present Note is not in the nature of a report. It is a summary examination of the problems inherent in draft article 8 of the draft articles, intended to present to the Working Group some reflections on how these problems could be solved. As things stand (see third report of the Special Rapporteur,[1] Annex), draft article 8 of the draft articles runs as follows:

Draft article 8: Mode of suspension or termination

In case of an armed conflict the mode of suspension or termination shall be the same as on those forms of suspension or termination included in the provision of articles 42 to 45 of the Vienna Convention on the law of treaties.

[1] *Yearbook ... 2007*, vol. II (Part One), document A/CN.4/578, annex.

2. Draft article 8 seeks to answer the question of whether articles 42 to 45 of the Vienna Convention on the law of treaties[2] (hereinafter the 1969 Vienna Convention) should apply in the context of the present draft articles, and the present Note only covers that question. The issue of notification, addressed by articles 65 and following of the 1969 Vienna Convention, is dealt with in the Special Rapporteur's fourth report[3] which, at paragraphs 43–47, offers three options.

[2] Signed in Vienna, 23 May 1969 (United Nations, *Treaty Series*, vol. 1155, No. 18232, p. 331).

[3] Document A/CN.4/589, reproduced in the present volume.

I. Situations covered by the draft articles

3. The present version of the articles basically covers three types of situations:

(*a*) international armed conflicts involving all or several of the parties to a treaty or one of them;

(*b*) internal armed conflicts susceptible of affecting the performance of a treaty by the State party to the conflict;

(*c*) international or internal armed conflicts involving one or several States members of an international organization which, on account of such a conflict, may experience difficulties in performing some of the obligations established by the organization's constitutive treaty or related agreements.

The last-mentioned instruments would seem to be within the purview of the present draft, unlike treaties concluded by international organizations.

4. The third hypothesis is not of central importance. If it were to arise, one could say that separability rather than withdrawal from or suspension of the whole treaty for the States concerned should be the rule; in addition, the fate of treaty obligations in that context is likely to be determined by the treaty itself. The second hypothesis comes close to the situation envisaged in article 62 of the 1969 Vienna Convention (fundamental change of circumstances), so that a reference to articles 42–45 does not appear wholly absurd. The essential problem arises in the first hypothesis, i.e. situations involving all or several States parties to a treaty whose relations are perturbed by armed conflict. It is here that the problem of the applicability of articles 42–45 of the Vienna Convention, especially of article 44 (separability of treaty provisions), arises in acute form. That problem can be approached and solved by a process of elimination.

II. References to be retained in draft article 8

A. The references to articles 42, 43 and 45 of the 1969 Vienna Convention

5. As far as article 42 of the 1969 Vienna Convention is concerned, one should point out immediately that article 73 of that same Convention prescribes that the provisions of the latter "shall not prejudge any question that may arise in regard to a treaty ... from the outbreak of hostilities between States". Whatever may be the precise meaning of "hostilities", it is evident that article 73 excludes the effects of armed conflicts on treaties from the purview of the Vienna Convention. Therefore, one cannot say, as is done in article 42, paragraph 2, that "the termination of a treaty, its denunciation or the withdrawal of a party may take place only as a result of the application of the provisions of the treaty or of the present [Vienna] Convention", or one may do so only in the framework of the Vienna Convention, but not in that of separate articles on the effects of armed conflicts on treaties. In other words, article 42 is not relevant in the present context, which is why it should not be mentioned in the future draft article 8 of the draft articles.

6. Under article 43 of the 1969 Vienna Convention, the termination of a treaty, withdrawal and the suspension of its operation, as a result of "the application of the present Convention" or of the provisions of the treaty "shall not in any way impair the duty of any State to fulfil any obligation embodied in the treaty to which it would be subject under international law independently of the treaty". This provision reflects a rule of general international law which applies even in the absence of article 43; but there was certainly no harm in including it in the Vienna Convention. Nor would there be any harm in restating it in the draft articles on the Effect of Armed Conflicts on Treaties, were it not for the phrase "as a result of the application of the present Convention". This is why, if the future draft article 8 of the draft articles is to embody a reference to article 43, it would be prudent to add to the reference the expression "*mutatis mutandis*" or language to a similar effect.

7. Article 45 appears relevant: if a State expressly agrees that a treaty remains in force or continues to operate, or if that treaty must be considered as being maintained by reason of that State's conduct despite the outbreak of an armed conflict, there is no reason not to recognize that such circumstances deprive the State concerned of the right to terminate or suspend the treaty or to withdraw from it. Accordingly, a reference to article 45 seems possible unless the third option proposed on page 20 of the Special Rapporteur's fourth report is retained. Moreover, the inclusion of the words "*mutatis mutandis*" seems appropriate since the scope of article 45 is limited to the grounds of invalidation, termination, withdrawal or suspension listed in articles 45–50 and 50–52, respectively, of the Vienna Convention.

B. The reference to article 44 of the 1969 Vienna Convention

8. It now remains to examine the problems connected with article 44 of the 1969 Vienna Convention (separability). Here again, one may proceed by elimination.

9. Article 44, paragraphs 1 and 2, establish a principle or presumption of non-separability. As the Special Rapporteur points out in his fourth report, armed conflicts are cataclysmal events in the life of treaties, certainly more so than other grounds of termination, withdrawal or suspension. Accordingly, and *a fortiori*, the principle of non-separability should be retained in the context of armed conflict as well. In other words, draft article 8 of the draft articles may include a reference to article 44, paragraphs 1 and 2 of the 1969 Vienna Convention.

10. Article 44, paragraph 5 of that Convention concerns the specific grounds set forth in articles 51–53 (coercion of State representative, coercion of State, conflict with existing *jus cogens*). This has nothing to do with the effect of armed conflicts on treaties, which is why no reference should be made to that provision.

11. The same situation prevails in respect of article 44, paragraph 4 of the 1969 Vienna Convention, which relates to the specific grounds set forth in articles 49 and 50 of that instrument (fraud, corruption of a representative of a State). This being the case, no mention of article 44, paragraph 4 should appear in draft article 8 of the draft articles.

12. It now remains to examine article 44, paragraphs 3 of the 1969 Vienna Convention, which allows Contracting States to terminate, suspend, or withdraw from a treaty only with respect to particular clauses if all the following conditions are met: (*a*) the ground of termination, suspension

or withdrawal exclusively relates to a particular clause, or particular clauses, of the treaty (article 44, paragraph 3, chapeau); (*b*) the clause or clauses are separable from the remainder of the treaty with regard to their application; (*c*) the clause(s) to be terminated, suspended or withdrawn from were not an essential basis of the consent of the other party or parties to be bound by the treaty as a whole; and (*d*) the performance of the treaty's surviving clauses would not be unjust.

13. A first question to be raised is whether the outbreak of an armed conflict can affect only a particular clause, or particular clauses, of a treaty. That this is possible can be shown by taking the example of a treaty on boundaries and a boundary regime between two States now at war: the boundary provisions undoubtedly survive, whereas the boundary regime will at least be suspended. Similarly, part at least of a treaty will survive in situations where only one of the contracting parties is involved in the armed conflict. The same is true for States parties so involved which are members of international organizations. Here, in fact, things are "the other way around": the organization's constitutive treaty and related agreements survive, also for belligerent States (see the Iraq/Islamic Republic of Iran war), but the belligerents may have become unable to meet certain treaty obligations.

14. So, although armed conflicts are cataclysmic in nature, it seems possible that treaty clauses survive if the parties so agree despite the conflict, or if the cumulative conditions of article 44, paragraph 3 are met.

15. The conditions listed in article 44, paragraph 3, will have to be interpreted taking account of the specific circumstances of the case. The question of how to interpret these conditions is beyond the scope of this Note. But it can certainly not be said that they are wholly irrelevant when it comes to gauging the effects of armed conflicts on treaties.

III. Conclusion: Possible solutions

16. The brief examination in this Note shows:

(*a*) that no reference should be made to article 42 of the 1969 Vienna Convention;

(*b*) that a reference to article 43 of the 1969 Vienna Convention is possible if the words "*mutatis mutandis*" are added;

(*c*) that reference can be made to article 45 of the 1969 Vienna Convention, also adding the words "*mutatis mutandis*", provided that the language to be used in matters of notification is not borrowed from article 45 (option 3 in the Special Rapporteur's fourth report[4]); and

(*d*) that regarding article 44 of the 1969 Vienna Convention, reference may be made to paragraphs 1 to 3 but not paragraphs 4 and 5.

17. On the basis of the above conclusions, the following options could be discussed:

(*a*) *Option A*—No reference to articles of part V, section 1, of the 1969 Vienna Convention. The rationale of this option would be that it is not necessary to say everything in the draft articles, the drawback being, of course, that the question of separability would be eluded;

(*b*) *Option B*—Inclusion in the draft articles of a provision fully reproducing the (adapted) provisions of articles 43; 44, paragraphs 1–3; and 45 (unless the language of article 45 is used for the article on notification). Advantages: greatest possible clarity, especially about separability. Drawback: relative complexity;

(*c*) *Option C*—Language along the lines of draft article 8 of the draft articles as presented in the Special Rapporteur's third report[5] and reference to articles 43 (*mutatis mutandis*); 44, paragraphs 1–3; and 45 (*mutatis mutandis*), unless the latter's language is used in the article on notification.[6] Advantages: relative clarity, in particular, on the issue of separability; relative simplicity. Drawback: the clarity is not complete.

18. In the context of options B and C, it would be desirable entirely to separate the reference to part V, section 1, of the 1969 Vienna Convention from the issue of notification.

[4] If that option were chosen, the language of article 45 to be used in a possible new provision on notification would have to be adapted as well as by eliminating the references to articles 45–50, 60 and 62 of the 1969 Vienna Convention.

[5] *Yearbook ... 2007*, vol. II (Part One), document A/CN.4/578, Annex, p. 66. Perhaps that language ought to be modified somewhat. The expression "mode of suspension or termination" ("withdrawal" should be added) could be changed into "modes".

[6] "*Mutatis mutandis*" could also be used so as to apply to all the references made in draft article 8. And if recourse to such language in the body of the article were regarded as cumbersome, qualifications could be formulated in the commentary on draft article 8.

EXPULSION OF ALIENS

[Agenda item 6]

DOCUMENT A/CN.4/594

Fourth report on the expulsion of aliens,* by Mr. Maurice Kamto, Special Rapporteur

[*Original: French*]
[*24 March 2008*]

CONTENTS

Multilateral instruments cited in the present report

	Source
Convention regarding the Status of Aliens in the respective Territories of the Contracting Parties (Havana, 20 February 1928)	League of Nations, *Treaty Series*, vol. CXXXII, No. 3045, p. 301.
Convention on Certain Questions relating to the Conflict of Nationality Laws (The Hague, 12 April 1930)	*Ibid.*, vol. CLXXIX, No. 4137, p. 89.
Convention on the Reduction of Statelessness (New York, 30 August 1961)	United Nations, *Treaty Series*, vol. 989, No. 14458, p. 175.
Convention on reduction of cases of multiple nationality and military obligations in cases of multiple nationality (Strasbourg, 6 May 1963)	*Ibid.*, vol. 634, No. 9065, p. 221.
Second Protocol amending the above-mentioned Convention (Strasbourg, 2 February 1993)	*Ibid.*, vol. 1967, No. 9065, p. 338.
International Covenant on Civil and Political Rights (New York, 16 December 1966)	*Ibid.*, vol. 999, No. 14668, p. 171.
Convention on the Rights of the Child (New York, 20 November 1989)	*Ibid.*, vol. 1577, No. 27531, p. 3.
European Convention on Nationality (Strasbourg, 6 November 1997)	*Ibid.*, vol. 2135, No. 37248, p. 213.

* The Special Rapporteur warmly acknowledges the contribution of Mr. William Worster to the preparation of the present report, in particular his important research on State practice with respect to loss of nationality and denationalization in the context of expulsion. The Special Rapporteur takes sole responsibility for the content of the present report.

Works cited in the present report

ABEL, Paul

"Denationalization", *Modern Law Review* (London), vol. VI, 1942–1943.

AMNESTY INTERNATIONAL

Myanmar—The Rohingya Minority: Fundamental Rights Denied, 18 May 2004. 38 p.

BICKERTON, Ian

"Dutch murders bring tighter terror laws", *Financial Times*, 15 July 2005, p. 6.

BOLL, Alfred M.

Multiple Nationality and International Law. Leiden, Martinus Nijhoff, 2007. 626 p. (Developments in International Law, vol. 57)

CHIROT, Daniel

"The debacle in Côte d'Ivoire", *Journal of Democracy*, vol. 17, No. 2, April 2006, pp. 63–77.

FERRETT, Grant

"Citizenship choice in Zimbabwe", BBC News, 28 February 2003 (http://news.bbc.co.uk).

GEARING, Julian

"The struggle for the Highlands: accused of endangering the environment, Thailand's tribespeople face eviction and an uncertain future", *Asiaweek*, vol. 25, No. 43, 29 October 1999.

HUMAN RIGHTS WATCH

Malaysia/Burma—Living in Limbo: Burmese Rohingyas in Malaysia, vol. 12, No. 4 (C), 1 August 2000. 78 p.

Kuwait: Promises Betrayed—Denial of Rights of Bidun, Women, and Freedom of Expression, vol. 12, No. 2 (E), 1 October 2000. 30 p.

Côte d'Ivoire—The New Racism: The Political Manipulation of Ethnicity in Côte d'Ivoire, vol. 13, No. 6 (A), 28 August 2001 (http://hrw.org). 68 p.

Eritrea and Ethiopia—The Horn of Africa War: Mass Expulsions and the Nationality Issue, vol. 15, No. 3 (A), 29 January 2003. 64 p.

KIDANE, Won

"Civil liability for violations of international humanitarian law: the jurisprudence of the Eritrea–Ethiopia Claims Commission in The Hague", *Wisconsin International Law Journal*, vol. 25, 2007–2008, pp. 23–87.

KOJANEC, Giovanni

"Multiple nationality", *Proceedings of the First European Conference on Nationality: Trends and Developments in National and International Law on Nationality, Strasbourg*, 18–19 October 1999, Council of Europe, (CONF/NAT (99) PRO 1, of 3 February 2000), pp. 35–47.

KOSLOWSKI, Rey

"Challenges of international cooperation in a world of increasing dual nationality", in David A. Martin and Kay Hailbronner, eds., *Rights and Duties of Dual Nationals: Evolution and Prospects*. The Hague, Kluwer Law International, 2003, pp. 157–182.

MACAN-MARKAR, Marwaan

"Thailand: fear of expulsion haunts hill tribes", *Asia Times*, 30 July 2003.

MAYER, Ann Elizabeth

"A 'benign' apartheid: how gender apartheid has been rationalized", *UCLA Journal of International Law and Foreign Affairs*, vol. 5, No. 2, 2000–2001, pp. 237–338.

MBARIA, John

"Meet the Nubians, Nairobi's fifth-generation 'foreigners'", *East African* (Kenya), 15 July 2002, part 2, p. 1.

MCDOUGAL, Myres S., Harold D. LASSWELL and Lung-chu CHEN

"Nationality and human rights: the protection of the individual in external arenas", *Yale Law Journal*, vol. 83, No. 5, April 1974, pp. 900–908.

MEYER, Peter and others

The Jews in the Soviet Satellites. Syracuse, N.Y., Syracuse University Press, 1953. 637 p.

PIOTROWICZ, Ryszard W.

"The Australian–Hungarian consular treaty of 1988 and the regulation of dual nationality", *Sydney Law Review*, vol. 12, No. 2/3, March 1990, pp. 569–583.

ROTH, Cecil

The History of the Jews of Italy. Philadelphia, Jewish Publication Society of America, 1946. 575 p.

RUDKO, Mykola

"Regulation of multiple nationality by bilateral and multilateral agreements", *Proceedings of the Second European Conference on Nationality: Challenges to National and International Law at the Beginning of the New Millennium, Strasbourg, 8–9 October 2001*, Council of Europe, (CONF/NAT (2001) PRO of 10 December 2001), pp. 109–128.

SALMON, Jean, ed.

Dictionnaire de droit international public. Brussels, Bruylant, 2001. 1198 p.

SARKIN, Jeremy

"Towards finding a solution for the problems created by the politics of identity in the Democratic Republic of the Congo (DRC): designing a constitutional framework for peaceful cooperation", *Politics of Identity and Exclusion in Africa: From Violent Confrontation to Peaceful Cooperation*. Conference held at Senate Hall, University of Pretoria, South Africa, 25–26 July 2001, pp. 67–80.

SHAVER, Lynn

"The revocation of dual citizenship in Turkmenistan", *Human Rights Brief*, vol. 11, No. 1, 2003, pp. 4–6.

UNITED NATIONS

The United Nations and Independence of Eritrea. United Nations publication, Sales No. E.96.I.10. (Blue Books Series, vol. XII)

UNITED STATES OF AMERICA DEPARTMENT OF STATE

"Kuwait", *Country Reports on Human Rights Practices for 2003*. Vol. II. Washington, D.C., U.S. Government Printing Office, 2004, pp. 1941–1963.

UNITED STATES OFFICE OF PERSONNEL MANAGEMENT

Investigations Service. *Citizenship Laws of the World* (IS–1 of March 2001). Washington D.C., Library of Congress, 2001. 233 p.

Introduction

1. During the International Law Commission's consideration, at its fifty-ninth session (7 May–5 June and 9 July–10 August 2007), of the third report on the expulsion of aliens,[1] in particular draft article 4 (Non-expulsion by a State of its own nationals), it was observed that the issue of the expulsion of persons having two or more nationalities should be studied in more detail and resolved within draft article 4, or in a separate draft article.[2] Another viewpoint, supported by several members, was that it was not appropriate to address the topic in that context, especially if the Commission's intention was to help strengthen the rule prohibiting the expulsion of nationals.[3] However, the Commission cannot dismiss the issue without first exploring it in more depth.

[1] *Yearbook ... 2007*, vol. II (Part One), document A/CN.4/581.

[2] *Yearbook ... 2007*, vol. II (Part Two), p. 57, para. 227.

[3] *Ibid.*, p. 57, para. 228.

2. It was also observed that the issue of deprivation of nationality, which was sometimes used as a preliminary to expulsion, deserved thorough study.[4]

3. With regard to his third report on the expulsion of aliens, the Special Rapporteur observed that it was not desirable to deal with the issue of dual nationals in connection with draft article 4, as protection from expulsion should be provided in respect of any State of which a person was a national. He believed that the issue could, in particular, have an impact in the context of diplomatic protection in cases of unlawful expulsion. However, in order to respond to the questions posed by several members, the Special Rapporteur planned to analyse further the issue of expulsion of dual nationals and the question of deprivation of nationality as a prelude to expulsion.[5] Such is the purpose of the present report.

[4] *Ibid.*, p. 57, para. 227.

[5] *Ibid.*, p. 60, para. 261.

Chapter I

Expulsion in cases of dual or multiple nationality

4. Nationality is essentially governed by internal law, albeit within the limits set by international law. This language from the preamble to the Commission's articles on the nationality of natural persons in relation to the succession of States[6] reflects an old idea expressed, *inter alia*, in the Convention on Certain Questions relating to the Conflict of Nationality Laws, which provides that:

> It is for each State to determine under its own law who are its nationals. This law shall be recognised by other States in so far as it is consistent with international conventions, international custom, and the principles of law generally recognised with regard to nationality.[7]

5. It is felt that in matters of nationality, the legitimate interests of both States and individuals must be duly taken into account. Concerning the interests of individuals, the Universal Declaration of Human Rights of 10 December 1948 stipulates that everyone has the right to a nationality;[8] the International Covenant on Civil and Political Rights[9] and the Convention on the Rights of the Child[10] recognize that every child has the right to acquire a nationality; and on 30 August 1961 States adopted a Convention on the reduction of statelessness. Likewise, the European Convention on Nationality[11] and the Commission's articles on nationality of natural persons in relation to the succession of States, of which the General Assembly took note,[12] are based on the principle of the right to a nationality. At the same time, the legitimate interests of States require acknowledgement of their freedom to confer their nationality on or withdraw it from an individual insofar as those measures are consistent with the relevant principles laid down in international law in this area. A State is thus free to establish by law the rule of sole and exclusive nationality or, conversely, to allow cases of dual or multiple nationality.

[6] See General Assembly resolution 55/153 of 12 December 2000, annex.

[7] Art. I of the Convention, which entered into force on 1 July 1937.

[8] See General Assembly resolution 217 (III) A, art. 15, para. 1.

[9] Art. 24, para. 3.

[10] Art. 7, para. 1.

[11] See article 4.

6. It should be noted that the recognition of dual or multiple nationality is a relatively recent trend. In the past, the acquisition of two or more nationalities by a single individual was discouraged in international law. In fact, until recently opposition to dual nationality was as strong as the movement to prevent statelessness. Cases of dual nationality have increased in the past few decades. Some authors have attributed this to the marital situation of women who acquire a second nationality through marriage.[13] Another factor that could be added, in this era of globalization, is the intensity of international migration and migrants' tendency to become long-term residents of their host countries, where acquisition of the nationality of those countries enables them to become better integrated into the social, political and economic system.

A. Are dual or multiple nationals aliens?

7. The issue of the expulsion of aliens poses particular legal problems when it relates to persons with dual or

[12] Art. 1 (see footnote 6 above).

[13] See Koslowski, "Challenges of international cooperation in a world of increasing dual nationality".

multiple nationality. First of all, if the individual subject to expulsion has the nationality of the expelling State, is the principle of non-expulsion of nationals strictly applicable? In other words, can a person liable to expulsion be considered an alien if he or she has not lost any of his or her nationalities? Secondly, in the light of this question, is a State in violation of international law if it expels an individual with dual nationality without first withdrawing its own nationality from that individual?

8. On the first point, some States do, in fact, treat their nationals who also hold another nationality as aliens for purposes other than expulsion. For example, Australia and Hungary have effected an exchange of notes in relation to their consular treaty under which their citizens with dual nationality are treated as aliens in the other country if they enter that country for a temporary stay using the passport of the other State with the appropriate visa.[14] Australia had already held that it could limit certain rights of its nationals, *inter alia*, by treating Australian nationals who simultaneously possessed another nationality as aliens.[15] Poland and the United States of America,[16] as well as Canada and Hungary,[17] have effected exchanges of notes relative to their respective consular treaties that contain similar provisions. It seems that these agreements were concluded to ensure that the citizens of the States concerned could return to their countries of origin after a stay abroad while retaining the nationality of the visited country.

9. In the 1928 *Georges Pinson* case before the French-Mexican Mixed Claims Commission, France submitted a claim lodged by an individual with dual French and Mexican nationality. The Commission held that "even if the case were recognised as one of double nationality from the strictly legal point of view, it would be very doubtful if the claimant could not have invoked the Convention notwithstanding, owing to the fact that the Mexican Government itself had always considered him, officially and exclusively, as a French subject".[18] It appears, in the light of this case, that States can in fact consider their nationals to be aliens if the said nationals have an additional nationality. Such an attitude tends to facilitate the expulsion of dual nationals by the State in question. It will be shown later in this report that this behaviour is not sufficient in itself to serve as a basis for expulsion insofar as the individual concerned remains a national of the expelling State until such time as the latter formally deprives him or her of its nationality, and such an individual may claim that nationality to contest the legality of the expulsion.

10. On the second point, specifically concerning the legality of expelling a person with more than one nationality if that person has not first been denationalized by the expelling State, the rule prohibiting the expulsion of a State's own nationals, proposed by the Special Rapporteur in his third report[19] and unanimously supported by the members of the Commission, tends to support the idea that such an expulsion would be contrary to international law. Yet cases of expulsion of dual nationals without prior denationalization by the expelling State are not unusual in practice. In many cases, the nationality of the individual subject to expulsion is not clear. In order to comply with the obligation of States not to expel their own nationals, some expelling States take the legal precaution of denationalizing the person concerned or refusing to recognize that the person has the nationality of that State on the ground that it has not been sufficiently established. At the same time, practices tending in the opposite direction can also be observed.

11. Requiring the expelling State to denationalize dual nationals prior to expulsion is not without risks, however: the imposition of such an obligation could undermine the expelled person's right of return. Were the expelled person to return to the expelling State, for example as a result of a change of government, this action would be complicated by the denationalization, since such a person would be treated as an alien requesting admission to a foreign State, or else the expelling State would have to restore its nationality to the person in order to enable the latter to exercise the right of return. It therefore appears that the application of a requirement to change a person's status from that of a dual national to that of an alien, by means of denationalization, prior to expulsion is not necessarily in the interest of the expelled person, whose rights the Commission seeks to offer the best possible protection through its work on the issue of the expulsion of aliens.

12. In the light of the foregoing, the Special Rapporteur is of the view that:

(*a*) The principle of the non-expulsion of nationals does not apply to persons with dual or multiple nationality unless the expulsion can lead to statelessness;

(*b*) The practice of some States and the interests of expelled persons themselves do not support the enactment of a rule prescribing denationalization of a person with dual or multiple nationality prior to expulsion.

[14] See Piotrowicz, "The Australian-Hungarian consular treaty of 1988 and the regulation of dual nationality", especially pp. 572–576.

[15] See Kojanec, "Multiple nationality". The author adds (*ibid.*, p. 43, para. 5.1): "The decision of the High Court of Australia in June 1999, according to which an Australian national possessing simultaneously another nationality may not, in application of Art. 44 of the Constitution, be elected to the Federal Parliament because of his ties to a 'foreign power', illustrates this conception."

[16] Exchange of notes (Note No. 38) of 31 May 1972 (pursuant to the Consular Convention of 31 May 1972 between Poland and the United States, entry into force on 6 July 1973, *United States Treaties and Other International Agreements*, vol. 24, part 2, no. 7642, p. 1231 (Washington, D.C., U.S. Government Printing Office, 1974): "Persons entering the Polish People's Republic for temporary visits on the basis of United States passports containing Polish entry visas will, in the period for which temporary visitor status has been accorded (in conformity with the visa's validity), be considered United States citizens by the appropriate Polish authorities for the purpose of ensuring the consular protection provided for in Article 29 of the Convention and the right of departure without further documentation, regardless of whether they may possess the citizenship of the Polish People's Republic", and vice versa.

[17] "Exchange of letters between Canada and Hungary constituting an agreement concerning certain consular matters and passports (Ottawa, 11 June 1964)" (entry into force on 25 May 1965, United Nations, *Treaty Series*, vol. 862, No. 12356, p. 257), accompanying the Trade Agreement signed the same day, *ibid.*, No. 12355, p. 233.

[18] Case No. 195, vol. 4, *Annual Digest of Public International Law Cases* (1927–1928), p. 300; see also UNRIAA, vol. V (Sales No. 1952.V.3), p. 327; see further McDougal, Lasswell and Chen, "Nationality and human rights: the protection of the individual in external arenas", pp. 900–908.

[19] *Yearbook ... 2007*, vol. II (Part One), document A/CN.4/581, p. 121, para. 57.

13. The legal issues raised by expulsion can be still more complex, depending on whether or not the expelling State is the State of dominant or effective nationality of the person subject to expulsion.

B. Is the expelling State the State of dominant or effective nationality of the person being expelled?

14. As the Special Rapporteur had already stated in his second report,[20] he will refrain from entering into a study of the conditions for acquiring nationality, the topic under examination being the expulsion of aliens and not the legal regime of nationality. The Special Rapporteur on diplomatic protection, Mr. John R. Dugard, had shown in his first report[21] the difficulties of this exercise by indicating the limits to the scope of the *Nottebohm* case, from which, in his view, a general rule should not be inferred.[22] Incidentally, the Commission's articles on nationality of natural persons in relation to the succession of States retain "habitual residence in the territory"[23] as a criterion for presumption of nationality.

15. The concept of dominant or effective nationality is established in international law and there is no need to discuss it at length here. It is sufficient to recall that it means the character the nationality possesses when it expresses the attachment of a person to a State by ties (social, cultural, linguistic, etc.) stronger than those which might link the person to another State.[24] Although in the practice of States and in the literature a preference for the expression "effective nationality" can be observed, nevertheless the two expressions are used to refer to a rule of international law applicable in the event of multiple nationality. Thus, in the *Nasser Esphahanian* v. *Bank Tejarat* case, the Iran-United States Claims Tribunal stated that the applicable rule of international law was that of dominant or effective nationality.[25]

16. The criterion of effective nationality is applied in cases of conflict of nationalities arising from multiple nationality. The principle is that the dominant nationality prevails over the other nationality or nationalities in a case of conflict of nationalities. Relating to expulsion, a distinction should be made between cases of dual nationality and multiple nationality.

17. In the case of dual nationality, it is a question of knowing which of the two States is the State of dominant nationality of the person facing expulsion. If the expelling State is the State of dominant nationality of the person in question, then in principle and logically, the State cannot expel its own national, by virtue of the rule of non-expulsion by a State of its own nationals. Contrary to the view expressed by a member of the Commission, however, this rule is not absolute, as the Special Rapporteur indicated in his third report.[26] In his final report of 20 June 1988, "The right of everyone to leave any country, including his own, and to return to his country", for the Economic and Social Council/Commission on Human Rights, Mr. C. L. C. Mubanga-Chipoya discusses a similar point of view, stating that a national of a State may be expelled from his own State with the consent of the receiving country. He writes:

> The expulsion of a national may therefore be carried out with the explicit or implicit consent of the receiving state upon whose demand the state of the national has the duty to readmit its nationals to its territory.[27]

18. According to the Special Rapporteur, however, while the consent of the State receiving the expelled person is necessary when the person does not have the nationality of that State, this requirement does not appear to apply when the aforementioned receiving State is also one of the two States of which the expelled person has nationality. For even if the receiving State is not the State of dominant or effective nationality of the expelled person, nonetheless there exists between the latter and that State formal legal ties of nationality which the expelled person can invoke if necessary. This State is required to accept its national expelled by the State of dominant nationality by virtue of a rule of international law found, for example, in the Convention regarding the Status of Aliens in the respective Territories of the Contracting Parties, whose article 6 provides that "States are required to receive their nationals expelled from foreign soil who seek to enter their territory".

19. The consent of a State to expulsion can be implicit or presumed. In the *Jama* v. *Immigration and Customs Enforcement* case,[28] the Supreme Court of the United States interpreted United States law as not prescribing prior consent of the receiving country when the United States expelled an alien. While prior consent was considered preferable, the Court ruled that the law did not require it and that it could not presume otherwise. It must be said that in this case the Government of the United States had not sought prior consent because it could not request such consent, the receiving State, Somalia, being in total decay at the time and lacking a functioning government. This interpretation could have been motivated mainly by the fact that the Court felt that the Government could not detain indefinitely an alien awaiting expulsion when the receiving State had categorically refused to accept the expelled person.[29] The Court says no more than that, for it refrained from specifically examining obligations under international law.

20. However well founded it may appear, this argument based on the general political situation in the receiving State loses sight of the rights of the individual, in particular the requirement to protect the rights of the expelled person. The chaotic situation of a country with a non-functioning government and general insecurity would not appear to be an appropriate context to receive a person

[20] *Yearbook ... 2006*, vol. II (Part One), document A/CN.4/573.

[21] *Yearbook ... 2000*, vol. II (Part One), p. 205, document A/CN.4/506 and Add.1.

[22] *Ibid.*, vol. II (Part Two), pp. 82–85.

[23] Art. 5 (see footnote 6 above).

[24] See Salmon, *Dictionnaire de droit international public*, p. 725.

[25] See *Iran–United States Claims Tribunal Reports*, vol. 2 (Cambridge, Grotius, 1984), p. 157, case no. 157, judgement of 29 March 1983.

[26] *Yearbook ... 2007*, vol. II (Part One), document A/CN.4/581, pp. 120–121, paras. 49–56.

[27] E/CN.4/Sub.2/1988/35 and Add.1 and Add.1/Corr.1, para. 116.

[28] See 543 U.S. 335 (2005).

[29] See, in this connection, *Zadvydas* v. *Davis*, 533 U.S. 678 (2001) (discussing the case of two aliens, one born in Lithuania and refused entry into Germany, and the other born in Cambodia and also refused entry by Germany, as no repatriation agreement existed).

expelled from abroad. On the contrary, the collapse of the State in a Somalia handed over to the warlords and the widespread violence of armed groups acting with extreme cruelty (the case of the United States soldiers tied to vehicles and dragged through the streets of Mogadishu comes to mind) was likely to endanger the life of the expelled person. Consequently, beyond the relationship strictly between States, the fate of the individual concerned should have been taken into account.

21. The determination of dominant nationality can prove to be particularly difficult in certain cases, as the person subject to expulsion can have more than one dominant nationality, considering that the criterion is "habitual residence", or even, in addition, economic interests. Indeed, it is not unusual for a person to spend half the year in another country where he or she also has nationality, and moreover, to hold economic interests in both countries. Expelling such a dual national to a third State does not raise any particular legal problems: if draft article 4, paragraph 2, contained in the third report[30] were to be retained, expulsion could take place in such cases only for exceptional reasons and with the consent of the receiving State. Then there is expulsion to the other State of nationality. Is such expulsion possible? And on what legal grounds? Can it take place without the consent of this receiving State or is such consent required?

22. In the view of the Special Rapporteur, when the person concerned has two equally dominant nationalities and there is no risk of statelessness arising from his or her expulsion to the other State where he or she also has nationality, expulsion can be envisaged only in two hypothetical cases:

(*a*) The expelling State allows the person concerned to retain his or her nationality: in this case it should be able to expel the person to the other State of nationality only with its consent;

(*b*) The expelling State deprives the person of his or her nationality, thereby transforming the person into an alien: in this case the ordinary law on the expulsion of aliens applies, since the expelled person becomes a person with a single nationality, now possessing only the nationality of the receiving State.

[30] *Yearbook ... 2007*, vol. II (Part One), document A/CN.4/581, p. 121, para. 57.

These reflections, which are based neither on State practice nor on any sort of jurisprudence, could at best lead to the progressive development of international law on that subject. It would still be necessary to establish the practical need for such development of the law, which the Special Rapporteur doubts.

23. The problem appears even more complex when the expulsion involves a person with several nationalities. In this case, the conflict of nationalities would concern not just two States as in the case of dual nationality, but at least three States, or even more. If only one or two of these States is the State of dominant nationality of the person facing expulsion, the preceding reasoning in the event of expulsion by one of the States of dominant nationality to the other State of dominant nationality should apply. On the other hand, different problems arise if the expulsion takes place from a State of dominant nationality to a State that is not the State of dominant nationality, or from the latter to a State of dominant nationality. In the first example, should the expelling State denationalize the person facing expulsion so that it is not in the position of expelling its own national or so that it need not obtain the prior consent of the receiving State which is not a State of dominant nationality? In the second example, can the expelling State, which is not the State of dominant nationality, expel the person to a receiving State that is the State of dominant nationality without requesting the latter's consent or denationalizing the person in advance, since the receiving State is the State of effective nationality?

24. These are just some of the questions that can be raised by these considerations based on the nationality of the person facing expulsion, taking into account, in cases of multiple nationality entailing a positive conflict of nationalities, the criterion of dominant or non-dominant nationality. The Special Rapporteur continues to doubt the interest and practical utility of entering into such considerations at this stage. He believes that these various scenarios could more appropriately be addressed in the framework of a study on protection of the property rights of expelled persons, which he plans to undertake later, in a report devoted to that question among others.

Chapter II

Loss of nationality, denationalization and expulsion

25. Loss of nationality and denationalization do not refer to exactly the same legal mechanism, even though their consequences are similar in the case of expulsion.

A. Loss of nationality and denationalization

1. Loss of nationality

26. A large number of States prevent their nationals from holding another nationality. In these cases, the acquisition of another nationality automatically leads to a loss of the nationality of the State whose legislation proscribes such acquisition.[31]

[31] For example, after listing the various cases in which Cameroonian nationality is acquired "by virtue of filiation" and "by virtue of birth in Cameroon", Law No. 68–LF–3 of 11 June 1968, establishing the Cameroon Nationality Code (*Journal officiel de la République fédérale du Cameroun*, 15 July 1968), provides in section 12 that: "The acquisition of Cameroon nationality extends automatically to any person unable to claim any other nationality of origin if that person was born

27. Loss of nationality is the consequence of an individual's voluntary act, whereas denationalization is a State decision of a collective or individual nature. Legislation pertaining to the loss of nationality can be found in various countries on all continents: Algeria,[32] Andorra,[33] Angola,[34] Argentina,[35] Armenia,[36] Austria,[37] Azerbaijan,[38] Bahamas,[39] Bahrain,[40] Bangladesh,[41] Belgium,[42] Bhutan,[43] Bolivia,[44] Botswana,[45] Brazil,[46] Brunei Darussalam,[47] Burundi,[48] Cambodia,[49] Cameroon,[50] China,[51] Congo,[52] Croatia,[53] Cuba,[54] Czech Republic,[55] Democratic People's Republic of Korea,[56] Democratic Republic of the Congo,[57] Denmark,[58] Djibouti,[59] Dominican Republic,[60] Ecuador,[61] Egypt,[62] Equatorial Guinea,[63] Eritrea,[64] Estonia,[65] Fiji,[66]

in Cameroon." Section 31, contained in chapter IV, entitled "Loss and forfeiture", is more specifically concerned with loss of nationality and provides that:

"Cameroon nationality is lost by:

"(*a*) Any Cameroon adult national who wilfully acquires or keeps a foreign nationality;

"(*b*) ...;

"(*c*) Any person who, occupying a post in a public service of an international or foreign body, retains that post notwithstanding an injunction by the Cameroonian Government to resign it."

[32] United States Office of Personnel Management, Investigations Service, *Citizenship Laws of the World* (IS–1 of March 2001), p. 15 (citing the Code of Algerian Nationality of 15 December 1978).

[33] *Ibid.*, p. 16.

[34] *Ibid.*, p. 17 (citing Law No. 13/91 of 13 May 1991).

[35] *Ibid.*, p. 19 (citing Argentine Citizenship Law No. 346) (except for dual nationality with Spain); see, however, Boll, *Multiple Nationality and International Law*, pp. 311–313 (affirming that only citizenship or political rights are lost rather than nationality).

[36] *Citizenship Laws of the World* (see footnote 32 above), p. 20 (citing the Constitution of Armenia of 5 July 1995 and the Citizenship Law of 26 November 1995); see also Rudko, "Regulation of multiple nationality by bilateral and multilateral agreements", citing article 14 of the Constitution of Armenia, p. 112).

[37] Boll, *op. cit.*, p. 320 (indicating that a request to retain nationality must be submitted in advance, and that approval is given only if this is in the national interest); see also *Citizenship Laws of the World* (footnote 32 above), p. 24 (citing the Citizenship Law of 1965, as amended, although exceptions are provided for).

[38] *Citizenship Laws of the World* (see footnote 32 above), p. 25 (although exceptions are provided for, particularly concerning treaties); see also Rudko, *loc. cit.* (citing the Law on Citizenship and the Constitution, sect. 32, art. 109).

[39] *Citizenship Laws of the World* (see footnote 32 above), p. 26 (citing the Constitution of the Bahamas of 10 July 1973).

[40] *Ibid.*, p. 27 (citing the Bahraini Nationality Law of 16 September 1963).

[41] *Ibid.*, p. 28 (citing the Bangladesh Citizenship Order of 1972, although exceptions are provided for).

[42] *Ibid.*, p. 31 (citing the Code of Belgian Nationality of 28 June 1984, amended on 1 January 1992); see also Boll, *op. cit.*, pp. 330–331 (noting the exception of nationality imposed on an individual without voluntary action and that in certain circumstances nationality may be retained by submitting a petition to that effect once every 10 years).

[43] *Citizenship Laws of the World* (see footnote 32 above), p. 35 (citing the 1958 Nationality Law of Bhutan and the Bhutan Citizenship Act of 1977, amended in 1985).

[44] *Ibid.*, p. 36 (although exceptions are provided for, particularly for Latin American States and Spain).

[45] *Ibid.*, p. 38 (citing the Constitution and Citizenship Act of Botswana of 31 December 1982).

[46] *Ibid.*, p. 39 (citing Constitutional Amendment No. 3 of 6 June 1994 and Law No. 818 of 18 September 1949, amended by Decree Law No. 961 of 13 October 1969, although exceptions are provided for).

[47] *Ibid.*, p. 40 (citing information provided by the diplomatic mission to the United States).

[48] *Ibid.*, p. 43 (citing the Burundian Nationality Code of 10 August 1971).

[49] *Ibid.*, p. 44 (citing Decree No. 913–NS of 20 November 1954 and Law No. 904–NS of 27 September 1954).

[50] *Ibid.*, p. 45 (citing Ordinances No. 2 of 1959 and No. 68 of 1968, providing for an exception in the case of marriage to a foreign national).

[51] *Ibid.*, p. 51 (citing the Nationality Law of the People's Republic of China of 10 September 1980; and the Interpretations of the Standing Committee of the National People's Congress on the Implementation of the Nationality Law of the People's Republic of China in the Macao Special Administrative Region of 20 December 1999 (on citizenship laws concerning Macao); see also Boll, *op. cit.*, p. 343.

[52] *Ibid.*, p. 56 (citing the Congolese Nationality Code and the Regulation bringing it into effect on 29 July 1961).

[53] *Ibid.*, p. 59 (citing the Law of Croatian Citizenship of June 1991) (however, revocation of nationality is not automatic upon the adoption of a subsequent nationality but dependent on the State's releasing the individual from nationality).

[54] *Ibid.*, p. 60 (citing information provided by the Cuban Interest Section of the Swiss diplomatic mission to the United States) (however, revocation of nationality is not automatic upon the adoption of a subsequent nationality but dependent on the State's releasing the individual from nationality).

[55] *Ibid.*, p. 62 (citing the Act on the Acquisition and Loss of Citizenship of 1 January 1993, as amended by Law No. 272 of 12 October 1993, Law No. 140 of 28 June 1995 and Law No. 139 of 26 April 1996) (although exceptions are provided for, including in the case of marriage to a foreign national); see also Boll, *op. cit.*, p. 360 (noting an exception in the case of marriage).

[56] *Citizenship Laws of the World* (see footnote 32 above), p. 109 (citing the Nationality Law of 9 October 1963) (although revocation of nationality is not automatic upon adoption of a subsequent nationality but dependent on the State's releasing the individual from nationality).

[57] *Ibid.*, p. 55 (citing the Congolese Civil Code and the Special Law on Congolese Nationality, although exceptions are provided for).

[58] *Ibid.*, p. 64 (citing the Danish Nationality Law); (although an exception is provided for in the case of marriage to a foreign national). See, however, the report of the Secretary-General of 28 December 1998 on human rights and arbitrary deprivation of nationality (E/CN.4/1999/56 and Add.1–2, para. 4) (citing Denmark's reply of 22 October 1998: "Denmark signed the European Convention on Nationality on 6 November 1997 in Strasbourg ... Arbitrary deprivation of nationality does not occur in Denmark.").

[59] *Citizenship Laws of the World* (see footnote 32 above), p. 65 (citing Law No. 200/AN/81 of 24 October 1981).

[60] *Ibid.*, p. 67 (citing article 11 of the Constitution of the Dominican Republic).

[61] *Ibid.*, p. 68 (citing the Constitution of Ecuador of 1998) (although an exception is provided for concerning the treaty with Spain).

[62] *Ibid.*, p. 69 (citing Law No. 17 of 22 June 1958) (however, revocation of nationality is not automatic upon the adoption of a subsequent nationality but dependent on the State's releasing the individual from nationality); see also Boll, *op. cit.*, p. 369 (noting that Egyptian nationality is retained if the individual does not obtain permission to naturalize elsewhere, or if such permission is obtained and the individual files a declaration of retention).

[63] *Citizenship Laws of the World* (see footnote 32 above), p. 72 (citing information provided by the diplomatic mission to the United States).

[64] *Ibid.*, p. 73 (citing the Eritrean Nationality Proclamation) (although exceptions could be provided for in the future).

[65] *Ibid.*, p. 74 (citing the Estonian Law of 19 January 1995 (in force as of 1 April 1995)); see also Rudko, *loc. cit.* (citing articles 1 and 3 of the Law on Citizenship); see further E/CN.4/1999/56 and Add.1–2 (footnote 58 above), mentioning articles 22 and 26–29 of the Law of Citizenship (para. 7) and citing Estonia's reply of 29 September 1998: "As of today no cases of arbitrary deprivation of nationality have been brought before Estonian courts" (para. 10).

[66] *Citizenship Laws of the World* (see footnote 32 above), p. 76 (citing the 1997 Federal Constitution); see also Boll, *op. cit.*, p. 373.

Finland,[67] Gabon,[68] Gambia,[69] Georgia,[70] Germany,[71] Ghana,[72] Guatemala,[73] Guinea,[74] Guinea-Bissau,[75] Guyana,[76] Haiti,[77] Honduras,[78] India,[79] Indonesia,[80] Japan,[81] Kazakhstan,[82] Kenya,[83] Kiribati,[84] Kuwait,[85] Kyrgyzstan,[86] Lao People's Democratic Republic,[87] Latvia,[88] Lesotho,[89] Liberia,[90] Libyan Arab Jamahiriya,[91] Lithuania,[92] Luxembourg,[93] Madagascar,[94] Malawi,[95] Malaysia,[96] Malta,[97] Marshall Islands,[98] Mauritania,[99] Micronesia (Federated States of),[100] Moldova,[101] Monaco,[102] Mongolia,[103]

[67] *Citizenship Laws of the World* (see footnote 32 above), p. 77 (citing the Finnish Citizenship Act of 28 June 1968, amended in 1984) (although exceptions are provided for); see also Boll, *op. cit.*, p. 377 (noting that Finland modified its legislation in 2003 in order to accept dual nationality when sufficient links are maintained with Finland).

[68] *Citizenship Laws of the World* (see footnote 32 above), p. 79 (citing information provided by the diplomatic mission to the United States).

[69] *Ibid.*, p. 80 (citing the Constitution) (although an exception is provided for in the case of marriage to a foreign national).

[70] See Rudko, *loc. cit.* (citing article 12 of the Constitution and article 1 of its law on citizenship).

[71] *Ibid.*, p. 82 (citing German citizenship law) (although exceptions are provided for); see also Boll *op. cit.*, p. 385 (also noting the exceptions to the rule of revocation).

[72] *Citizenship Laws of the World* (see footnote 32 above), p. 83 (citing the Constitution of Ghana of April 1992) (although an exception is provided for in the case of marriage to a foreign national); see also the report of the Secretary-General E/CN.4/1999/56 and Add.1–2 (footnote 58 above), para. 15 (citing Ghana's reply of 9 November 1998: "While a lot is to be said for the right to a nationality as a human right one cannot overlook the other side of the coin, namely the effect of such a right on the principle of State sovereignty").

[73] *Citizenship Laws of the World* (see footnote 32 above), p. 86 (citing the Constitution of Guatemala) (although exceptions are provided for where treaties with some other Central and South American States are concerned).

[74] *Ibid.*, p. 87.

[75] *Ibid.*, p. 88 (citing the Law of Nationality of 1973).

[76] *Ibid.*, p. 89 (citing the Constitution of Guyana of 1980) (although an exception is provided for in the case of marriage to a foreign national).

[77] *Ibid.*, p. 90 (citing the Constitution of Haiti).

[78] *Ibid.*, p. 91 (citing the Constitution of Honduras) (although many exceptions are provided for, including on the basis of treaties).

[79] *Ibid.*, p. 94 (citing the Citizenship Act of 1955); see also Boll, *op. cit.*, p. 409.

[80] *Citizenship Laws of the World* (see footnote 32 above), p. 95 (citing the Nationality Laws of 1 January 1946, as amended on 1 August 1958) (although exceptions are provided for); see also Boll, *op. cit.*, p. 412 (noting the existence of exceptions).

[81] *Citizenship Laws of the World* (see footnote 32 above), p. 103 (citing the Nationality Act of 4 May 1950); see also Boll, *op. cit.*, p. 436.

[82] *Citizenship Laws of the World* (see footnote 32 above), p. 105 (citing the Law on Citizenship for the Republic of Kazakhstan of 1 March 1992) (although exceptions are possible under treaties concluded with some former Soviet republics).

[83] *Ibid.*, p. 106 (citing the Kenyan Constitution); see also Boll, *op. cit.*, p. 439.

[84] *Citizenship Laws of the World* (see footnote 32 above), p. 108 (citing the Kiribati Independence Order of 12 July 1979) (although an exception is provided for in the case of marriage to a foreign national).

[85] *Ibid.*, p. 112 (citing the Constitution of Kuwait); see also E/CN.4/1999/56 and Add.1–2 (footnote 58 above), citing Amiral Decree No. 15 of 1959, as amended, art. 4, para. 5, and arts. 13, 14 and 21 *bis* (para. 20) and Kuwait's reply of 30 October 1998: "Matters relating to nationality are of great importance to the State insofar as they involve aspects that affect the homeland, as well as considerations concerning the sovereign entity of the State, its internal and external security and its social and economic situation and circumstances, in addition to the fact that nationality implies a bond of loyalty and a sense of patriotism in the absence of which it becomes necessary and even essential to withdraw citizenship status from a person who has acquired it" (para. 19).

[86] *Citizenship Laws of the World* (see footnote 32 above), p. 113 (citing the draft Constitution of 5 May 1993) (although exceptions are possible under treaties concluded with former Soviet republics); see also Rudko, *loc. cit.*, citing the Constitution, art. 13; the law of the Kyrgyz Republic, art. 5; the Agreement between Belarus, Kazakhstan, Kyrgyzstan and the Russian Federation; and the Russian Federation-Kyrgyzstan Agreement (simplified procedure for acquiring citizenship)).

[87] *Citizenship Laws of the World* (see footnote 32 above), p. 114 (citing the Law of Laotian Citizenship of 29 November 1990) (although revocation of nationality is not automatic upon adoption of a subsequent nationality but dependent on the State's releasing the individual from nationality).

[88] *Ibid.*, p. 115 (citing the Citizenship Law of the Republic of Latvia); see also Rudko, *loc. cit.* (citing the Constitutional Law, art. 5, and the Law on Citizenship, arts. 1 and 9) (although revocation of nationality is not automatic upon adoption of a subsequent nationality but dependent on the State's releasing the individual from nationality); see further Boll, *op. cit.*, p. 445 (indicating that revocation of Latvian nationality is possible through a court decision).

[89] *Citizenship Laws of the World* (see footnote 32 above), p. 118 (citing the 1993 revised Constitution and the 1971 Lesotho Citizenship Order) (although exceptions are provided for in the case of marriage to a foreign national).

[90] *Ibid.*, p. 119 (citing the Constitution of the Republic of Liberia).

[91] *Ibid.*, p. 120 (citing the 1954 Nationality Law No. 17 and the 1979 Law No. 3).

[92] *Ibid.*, p. 122 (citing the Law on Citizenship of the Republic of Lithuania of 5 December 1991); see also Rudko, *loc. cit.* (citing the Constitution, art. 12, and the Law of the Lithuanian Republic, art. 1).

[93] *Citizenship Laws of the World* (see footnote 32 above), p. 123 (citing the Law of 1 January 1987); see also Boll, *op. cit.*, p. 450.

[94] *Citizenship Laws of the World* (see footnote 32 above), p. 124 (citing Ordinance No. 60–064 of 22 July 1960) (although exceptions are provided for in the case of marriage to a foreign national).

[95] *Ibid.*, p. 125 (citing the Malawi Citizenship Act of 6 July 1966) (although exceptions are provided for in the case of marriage to a foreign national).

[96] *Ibid.*, p. 126 (citing the Constitution of Malaysia); see also Boll, *op. cit.*, p. 454 (noting that revocation is discretionary).

[97] *Citizenship Laws of the World* (see footnote 32 above), p. 129 (citing the 1964 Constitution, as amended, and the Maltese Citizenship Act) (although exceptions are provided for).

[98] *Ibid.*, p. 130 (citing the Constitution of the Marshall Islands of 21 December 1978 and its Immigration Law) (although exceptions are provided for in the case of marriage to a foreign national).

[99] *Ibid.*, p. 131 (citing the Nationality Code of 12 June 1961) (although an exception is provided for in the case of marriage to a foreign national).

[100] *Ibid.*, p. 134 (citing the Citizenship and Naturalization Act of 10 May 1979).

[101] *Ibid.*, p. 135 (citing the Law of Citizenship of 23 June 1990); see also Rudko, *loc. cit.* (citing the Constitution, art. 18, and the Law on Citizenship of Moldova, art. 4).

[102] *Citizenship Laws of the World* (see footnote 32 above), p. 136 (citing the Acquisition of Monegasque Nationality of 1 January 1987); see also E/CN.4/1999/56 and Add.1–2 (footnote 58 above), paras. 21–23 (citing Monaco's reply of 19 September 1998); the Constitution of 17 December 1962, art. 18 ("Loss of Monegasque nationality in any other circumstances may occur only as a result of the intentional acquisition of another nationality or of service unlawfully carried out in a foreign army"); Act No. 572 of 18 November 1952, arts. 5 and 6 (concerning the acquisition of Monegasque nationality); Act No. 1155 of 18 December 1992, chaps. III–V, sect. I (concerning nationality); and Ordinance No. 10.822 of 22 February 1993.

[103] *Citizenship Laws of the World* (see footnote 32 above), p. 137 (citing the Constitution of Mongolia of 13 January 1992) (although revocation of nationality is not automatic upon adoption of a subsequent nationality but dependent on the State's releasing the individual from nationality upon application).

Mozambique,[104] Myanmar,[105] Namibia,[106] Nauru,[107] Nepal,[108] the Netherlands,[109] Nicaragua,[110] the Niger,[111] Norway,[112] Oman,[113] Pakistan,[114] Palau,[115] Panama,[116] Papua New Guinea,[117] Philippines,[118] Qatar,[119] Republic of Korea,[120] Russian Federation,[121] Rwanda,[122] Sao Tome and Principe,[123] Saudi Arabia,[124] Senegal,[125] Seychelles,[126] Sierra Leone,[127] Singapore,[128] Solomon Islands,[129] South Africa,[130] Spain,[131] Sri Lanka,[132] Sudan,[133] Swaziland,[134] Syrian Arab Republic,[135] Thailand,[136] Tonga,[137] Turkey,[138] Uganda,[139] Ukraine,[140] United Arab Emirates,[141] United Republic of Tanzania,[142] Uzbekistan,[143] Vanuatu,[144]

---

[104] *Ibid.*, p. 139 (citing the 1975 Law of Nationality, as amended in November 1990).

[105] *Ibid.*, p. 140 (citing information provided by the diplomatic mission to the United States).

[106] *Ibid.*, p. 141 (citing the Constitution of the Republic of Namibia of 21 March 1990).

[107] *Ibid.*, p. 142 (citing the Constitution of 30 January 1968 and the Nauruan Community Ordinance of 1956–1966).

[108] *Ibid.*, p. 143 (citing the Constitution, as amended in 1990, and the Nepal Citizenship Act of 1964).

[109] *Ibid.*, p. 144 (citing the Nationality Act of 1984) (although exceptions are provided for); see also Boll, *op. cit.*, p. 465 (noting exceptions to revocation if the nationality acquired is based on birth in another State or if the individual has only lived in the foreign State as a minor for not more than five years; these exceptions do not apply, however, to certain nationalities such as those of Austria, Belgium, Denmark, Luxembourg and Norway).

[110] *Citizenship Laws of the World* (see footnote 32 above), p. 147 (citing the Constitution of Nicaragua) (although exceptions are provided for under treaties with Central American and other countries).

[111] *Ibid.*, p. 148 (citing information provided by the diplomatic mission to the United States).

[112] *Ibid.*, p. 150 (citing the Norwegian Nationality Act of 8 December 1950) (although exceptions are provided for); see also Boll, *op. cit.*, p. 475 (noting that exceptions are provided for).

[113] *Citizenship Laws of the World* (see footnote 32 above), p. 151 (citing information provided by the diplomatic mission to the United States) (although revocation of nationality is not automatic upon adoption of a subsequent nationality but dependent on the State's releasing the individual from nationality).

[114] *Ibid.*, p. 152 (citing the Pakistan Citizenship Act of 13 April 1951).

[115] *Ibid.*, p. 153 (citing the 1994 Constitution).

[116] *Ibid.*, p. 155 (citing the Panamanian Constitution).

[117] *Ibid.*, p. 156 (citing the Constitution of 16 September 1975 and the Citizenship Act of 13 February 1976) (although exceptions are provided for in the case of marriage to a foreign national).

[118] *Ibid.*, p. 159 (citing the Constitution of the Philippines of 2 February 1987); see also Boll, *op. cit.*, p. 484 (noting that revocation applies only if the person concerned must swear an oath of allegiance in another country and that persons who are Philippine nationals by birth may resume nationality later).

[119] *Citizenship Laws of the World* (see footnote 32 above), p. 162 (citing Law No. 2 of 1961, as amended by Law No. 19 of 1963 and Law No. 17 of 1966).

[120] *Ibid.*, p. 110 (citing the Nationality Act of 13 December 1997, later amended); see also Boll, *op. cit.*, p. 442.

[121] *Citizenship Laws of the World* (see footnote 32 above), pp. 164–165 (citing the Law on Citizenship of 6 February 1992) (although exceptions are provided for under treaties with other States); see also Rudko, *loc. cit.* (citing the Constitution, arts. 6 and 62; the Law on Dual Citizenship, art. 3; the 1993 Agreement between the Russian Federation and Turkmenistan on the regulation of dual citizenship matters, Diplomaticheskii vestnik (1994), No. 1–2, pp. 24–25; and the 1995 Agreement between the Russian Federation and the Republic of Tajikistan on regulation of dual citizenship matters, *ibid.* (October 1995), No. 10, pp. 23–26).

[122] *Citizenship Laws of the World* (see footnote 32 above), p. 166 (citing the Code of Rwandese Nationality of 28 September 1963).

[123] *Ibid.*, p. 171 (citing the Law of Nationality of 13 September 1990).

[124] *Ibid.*, p. 172 (citing the Saudi Nationality Law).

[125] *Ibid.*, p. 173 (citing the 1960 Code of Nationality, as amended in 1989) (although revocation of nationality is not automatic upon adoption of a subsequent nationality but dependent on the State's releasing the individual from nationality).

[126] *Ibid.*, p. 174 (citing the 1970 Constitution and the Citizenship of Seychelles Act of 29 June 1976).

[127] *Ibid.*, p. 175 (citing the 1961 Law of Citizenship).

[128] *Ibid.*, p. 176 (citing the Constitution of Singapore of 9 August 1965); see also Boll, *op. cit.*, p. 503.

[129] *Citizenship Laws of the World* (see footnote 32 above), p. 180 (citing the Solomon Islands Independence Order No. 783 of 7 July 1978).

[130] *Ibid.*, p. 182 (citing the South African Citizenship Act, 1995 (Act No. 88 of 1995), as amended) (although exceptions are provided for); see also Boll, *op. cit.*, p. 512 (noting that nationality may be retained provided permission has been granted).

[131] *Citizenship Laws of the World* (see footnote 32 above), p. 184 (citing articles 17–26 of the Civil Code, modified by Laws Nos. 18/1990 and 29/1995) (although exceptions are made under treaties with Argentina, Bolivia, Chile, Costa Rica, the Dominican Republic, Ecuador, Guatemala, Honduras, Nicaragua, Paraguay and Peru); see also Boll *op. cit.*, p. 515 (noting that revocation is possible only if the person concerned resides abroad for three years, unless Spain is at war or the person concerned has notified the authorities of his or her intention to preserve Spanish nationality).

[132] *Citizenship Laws of the World* (see footnote 32 above), p. 185 (citing the Citizenship Act of Sri Lanka of 22 May 1972, as amended in 1987) (although exceptions are provided for).

[133] *Ibid.*, p. 186 (citing the Law of Sudanese Nationality No. 22 of 1957; Law No. 55 of 1970; and Law No. 47 of 1972).

[134] *Ibid.*, p. 188 (citing information provided by the diplomatic mission to the United States) (although an exception is provided for in the case of nationality acquired by birth, which cannot be revoked).

[135] *Ibid.*, p. 192 (citing information provided by the diplomatic mission to the United States); see also Boll, *op. cit.*, p. 527 (noting that the person concerned may be permitted to retain nationality, but that foreign nationality is usually not recognized and nationality is retained regardless).

[136] *Citizenship Laws of the World* (see footnote 32 above), p. 196 (citing the Nationality Act of 1965, with amendments Nos. 2 AD 1992 and 3 AD 1993); see also Boll, *op. cit.*, p. 533.

[137] *Citizenship Laws of the World* (see footnote 32 above), p. 199 (citing the Nationality Act, as amended 1915 through 1988; 2 Laws of Tonga, chap. 59 (1988 rev. ed.)); see also Boll, *op. cit.*, p. 536.

[138] *Citizenship Laws of the World* (see footnote 32 above), p. 202 (citing the Turkish Constitution, art. 66, and Law No. 403 of the 1964 Turkish Citizenship Law); see also Boll, *op. cit.*, p. 542 (revocation is discretionary; authorization to retain nationality is possible).

[139] *Citizenship Laws of the World* (see footnote 32 above), p. 205 (citing the Constitution of Uganda).

[140] *Ibid.*, p. 206 (citing the 1991 Statute on Citizenship); see also Rudko, *loc. cit.* (citing the Law on Succession of Ukraine of 12 September 1991, arts. 6–7; the Convention between Ukraine and the Socialist Federal Republic of Yugoslavia of 22 May 1956 (succession to convention assumed); the Convention between Ukraine and Hungary of 24 August 1957; the Convention between Ukraine and Romania of 4 September 1957; the Convention between Ukraine and Albania of 18 September 1957; the Convention between Ukraine and Czechoslovakia of 5 October 1957; the Convention between Ukraine and Bulgaria of 12 December 1957; the Convention between Ukraine and the Democratic People's Republic of Korea of 16 December 1957; the Convention between Ukraine and Poland of 21 January 1958; and the Convention between Ukraine and Mongolia of 25 August 1958).

[141] *Citizenship Laws of the World* (see footnote 32 above), p. 207 (citing Nationality Law No. 17 of 1 January 1972, as amended by Law No. 10 of 1975).

[142] *Ibid.*, p. 195 (citing the Tanzanian Citizenship Act No. 6 of October 1995) (although exceptions are provided for in case of marriage to a foreign national).

[143] *Ibid.*, p. 211 (citing the Citizenship Law).

[144] *Ibid.*, p. 212 (citing the Constitution of 30 July 1983, sect. 10); see also Boll, *op. cit.*, p. 559.

Venezuela (Bolivarian Republic of),[145] Viet Nam,[146] Yemen,[147] Zambia[148] and Zimbabwe;[149] in other words, the vast majority of States.[150] In principle, these legal provisions entail no risk of statelessness, insofar as the person concerned can retain the nationality which he or she

[145] *Citizenship Laws of the World* (see footnote 32 above), p. 213 (citing the Constitution).

[146] *Ibid.*, p. 214 (citing the Law of Vietnamese Nationality, as revised on 15 July 1988).

[147] *Ibid.*, p. 216 (citing Citizenship Law No. 2 of 1975).

[148] *Ibid.*, p. 218 (citing the Constitution) (although an exception is provided for in case of marriage to a foreign national).

[149] *Ibid.*, p. 219 (citing the Constitution); see also Boll, *op. cit.*, p. 565.

[150] The following States do not withdraw their nationality from individuals possessing another nationality: Antigua and Barbuda (*Citizenship Laws of the World* (see footnote 32 above), p. 18 (citing the Citizenship Law of 1 November 1981)); Australia (*ibid.*, pp. 22–23 (citing the Australian Citizenship Act of 1948)); Barbados (*ibid.*, p. 29 (citing the Constitution)); Belarus (*ibid.*, p. 30 (citing the Law of the Republic of Belarus, Laws of Citizenship of 18 October 1991); see also Rudko, *loc. cit.*, citing the Law on Citizenship, art. 1, and the Agreement between Belarus and Kazakhstan; and Boll, *op. cit.*, p. 327 (indicating that Belarus amended its legislation in 2002 to abolish automatic revocation of nationality in case of naturalization in another State); Belize (*Citizenship Laws of the World* (see footnote 32 above), pp. 32–33 (citing the Belize Nationality Act, chap. 127A of the Laws of Belize, R.E. 1980–1990)); Benin (*ibid.*, p. 34 (citing the Law of Civil Rights)); Bulgaria (*ibid.*, p. 41 (citing the Law on Bulgarian Citizenship of November 1998)); Burkina Faso (*ibid.*, p. 42 (not prohibited)); Canada (*ibid.*, p. 46 (citing the Canadian Citizenship Act of 1947, the Citizenship Act and the Citizenship Regulations of 1977)); Cape Verde (*ibid.*, p. 47 (citing information provided by the diplomatic mission to the United States)); Central African Republic (*ibid.*, p. 48 (citing the Constitution of 7 January 1995)); Chile (*ibid.*, p. 50 (citing information provided by the diplomatic mission to the United States) (although exceptions are provided for by treaty with respect to Spanish nationality); see also the July 1991 repatriation agreement between Chile, IOM and UNHCR, *Diario oficial de la Republica de Chile* (19 February 1992), art. II (allowing the return of Chilean refugees, including those who had lost Chilean nationality through naturalization abroad in the asylum State); see further Boll, *op. cit.*, p. 340 (noting that Chile revised its constitutional provisions in 2005 to allow dual nationality); Colombia (*Citizenship Laws of the World* (see footnote 32 above), p. 53 (citing the Constitution of July 1991 and Citizenship Law No. 43 of 1 February 1993)); Costa Rica (*ibid.*, p. 57 (citing the Constitution)); Côte d'Ivoire (*ibid.*, p. 58 (citing information provided by the diplomatic mission to the United States); see also Boll, *op. cit.*, p. 429); Cyprus (*Citizenship Laws of the World* (see footnote 32 above), p. 61 (citing the Republic Law of 1967)); Timor-Leste (Boll, *op. cit.*, p. 363 (citing the Constitution of 20 May 2002 and Law No. 9/2002 on citizenship of 5 November 2002)); El Salvador (*Citizenship Laws of the World* (see footnote 32 above), p. 71 (citing the Salvadoran Constitution) (although only those who are Salvadorans by birth have the right to enjoy dual nationality)); France (*ibid.*, p. 78 (citing the French Nationality Code); see also Boll *op. cit.*, p. 382 (noting, however, that France is a party to the Convention on reduction of cases of multiple nationality and military obligations in cases of multiple nationality and its Second Protocol)); Greece (*Citizenship Laws of the World* (see footnote 32 above), p. 84 (citing the Code of Greek Citizenship, as amended in 1968 and 1984) (although revocation of nationality is not automatic upon adoption of a subsequent nationality but dependent on the State's releasing the individual from nationality)); see also Boll, *op. cit.*, p. 391 (noting that nationality is not automatically lost upon naturalization elsewhere, although some exceptions to this rule are provided for). Greece could alternatively be placed in the automatic revocation list because it apparently reserves the power to revoke; Grenada (*Citizenship Laws of the World* (see footnote 32 above), p. 85 (citing the Grenada Constitution Order of 19 December 1973)); Hungary (*ibid.*, p. 92 (citing Law No. 55 of 1 June 1993)); Iceland (*ibid.*, p. 93 (citing the Icelandic Nationality Act of 23 December 1952, as amended on 11 May 1982 and 12 June 1998) (although some exceptions are provided for); see also Boll, *op. cit.*, p. 406 (noting that the legislation was amended in 2003 to allow the retention of dual nationality provided that the individual had ties to Iceland)); Ireland (*Citizenship Laws of the World* (see footnote 32 above), p. 99 (citing the Irish Nationality and Citizenship Act of 1956)); Iran (Islamic Republic of) (*ibid.*, p. 97 (citing the Iranian Civil Code) (although revocation of nationality is not automatic upon adoption of a subsequent nationality but dependent on the State's releasing the individual from nationality)); see also Boll, *op. cit.*, p. 415 (noting that naturalization elsewhere may lead to loss of property and disqualification from holding government office)); Israel (*Citizenship Laws of the World* (see footnote 32 above), p. 100 (citing the Citizenship Law of 1952, as amended in 1968); see also Boll, *op. cit.*, p. 423 (noting an exception for the acquisition of the nationality of a "hostile" State, which leads to revocation)); Italy (*Citizenship Laws of the World* (see footnote 32 above), p. 101 (citing the Italian Law on Nationality, as amended on 5 February 1992); see also Boll, *op. cit.*, p. 427 (noting an exception with regard to a State at war with Italy, and pointing out that Italy is a party to the Convention on reduction of cases of multiple nationality and military obligations in cases of multiple nationality) (also noting that failure to notify the Italian authorities of the acquisition of another nationality is subject to a fine)); Jamaica (*Citizenship Laws of the World* (see footnote 32 above), p. 102 (citing the Jamaican Nationality Act of 1962, as amended on 2 March 1993)); Jordan (*ibid.*, p. 104 (citing the Jordanian Citizenship Act of 1954) (although acquisition of a second nationality is subject to prior authorization unless it is the nationality of an Arab State)); Lebanon (*ibid.*, p. 117 (citing information provided by the diplomatic mission to the United States)); Maldives (*ibid.*, p. 127); Mali (*ibid.*, p. 128 (citing the Code of Nationality, regulation No. 95–098 of 1995)); Mauritius (*ibid.*, p. 132 (citing the Mauritius Independence Order of 4 March 1968)); Mexico (*ibid.*, p. 133 (citing the Federal Constitution, as amended on 20 March 1998); see also Boll, *op. cit.*, p. 457 (noting an exception for naturalized Mexican nationals, who do lose Mexican nationality)); Morocco (*Citizenship Laws of the World* (see footnote 32 above), p. 138 (citing the Code of Moroccan Nationality of 6 September 1958)); New Zealand (*ibid.*, p. 145 (citing the Constitution of 1 January 1949). However, see Boll, *op. cit.*, p. 468 (noting an exception when the naturalization abroad is by voluntary act and the individual commits acts against the State or exercises rights contrary to State interests)); Nigeria (*Citizenship Laws of the World* (see footnote 32 above), p. 149 (citing the Constitution of 1989); see also Boll, *op. cit.*, p. 471 (noting an exception for naturalized citizens)); Paraguay (*Citizenship Laws of the World* (see footnote 32 above), p. 157 (citing the Constitution) (although the rule concerning the revocation of nationality applies only to naturalized citizens); see also Boll, *op. cit.*, p. 478 (noting that it only applies to naturalized nationals and that nationals by birth are deprived of rights of citizenship upon naturalization elsewhere, not revocation of nationality)); Peru (*Citizenship Laws of the World* (see footnote 32 above), p. 158 (citing the Constitution of 31 October 1993 and Nationality Law No. 26574 of January 1996)); Poland (*ibid.*, p. 160 (citing the Constitution and the Citizenship Act of 15 February 1962) (although revocation of nationality is not automatic upon adoption of a subsequent nationality but dependent on the State's releasing the individual from nationality)); Portugal (*ibid.*, p. 161 (citing Citizenship Law No. 37/81 of 1981 and Decree-Law No. 322/82); see also E/CN.4/1999/56 and Add.1–2 (footnote 58 above), para. 25 (citing Portugal's reply of 3 December 1998: "In accordance with the Portuguese Law on Nationality (art. 8), no Portuguese citizen shall be deprived of his or her nationality unless he or she, being a national of another State, declares that he or she does not wish to be Portuguese. Therefore, no arbitrary deprivation of nationality is possible within the Portuguese legal framework")); Romania (*Citizenship Laws of the World* (see footnote 32 above), p. 163 (citing Law No. 21 of 1991)); Saint Kitts and Nevis (*ibid.*, p. 167 (citing the Constitution)); Saint Lucia (*ibid.*, p. 168 (citing the Citizenship Act of 5 June 1979)); Saint Vincent and the Grenadines (*ibid.*, p. 169 (citing the Constitution of 27 October 1979 and the Citizenship Act of 1984)); Samoa (*ibid.*, p. 170 (citing the Citizenship Act of 9 August 1972) (although exceptions are provided for in case of marriage to a foreign national); however, see also Boll, *op. cit.*, p. 501 (indicating that the legislation was amended in 2004 to allow dual nationality)); Slovakia (*Citizenship Laws of the World* (see footnote 32 above), p. 177 (citing the National Council of the Slovak Republic Law No. 40 of 19 January 1993)); Slovenia (*ibid.*, p. 178 (citing the Citizenship Act of 25 June 1991) (although exceptions are provided for); see also Boll, *op. cit.*, p. 508); Sweden (*Citizenship Laws of the World* (see footnote 32 above), p. 189 (citing the Swedish Nationality Law); see also Boll, *op. cit.*, p. 518 (citing the Swedish Citizenship Act of 1 July 2001); Switzerland (*Citizenship Laws of the World* (see footnote 32 above), p. 190 (citing the Swiss Citizenship Law of 29 September 1952, as amended in 1984 and 1990)); Togo (*ibid.*, p. 198 (citing information provided by the diplomatic mission to the United States)); Trinidad and Tobago (*ibid.*, p. 200 (citing the Constitution, as revised in 1976, and the

would lose upon adopting another nationality by repudiating that other nationality.

2. Denationalization

28. Unlike loss of nationality, which, as seen above, is the consequence of a voluntary act on the part of the individual concerned, denationalization is a State decision that deprives a class of people, or one or more individuals, of the nationality of that State. In practice, some States, in special circumstances such as war, succession of States or the reprehensible conduct of a given individual, have in fact deprived the persons involved in these situations or engaged in such conduct of their nationality. Denationalization may take any of the following forms:

(*a*) Collective withdrawal of nationality through the enactment of a restrictive nationality law that takes away the nationality of a given State, for ethnic or other reasons, from a large number of citizens or permanent or long-term residents of the territory of that State. The cases generally cited are those of Czechoslovakia, Germany,[151] Hungary, Italy,[152] and Romania[153] in the period preceding the Second World War. Situations of this type have arisen more recently in States such as Bhutan,[154] Côte d'Ivoire,[155] the Democratic Republic of the Congo,[156] the Dominican Republic,[157] Kenya,[158] Kuwait,[159] Myanmar,[160] the Russian Federation,[161] Thailand,[162] Zambia[163] and Zimbabwe;[164]

(*b*) Denaturalization, which is an option made available under some bilateral conventions between countries of emigration and countries of immigration authorizing emigrants who had acquired the nationality of the host country through naturalization to revert to their nationality of origin if they subsequently establish residency in their country of origin.[165] Such individuals then revert to the status of aliens with respect to the country to which they had emigrated and are subject to expulsion therefrom under ordinary law;

(*c*) Deprivation of nationality, which is the withdrawal by a State of its nationality from an alien who has acquired it, for security reasons or any other grounds generally provided for in its domestic criminal law. Such legislation may provide that an alien who has acquired the nationality of the State concerned may be deprived of that nationality: (i) if the person has been convicted of a crime or offence against the domestic or external security of that

Citizenship Act of 30 August 1962)); Tunisia (*ibid.*, p. 201 (citing the Code of Nationality of 26 January 1956)); Tuvalu (*ibid.*, p. 204 (citing the Constitution of Tuvalu Ordinance of 15 September 1986 and the Citizenship Ordinance of 1979); see also Boll, *op. cit.*, p. 545 (with the exception of naturalized citizens)); United Kingdom of Great Britain and Northern Ireland (*Citizenship Laws of the World* (see footnote 32 above), pp. 208–209 (citing the British Nationality Act of 1984); see also E/CN.4/1999/56 and Add.1–2 (footnote 58 above), para. 31 (*b*) (citing the United Kingdom's reply of 26 October 1998: "A person who acquired [one of the various forms of British nationality] by or as a result of naturalization or registration otherwise than under the British Nationality Acts 1948 to 1964 may additionally be deprived of that citizenship or status if he or she: ... (iii) Has, within five years of the date of registration or naturalization, been sentenced to imprisonment for at least 12 months and would not, on losing British nationality, become stateless"); British Nationality Act 1981, sect. 40 (c. 61), Hong Kong (British Nationality) Order 1986 (No. 948), art. 7); United States (E/CN.4/1999/56 and Add.1–2 (see footnote 58 above), para. 39 (citing the reply of the United States of 9 October 1998)); and Uruguay (*Citizenship Laws of the World* (see footnote 32 above), p. 210 (citing the Constitution) (although this rule applies only to those who are Uruguayan by birth); see also Boll, *op. cit.*, p. 556 (noting an exception for naturalized citizens, but only if they do not maintain residency or other ties to Uruguay) (also noting that nationals do lose citizenship rights, though not nationality, when they are naturalized elsewhere)).

[151] Reich Citizenship Law of 15 September 1935 (Nuremberg, Germany) (sometimes referred to as the "Law on the Retraction of Naturalizations and the Derecognition of German Citizenship" or the "Nuremberg Laws") (denationalizing any German national who acquired German nationality between the end of the First World War and Hitler's assumption of power in January 1933), Nazi Conspiracy and Aggression, vol. IV (Washington, D.C., U.S. Government Printing Office, 1946). See also Abel, "Denationalization", especially pp. 59–61; and McDougal, Lasswell and Chen, *loc. cit.*

[152] See Roth, *The History of the Jews of Italy*, pp. 524–527 (withdrawal of all naturalization certificates issued to Jews between 1 January 1919 and 17 December 1938).

[153] See Meyer and others, *The Jews in the Soviet Satellites*, pp. 384 and 500.

[154] See Amnesty International, *Nepal—Bhutanese Refugees Rendered Stateless: Leading Global NGOs Criticize Screening Process* (19 June 2003), press release available at www.amnesty.org (individuals of Nepalese origin). But see below for discussion of the fact that some regard the expelled individuals as never having had Bhutanese nationality.

[155] See Chirot, "The debacle in Côte d'Ivoire", p. 68; and Human Rights Watch, *The New Racism: The Political Manipulation of Ethnicity in Côte d'Ivoire* (requirement that both parents be natives of Côte d'Ivoire in order to transmit that nationality to their children).

[156] See Sarkin, "Towards finding a solution for the problems created by the politics of identity in the Democratic Republic of the Congo (DRC): designing a constitutional framework for peaceful cooperation" (discussion of the Banyamulenge people concentrated in the north-east).

[157] See *Dilcia Yean and Violeta Bosica* v. *Dominican Republic*, case No. 12.189 of 22 February 2001, report No. 28/01, OAS document OEA/Ser.L/V/II.111, doc. 20 rev., p. 252 (Inter-American Commission on Human Rights (alleging that two girls of Haitian ancestry who were born in the State were denied Dominican nationality notwithstanding the fact that the Dominican Republic's Constitution grants nationality *jus soli*).

[158] See the oral intervention by the African Society of International and Comparative Law and Minority Rights Group International, United Nations Commission on Human Rights, fifty-ninth session (2 April 2003) (discussing the Nubian community forcibly resettled by the British from the Sudan (www.minorityrights.org)); Mbaria, "Meet the Nubians, Kenya's fifth-generation 'foreigners' "; and United Nations press release (HR/CN/1017) of 3 April 2003, "Commission on Human Rights hears from NGOs charging violations around the world".

[159] See Human Rights Watch, *Kuwait—Promises Betrayed: Denial of Rights of Bidun, Women, and Freedom of Expression*; and United States Department of State, Country Reports on Human Rights Practices for 2003: Kuwait (25 February 2004) (discussing the Bedoun groups).

[160] See Amnesty International, *Myanmar—The Rohingya Minority: Fundamental Rights Denied*; and Human Rights Watch, *Living in Limbo: Burmese Rohingyas in Malaysia* (discussing the Rohingya Muslim minority in Ankara state).

[161] The Meskhetian minority in the Krasnodar Krai region were considered nationals of the Union of Soviet Socialist Republics, but nationality under the 1991 Law No. 1948–I of the Russian Federation was refused, although the law appears to grant it under article 13, paragraph 1.

[162] See Macan-Markar, "Thailand: fear of expulsion haunts hill tribes"; and Gearing, "The struggle for the Highlands: accused of endangering the environment, Thailand's tribespeople face eviction and an uncertain future".

[163] See *Legal Resources Foundation* v. *Zambia*, 211/98 of 7 May 2001, *Fourteenth Annual Activity Report of the African Commission on Human and Peoples' Rights (2000–2001)*, thirty-seventh session, OAU document AHG/229(XXXVII) (2–12 July 2001), pp. 86–97.

[164] See Ferrett, "Citizenship choice in Zimbabwe".

[165] See Salmon, *op. cit.*, p. 320.

State; (ii) if the person has committed acts contrary to the interests of that State.[166].

29. Neither loss of nationality nor denationalization should lead to statelessness. In the case of denationalization in particular, there is a general obligation not to denationalize a citizen who does not have any other nationality. Likewise, nationality cannot effectively be lost unless the person concerned has effectively adopted another nationality. In addition, denationalization should not be arbitrary or based on discriminatory grounds. In all cases, both loss of nationality and denationalization change a person's status from that of a national to that of an alien and make him or her subject to expulsion from the State whose nationality he or she possessed until that time.

B. Expulsion in cases of loss of nationality or denationalization

30. Although dual or multiple nationality is widely recognized today, it does not seem possible to establish the existence of a rule of customary law in this regard. In the *Eritrea* v. *Ethiopia* case, the Claims Commission considered that revocation of nationality in the case of dual nationals was a permissible practice if it was not arbitrary or discriminatory. The Commission rejected Eritrea's argument that the denationalization and subsequent expulsion of persons with dual Eritrean and Ethiopian nationality were contrary to international law.[167] It held that the persons concerned had in fact acquired dual Eritrean and Ethiopian nationality as a result of the proclamation issued by Eritrea's Provisional Government on eligibility for citizenship for the purposes of the referendum and the establishment of the new State.[168] Thus, Ethiopia did not violate international law by denationalizing those of its citizens who had become dual nationals by acquiring Eritrean nationality.[169] On the other hand, the Commission held that the expulsion from Ethiopia of dual nationals—largely from small towns—by the local authorities for security reasons, and the expulsion of many others against their will, were arbitrary and thus contrary to international law. In other words, what the Commission objected to in this case was not expulsion on the ground of dual nationality, but the arbitrary nature of that expulsion.

31. A number of scenarios can be envisaged with respect to expulsion following loss of nationality or denationalization.

32. In cases of dual nationality, must the person concerned necessarily be expelled to the State of the remaining nationality if it is not the "denationalizing" State? Can the expelled person object to this? If so, what action is taken?

33. In principle, the expelling State in such cases has the right to expel the person to the State of the remaining nationality because denationalization ends the situation of dual nationality; the expelled person henceforth has only the nationality of the latter State, whether or not it was the dominant nationality prior to denationalization. Recent examples illustrating actual denationalization on the basis of dual nationality are those of Turkey[170] and Turkmenistan[171], while examples of the threatened denationalization of dual nationals are found in France,[172] the Netherlands[173] and the United Kingdom, particularly when the persons in question are linked to radical Islamic movements. The United Kingdom has specified that its legislation allows the Government to denaturalize individuals who have been convicted of a serious crime unless such persons would thereby become stateless.[174] However, if the person subject to expulsion does not want to be expelled to the State of which he or she now has sole nationality or if the person has reason to fear for his or her life or risks being subjected to torture or degrading treatment in that country, he or she may be expelled to a third State with the latter's consent.

34. For cases of multiple nationality, one scenario to consider is that in which the "denationalizing" State is the State of dominant nationality. In such a case, the same reasoning outlined above in respect of dual nationality could apply, with the sole difference that there would be not one but two or more States of remaining nationality. Another scenario would be one in which the expelling State is not the State of dominant nationality. In this case, expulsion should preferably be to the State of dominant nationality.

35. The Special Rapporteur is not convinced of the necessity or even the practical utility of proposing one or more draft articles on the issues dealt with in the present report, primarily for the following reasons:

(*a*) As the power to confer nationality is within the sovereign jurisdiction of each State, the State may

---

[166] See, for example, Law No. 68-LF-3 (footnote 31 above), art. 34.

[167] See Eritrea–Ethiopia Claims Commission, Partial Award—Civilians Claims: Eritrea's Claims 15, 16, 23 and 27–32 , paras. 79–80; see also ILM, vol. 44 (May 2005), p. 601. See further Kidane, "Civil liability for violations of international humanitarian law: the jurisprudence of the Eritrea–Ethiopia Claims Commission in The Hague", especially p. 52.

[168] See Partial Award … (footnote 167 above), paras. 40 and 45. See also Proclamation No. 21/1992 of the Provisional Government of Eritrea (6 April 1992) (establishing various means of acquiring Eritrean nationality, including birth, marriage and naturalization), United Nations, *The United Nations and the Independence of Eritrea*, pp. 156–158.

[169] See Partial Award … (footnote 167 above), paras. 43 and 46. See also Human Rights Watch, *Eritrea and Ethiopia—The Horn of Africa War: Mass Expulsions and the Nationality Issue*.

[170] See Mayer, "A 'benign' apartheid: how gender apartheid has been rationalized", especially pp. 312–313 (discussing the denationalization case of Member of Parliament, Merve Kavakci, who was a member of the Islamist Virtue Party, wore a headscarf to Parliament and acquired United States nationality without Government permission), citing "Headscarf deputy is stripped of Turkish citizenship", *Deutsche Presse-Agentur* (15 May 1999).

[171] See Shaver, "The revocation of dual citizenship in Turkmenistan" (President Niyazov announced that Turkmenistan was renouncing the 1993 bilateral agreement with the Russian Federation allowing for dual Russian-Turkmen nationality, which results in denationalization and potential expulsion of former nationals.)

[172] "The French lesson", *The Economist* (13 August 2005) (discussing Nicolas Sarkozy's speculation, as Minister of the Interior, that France could revoke the nationality of dual nationals who were radical imams promoting terrorism).

[173] See, for example, Bickerton, "Dutch murders bring tighter terror laws"; and "Dealing with traitors", *The Economist* (see footnote 172 above) (discussing proposals in the Netherlands and the United Kingdom to adopt laws on revocation of the nationality of dual nationals who embrace radical Islam).

[174] See E/CN.4/1999/56 and Add.1–2, para. 31 (*b*) (footnote 58 above).

establish in its domestic legislation conditions for the loss of its nationality and for the denationalization of its nationals provided that this does not result in statelessness and the denationalization is not arbitrary or discriminatory. This is not, strictly speaking, connected to the issue of expulsion of aliens, since the rules referred to above would apply even if the loss of nationality or denationalization were not followed by expulsion. These rules therefore pertain more to the laws governing nationality than to the laws governing the expulsion of aliens;

(*b*) Specifically with respect to expulsion, it has been noted that in cases of dual nationality where there is no risk of statelessness, the loss of nationality or denationalization brings about a situation of sole nationality in which the person in question is subject to ordinary-law provisions concerning expulsion. There is thus no need to set out rules specific to this scenario;

(*c*) Only in cases of multiple nationality do special situations arise: the first is one in which it is necessary to decide to which other State of nationality a State can expel a person who has lost the nationality of the expelling State or has been denationalized, particularly when the expelling State is not the State of dominant nationality of the person in question; the second is one in which the expelled person, exercising his or her right to choose, particularly in the case of succession of States, decides to be a national of the State that intends to expel the person by reason of his or her adoption of a new nationality. In both cases, however, past practice is sorely lacking, although this issue, too, essentially concerns the rules on the nationality of natural persons.

Accordingly, the Special Rapporteur is not convinced that it would be worthwhile for the Commission to prepare draft rules for these situations, even in the interest of the progressive development of international law.

THE OBLIGATION TO EXTRADITE OR PROSECUTE (*AUT DEDERE AUT JUDICARE*)

[Agenda item 7]

DOCUMENT A/CN.4/603

Third report on the obligation to extradite or prosecute (*aut dedere aut judicare*), by Mr. Zdzislaw Galicki, Special Rapporteur

[*Original: English*]
[*10 June 2008*]

CONTENTS

Multilateral instruments cited in the present report

	Source
Convention on Extradition (Montevideo, 26 December 1933)	League of Nations, *Treaty Series*, vol. CLXV, No. 3803, p. 45.
Convention on the Prevention and Punishment of the Crime of Genocide (Paris, 9 December 1948)	United Nations, *Treaty Series*, vol. 78, No. 1021, p. 277.
European Convention on Extradition (Paris, 13 December 1957)	*Ibid.*, vol. 359, No. 5146, p. 273.
Convention on offences and certain other acts committed on board aircraft (Tokyo, 14 September 1963)	*Ibid.*, vol. 704, No. 10106, p. 219.
Vienna Convention on the Law of Treaties (Vienna, 23 May 1969)	*Ibid.*, vol. 1155, No. 18232, p. 331.
Convention for the suppression of unlawful seizure of aircraft (The Hague, 16 December 1970)	*Ibid.*, vol. 860, No. 12325, p. 105.
Convention for the suppression of unlawful acts against the safety of civil aviation (Montreal, 23 September 1971)	*Ibid.*, vol. 974, No. 14118, p. 177.
The Convention against torture and other cruel, inhuman or degrading treatment or punishment (New York, 10 December 1984)	*Ibid.*, vol. 1465, No. 24841, p. 85.
South Asian Association for Regional Cooperation (SAARC) Regional Convention on Suppression of Terrorism (Kathmandu, 4 November 1987)	*International Instruments related to the Prevention and Suppression of International Terrorism* (United Nations publication, Sales No. E.08.V.2), p. 174.
Additional Protocol to the South Asian Association for Regional Cooperation (SAARC) Regional Convention on Suppression of Terrorism (Islamabad, 6 January 2004)	*Ibid.*, p. 250.
Convention for the suppression of unlawful acts against the safety of maritime navigation (Rome, 10 March 1988)	United Nations, *Treaty Series*, vol. 1678, No. 29004, p. 201.
United Nations Convention against Illicit Traffic in Narcotic Drugs and Psychotropic Substances (Vienna, 20 December 1988)	*Ibid.*, vol. 1582, No. 27627, p. 95.
Rome Statute of the International Criminal Court (Rome, 17 July 1998)	*Ibid.*, vol. 2187, No. 38544, p. 3.
United Nations Convention against Transnational Organized Crime (New York, 15 November 2000)	*Ibid.*, vol. 2225, No. 39574, p. 209.
Protocol to Prevent, Suppress and Punish Trafficking in Persons, Especially Women and Children, supplementing the United Nations Convention against Transnational Organized Crime (New York, 15 November 2000)	*Ibid.*, vol. 2237, No. 39574, p. 319.
Protocol against the Smuggling of Migrants by Land, Sea and Air, supplementing the United Nations Convention against Transnational Organized Crime (New York, 15 November 2000)	*Ibid.*, vol. 2241, No. 39574, p. 480.
Protocol against the Illicit Manufacturing of and Trafficking in Firearms, Their Parts and Components and Ammunition, supplementing the United Nations Convention against Transnational Organized Crime (New York, 31 May 2001)	*Ibid.*, vol. 2326, No.39574, p. 211.
United Nations Convention on Jurisdictional Immunities of States and Their Property (New York, 2 December 2004)	*Official Records of the General Assembly, Fifty-ninth session, Supplement No. 49* (A/59/49), vol. I, resolution 59/38, annex.

Works cited in the present report

ENACHE-BROWN, Colleen and Ari FRIED

"Universal Crime, Jurisdiction and Duty: The Obligation of *Aut Dedere Aut Judicare* in International Law", *McGill Law Journal*, vol. 43 (1997–1998), p. 613–633.

INSTITUTE OF INTERNATIONAL LAW

Yearbook, vol. 71–II, Session of Krakow, 2005, Second Part, Paris, Pedone, p. 297.

WISE, Edward M.

"The obligation to extradite or prosecute", *Israel Law Review*, vol. 27 (1993), pp. 268–287.

Introduction

1. The present report is the third report on the obligation to extradite or prosecute (*aut dedere aut judicare*) presented by the Special Rapporteur. It is aimed at continuing the process undertaken in the preliminary report of 2006[1] and the second report, of 2007,[2] which is to formulate questions addressed both to States and to the members of the International Law Commission concerning the most essential aspects of the topic. These questions, which to

[1] *Yearbook ... 2006*, vol. II (Part One), document A/CN.4/571.

[2] *Yearbook ... 2007*, vol. II (Part One), document A/CN.4/585.

some extent have been repeated each year, are intended to enable the Special Rapporteur to draw some final conclusions regarding the main problem of this exercise, namely, whether the obligation *aut dedere aut judicare* exists as a matter of customary international law.

2. Although a fully convincing answer to this question cannot be found yet at this stage, the results of this research seem now to be much more promising than at the beginning, when some voices expressing doubts about existence of the said obligation could be heard (see paras. 60 and 61 below). The topic itself requires a wide analysis of various instruments, such as treaties and their *travaux preparatoires*, jurisprudence, national legislation and doctrine.

Chapter I

The follow-up to the second report of the Special Rapporteur

3. The second report, presented by the Special Rapporteur during the fifty-ninth session of the International Law Commission, in 2007, was in fact closely connected to the preliminary report presented to the Commission in 2006. Readers could even find that certain fragments of both reports were almost identical. There were, however, at least three reasons justifying such repetitions.

4. The first one derived from the simple fact that around half the members of the Commission had been replaced as a result of the election held by the General Assembly at the end of 2006. Therefore, it was worthwhile to recapitulate in the second report, for the benefit of newly elected members, the main ideas and concepts presented by the Special Rapporteur in the preliminary report, together with a summary of the discussion which had subsequently taken place first in the Commission, and later in the Sixth Committee.

5. Secondly, as mentioned in paragraph 3 of the second report,[3] it appeared to be necessary to obtain the views of the new members of the Commission on the most controversial matters covered in the preliminary report before proceeding to a substantive elaboration of possible draft rules or articles concerning the obligation to extradite or prosecute.

6. Finally, there was the unquestioned need for a wider response to be obtained from States on the issues identified by the Commission in the relevant part of its 2006 report.[4] Unfortunately, only seven States had responded to this request and had transmitted their comments and opinions concerning those issues at the moment the Special Rapporteur finalized the second report. Consequently, only those seven comments and opinions could be considered in the second report. Subsequently, the number of comments, opinions and information has increased to about 20, but the repetition of the request to States still seemed, as it seems now, necessary to obtain, as far as possible, a full and actual picture of States' internal regulations and international commitments concerning the obligation to extradite or prosecute.

[3] *Ibid.*, p. 68, para. 3.

[4] *Yearbook ... 2006*, vol. II (Part Two), p. 21, paras. 30 and 31.

A. Consideration of the topic at the fifty-ninth session of the International Law Commission

1. Specific nature of the second report

7. The second report,[5] consisted of a preface, an introduction and two chapters. The preface and the introduction were of an introductory character, recounting briefly the history of the topic in the work of the International Law Commission. The Special Rapporteur now feels free from repeating this history once again.

8. Chapter I of the second report expressed—already in its title—the intention of the Special Rapporteur to address some old and new questions concerning the topic to newly elected members of the Commission, and to have the preliminary report revisited.

9. Consequently, two sections of this chapter of the second report concentrated on the reconsideration of the topic at the fifty-eighth session of the International Law Commission in 2006 and the identification of specific issues on which comments of States were of particular interest to the Commission. It is worth recalling that during the debate in the Commission at its 2006 session, some important questions had already been raised, such as:[6]

(*a*) Is the obligation *aut dedere aut judicare* derived exclusively from international treaties formulating it, or can it be considered also to be based on an already existing, or just emerging, principle of international customary law?[7]

(*b*) Can we find a sufficient customary basis for the application of the said obligation at least to some categories of crimes, for instance, to the most serious crimes recognized under international customary law, such as war crimes, piracy, genocide and crimes against humanity?

[5] *Yearbook ... 2007*, vol. II (Part One), document A/CN.4/585.

[6] *Yearbook ... 2006*, vol. II (Part Two), chap. XI, sect. B.2, p. 172, paras. 220–229.

[7] A similar request was already made in the preliminary report, in which the members of the Commission were asked "to find a generally acceptable answer to the question of whether the legal source of the obligation to extradite or prosecute should be limited to the treaties which are binding the States concerned, or be extended to appropriate customary norms or general principles of law" (see *Yearbook ... 2006*, vol. II (Part One), document A/CN.4/571, p. 266, para. 40).

(*c*) Is it generally acceptable to draw a clear distinction between the concepts of the obligation to extradite or prosecute and that of universal criminal jurisdiction, or perhaps should the Commission embark—in connection with the obligation *aut dedere aut judicare*—on a consideration of the question of universal jurisdiction, at least to some extent, and if so, to what extent?

(*d*) Which part of the alternative obligation to extradite or prosecute should have priority in the process of fulfilling this obligation, or should both parts be treated by States on equal level? And, consequently, to what extent does fulfilment of one part of the said alternative obligation make the State concerned free from fulfilling another part?

(*e*) Should the concept of "triple alternative", involving also the jurisdiction of international tribunals, be totally excluded from our considerations, or—on the basis of a developing practice of States—should it be included as a possible, at least in some cases, third path?

(*f*) Should a final product of the work of the Commission on the topic in question, whenever it is going to be elaborated, take the form of draft articles, rules, principles, guidelines or recommendations, or is it still too early to decide about it?

10. Since not all of these questions obtained concurring answers from the members of the Commission in 2006, it was of great importance for the Special Rapporteur to receive a more decisive response in 2007 from the newly elected Commission.

11. The substantive contents of this response could be also enriched with the views and opinions of the delegations in the Sixth Committee, which have been summarized—thanks to the kind assistance of the Secretariat—in section C of chapter I of the second report and in section C of chapter I of the present report. The Special Rapporteur retained in both cases the systematic arrangement of these sections, together with the subheadings, as introduced by the Secretariat.

12. It has to be stressed that, despite the discussion on these questions during two sessions of the International Law Commission and two sessions of the Sixth Committee, all problems raised above still seem to be open for further consideration.

13. As the members of the Commission may recall, the Special Rapporteur decided to give, in section D of chapter I of the second report,[8] his personal concluding remarks concerning the debate on the preliminary report which had taken place in 2006 in the Commission and in the Sixth Committee. The Special Rapporteur noticed that, taking into account the specific nature of the preliminary report, the comments of the members of the Commission and of the Sixth Committee had concentrated, in general, on the main issues to be considered by the Commission and by the Special Rapporteur in their future work on the topic.

14. There was a great variety of opinions, remarks and suggestions expressed by the members of the Commission and the Sixth Committee during the debate on the topic, dealing with both the substance and the formal side of this exercise, starting with its very title and ending on the choice of the final form of the work of the Commission in this field. A detailed presentation of those opinions, remarks and suggestions, as well as their assessment by the Special Rapporteur, was contained in paragraphs 40 to 60 of the second report.

15. Section E of chapter I of the second report, and section B of chapter I of the present report, contain a summarized presentation of comments and information received from Governments in response to the request addressed to them in the report of the International Law Commission on its fifty-eighth session. These responses have been compiled by the Secretariat in document A/CN.4/579.[9]

16. It has to be stressed that materials received from States were organized by the Secretariat in a transparent manner, in four clusters of information, in accordance with the order of questions formulated earlier in the report of the Commission. Section B of this chapter below follows the same organization: (*a*) international treaties containing the obligation *aut dedere aut judicare*; (*b*) domestic legal regulations; (*c*) judicial practice; and (*d*) crimes or offences.

17. This organization has made it much easier, for the Commission and the Special Rapporteur, to perform now and in the future any comparative exercise necessary for further elaboration of the topic. The Special Rapporteur would like to express, once again, his gratitude to the Secretariat for its kind assistance and cooperation. The comments and information contained in *Yearbook ... 2007*, vol. II (Part One), document A/CN.4/579 and Add. 1–4, because of their delayed presentation by States, could not be considered by the Special Rapporteur in his second report. Therefore, they only have been considered and analysed in the present report (see paras. 57–87 below).

18. Chapter II of the second report[10] brought us to the core of the work performed traditionally by the Commission over each substantial topic elaborated by the Commission in the process of the codification and progressive development of international law. It contains a formulation of draft articles, rules, principles, guidelines or recommendations—whatever form is chosen by the Commission—which is intended to reflect the actual status quo of international law and of the practice of States in a given area of international relations.

19. During the preparation of the second report, the Special Rapporteur was of the opinion that, although the comments and information delivered by States were still far from being complete and from giving a solid and definite basis for constructive conclusions, it was possible,

[8] *Yearbook ... 2007*, vol. II (Part One), document A/CN.4/585.

[9] *Yearbook ... 2007*, vol. II (Part One), document A/CN.4/579 and Add.1–4.

[10] *Yearbook ... 2007*, vol. II (Part One), document A/CN.4/585.

already at that stage, to formulate provisionally a draft article concerning the scope of application of future draft articles on the obligation to extradite or prosecute. Section A of chapter II of the second report was intended to deal with this task.

20. Consequently, in paragraph 76 of the second report,[11] taking into account considerations evoked in the preliminary report, as well as in the second report, the Special Rapporteur suggested that the first article be formulated in the following way:

"*Article 1. Scope of application*

"The present draft articles shall apply to the establishment, content, operation and effects of the alternative obligation of States to extradite or prosecute persons under their jurisdiction."

21. In paragraphs 79 to 104 of the second report,[12] the Special Rapporteur gave a short survey of three main elements proposed in draft article 1 and tried to identify principal problems connected to them which, in his opinion, could become a subject of discussion by the members of the Commission. They were:

(*a*) The time element: extension of the application of the future draft articles to the periods of establishment, operation and production of effects of the obligation in question;

(*b*) The substantive element: a specific alternative obligation of States to extradite or prosecute;

(*c*) The personal element: the persons against whom the above-mentioned obligation of States may be exercised.

22. As was stressed in paragraph 80 of the second report,[13] there are at least three specific periods of time connected with the establishment, operation and effects of the obligation *aut dedere aut judicare*, each possessing its own particular characteristic, which should be reflected later in the draft articles. Furthermore, particularly as it concerns the period of establishment of the obligation to extradite or prosecute, a matter of paramount importance seems to be the question of sources from which this obligation may derive. Then, if ever a customary way of formulation of the said obligation is going to be finally accepted, the practice of States required for such formulation has to be considered in the context of the period of time necessary for a sufficient development of such practice.

23. With reference to the substantive element, as was noted in paragraph 89 of the second report,[14] the Commission has to decide whether and to what extent an obligation to extradite or prosecute exists and whether it is an absolute or a relative one. There are numerous questions which may appear in connection with the said alternative. Three of them have been raised in paragraphs 90 to 92 of the second report:[15]

(*a*) Which part of the alternative should have a priority in the practice of exercising this obligation by States, or do States have freedom of choice between the extradition and the prosecution of the persons concerned?

(*b*) Does the custodial State which receives the extradition request have a sufficient margin of discretion to refuse it when it is ready to enforce its own means of prosecution in the case, or when the arguments of the extradition request appear to be wrong and contrary to the legal system of the custodial State?

(*c*) Does the obligation *aut dedere aut judicare* include or exclude a possibility of a third choice? This question has a special importance, in particular in the light of the alternative competence of the International Criminal Court established on the basis of the Rome Statute of 1998.

24. Finally, considering the third, personal element of the proposed draft article 1, it is necessary to remember, as was stressed in paragraph 94 of the second report,[16] that the obligation of States to extradite or prosecute is not an abstract one, but is always connected with necessary activities to be undertaken by States *vis-à-vis* particular natural persons. The choice to make between extradition or prosecution in a given case has to be addressed to defined persons.

25. A further condition for natural persons to be covered under the obligation *aut dedere aut judicare* is that they should be under the jurisdiction of States bound by this obligation. The term "under their jurisdiction", proposed in draft article 1, means both actual jurisdiction that is effectively exercised and potential jurisdiction that a State is entitled to establish over persons committing particular offences. At a later stage, the Commission will have to decide precisely to what extent the concept of universal jurisdiction should be used for a final description of the scope of the obligation *aut dedere aut judicare*.

26. Together with the personal element, it will be impossible to avoid considering at a later stage the question of crimes and offences, to which the substantive obligation is going to extend, committed by the persons concerned (or, at least which those persons are suspected or accused of having committed). However, as was stated in paragraph 100 of the second report,[17] the Special Rapporteur is of the opinion that, for the purposes of elaboration of the provision dealing with the scope of application of the draft articles on the obligation *aut dedere aut judicare*, it does not seem to be essential to include any direct remark concerning those crimes or offences in the actual text of draft article 1.

27. Section B of chapter II of the second report was entitled "Plan for further development". It was the specific part of the report in which the Special Rapporteur wanted to share with the members of the Commission his ideas and concepts concerning other draft articles, following the initial one. These ideas and concepts remain actual matters for the purposes of the present report.

[11] *Ibid.*, p. 76, para. 76.

[12] *Ibid.*, p. 76–79, paras. 79–104.

[13] *Ibid.*, p. 76, para. 80.

[14] *Ibid.*, p. 77, para. 89.

[15] *Ibid.*, p. 77, para. 90–92.

[16] *Ibid.*, p. 77, para. 94.

[17] *Ibid.*, p. 78, para. 100.

28. It seemed rather indisputable that the next draft article to be elaborated, which could be entitled "Use of terms", should include a definition or description of the terms used for the purposes of the draft articles. The list of such terms should remain open and its content depends on particular needs which may appear in the process of elaboration of other draft articles. Proposals given in the second report by the Special Rapporteur were limited, for instance, to such terms as "jurisdiction", "prosecution", "extradition" or "persons under jurisdiction". They have served, however, as a useful basis for draft article 3 proposed in the present report.

29. As was noted in paragraph 107 of the second report,[18] another draft article, or even a set of draft articles, that may already be foreseen, could be connected with a more detailed description of the principal obligation *aut dedere aut judicare*, as well as of its alternative elements.

30. Taking into account that there is a rather general consensus as to the fact that international treaties are treated as a generally recognized source of the obligation to extradite or prosecute, it seems possible—at the beginning—to formulate in the future a draft article stating, "Each State is obliged either to extradite or to prosecute an alleged offender if such an obligation is provided for by a treaty to which such State is a party". Such an article would be, of course, without any prejudice to the recognition of international customary norms as a possible source of criminalization of certain acts, and as a source of the obligation to extradite or to prosecute, to be exercised by States, at least towards the offenders committing such crimes.

31. Finally, as was noted in paragraphs 113 and 114 of the second report,[19] another source of interesting suggestions concerning the formulation of subsequent draft articles may be found in the draft Code of Crimes against the Peace and Security of Mankind, which was adopted by the Commission in 1996.[20] That Code incorporated the *aut dedere aut judicare* rule and, in explanations accompanying the rule, gave *sui generis* directives for possible further draft articles on the obligation to extradite or prosecute.

32. Four of these quasi-rules were presented in paragraph 114 of the second report. However, the Special Rapporteur had already stressed that those rules were not yet formally included as proposals for draft articles. As they have been evoked earlier by the Commission, although in a different context, the Special Rapporteur just saw a reason to bring them again to the attention of the members of the Commission. Although they are not actually repeated in the present report, the Special Rapporteur plans to return to them at an appropriate time and place.

33. In his introduction of the second report on the obligation to extradite or prosecute before the Commission, the Special Rapporteur confirmed that the "preliminary plan of action" formulated in 10 main points in the preliminary report[21] remained the main road map for his further work, including the continued analysis of highly informative materials concerning legislation (international and national), judicial decisions, practice of States and doctrine, collected with the kind assistance of the Secretariat. The Special Rapporteur was convinced that those elements, together with the further opinions and comments from Governments, should create a sufficient background for the effective elaboration of subsequent draft articles. Those expectations of the Special Rapporteur remain valid in the context of the present report, although the slow flow of the said opinions and comments from States affects the progress of the work in a rather negative way.

2. Summary of the debate in the Commission

34. It was the intention of the Special Rapporteur to include in the second report as many difficult problems and questions as possible, with the purpose of obtaining answers and suggestions, first from the members of the Commission and later from the members of the Sixth Committee. As a result of that approach, a great variety of views, opinions, remarks and suggestions was expressed by the members of the Commission during the debate on the topic, dealing with both the substance and the formal side of this exercise, starting with its very title and ending with the choice of the final form of the work of the Commission in this field.

35. As regards the title, among the members of the Commission, the concept of "obligation" seems to prevail over the "principle" to extradite or prosecute. Consequently, the Special Rapporteur shares the opinion that, at least at this stage, the title as it is now formulated should be retained. As already noted by the Special Rapporteur in 2006, the concept of the "obligation" *aut dedere aut judicare* seems to be a safer ground for continuing further constructive analysis than the concept of "principle". It does not exclude, of course, the possibility, and even a necessity, to consider the parallel question of the right of States to extradite or prosecute as a kind of *sui generis* counterbalance to the said obligation.

36. There were some doubts expressed by the members as to the use of the Latin formula "*aut dedere aut judicare*", especially as concerns the term "*judicare*", which does not reflect precisely the scope of the term "prosecute". The Special Rapporteur agrees with these remarks, though at this stage, he considers it rather premature to concentrate on the precise formulation of terms. Already in his preliminary report,[22] the Special Rapporteur gave a review of various terms used in different periods of development of the said obligation, starting with Grotius's phrase "*punire*".

37. It seems that a more precise meaning and exact scope of the term "*judicare*", which is mostly used now, should be defined, together with other terms, for the purposes of the draft articles, in the future draft article 2 ("Use of terms"). It also seems that the total elimination of the Latin origin of the obligation in question would not be appropriate since it is still retained in both the legislative practice and the doctrine.

---

[18] *Ibid.*, p. 79, para. 107.

[19] *Ibid.*, p. 80, paras. 113 and 114.

[20] *Yearbook ... 1996*, vol. II (Part Two), p. 30, art. 9 (Obligation to extradite or prosecute).

[21] *Yearbook ... 2006*, vol. II (Part One), document A/CN.4/571, p. 269, para. 61.

[22] *Ibid.*, p. 262, paras. 5 *et seq.*

38. The debate in the Commission during its fifty-ninth session, in 2007, revolved generally around three main problems,[23] although not all the members expressed concurring opinions in respect of these questions:

(*a*) How to approach the topic from the point of view of the sources of the obligation concerned;

(*b*) What kind of mutual relationship—if it is supposed that such a relationship exists—between the obligation *aut dedere aut judicare* and the concept of universal jurisdiction should be accepted for the purposes of draft articles on the obligation to extradite or prosecute;

(*c*) How the limits of the scope of the said obligation—and those of the application of future draft articles—should be established.

39. The Special Rapporteur notes with satisfaction that, although the questions listed above had already been posed during the debate at the fifty-eighth session, in 2006, there was a significant clarification of views expressed by members of the Commission during the fifty-ninth session, in 2007.

40. On the first question, although there is rather general consent that appropriate treaty provisions may at present be considered as the unquestioned source of the obligation *aut dedere aut judicare*, there seems to be a growing interest among the members of the Commission concerning a possibility of recognizing also a customary basis for the said obligation, at least in respect of some categories of crimes, for instance, the most serious crimes recognized under international customary law.

41. The Special Rapporteur agrees that, when giving some examples of such crimes, he omitted a category of "crimes against the peace and security of mankind". On the other hand, he feels satisfied with the fact that a number of members of the Commission added this category to those which could be considered as a possible background for the application of the obligation in question, without prejudice, of course, to the final results of such consideration.

42. During the 2006 session, the opinions expressed by the members of the Commission were much more cautious concerning the possibility of a customary basis for the said obligation. In 2007, their attitude to this problem seemed to be generally more permissive, although the Special Rapporteur agrees with warnings expressed by many members that such a conclusion should be based only on a very solid analysis of the international, legislative and judicial practice of States.

43. It was also stressed during the fifty-ninth session that for this purpose it was necessary to know both the practice and *opinio juris* of a large number of States. Therefore, the idea of continuing to request States to deliver appropriate information—either directly or through States' representatives in the Sixth Committee—seems to be accepted, though this last channel was criticized by some members.

[23] *Yearbook ... 2007*, vol. II (Part Two), p. 88, para. 365.

44. The number of opinions and comments concerning the preliminary report, sent by States over a period of more than one year, is still rather small, but is growing slowly, giving rise to some optimism that this source will eventually yield information that is sufficiently voluminous and representative to allow some constructive conclusions to be drawn in subsequent reports.

45. As to the second question, concerning universal jurisdiction, a specific evolution may also be noticed in comparison with the position taken last year by the members of the Commission. While at the fifty-eighth session of the Commission, the prevailing opinion, as noted by the Special Rapporteur in his second report, was that there should be a very careful treatment of the mutual relationship between the obligation to extradite or prosecute and the principle of universal jurisdiction, and that the distinction between universal jurisdiction and the obligation *aut dedere aut judicare* should be clearly drawn, during the fifty-ninth session a more permissive approach was taken by a large number of members.

46. It was suggested that these two institutions should be analysed in parallel. It was also stated, for instance, that universal jurisdiction had to be analysed in order to see whether and where that basis for jurisdiction might overlap with the obligation *aut dedere aut judicare*.

47. The Special Rapporteur agrees with these suggestions, especially in the light of interesting conclusions, contained in the resolution adopted by the Institute of International Law in Cracow, Poland, in 2005 on universal criminal jurisdiction with respect to the crime of genocide, crimes against humanity and war crimes.[24] A mutual relationship and—to some extent—an interdependence between universal jurisdiction and the obligation *aut dedere aut judicare* was rather clearly shown in that resolution.

48. However, the Special Rapporteur is convinced that the main current of further consideration should remain connected with the obligation to extradite or prosecute and should not be dominated in any case by the question of universal jurisdiction.

49. With regard to the third question, concerning, as the Special Rapporteur proposed in draft article 1, the scope of application of the draft articles and, as some members suggested, the scope of the obligation "*aut dedere aut judicare*", the Special Rapporteur could agree with the suggestion that the said obligation should not be treated as an alternative one and that the mutual relationship and interdependence between the two elements of this obligation—"*dedere*" and "*judicare*"—should be carefully and thoroughly analysed in the future.[25] As was suggested by some members, specific characteristics of both elements and conditions necessary for their application should be also considered.

[24] *Yearbook of the Institute of International Law*, p. 297.

[25] However, the Special Rapporteur would like to recall here that one of the best doctrinal specialists in the topic in question, Professor Edward M. Wise, in his well-known essay on the obligation to extradite or prosecute, starts with the statement: "This paper is concerned with the alternative obligation to extradite or prosecute contained in multilateral treaties requiring suppression of 'international offenses'." See Wise, "The obligation to extradite or prosecute", pp. 268–287.

50. Taking into account prevailing opinions expressed by the members of the Commission, the Special Rapporteur will consider withdrawing his initial concept of a possible "triple alternative", and will rather try to present and analyse possible particular situations connected with the surrender of persons to the International Criminal Court, which may have an impact on the obligation *aut dedere aut judicare*.

51. However, as concerns another disputable question, the Special Rapporteur is not fully convinced that "the time element" of the proposed draft article 1, dealing with the scope of application, should be treated in a comprehensive way, without any differentiation between the periods connected with the establishment, operation and effects of the obligation in question.

52. Numerous members of the Commission suggested referring draft article 1 to the Drafting Committee for further elaboration. The Special Rapporteur was not opposed in principle to this suggestion. However, for practical reasons, he would suggest that draft article 1 be referred together with other draft articles which are going to be presented later. The draft articles could be more easily considered by the Drafting Committee as a set, taking into account possible interdependence among them. Substantive suggestions concerning such future articles were given by the Special Rapporteur in chapter II of his second report, and it seems that they were rather positively evaluated by the members of the Commission.

53. Since the debate on the obligation to extradite or prosecute was attended by numerous members of the International Law Commission, the Special Rapporteur, in his concluding remarks presented to the Commission,[26] was able to address only the most general and most important problems and questions raised by the participants. Nevertheless, he can assure the members that all other remarks, opinions, views and comments—positive as well as critical—have been carefully noted and taken into account in the preparation of the present report.

B. Specific issues on which comments of States would be of particular interest to the Commission: comments and information received from Governments

54. The Commission included in chapter III of the report on its fifty-ninth session, as usual, a list of specific issues on which comments from States would be of particular interest. The obligation to extradite or prosecute (*aut dedere aut judicare*) was among the issues identified.[27]

55. To a great extent, the questions raised in this context were analogous to those formulated during the fifty-eighth session, in 2006.[28] The Commission declared that it would welcome any information that Governments might wish to provide concerning their legislation and practice, particularly the more contemporary, with regard to this topic. If possible, such information should concern:

(*a*) International treaties by which a State is bound, containing the principle of universal jurisdiction in criminal matters; is it connected with the obligation *aut dedere aut judicare*?

(*b*) Domestic legal regulations adopted and applied by a State, including constitutional provisions and penal codes or codes of criminal procedures, concerning the principle of universal jurisdiction in criminal matters; is it connected with the obligation *aut dedere aut judicare*?

(*c*) Judicial practice of a State reflecting the application of the principle of universal jurisdiction in criminal matters; is it connected with the obligation *aut dedere aut judicare*?

(*d*) Crimes or offences to which the principle of universal jurisdiction in criminal matters is applied in the legislation and practice of a State; is it connected with the obligation *aut dedere aut judicare*?

56. Furthermore, the Commission added in 2007 that it would also appreciate information on the following:[29]

(*a*) whether the State has authority under its domestic law to extradite persons in cases not covered by a treaty or to extradite persons of its own nationality;

(*b*) whether the State has authority to assert jurisdiction over crimes occurring in other States that do not involve one of its nationals;

(*c*) whether the State considers the obligation to extradite or prosecute as an obligation under customary international law and if so to what extent.

Finally, the Commission said that it would welcome any further information and views that Governments might consider relevant to the topic.

57. Unfortunately, with the exception of the written information received from States during the fifty-ninth session of the Commission that responded to the questions formulated in the preliminary report of 2006, there was practically no written response from States to the questions formulated in paragraph 20 of the second report in 2007. The list of States which have delivered written information in response to the questions formulated in either report (in most cases the preliminary report only) includes the following:

(*a*) Austria, Croatia, Japan, Monaco, Qatar, Thailand and United Kingdom of Great Britain and Northern Ireland (reflected in A/CN.4/579);

(*b*) Chile, Ireland, Kuwait, Latvia, Lebanon, Mexico, Poland, Serbia, Slovenia, Sri Lanka, Sweden, Tunisia and the United States of America.

58. The information from the seven States mentioned in (*a*) above was considered by the Special Rapporteur in his second report.[30] The information sent by the remaining

[26] *Yearbook ... 2007*, vol. II (Part Two), pp. 88–89, paras. 364–368.

[27] *Ibid.*, p. 6, paras. 31–33.

[28] *Yearbook ... 2006*, vol. II (Part Two), p. 21, para. 30.

[29] *Yearbook ... 2007*, vol. II (Part Two), p. 14, para. 32.

[30] *Yearbook ... 2007*, vol. II (Part One), document A/CN.4/585, pp. 74–76, paras. 61–72.

13 States, mentioned in *(b)* above, in the period between April and July 2007 (in response to the questions formulated in the preliminary report), could not be taken into account in the second report and will be used in the present report.

59. Although the questions addressed to States in both reports dealt with rather particular issues, the possibility of presenting more general observations concerning the topic was of course not excluded. In practice, this opportunity was used only by one State, the United States.

60. In its general comments, the United States stated its belief that "its practice, and that of other countries, reinforces the view that there is not a sufficient basis in customary international law or State practice to formulate draft articles that would extend an obligation to extradite or prosecute beyond binding international legal instruments that contain such obligations".[31]

61. The United States added that it "does not believe that there is a general obligation under customary international law to extradite or prosecute individuals for offences not covered by international agreements containing such an obligation. Rather, the United States believes that States only undertake such obligations by joining binding international legal instruments that contain extradite or prosecute provisions and that those obligations only extend to other States that are parties to such instruments".[32]

62. Although some States, through their delegates in the Sixth Committee or in their written comments, expressed some doubts about the customary basis for a legal obligation *aut dedere aut judicare*, such a decisive rejection *a priori* of a possibility to look for a customary background to the said principle, even as applicable to a limited group of offences, was generally not supported by other States.

1. International treaties by which a State is bound, containing the obligation to extradite or prosecute, and reservations made by that State to limit the application of this obligation

63. All 13 responding States conveyed a list of multilateral and bilateral[33] treaties establishing the obligation *aut dedere aut judicare*, except Sweden, which saw no need to list in its submission each international treaty containing the principle *aut dedere aut judicare*. The lists of multilateral treaties, both universal and regional,[34] followed the list of treaties and conventions mentioned by the Special Rapporteur in his preliminary report.[35] In addition, Chile mentioned two multilateral treaties concerning specific offences in view of their special relevance.[36]

64. Slovenia and Sri Lanka mentioned that they made no reservation to relevant multilateral treaties which limit the application of the obligation *aut dedere aut judicare*.

65. Mexico noted that, in signing the Convention on Extradition and in acceding to the Convention for the Suppression of Unlawful Acts against the Safety of Maritime Navigation, it had made reservations, but that those reservations did not affect the provisions setting out the obligation to extradite or prosecute in the multilateral treaties to which it was a party.

66. The United States noted that it had not made reservations to limit the application of the obligation to extradite or prosecute *per se*. When becoming a party to conventions, the United States had taken the position that the extradition obligations within the conventions applied only to expand the bases for extradition with countries with which the United States had bilateral extradition treaties.

67. Poland mentioned that it had made two declarations to the European Convention on Extradition concerning non-extradition of its own nationals.

68. Chile, Kuwait, Latvia, Lebanon, Mexico, Poland, Serbia, Slovenia, Sri Lanka and Tunisia listed bilateral treaties containing the obligation *aut dedere aut judicare*. Mostly, they were extradition treaties, although Kuwait and Tunisia mentioned also agreements on legal assistance and legal relations. Serbia stressed that the bilateral treaties did not specifically regulate matters related to extradition or prosecution. However, a number of them stated, as a reason to refuse extradition, the jurisdictional competence of the requested State to prosecute, and provided that, in the case when criminal proceedings had already been initiated for the same offence, the extradition request would be declined.

2. Domestic legal regulations adopted and applied by a State, including constitutional provisions and penal codes or codes of criminal procedures, concerning the obligation to extradite or prosecute (*aut dedere aut judicare*)

69. Some Governments mentioned that international treaties were applicable with no need for national regulations, in some cases directly (Chile) and in other cases following the hierarchy of legislation imposed by the State's constitution (Latvia, Mexico, Serbia and Slovenia).

70. Latvia, Lebanon, Mexico, Poland, Serbia, Slovenia, Sweden and Tunisia mentioned rules from their penal codes and codes of criminal procedures relating to the crimes and to the procedure of the extradition, as well as the cases when the extradition should be accepted or refused and providing who was the competent authority to make such decisions.

---

[31] *Yearbook … 2007*, vol. II (Part One), document A/CN.4/579 and Add.1–4, sect. A, p. 85, para. 1.

[32] *Ibid.*, p. 85, para. 2.

[33] Kuwait mentioned only bilateral agreements.

[34] Ireland, Latvia, Poland and Slovenia mentioned European conventions; Sri Lanka mentioned conventions elaborated within the South Asian Association for Regional Cooperation; and Mexico and Chile mentioned the Convention on Extradition signed in Montevideo in 1933.

[35] *Yearbook … 2006*, vol. II (Part One), document A/CN.4/571, pp. 265–266, paras. 35–39.

[36] United Nations Convention against Illicit Traffic in Narcotic Drugs and Psychotropic Substances; and the United Nations Convention against Transnational Organized Crime and its Protocols (General Assembly resolution 55/25).

71. Latvia, Lebanon, Poland, Serbia, Slovenia, Sweden and Tunisia established different regimes depending on whether the person whose extradition was requested was a national or not. Sweden stressed that it had different regimes regarding extradition, depending on the country to which a person was subject to the extradition.

72. The obligation to prosecute is closely linked to the refusal of the extradition, for example, in Ireland, where the obligation to extradite is considered paramount, recourse to prosecution is considered only when the extradition of an Irish citizen is not permitted because of the absence of reciprocal agreements.

73. In Serbia, in the case when the request for extradition is refused, the criminal legislation of the State provides for prosecution so that the foreigner can be held criminally liable and can face punishment. The criminal legislation of Serbia and the principle of universality will be applied only if no foreign country has requested the extradition of a foreigner or if the extradition request has been refused.

74. In Sweden, a prosecutor is involved in the extradition procedures and will be informed if a request is refused. In that case, the provisions of Swedish legislation and preliminary investigation and prosecution could be applicable in order to fulfil the obligation deriving from the principle *aut dedere aut judicare*.

75. Latvia, Mexico, Poland, Slovenia, Sweden and Tunisia established the rule of double criminality in the conditions to extradite. The offence must exist in accordance with their law and the law of the requesting State.

76. Mexico mentioned that all its extradition proceedings were conducted on the basis of bilateral treaties or of the Extradition Act and that, up to the present, it had not received any extradition request based on a multilateral treaty.

77. Sweden noted that there were additional situations, according to its penal code, where crimes committed outside Swedish territory were to be adjudged according to Swedish law and by a Swedish court, and in such cases, the law did not impose any requirement of double criminality.

78. Ireland mentioned its International Criminal Court Act of 2006, which provided for the surrender of individuals to the International Criminal Court for the prosecution of offences within the jurisdiction of the Court, and the International War Crimes Tribunal Act of 1998, which provided for the surrender of individuals where requested by an "international tribunal".

79. Poland noted that the final decision on the application of a foreign State for extradition was taken by the Minister of Justice and that only a ruling in which the court determined inadmissibility of extradition was binding on the Minister.

80. Sri Lanka recalled the Extradition Act No. 08 of 1977, which provided the basic legal regime to deal with requests for the extradition of offenders received from designated Commonwealth countries or treaty States. In addition, appropriate provisions amending that Act were mentioned, including the enabling legislations introduced to give effect to international treaties relating to the suppression of serious international crimes which contained the obligation to extradite or prosecute.

81. While Tunisia mentioned that its Code of Criminal Procedure recognized the active personality principle, the passive personality principle and the objective territoriality principle, Serbia noted that its criminal legislation applied the active personality principle.

82. Kuwait mentioned that the international agreements by which the Government had become bound constituted applicable legislation on the basis of which rulings were to be handed down by the courts and provisions of which were to be applied in all matters relating to extradition.[37]

83. The United States noted that it had no domestic legal provisions concerning the obligation to extradite or prosecute.

3. Judicial practice of a State reflecting the application of the obligation *aut dedere aut judicare*

84. Ireland, Latvia, Mexico and Slovenia have stated that there is not judicial practice reflecting the obligation *aut dedere aut judicare*.

85. Chile and Sri Lanka[38] mentioned cases where the judicial practice reflected the application of the obligation *aut dedere aut judicare*. The two cases presented by Chile concerned the refusal of extradition requests.

86. Serbia noted that its judicial practice allowed for the extradition of foreigners provided all requirements for it had been met. In the previous 10 years, extradition requests had been denied only in very few instances and mainly because nationals of Serbia were involved. When that was the case, the said individuals had not been prosecuted in Serbia since their offences had not fulfilled the conditions required to consider them as offences under international instruments providing for the obligation to extradite or prosecute.

87. The United States mentioned that its judicial practice was consistent with the understanding that the obligation to extradite or prosecute is tethered firmly to international conventions, giving one case as an example.[39]

---

[37] For instance, concerning such matters as the cases in which extradition is compulsory, the cases in which it is not permissible, and the conditions that must be fulfilled for an offence to be extraditable.

[38] In the Supreme Court in Colombo, in the judgment on *Ekanayake v. Attorney General* (SLR 1988 (1), p 46), the following international conventions which contain the obligation to extradite or prosecute were taken into consideration: (*a*) the Convention on Offences and Certain Other Acts committed on Board Aircraft; (*b*) the Convention for the Suppression of Unlawful Seizure of Aircraft and (*c*) the Convention for the Suppression of Unlawful Acts against the Safety of Civil Aviation.

[39] In *United States of America v. Yousef*, 327 F.3d 56 (2d Cir. 2003), a United States court of appeals held that the Montreal Convention created "a jurisdictional agreement among contracting States to extradite or prosecute offenders who commit the acts proscribed by the treaty" (p. 96).

88. The Special Rapporteur is convinced that the judicial practice of States may serve as one of the principal sources to confirm the developing customary background for the obligation *aut dedere aut judicare*. Although, within the written information submitted by States, one may find a relatively small amount of examples of judicial authorities applying the said principle in practice, there is a growing number of such cases reported by other sources. For instance:

(*a*) The Inter-American Court of Human Rights, in its ruling in the case of *Goiburú et al. v. Paraguay*, Judgment of September 22, 2006 (Merits, Reparations and Costs),[40] stated as follows:

> 132. Hence, extradition is an important instrument to this end. The Court therefore deems it pertinent to declare that the States Parties to the Convention should collaborate with each other to eliminate the impunity of the violations committed in this case, by the prosecution and, if applicable, the punishment of those responsible. Furthermore, based on these principles, a State cannot grant direct or indirect protection to those accused of crimes against human rights by the undue application of legal mechanisms that jeopardize the pertinent international obligations. Consequently, the mechanisms of collective guarantee established in the American Convention, together with the regional and universal international obligations on this issue, bind the States of the region to collaborate in good faith in this respect, either by conceding extradition or prosecuting those responsible for the facts of this case on their territory.

(*b*) The Guatemala Constitutional Court decided, on 12 December 2007, not to grant two extradition requests made by an investigating judge of Spain, because, in its view, Spain could not exercise universal jurisdiction in the case. The case in Spain, known as the *Ríos Montt* case, is mainly based on the alleged genocide of the Mayan population in Guatemala during the armed conflict and the killings committed in the Spanish embassy in Guatemala City by Guatemalan officials. The Constitutional Court stated, among other reasons for its decision, that the Convention on the Prevention and Punishment of the Crime of Genocide did not provide for universal jurisdiction by a third State without prior consent of the territorial State, Guatemala. However, the ruling contains a positive statement on the obligation to prosecute or extradite. The Court recalls, three times, that it is a duty of Guatemala to extradite or prosecute. The positive assertion by the Court, which does not seem to be based on any conventional provision nor any treaty, is quoted as a basis for such a statement. The Court simply refers to it as a rule or obligation;[41]

(*c*) The ruling by the National Court of Spain, rendered on 28 April 2008, gives another very fresh example of the appearance of the principle *aut dedere aut judicare* in the judicial acts. The National Court, in a first preliminary ruling, subject to appeal, found that the extradition request by Argentina to investigate María Estela Martínez de Perón (third wife of Juan Perón, and his widow) for a case of enforced disappearance and another case of imprisonment and torture, both committed in 1975, might not be conceded. The main reasons cited by the Court were the lack of jurisdiction by Argentina and the applicability of statutory limitations to the crimes committed in 1975. The Court found that those crimes were not widespread or systematic and therefore did not amount to crimes against humanity (to which the prohibition of statute of limitations does apply, according to the Court). In addition, the Court, while interpreting the extradition treaty between Spain and Argentina, asserted that if an extradition request is denied, the State where the suspect is found is under the obligation to try him or her before national courts. However, the Court also added a new and so far unknown condition: the trial before national courts may only take place if so required by the requesting State (in this case, Argentina).

89. The three judicial acts mentioned above, adopted after the beginning of our exercise concerning the obligation to extradite or prosecute, may create a good stimulation for further research in this direction, as they show that not only treaties, but also other sources may be treated as a basis for this obligation.

4. Crimes or offences to which the principle of the obligation *aut dedere aut judicare* is applied in the legislation or practice of a State

90. Chile, Slovenia and Poland mentioned that the obligation *aut dedere aut judicare* applies to all offences. In

---

[40] Inter-American Court of Human Rights, Series C, no. 153; available at www.corteidh.or.cr/docs/casos/articulos/seriec_153_ing.pdf (accessed 21 November 2013).

[41] See Guatemala, Constitutional Court, 2008. Furthermore, in the recent pronouncement (Spain, Audiencia Nacional, Juzgado Central de Instrucción Uno, D. Previas 331/1999) by Investigating Judge Santiago Pedraz Gómez, in charge of the *Ríos Montt* case in Madrid, he not only regrets the lack of cooperation in the investigations by Guatemalan authorities but makes a number of valuable statements of a legal nature, particularly on the customary and conventional nature of the *aut dedere aut judicare* principle, as well as its applicability to all *jus cogens* crimes:

"In the course of the investigation of the crimes (genocide, tortures, assassinations) the Kingdom of Spain requested of the Guatemalan authorities judicial collaboration by way of timely and appropriate rogatory commissions. Not one of these has been carried out, in spite of multiple attempts on the part of Spain to obtain said collaboration. The Guatemalan State has demonstrated a clear dilatory attitude, not only by the delays in moving the process forward, but also by claiming "problems" with signatures, footnotes, the financial resources of those charged.

"...

"At the same time, with this decision, the Constitutional Court lets it be known that the State of Guatemala assumes full responsibility for violating its international obligations and its own national laws, by ignoring the *erga omnes* (universally applicable) international obligation *aut dedere aut judicare* (extradite or prosecute) recognized by most authoritative doctrine since it was established in the XVII century by Grotius and, today, incorporated into both customary and conventional International Law and International Criminal Law. It bears noting that, beyond its application in customary International Criminal Law, conventional (treaty-based) International Law such as the Convention Against Torture and Other Cruel, Inhuman or Degrading Treatment or Punishment..., the requirement to extradite or prosecute is obligatory, and mentioned repeatedly.

"In spite of this obligation *erga omnes*, applicable to all international crimes that are *jus cogens* in nature, like those here charged, the highest Guatemalan court says or insinuates nothing about the full effect of these laws and of the obligation of its courts to execute them, and thus Guatemala incurs in a flagrant violation of its international obligations as a State.

"...

"Genocide is a crime under International Law. Therefore, its prosecution becomes obligatory for all the members of the international community. In its ruling, the Constitutional Court of Guatemala characterizes what took place against the Mayan people as a political crime, in the same way it considers the other crimes being investigated.

"...

"Consequently, it becomes even more necessary that the Spanish judicial system continue to investigate these crimes ... as it is clear that Guatemalan cooperation will not be forthcoming in the process against those presumed to be criminally responsible, by denying the request for their extradition, in violation of the already cited *aut dedere aut judicare* obligation."

the case of Chile, there are no limitations in national legislation that would prevent its application to certain crimes or offences. In Slovenia, it applies to all crimes proscribed in the Penal Code, including crimes which derive from international humanitarian law and international treaties. In Poland, its application is connected with the commission of any crimes or offences covered by international treaties binding on the Poland.

91. Ireland made a cross-reference to information given on the topic of domestic legislation.

92. In Mexico, according to the Judicial Authority Organization Act, individuals who commit federal crimes can be extradited, and crimes provided for in international treaties are federal crimes, which are heard by federal criminal judges.

93. As noted at the beginning of the present section B, the comments and information discussed in this section are those received in written form from a limited number of States. Consequently, a wider reaction of States to the questions formulated in the reports of the International Law Commission could be found in practice mostly in the observations presented by the delegates to the Sixth Committee of the General Assembly during its sixty-second session.

C. Discussion on the obligation to extradite or prosecute held in the Sixth Committee during the sixty-second session of the General Assembly

94. The present section is based, as was the corresponding section of the second report, on the topical summary prepared by the Secretariat of the discussion held in the Sixth Committee of the General Assembly.[42] The Special Rapporteur decided to retain, as before, the systematic arrangement of the material employed in the topical summary, including the subtitles applied by the Secretariat, thanks to which the presentation of Member States' views and opinions is much more clear and transparent. Because of a lack of written observations received from States in response to the request contained in chapter III of the 2007 report (see para. 54 above), the opinions expressed by delegations in the Sixth Committee gained special importance as a means of discerning the views of States and their practice in relation to the topic in question.

1. General remarks

95. During the sixty-second session of the General Assembly, in 2007, at the meetings of the Sixth Committee, some delegations emphasized that the obligation to extradite or prosecute was aimed at combating impunity, by ensuring that persons accused of certain crimes would be denied safe haven and be brought to trial for their criminal acts. It was noted that the application of that obligation should not compromise the jurisdiction of States or affect the immunity of State officials from criminal prosecution.

96. Some delegations welcomed the plan for further development of the topic proposed by the Special Rapporteur. Support was expressed for the idea that the Commission conduct a systematic survey of international treaties, national legislation and judicial decisions relevant to the obligation to extradite or prosecute, based on the information obtained from Governments. According to some delegations, the Commission should carry out the survey on a priority basis, before proceeding to the drafting of any articles on the topic. A number of delegations provided, during the debates, information on their laws and practice in the field, as requested by the Commission.

97. While it was pointed out that the Commission should examine the different modalities of the obligation to extradite or prosecute in international treaties, the view was expressed that, if the obligation only existed under conventional law, draft articles on the topic might not be appropriate.[43]

2. Customary character of the obligation

98. Some delegations expressed the view that the obligation to extradite or prosecute was based only on treaties and did not have a customary character. Some other delegations considered that the obligation had acquired customary status, at least for the most serious international crimes, or that it would soon attain such status in respect of such crimes.[44] It was argued that the jurisdiction entrusted to international criminal tribunals to try certain serious international crimes provided evidence of the emerging customary status of the obligation to extradite or prosecute for those crimes.[45] Some delegations emphasized that the question should be settled through an examination of the relevant State practice and supported further study of the issue by the Commission.[46] In

[42] See document A/CN.4/588, paras. 161–173. The Special Rapporteur would like to express, once again, his gratitude to the Secretariat for its very active assistance in collecting and systematizing materials necessary for the preparation of this report.

[43] See, for instance, the statement by the representative of the United States (*Official Records of the General Assembly, Sixty-second Session*, Sixth Committee, 22nd meeting, A/C.6/62/SR.22, para. 91).

[44] An interesting opinion was expressed by the representative of China, who said that "[w]hile the obligation to extradite or prosecute was basically a treaty obligation, it might also become an obligation under customary international law if the crime to which it was applied was a crime under the customary law universally acknowledged by the international community. The crimes covered by that obligation should be primarily international crimes, transnational crimes endangering the common interest of the international community under international law, and serious crimes endangering the national and public interest, under domestic law. Thought might be given to including in the draft articles a non-exhaustive list of such crimes" (*ibid.*, para. 62).

[45] For instance, the representative of Sweden, speaking on behalf of the Nordic Countries, stated that there were grounds to claim that the obligation to extradite or prosecute was acquiring customary status with regard to crimes such as genocide, crimes against humanity, war crimes, torture and terrorist crime. The Commission had concluded in its 1996 draft Code of Crimes against the Peace and Security of Mankind that genocide, crimes against humanity and war crimes would fall under the obligation *aut dedere aut judicare*. The importance of the practical commitment of States to ending impunity for these crimes was also reflected in the Rome Statute of the International Criminal Court, which built on the principle of complementarity (*ibid.*, para. 33).

[46] Such a suggestion was made by the representative of Argentina, who said that the customary law character of the principle would need to be shown on a case-by-case basis, according to the type of crime involved. While there existed an *opinio juris* with regard to the most serious crimes, namely genocide, crimes against humanity and war crimes, that did not warrant any conclusion as to the application to such crimes of the principle in question or of a universal jurisdiction (*ibid.*, 22nd meeting, A/C.6/62/SR.22, para. 58).

general, it may be said that in comparison with the reaction of States to the preliminary report of 2006, a critical approach of States to the idea of a possible customary basis for the obligation *aut dedere aut judicare* has been to some extent relaxed.

3. Crimes covered by the obligation

99. Some delegations suggested that the Commission should establish a non-exhaustive list of crimes covered by the obligation (see footnote 44 above). Among the offences that could be included in such a list, delegations mentioned genocide, war crimes, crimes against humanity and torture, as well as terrorism and corruption.

100. Other delegations supported the proposal that the Commission limit itself to a determination of criteria for the identification of the crimes subject to the obligation (using, for instance, the concept of "crimes against the peace and security of mankind" or referring to the interests of the international community as a whole).

4. Scope and content of the obligation

101. According to some delegations, the definition of the scope of the obligation should remain at the centre of the study by the Commission. It was indicated that the obligation arose for the State when the alleged offender was located on its territory.

102. It was also noted that, in case of concurring jurisdictions, priority should be given to the exercise of jurisdiction by the State on the territory of which the crime was committed or by that of the nationality of the alleged offender. Support was expressed for the Commission to examine, within the present topic, the scope and conditions of the obligation to prosecute, as well as the conditions of extradition (including under domestic law). Specific questions were also raised for further consideration by the Commission, such as the nature of the territorial link required to establish the applicability of the obligation.

103. Some delegations considered that the content of the obligation to extradite or prosecute, and in particular the relationship between the two options contained therein, should be interpreted in the context of each convention providing for that obligation.

104. It was suggested that, in studying the scope and content of the obligation, the Commission should consider in particular the relationship between the options to extradite and to prosecute. Some delegations emphasized the alternative character of the obligation, noting, for example, that the custodial State had discretion to decide which part of the obligation it would execute. Other delegations pointed to the conditional nature of the obligation or noted that the option of extradition took precedence over that of prosecution.

5. Relationship with universal jurisdiction

105. Some delegations emphasized the link between the obligation to extradite or prosecute and the principle of universality (pointing, in particular, to their common purpose), suggesting that the Commission should not exclude *a priori* the existence of such a link. Other delegations rejected the existence of such a link or considered that it was not substantial.

106. In that regard, some delegations were of the view that the concept of universal jurisdiction should not be the focus of the present study. While some delegations encouraged the Commission to analyse its relationship with the obligation to extradite or prosecute (either in a separate provision or in the commentary to the future draft articles), other delegations opposed that proposal. It was also argued that the Commission should clearly distinguish the two notions and that universal jurisdiction should be dealt with in the future draft articles only to the extent necessary for the study of the obligation to extradite or prosecute. The view was expressed that extending universal jurisdiction could be an effective way to implement the obligation to extradite or prosecute; it was indicated, in that regard, that, in order to have the possibility to choose between the two options of *aut dedere aut judicare*, the State should ensure that it had jurisdiction over the relevant offences.

6. Surrender of suspects to international criminal tribunals

107. Some delegations welcomed the decision of the Special Rapporteur to refrain from examining further the so-called "triple alternative" (i.e., the surrender of the alleged offender to an international criminal tribunal).[47] Other delegations, however, continued to believe that the "triple alternative" raised particular issues that should be considered within the present topic. It was noted that States must, in any event, meet their obligations with respect to international criminal jurisdiction.

7. Draft article 1 proposed by the Special Rapporteur

108. Some delegations welcomed draft article 1 proposed by the Special Rapporteur. It was noted, however, that the provision raised a number of issues still to be addressed by the Commission and that it required further clarification. The references made therein to the "alternative" character of the obligation and to different time periods relating to the obligation were criticized by some delegations.[48] A call was made for a further examination of the condition that the alleged offender be "under the jurisdiction" of the State; it was suggested, in that regard, that the draft articles should refer to persons present in the territory of the custodial State or under its control.

---

[47] See, for instance, the statement by the representative of the United Kingdom, who welcomed the said decision of the Special Rapporteur and recalled that the surrender of individuals to international criminal courts was governed by a distinct set of treaty arrangements and legal rules (*ibid.*, 24th meeting, A/C.6/62/SR.24, para. 63). A similar opinion was expressed by the representative of France, who said that her delegation approved of the decision of the Special Rapporteur to refrain from examining further the so-called "triple alternative", the surrender of an individual to an international criminal tribunal, in view of the special treaty rules applicable in that area (*ibid.*, 20th meeting, A/C.6/62/SR.20, para. 12).

[48] The representative of Mexico affirmed that the obligation deriving from the principle *aut dedere aut judicare* was not alternative but conditional. He therefore suggested that draft article 1 be redrafted to eliminate that alternative characteristic (*ibid.*, 24th meeting, A/C.6/62/SR.24, para. 9).

8. Final outcome of the work of the Commission

109. Some delegations indicated that they were flexible as to the final form of the outcome of the Commission's work. Some delegations pointed out that a decision on the matter would depend on the results of the Commission's subsequent examination of the topic. Generally, it was apparent that all delegations wanted to avoid prejudging the final form of the work of the Commission on the topic in question. Simultaneously, this leaves more freedom to the Commission as to the final decision in this matter.

Chapter II

Draft rules on the obligation to extradite or prosecute

110. Although neither the Commission nor the Sixth Committee decided about the formal shape of the exercise on the obligation to extradite or prosecute, it seems that both of them have expressed a rather positive attitude to the proposal made by the Special Rapporteur in his second report to elaborate draft articles on the obligation *aut dedere aut judicare*, including a proposal to formulate a few initial draft articles, starting with draft article 1 on the scope of application.

111. The formulation of the results of the work of the Commission on the obligation to extradite or prosecute in draft articles is without prejudice to a final decision of the Commission as to the kind of international instrument in which such draft articles should be incorporated (annex to a resolution, declaration, draft convention, etc.).

A. Article 1: Scope of application of the draft articles

112. Draft article 1, which has been quoted in paragraph 20 above, has got, in general, a positive evaluation by the members of the Commission and by the delegates in the Sixth Committee, though some remarks concerning its improvements have been made (see paras. 52 and 108 above).

113. Taking into account opinions expressed in the Commission and the Sixth Committee, the Special Rapporteur is ready to delete from the proposed text of the said article the adjective "alternative" (before "obligation"), although, as can be seen from footnote 25 above, the said adjective is used in the doctrinal description of the obligation to extradite or prosecute.

114. Another element of draft article 1 which caused some discussion was the enumeration of phases of formulation and application of the obligation in question ("establishment, content, operation and effects"). Here the Special Rapporteur is ready for further discussion as to the total elimination of this enumeration or its replacement by another formula (e.g., "formulation and application").

115. Finally, the personal element in draft article 1 ("persons under their jurisdiction") has met also with some criticism. There were proposals to replace this formula with others, such as "persons present in the territory of the custodial State" or "persons under the control of custodial State". It seems that this question may be the subject of further discussion, though the Special Rapporteur would rather favour his original proposal.

116. Taking into account comments made by the members of the Commission and delegates in the Sixth Committee, and the opinions of States, the Special Rapporteur would like at this stage to keep the discussion open and to propose an "alternative type" version of draft article 1:

"*Article 1. Scope of application*

"The present draft articles shall apply to the establishment, content, operation and effects of the legal obligation of States to extradite or prosecute persons [under their jurisdiction] [present in the territory of the custodial State] [under the control of custodial State]."

117. Instead of the criticized concept of "alternative" obligation, the Special Rapporteur would like to suggest the addition of "legal" before the "obligation", to stress the necessity of basing the said obligation on legal background and not to treat it as an obligation of moral or political nature. Considering the principle *aut dedere aut judicare* as a fundamental element of the suppression of criminality or as a limitation of power-based diplomacy, though justified to some extent, may create a tendency towards increasing its moral or political importance while diminishing its legal value.

118. The Special Rapporteur has some doubts concerning the suggested elimination of the listing of various phases in which the obligation in question may appear (establishment, content, operation and effects). It is possible, of course, to replace them by a shorter description (e.g. formulation and application), but it may cause some difficulties in the process of formulating draft rules applicable to the more detailed phases of appearance of the obligation *aut dedere aut judicare*. This question, however, has to be decided by the Commission as soon as possible, since it is a precondition for the further systematization of future draft rules.

B. Article 2: Use of terms

119. This article seems to be necessary to avoid misunderstandings and unnecessary repetitions in the process of formulating draft rules concerning the obligation to extradite or prosecute. Although the Special Rapporteur made some suggestions in the second report concerning the terms to be used in the draft articles which could require more detailed definitions, there was a rather weak response as to the possible catalogue of such terms. There was, however, no opposition to such an article and a rather positive approach to this concept.

120. As an example of such terms, the Special Rapporteur mentioned in the second report "extradition", "prosecution", "jurisdiction" and "persons". In connection with the last one, it will be probably useful to add some closer description of "crimes" and "offences" within the "scope of application" of the draft articles. The Special Rapporteur is still convinced that draft article 2 should remain open until the end of the exercise, as to give the opportunity to add other definitions and descriptions whenever necessary.

121. Meanwhile, the only part of draft article 2 which can be suggested now without any doubt would be as follows:

"*Article 2. Use of terms*

"1. For the purposes of the present draft articles:

(*a*) "extradition" means............................. ;

(*b*) "prosecution" means .... ;

(*c*) "jurisdiction" means............................ ;

(*d*) "persons under jurisdiction" means ..... ;

....

"2. The provisions of paragraph 1 regarding the use of terms in the present draft articles are without prejudice to the use of those terms or to the meanings which may be given to them [in other international instruments or] in the internal law of any State."

122. The members of the Commission are kindly requested to propose other terms which—in their opinion—should be specifically defined in draft article 2 for the purposes of the present draft articles. The bracketed part of paragraph 2 of draft article 2 follows various forms that similar articles take in international treaties (drafts of which were elaborated by the Commission).[49] The Special Rapporteur is of the opinion that, taking into account numerous international treaties which are connected with the obligation *aut dedere aut judicare*, draft article 2—apart from "the internal law of any State"—should extend its "without prejudice" clause also to "other international instruments".

[49] For instance, the 1969 Vienna Convention on the Law of Treaties deals only with "the internal law of any State" (art. 2, para. 2), while the United Nations Convention on Jurisdictional Immunities of States and Their Property of 2004 extends the "without prejudice" clause also to "other international instruments" (art. 2, para. 3).

C. Article 3: Treaty as a source of the obligation to extradite or prosecute

123. Draft article 3 proposed in the present report deals with the treaties as a source of the obligation to extradite or prosecute. This suggestion was made by the Special Rapporteur already in the second report, and since it was not opposed either in the Commission or in the Sixth Committee, it seems that the text of draft article 3 could be as follows:

"*Article 3. Treaty as a source of the obligation to extradite or prosecute*

"Each State is obliged either to extradite or to prosecute an alleged offender if such an obligation is provided for by a treaty to which such State is a party."

124. There is a rather general consensus as to the fact that international treaties are a generally recognized source of the obligation to extradite or prosecute. The number of international treaties containing the obligation *aut dedere aut judicare* is growing every year. That formulation alone cannot serve as sufficient background for the codification of a generally binding customary rule, but the development of international practice based on the growing number of treaties establishing and confirming such an obligation may lead at least to the beginning of the formulation of an appropriate customary norm.

125. The Special Rapporteur would like to recall here a doctrinal statement: "If a State accedes to a large number of international treaties, all of which have a variation of the *aut dedere aut judicare* principle, there is strong evidence that it intends to be bound by this generalizable provision, and that such practice should lead to the entrenchment of this principle in customary law."[50]

[50] Enache-Brown and Fried, "Universal Crime, Jurisdiction and Duty: The Obligation of *Aut Dedere Aut Judicare* in International Law", p. 629.

Chapter III

Conclusions

126. The present report on the obligation to extradite or prosecute, as noted at the beginning, is closely connected with its two predecessors—the preliminary report of 2006 and the second report of 2007. Reading carefully all three reports, it is easy to notice the sequence of presented problems and their continuation in subsequent reports. Such a connected approach, even with some repetitions, seems to be suitable for reaching a final result in the form of draft rules truly reflecting existing legal reality. This reality is also changing, even during the not-so-long period of our exercise, as can be noticed, for instance, in the growing number of national legal acts and judicial decisions dealing with the matter concerned. This creates and develops legal practice, which is a crucial element for establishing and accepting emerging customary norms. And proving the existence of a customary basis for the obligation *aut dedere aut judicare* is precisely the main purpose of our endeavour. It seems that during the last three years a growing degree of acceptability for these efforts can be noticed on behalf of States.

127. Among the initial questions which still remain unsolved, appears the problem of the mutual relationship between the obligation *aut dedere aut judicare* and the principle of universal jurisdiction. Despite the efforts

to obtain some convincing opinions from States—especially on the basis of the questions added in paragraph 20 of the second report—the response from States was, first of all, highly insufficient as far as the number of answers obtained is concerned, and secondly, not convincing because of the significant differentiation among those answers (see paras. 45–48, 107 and 108 above). Finally, it seems that, in our exercise, we should avoid any exaggeration in presenting problems connected with universal jurisdiction. On the other hand, it is impossible to eliminate or even marginalize the question of universal jurisdiction whenever and wherever it appears in connection with the fulfilment of the obligation to extradite or prosecute. The compromise solution should be elaborated and it depends to a great extent on the positive reaction of States to the request formulated in this area by the Commission.

128. Another important problem—as yet unresolved—exists in connection with the decision undertaken by the Special Rapporteur in the second report to refrain from examining further the so-called "triple alternative", which means the surrender of the alleged offender to an international criminal tribunal. Although many States supported this decision, it seems that a total rejection of this question could be slightly premature.

129. It may be recalled here that, on 9 January 2007, the act implementing the Rome Statute in Argentina was issued in the *Boletín Oficial de la República Argentina* (Official Gazette), which includes a provision on the *aut dedere aut judicare* obligation closely connected with the question of surrender. It reads as follows:

Article 4.

The aut dedere aut judicare principle

Where a person suspected of having committed a crime as defined in this Act is in the territory of the Argentine Republic or in a place subject to its jurisdiction and that person is not extradited or handed over to the International Criminal Court, the Argentine Republic shall take all necessary steps to exercise its jurisdiction with respect to that crime.[51]

130. Some laws recently enacted in Uruguay, Panama and Peru to implement the Rome Statute also provide for the *aut dedere aut judicare* obligation in the context of the institution of surrender. There is an impression that the "triple alternative" is still alive and closely related to the obligation to extradite or prosecute.

131. Concluding these considerations, the Special Rapporteur would like to request both the members of the Commission and the delegates in the Sixth Committee to respond openly to all questions and problems raised in this report, or in the second report and even in the preliminary report. That will make it possible to continue and complete our joint work on the draft articles on the obligation to extradite or prosecute. The positive effects of this work seem to be more and more important for the international community of States facing growing threats from national and international crime.

[51] *Boletín Oficial de la República Argentina*, año CXV, no. 31069, 9 January 2007, Act No. 26200 implementing the Rome Statute (adopted by Act No. 25390 and ratified on 16 January 2001) of the International Criminal Court. General provisions. General penalties and principles. Offenses against the administration of justice by the International Crimi-nal Court. Relations with the International Criminal Court. Ratified on 13 December 2006, *de facto* promulgation on 5 January 2007.

THE OBLIGATION TO EXTRADITE OR PROSECUTE (*AUT DEDERE AUT JUDICARE*)

[Agenda item 7]

DOCUMENT A/CN.4/599

Comments and observations received from Governments

[*Original: English/Russian/Spanish*]
[*30 May 2008*]

CONTENTS

Multilateral instruments cited in the present report

	Source
Central American Convention on Extradition (Washington, D. C., 7 February 1923)	*Supplement to the American Journal of International Law*, vol. 17, 1923, p. 76.
Convention on Private International Law (Havana, 20 February 1928)	League of Nations, *Treaty Series*, vol. LXXXVI, No. 1950, p. 111.
International Convention for the Suppression of Counterfeiting Currency (Geneva, 20 April 1929)	*Ibid.*, vol. CXII, No. 2623, p. 371.
Convention on Extradition (Montevideo, 26 December 1933)	*Ibid.*, vol. CLXV, No. 3803, p. 45.
Convention of 1936 for the Suppression of the Illicit Traffic in Dangerous Drugs (Geneva, 26 June 1936)	*Ibid.*, vol. CXCVIII, No. 4648, p. 299.
Convention on the prevention and punishment of the crime of genocide (New York, 9 December 1948)	United Nations, *Treaty Series*, vol. 78, No. 1021, p. 277.
Geneva Conventions for the protection of war victims (Geneva, 12 August 1949)	*Ibid.*, vol. 75, Nos. 970–973.
Geneva Convention for the Amelioration of the Condition of the Wounded and Sick in Armed Forces in the Field (Geneva, 12 August 1949)	*Ibid.*, vol. 75, No. 970, p. 31.
Geneva Convention for the Amelioration of the Condition of the Wounded, Sick and Shipwrecked Members of the Armed Forces at Sea (Geneva, 12 August 1949)	*Ibid.*, vol. 75, No. 971, p. 85.
Geneva Convention relative to the Treatment of Prisoners of War (Geneva, 12 August 1949)	*Ibid.*, vol. 75, No. 972, p. 135.
Geneva Convention relative to the Protection of Civilian Persons in Time of War (Geneva, 12 August 1949)	*Ibid.*, vol. 75, No. 973, p. 287.

	Source
Protocol additional to the Geneva Conventions of 12 August 1949, and relating to the protection of victims of international armed conflicts (Protocol I) (Geneva, 8 June 1977)	*Ibid.*, vol. 1125, No. 17512, p. 3.
Protocol additional to the Geneva Conventions of 12 August 1949, and relating to the protection of victims of non-international armed conflicts (Protocol II) (Geneva, 8 June 1977)	*Ibid.*, No. 17513, p. 609.
European Convention on Extradition (Paris, 13 December 1957)	*Ibid.*, vol. 359, No. 5146, p. 273.
Additional Protocol to the European Convention on Extradition (Strasbourg, 15 October 1975)	*Ibid.*, vol. 1161, No. A-5146, p. 450.
Second Additional Protocol to the European Convention on Extradition (Strasbourg, 17 March 1978)	*Ibid.*, vol. 1496, No. A-5146, p. 328.
Convention on the High Seas (Geneva, 29 April 1958)	*Ibid.*, vol. 450, No. 6465, p. 11.
Single Convention on Narcotic Drugs, 1961 (New York, 30 March 1961)	*Ibid.*, vol. 520, No. 7515, p. 151.
Convention on offences and certain other acts committed on board aircraft (Tokyo, 14 September 1963)	*Ibid.*, vol. 704, No. 10106, p. 219.
Convention for the suppression of unlawful seizure of aircraft (The Hague, 16 December 1970)	*Ibid.*, vol. 860, No. 12325, p. 105.
Convention to prevent and punish the acts of terrorism taking the form of crimes against persons and related extortion that are of international significance (Washington, D. C., 2 February 1971)	*Ibid.*, vol. 1438, No. 24381, p. 191.
Convention on psychotropic substances (Vienna, 21 February 1971)	*Ibid.*, vol. 1019, No. 14956, p. 175.
Convention for the suppression of unlawful acts against the safety of civil aviation (Montreal, 23 September 1971)	*Ibid.*, vol. 974, No. 14118, p. 177.
Protocol for the suppression of unlawful acts of violence at airports serving international civil aviation, supplementary to the Convention for the suppression of unlawful acts against the safety of civil aviation (Montreal, 24 February 1988)	*Ibid.*, vol. 1589, No. 14118, p. 474.
International Convention for the Prevention of Pollution from Ships (MARPOL Convention) (London, 2 November 1973), as amended by the Protocol of 1978 (London, 17 February 1978)	United Nations, *Treaty Series*, vol. 1340, No. 22484, p. 61 .
International Convention on the Suppression and Punishment of the Crime of Apartheid (New York, 30 November 1973)	*Ibid.*, vol. 1015, No. 14861, p. 243.
Convention on the prevention and punishment of crimes against internationally protected persons, including diplomatic agents (New York, 14 December 1973)	*Ibid.*, vol. 1035, No. 15410, p. 167.
European Convention on the suppression of terrorism (Strasbourg, 27 January 1977)	*Ibid.*, vol. 1137, No. 17828, p. 93.
Protocol amending the European Convention on the Suppression of Terrorism (Strasbourg, 15 May 2003)	Council of Europe, *European Treaty Series*, No. 190.
Convention on the physical protection of nuclear material (Vienna, 26 October 1979)	*Ibid.*, vol. 1456, No. 24631, p. 101.
International Convention against the taking of hostages (New York, 17 December 1979)	*Ibid.*, vol. 1316, No. 21931, p. 205.
Inter-American Convention on extradition (Caracas, 25 February 1981)	*Ibid.*, vol. 1752, No. 30597, p. 177.
United Nations Convention on the Law of the Sea (Montego Bay, 10 December 1982)	*Ibid.*, vol. 1833, No. 31363, p. 3.
Convention against torture and other cruel, inhuman or degrading treatment or punishment (New York, 10 December 1984)	*Ibid.*, vol. 1465, No. 24841, p. 113.
Inter-American Convention to Prevent and Punish Torture (Cartagena de Indias, 9 December 1985)	Organization of American States, *Treaty Series*, No. 67.
Convention for the suppression of unlawful acts against the safety of maritime navigation (Rome, 10 March 1988)	United Nations, *Treaty Series*, vol. 1678, No. 29004, p. 201.
Protocol to the above-mentioned Convention for the suppression of unlawful acts against the safety of fixed platforms located on the continental shelf (Rome, 10 March 1988)	*Ibid.*,
United Nations Convention against Illicit Traffic in Narcotic Drugs and Psychotropic Substances (Vienna, 20 December 1988)	*Ibid.*, vol. 1582, No. 27627, p. 95.
Convention on the prohibition of the development, production, stockpiling and use of chemical weapons and on their destruction (Paris, 13 January 1993)	*Ibid.*, vol. 1974, No. 33757, p. 45.
Inter-American Convention on Forced Disappearance of Persons (Belém do Pará, 9 June 1994)	*International Legal Materials*, vol. 33, No. 6, 1994, p. 1529.
Convention on the Safety of United Nations and Associated Personnel (New York, 9 December 1994)	United Nations, *Treaty Series*, vol. 2051, No. 35457, p. 363.
Inter-American Convention against Corruption (Caracas, 29 March 1996)	*International Legal Materials*, vol. 35, 1996, p. 727.
International Convention for the Suppression of Terrorist Bombings (New York, 15 December 1997)	United Nations, *Treaty Series*, vol. 2149, No. 37517, p. 256.

	Source
Convention on Combating Bribery of Foreign Public Officials in International Business Transactions (Paris, 17 December 1997)	*International Legal Materials*, vol. 37, 1998, p. 4.
Rome Statute of the International Criminal Court (Rome, 17 July 1998)	United Nations, *Treaty Series*, vol. 2187, No. 38544, p. 3.
Criminal Law Convention on Corruption (Strasbourg, 27 January 1999)	*Ibid.*, vol. 2216, No. 39391, p. 225.
International Convention for the Suppression of the Financing of Terrorism (New York, 9 December 1999)	*Ibid.*, vol. 2178, No. 38349, p. 197.
United Nations Convention against Transnational Organized Crime (New York, 15 November 2000)	*Ibid.*, vol. 2225, No. 39574, p. 209.
Protocol against the Smuggling of Migrants by Land, Sea and Air, supplementing the United Nations Convention against Transnational Organized Crime (New York, 15 November 2000)	*Ibid.*, vol. 2241, No. 39574, p. 480.
Protocol to Prevent, Suppress and Punish Trafficking in Persons, Especially Women and Children, supplementing the United Nations Convention against Transnational Organized Crime (New York, 15 November 2000)	*Ibid.*, vol. 2237, No. 39574, p. 319.
Convention on Cybercrime (Budapest, 23 November 2001)	*Ibid.*, vol. 2296, No. 40916, p. 167.
United Nations Convention against Corruption (New York, 31 October 2003)	*Ibid.*, vol. 2349, No. 42146, p. 41.
International Convention for the Suppression of Acts of Nuclear Terrorism (New York, 13 April 2005)	*Ibid.*, vol. 2445, No. 44004, p. 89.
Central American Treaty on Arrest Warrants and Simplified Extradition (León, 2 December 2005)	Secretaría General del Sistema de la Integración Centroamericana, *Instrumentos jurídicos del Sistema de la Integración Centroamericana*, 1st ed., 2008, p. 419.

Introduction

1. The present report has been prepared pursuant to General Assembly resolution 62/66 of 6 December 2007, in which the Assembly, *inter alia*, invited Governments to provide to the International Law Commission information on practice regarding the topic "The obligation to extradite or prosecute (*aut dedere aut judicare*)".

2. At its fifty-eighth session, in 2006, the Commission decided in accordance with article 19 (2) of its Statute (General Assembly resolution 174 (II), 21 November 1947, annex) to request, through the Secretary-General, Governments to submit information concerning their legislation and practice, particularly the more contemporary, with regard to this topic. More specifically, Governments were requested to provide information concerning:

(*a*) International treaties by which a State is bound, containing the obligation to extradite or prosecute, and reservation made by that State to limit the application of this obligation;

(*b*) Domestic legal regulation adopted and applied by a State, including constitutional provisions and penal codes of criminal procedures, concerning the obligation to extradite or prosecute (*aut dedere aut judicare*);

(*c*) Judicial practice of a State reflecting the application of the obligation *aut dedere aut judicare*;

(*d*) Crimes or offences to which the principle of the obligation *aut dedere aut judicare* is applied in the legislation or practice of a State.[1]

3. At its fifty-ninth session, in 2007, the Commission further requested Governments to submit information concerning their relevant legislation and practice, particularly the more contemporary, more specifically on:

(*a*) International treaties by which a State is bound, containing the principle of universal jurisdiction in criminal matters; is it connected with the obligation *aut dedere aut judicare*?

(*b*) Domestic legal regulations adopted and applied by a State, including constitutional provisions and penal codes or codes of criminal procedures, concerning the principle of universal jurisdiction in criminal matters; is it connected with the obligation *aut dedere aut judicare*?

(*c*) Judicial practice of a State reflecting the application of the principle of universal jurisdiction in criminal matters; is it connected with the obligation *aut dedere aut judicare*?

(*d*) Crimes or offences to which the principle of universal jurisdiction in criminal matters is applied in the legislation and practice of a State; is it connected with the obligation *aut dedere aut judicare*?[2]

4. At the same session, the Commission also indicated that it would appreciate information on:

(*a*) Whether the State has authority under its domestic law to extradite persons in cases not covered by a treaty or to extradite persons of its own nationality?

(*b*) Whether the State has authority to assert jurisdiction over crimes occurring in other States that do not involve one of its nationals?

(*c*) Whether the State considers the obligation to extradite or prosecute as an obligation under customary international law and if so to what extent?[3]

5. Comments received at the fifty-ninth session of the Commission were reproduced in *Yearbook ... 2007*, vol. II (Part One), document A/CN.4/579 and Add. 1 to 4. Since then, and as at 30 May 2008, written observations have been received from the following five States: Chile, Guatemala, Mauritius, the Netherlands and the Russian Federation.

---

[1] See *Yearbook ... 2006*, vol. II (Part Two), p. 21, para. 30.

[2] *Yearbook ... 2007*, vol. II (Part Two), p. 6, para. 31.

[3] *Ibid.*, p. 6, para. 32.

Comments and observations received from Governments

A. Chile

As a complement to the information reproduced in *Yearbook ... 2007*, vol. II (Part One), document A/CN.4/579 and Add. 1 to 4, Chile submitted a list of multilateral treaties to which it is party, containing the obligation to extradite or prosecute: Convention against torture and other cruel, inhuman or degrading treatment or punishment, adopted on 10 December 1984 and promulgated by supreme decree of the Ministry of Foreign Affairs No. 808 of 7 October 1988, *Diario Oficial*, 26 November 1988; Inter-American Convention to Prevent and Punish Torture, adopted on 9 December 1985 and promulgated by supreme decree of the Ministry of Foreign Affairs No. 809 of 7 October 1988, *Diario Oficial*, 26 November 1988; Convention on the prevention and punishment of crimes against internationally protected persons, including diplomatic agents, adopted on 14 December 1973 and promulgated by supreme decree of the Ministry of Foreign Affairs No. 129 of 28 February 1977, *Diario Oficial*, 29 March 1977; Geneva Convention for the Amelioration of the Condition of the Wounded and Sick in Armed Forces in the Field, adopted on 12 August 1949 and promulgated by supreme decree of the Ministry of Foreign Affairs No. 752 of 5 December 1950, *Diario Oficial*, 17 April 1951; Geneva Convention for the Amelioration of the Condition of the Wounded, Sick and Shipwrecked Members of the Armed Forces at Sea, adopted on 12 August 1949 and promulgated by supreme decree of the Ministry of Foreign Affairs No. 752 of 5 December 1950, *Diario Oficial*, 17 April 1951; Geneva Convention relative to the Treatment of Prisoners of War, adopted on 12 August 1949 and promulgated by supreme decree of the Ministry of Foreign Affairs No. 752 of 5 December 1950, *Diario Oficial*, 18 April 1951; Geneva Convention relative to the Protection of Civilian Persons in Time of War, adopted on 12 August 1949 and promulgated by supreme decree of the Ministry of Foreign Affairs No. 752 of 5 December 1950, *Diario Oficial*, 19 and 20 April 1951; International Convention for the Suppression of the Financing of Terrorism, adopted by the United Nations General Assembly on 9 December 1999 and promulgated by supreme decree of the Ministry of Foreign Affairs No. 163 of 3 July 2002, *Diario Oficial*, 13 September 2002; International Convention for the Suppression of Terrorist Bombings, adopted by the United Nations General Assembly on 15 December 1997 and promulgated by supreme decree of the Ministry of Foreign Affairs No. 519 of 20 November 2001, *Diario Oficial*, 6 February 2002; International Convention against the taking of hostages, adopted by the United Nations General Assembly on 17 December 1979 and promulgated by supreme decree of the Ministry of Foreign Affairs No. 989 of 16 November 1981, *Diario Oficial*, 8 January 1982; Convention for the suppression of unlawful seizure of aircraft, signed at The Hague on 16 December 1970 and promulgated by supreme decree of the Ministry of Foreign Affairs No. 147 of 20 March 1972, *Diario Oficial*, 19 April 1972; Convention for the suppression of unlawful acts against the safety of civil aviation, signed at Montreal on 23 September 1971 and promulgated by supreme decree of the Ministry of Foreign Affairs No. 736 of 4 November 1975, *Diario Oficial*, 11 December 1975; Protocol for the suppression of unlawful acts of violence at airports serving international civil aviation, supplementary to the Montreal Convention of 1971, signed at Montreal on 24 February 1988 and promulgated by supreme decree of the Ministry of Foreign Affairs No. 519 of 10 July 1989, *Diario Oficial*, 9 September 1989; Convention for the suppression of unlawful acts against the safety of maritime navigation and its Protocol to the above-mentioned Convention for the suppression of unlawful acts against the safety of fixed platforms located on the continental shelf, adopted in Rome on 10 March 1988 and promulgated by supreme decree of the Ministry of Foreign Affairs No. 793 of 3 June 1994, *Diario Oficial*, 8 August 1994; Convention on the Safety of United Nations and Associated Personnel, adopted in New York on 9 December 1994 and promulgated by supreme decree of the Ministry of Foreign Affairs No. 712 of 12 May 1999, *Diario Oficial*, 21 July 1999; United Nations Convention against Corruption, adopted in New York on 31 October 2003 and promulgated by supreme decree of the Ministry of Foreign Affairs No. 375 of 23 November 2006, *Diario Oficial*, 30 January 2007; Inter-American Convention Against Corruption, adopted in Caracas on 29 March 1996 and promulgated by supreme decree of the Ministry of Foreign Affairs No. 1879 of 29 October 1998, *Diario Oficial*, 2 February 1999.

B. Guatemala

International treaties by which Guatemala is bound, containing the obligation to extradite or prosecute, and reservations made by that State to limit the application of this obligation

1. Guatemala submitted the following list of relevant multilateral treaties: the four Geneva Conventions of 12 August 1949 (Convention for the Amelioration of the Condition of the Wounded and Sick in Armed Forces in the Field (Convention I); Convention for the Amelioration of the Condition of Wounded, Sick and Shipwrecked Members of Armed Forces at Sea (Convention II); Convention relative to the Treatment of Prisoners of War (Convention III); and Convention relative to the Protection of Civilian Persons in Time of War (Convention IV)); Single Convention on Narcotic Drugs of 30 March 1961; Convention for the suppression of unlawful seizure of aircraft of 16 December 1970; Convention on psychotropic substances of 21 February 1971; Convention for the suppression of unlawful acts against the safety of civil aviation of 23 September 1971; Convention on the prevention and punishment of crimes against internationally protected persons, including diplomatic agents of 14 December 1973; International Convention against the taking of hostages of 17 December 1979; Convention on the physical protection of nuclear material of 3 March 1980; International Convention for the Suppression of Terrorist Bombings of 15 December 1997; International Convention for the Suppression of the Financing of Terrorism of 9 December 1999; United Nations Convention against Transnational Organized Crime of 15 November 2000;

United Nations Convention against Corruption of 31 October 2003; Convention against torture and other cruel, inhuman or degrading treatment or punishment of 10 December 1984.

2. Guatemala further noted that it is a party to the Convention on the prevention and punishment of the crime of genocide of 9 December 1948 and to the International Convention on the Suppression and Punishment of the Crime of *Apartheid* of 30 November 1973, neither of which contains an obligation to extradite or prosecute, but both of which oblige States parties to establish jurisdiction over the corresponding offences and to extradite in accordance with the legislation of each State. In addition, Guatemala has signed, but not ratified, the Rome Statute of the International Criminal Court of 17 July 1998 and the Inter-American Convention on extradition of 25 February 1981.

3. Guatemala also submitted a list of relevant regional treaties: Convention on Private International Law (Bustamante Code) of 20 February 1928; Convention to prevent and punish the acts of terrorism taking the form of crimes against persons and related extortion that are of international significance of 2 February 1971; Inter-American Convention to Prevent and Punish Torture of 9 December 1985; Inter-American Convention on Forced Disappearance of Persons of 9 June 1994; Inter-American Convention against Corruption of 29 March 1996; Convention on Extradition of 26 December 1933; Central American Convention on Extradition of 7 February 1923.

4. Guatemala noted that its reservations to the multilateral and regional treaties listed above did not affect their provisions relating to the obligation to extradite or prosecute.

5. Guatemala further submitted a list of relevant bilateral treaties: Treaty on Extradition of Criminals between Guatemala and Belgium; Additional Convention to the Treaty on Extradition between Guatemala and Belgium; Additional Protocol to the Convention on Extradition between Guatemala and Belgium; Treaty on Extradition between Guatemala and Spain; Additional Protocol to the Treaty on Extradition between Guatemala and Spain; Treaty on Extradition between Guatemala and the United States of America; Supplementary Convention to the Treaty on Extradition between Guatemala and the United States; Treaty on Extradition between Guatemala and the United Kingdom of Great Britain and Northern Ireland; Additional Protocol to the Treaty on Extradition between Guatemala and the United Kingdom; Exchange of notes extending the provisions of the Treaty on Extradition to certain territories under the mandate of the United Kingdom; Treaty on Extradition between Guatemala and Mexico; Treaty on Extradition between Guatemala and the Republic of Korea.

6. Lastly, Guatemala reported that it had signed three treaties that have not yet entered into force: Agreement on Extradition between Guatemala and Brazil; Treaty on Extradition between Guatemala and Peru; Central American Treaty on Arrest Warrants and Simplified Extradition Procedures.

Domestic legal regulations adopted and applied by Guatemala, including constitutional provisions and penal codes or codes of criminal procedures, concerning the obligation to extradite or prosecute

7. Extradition is dealt with in article 27 of the Political Constitution of the Republic of Guatemala, which states that extradition is governed by the provisions of international treaties. This provision also states that extradition of Guatemalans shall not be attempted for political offences, and in no case will they be handed over to a foreign Government, except as established in treaties and conventions with respect to crimes against humanity or against international law. This article is the basis for ordinary domestic legislation on the subject, such as articles 5 and 8 of the Penal Code[1] (Decree No. 17-73 of the Congress of the Republic and its amendments) and other legal and regulatory provisions, such as articles 68 and 69 of the Act to Combat Trafficking in Narcotic Drugs, Agreement No. 8-2005 of the Supreme Court of Justice—which establishes which courts are competent to rule on extradition requests—and Supreme Court of Justice Registry Circular No. 3426-B of 13 May 1952.

8. Owing to the fact that under the Constitution extradition is governed by international treaties, the few domestic provisions in force on the subject are largely procedural in nature and supplementary to those treaties. Domestic legislation must comply with recognized international principles concerning extradition, for example, that extradition shall not be granted in the case of nationals of the requested country, for misdemeanours or minor offences punishable by less than one year in prison or for political offences or related ordinary offences, and that the person being extradited will not be given a harsher sentence than the sentence applicable in the requested country or the death sentence.

9. As regards the obligation not to hand over nationals, article 27 of the Constitution prohibits the extradition of nationals only in the case of political offences, but makes an exception for crimes against humanity or against international law, in accordance with the international treaties to which Guatemala is a party. Accordingly, it may be inferred by exclusion that the Constitution does not prohibit the handover of nationals, since the Guatemalan authorities have discretion to grant or deny extradition. If they deny an extradition request, however, there is an obligation to prosecute.

10. In the same vein, article 5, paragraph 3, of the Penal Code provides an example of a specific case in which Guatemala accepts the obligation *aut dedere aut judicare*, since it states that Guatemalan penal law shall apply to "acts committed outside Guatemala by a Guatemalan where a request for extradition has been denied".

11. Unlike the Penal Code, which deals with ordinary offences, articles 68 and 69 of Guatemala's Act to

[1] Article 5, paragraph 3, reads as follows: "Acts committed outside Guatemala by a Guatemalan where a request for extradition has been denied." Article 8 reads as follows: "Extradition may be attempted or granted only for ordinary offences. Extradition in accordance with international treaties may be granted only if there is reciprocity..."

Combat Trafficking in Narcotic Drugs establish a number of parameters for drugs-related offences, as follows:

Article 68. Extradition and procedure for dealing with extradition requests. [...]

(i) In the event that extradition is denied, either by judicial ruling or by decision of the executive branch, Guatemala shall be obliged to prosecute the person whose extradition has been denied and to send a certified copy of the sentence to the requesting State.

This article shall apply to the offences characterized in this law.

Article 69. The right to waive extradition proceedings. The State of Guatemala may hand over the person being sought to the requesting party without conducting formal extradition proceedings, provided that the person being sought expresses his or her consent to being handed over before a competent judicial authority.

12. In practice, extradition is not granted simply out of reciprocity in Guatemala. Article 8 of Guatemala's Penal Code establishes that extradition may be attempted or granted only for ordinary offences. It also establishes that extradition in accordance with international treaties may be granted only if there is reciprocity. However, this provision has been superseded by article 27 of the Constitution, which states that extradition is governed by international treaties. Moreover, Guatemalan criminal legislation does not define what is meant by ordinary offences or specify when they are deemed to be political offences. In practice and according to the jurisprudence of the courts, however, the term "political offence" refers to crimes against the security of the State or against the institutional order (Titles XI and XII of the Penal Code).

Crimes or offences to which the principle of the obligation to extradite or prosecute is applied in the legislation or practice of Guatemala

13. Guatemala explained that any offence that is extraditable under one or more of the treaties listed above implicitly carries an obligation *aut dedere aut judicare*, provided that no exception is made with respect to the obligation to prosecute in the event that extradition is denied.

C. Mauritius

1. Mauritius submitted a list of international treaties, to which it is party, containing the obligation to extradite or prosecute: the four Geneva Conventions of 12 August 1949 (Geneva Convention for the Amelioration of the Condition of the Wounded and Sick in Armed Forces in the Field; Geneva Convention for the Amelioration of the Condition of the Wounded, Sick and Shipwrecked Members of the Armed Forces at Sea; Geneva Convention relative to the Treatment of Prisoners of War; Geneva Convention relative to the Protection of Civilian Persons in Time of War, 1949); Protocol additional to the Geneva Conventions of 12 August 1949, and relating to the protection of victims of international armed conflicts (Protocol I) (Geneva, 8 June 1977), done at Geneva on 10 June 1977; Protocol additional to the Geneva Conventions of 12 August 1949, and relating to the protection of victims of non-international armed conflicts (Protocol II) (Geneva, 8 June 1977), done at Geneva on 10 June 1977; Convention for the suppression of unlawful seizure of aircraft, The Hague, 1970 (ratified on 25 April 1983); Convention for the suppression of unlawful acts against the safety of civil aviation, Montreal, 1971 (ratified on 25 April 1983); Convention on psychotropic substances, Vienna, 1971 (acceded on 8 May 1973); Convention on the prevention and punishment of crimes against internationally protected persons, including diplomatic agents, New York, 1973 (acceded on 24 September 2003); International Convention against the taking of hostages, New York, 1979 (ratified on 17 October 1980); Convention against torture and other cruel, inhuman or degrading treatment or punishment, New York, 1984 (acceded on 9 December 1992); Convention for the suppression of unlawful acts against the safety of maritime navigation, Rome, 1988 (acceded on 21 July 2004); United Nations Convention against Illicit Traffic in Narcotic Drugs and Psychotropic Substances, Vienna, 1988 (acceded on 6 March 2001); International Convention for the Suppression of Terrorist Bombings, New York, 1997 (acceded on 24 January 2003); International Convention for the Suppression of the Financing of Terrorism, New York, 1999 (ratified on 14 December 2004); United Nations Convention against Transnational Organized Crime, New York, 2000 (ratified on 18 April 2003); the Protocol to Prevent, Suppress and Punish Trafficking in Persons, Especially Women and Children, supplementing the United Nations Convention against Transnational Organized Crime, 2000, (acceded on 24 September 2003); United Nations Convention against Corruption, New York, 2003 (ratified on 14 December 2004).

2. Mauritius also ratified, on 5 April 1983, the Convention on offences and certain other acts committed on board aircraft, Tokyo, 1963. However, that Convention did not impose an obligation to extradite or prosecute, but only required each Contracting State to take such measures as may be necessary to establish its jurisdiction as the State of registration over offences committed on board aircraft registered in such State.

3. Mauritius further indicated that it had concluded a few bilateral extradition treaties with some countries. However, those bilateral treaties on extradition merely created an obligation to extradite under certain conditions as opposed to an obligation to extradite or prosecute.

4. Mauritius explained that it did not have any specific domestic legislation on the obligation to extradite or prosecute. Even the Extradition Act 1970, which regulated extradition practice in Mauritius, did not contain any provision on *aut dedere aut judicare*. On the other hand, the Extradition Act did not prohibit the extradition of Mauritian nationals; usually in countries where extradition was refused on the basis of nationality, the application of the principle of *aut dedere aut judicare* was required to prevent impunity on the basis of nationality. Under the Prevention of Corruption Act (2002), corruption offences were merely extraditable. The Act did not create an obligation to extradite or prosecute. In that connection, section 80 of the Act provided: "Any corruption offence shall be deemed to be an extradition crime for which extradition may be granted or obtained under the Extradition Act." Similarly, section 29 of the Financial Intelligence and Anti-Money-Laundering Act 2002 stated that money-laundering offences were extraditable. The Act did not stipulate an obligation to extradite or prosecute.

5. Mauritius has a few statutory provisions creating jurisdiction for specified crimes, thus enabling the Director of Public Prosecutions to prosecute. In this connection, the Convention for the Suppression of the Financing of Terrorism Act 2003, which implements the International Convention for the Suppression of the Financing of Terrorism, provides for the application of the principle of *aut dedere aut judicare*. The financing of terrorism, whether committed in Mauritius or overseas, constitutes an offence under section 4 of the Convention for the Suppression of the Financing of Terrorism Act 2003. Section 7(*i*)(*h*) of the said Act confers jurisdiction upon a Mauritian Court to try a person suspected of financing terrorism provided the suspect is, after the commission of the act, present in Mauritius whether the act constituting the offence is committed within or outside Mauritius and the person cannot be extradited to a foreign State having jurisdiction over the offence. In the light of the foregoing, it would appear that Mauritian courts are empowered to exercise extraterritorial jurisdiction over foreign nationals suspected to have committed the offence of financing terrorism overseas. The Act creates jurisdiction for the Mauritian Courts to try the offence of financing terrorism, but because any such prosecution is subject to the inability of Mauritius to extradite the suspect, it is clear that the Act provides for the application of the principle of *aut dedere aut judicare*. Similarly, the obligation to extradite or prosecute is equally found under section 30(*c*) of the Prevention of Terrorism Act 2002, which provides that a Mauritian Court shall have jurisdiction to try an offence and inflict the penalties specified in the Act where the act constituting the offence as defined thereunder has been done or completed outside Mauritius and the alleged offender is in Mauritius, and Mauritius does not extradite the alleged offender.

6. Furthermore, Mauritius observed that there were other instruments of cooperation in place to facilitate international cooperation in criminal matters. For example, the Mutual Assistance in Criminal and Related Matters Act 2003 provided for a broad range of assistance including, *inter alia*, taking of evidence or statements of persons, search and seizure, the provision of documents or evidentiary items, the service of documents and the temporary transfer of persons to assist an investigation or appear as a witness.

D. The Netherlands

International treaties by which a State is bound, containing the obligation to extradite or prosecute, and reservations made by that State to limit the application of this obligation

1. The Netherlands listed the following relevant treaties: International Convention for the Suppression of Counterfeiting Currency, Geneva, 1929; Convention of 1936 for the Suppression of the Illicit Traffic in Dangerous Drugs, Geneva, 1936; Geneva Conventions of 1949 (the Geneva Convention for the Amelioration of the Condition of the Wounded and Sick in Armed Forces in the Field; Geneva Convention for the Amelioration of the Condition of the Wounded, Sick and Shipwrecked Members of Armed Forces at Sea; Geneva Convention relative to the Treatment of Prisoners of War; and Geneva Convention relative to the Protection of Civilian Persons in Time of War); Convention on the High Seas, Geneva, 1958; Single Convention on Narcotic Drugs, New York, 1961; Convention for the suppression of unlawful seizure of aircraft, The Hague, 1970; Convention for the suppression of unlawful acts against the safety of civil aviation, Montreal, 1971; Convention on psychotropic substances, Vienna, 1971; International Convention for the Prevention of Pollution from Ships, 1973 (MARPOL Convention); Convention on the prevention and punishment of crimes against internationally protected persons, including diplomatic agents, New York, 1973; Protocol additional to the Geneva Conventions of 12 August 1949, and relating to the protection of victims of international armed conflicts (Protocol I), Geneva, 1977; European Convention on the suppression of terrorism, Strasbourg, 1977; International Convention against the taking of hostages, New York, 1979; Convention on the physical protection of nuclear material, Vienna, New York, 1980; United Nations Convention on the Law of the Sea, Montego Bay, 1982; Convention against torture and other cruel, inhuman or degrading treatment or punishment, New York, 1984; United Nations Convention against Illicit Traffic in Narcotic Drugs and Psychotropic Substances, Vienna, 1988; Convention for the suppression of unlawful acts against the safety of maritime navigation, Rome, 1988; Protocol for the suppression of unlawful acts of violence at airports serving international civil aviation, supplementary to the Montreal Convention, Montreal, 1988; Protocol to the above-mentioned Convention for the suppression of unlawful acts against the safety of fixed platforms located on the continental shelf, Rome, 1988; Convention on the prohibition of the development, production, stockpiling and use of chemical weapons and on their destruction, New York, 1992; Convention on the Safety of United Nations and Associated Personnel, New York, 1994; Convention on Combating Bribery of Foreign Public Officials in International Business Transactions, Paris, 1997; International Convention for the Suppression of Terrorist Bombings, New York, 1997; International Convention for the Suppression of the Financing of Terrorism, New York, 1999; Criminal Law Convention on Corruption, Strasbourg, 1999; United Nations Convention against Transnational Organized Crime, New York, 2000; Protocol to Prevent, Suppress and Punish Trafficking in Persons, Especially Women and Children, New York, 2000, supplementary to the United Nations Convention against Transnational Organized Crime; Protocol against the Smuggling of Migrants by Land, Sea and Air, New York, 2000, supplementing the United Nations Convention against Transnational Organized Crime; Convention on Cybercrime, Budapest, 2001; Council framework decision of 13 June 2002 on the European arrest warrant and the surrender procedures between Member States, Luxembourg, 2002;[1] United Nations Convention against Corruption, New York, 2003.

2. The Netherlands has signed the Protocol amending the European Convention on the suppression of terrorism and the International Convention for the Suppression of Acts of Nuclear Terrorism and is in the process of ratifying these treaties.

[1] *Official Journal of the European Communities*, No. L 190, vol. 45 (18 July 2002), p. 1.

3. The Netherlands is also a party to the European Convention on Extradition (1957) and both its additional protocols (1975, 1978), which do not contain an obligation *aut dedere aut judicare*, but further international judicial cooperation in the area of criminal law.

4. The Netherlands has also concluded several bilateral extradition agreements.

5. Finally, the Netherlands noted that it is party to the Convention on the prevention and punishment of the crime of genocide, 1948 and the Convention on offences and certain other acts committed on board aircraft, 1963, which do not contain an obligation to extradite or prosecute, but require States to establish jurisdiction in respect of certain offences.

Domestic legal regulations adopted and applied by a State, including constitutional provisions and penal codes of criminal procedures, concerning the obligation to extradite or prosecute

6. In October 2003, a new law with regard to international crimes entered into force in the Netherlands, which provides for the possibility to prosecute persons suspected of having committed international crimes if the suspect committed international crimes abroad but is arrested on Dutch territory; the suspect committed international crimes abroad against Dutch nationals; the suspect has Dutch nationality. The international crimes considered in this law are genocide, crimes against humanity, war crimes and torture.

Judicial practice of a State reflecting the application of the obligation aut dedere aut judicare

7. The Netherlands observed that the international developments at the time of the emergence of the International Criminal Court had prompted the decision to increase the means available to the public prosecutor's department for such complex prosecutions. Since then, a member of the military from the Democratic Republic of the Congo and two former members of the military from Afghanistan, who had sought asylum in the Netherlands, had been prosecuted for international crimes and sentenced accordingly. Additionally, two Dutch citizens had been arrested on charges of complicity in war crimes and genocide. Some of them had appealed the decision taken by the court in the first instance. More recently, another former Afghan officer and a Rwandan refugee had been arrested and charged with war crimes and torture. The case against the Rwandan national had initially involved charges for war crimes and genocide. The court in the first instance, however, had found the genocide charge inadmissible. Under the new International Crimes Act it was now possible to prosecute foreign nationals for genocide if they were arrested on Dutch territory. However, in 1994, when the suspect had allegedly committed genocide, there had been no such law in force in the Netherlands (*nullum crimen sine lege*). The Public Prosecutor had filed for appeal but there was no verdict yet.

E. Russian Federation

International treaties to which the Russian Federation is a party that contain the principle of universal jurisdiction in criminal matters

1. The Russian Federation is a party to the Geneva Conventions of 1949 and Additional Protocol I thereto, which establish universal criminal jurisdiction with regard to war crimes (arts. 49 and 50 of the first Geneva Convention; arts. 50 and 51 of the second Geneva Convention; arts. 129 and 130 of the third Geneva Convention; arts. 146 and 147 of the fourth Geneva Convention; art. 85 of Additional Protocol I of 1977 to the Geneva Conventions).

2. The Russian Federation is also a party to most of the universal and regional international treaties for the suppression of individual crimes that contain the *aut dedere aut judicare* principle. These include, in particular, the Convention for the suppression of unlawful seizure of aircraft of 1970; the Convention for the suppression of unlawful acts against the safety of civil aviation of 1971; the Convention on the prevention and punishment of crimes against internationally protected persons, including diplomatic agents of 1973; the European Convention on the Suppression of Terrorism of 1977; the Convention on the physical protection of nuclear material of 1979; the United Nations Convention against Illicit Traffic in Narcotic Drugs and Psychotropic Substances of 1988; the Convention for the suppression of unlawful acts against the safety of maritime navigation of 1988; the International Convention for the Suppression of Terrorist Bombings of 1997; the International Convention for the Suppression of the Financing of Terrorism of 1999; the United Nations Convention against Transnational Organized Crime of 2000; and the United Nations Convention against Corruption of 2003.

3. The Russian Federation is a party to the United Nations Convention on the Law of the Sea, article 105 of which establishes universal criminal jurisdiction with regard to piracy.

4. In addition, the Russian Federation is a party to a number of international treaties which contain the principle of universal jurisdiction, though not in connection with the non-extradition of alleged offenders. These include the Convention on the prevention and punishment of the crime of genocide of 1948 and the International Convention on the Suppression and Punishment of the Crime of *Apartheid* of 1973. The Russian Federation has signed but not yet ratified the Rome Statute of the International Criminal Court.

5. In some international treaties to which the Russian Federation is a party, the *aut dedere aut judicare* principle is not connected with the establishment of universal criminal jurisdiction. For example, article 8 of the International Convention for the Suppression of Counterfeiting Currency of 1929 provides that "in countries where the principle of the extradition of nationals is not recognized, nationals who have returned to the territory of their own country after the commission abroad of an offence referred to in Article 3 should be punishable in

the same manner as if the offence had been committed in their own territory, even in a case where the offender has acquired his nationality after the commission of the offence".

Legislation of the Russian Federation concerning the principle of universal jurisdiction in criminal matters; is it connected with the obligation aut dedere aut judicare?

6. In accordance with article 15, paragraph 4, of the Constitution of the Russian Federation, generally recognized principles and rules of international law and the international treaties to which the Russian Federation is a party shall be an integral part of its legal system. If an international treaty to which the Russian Federation is a party establishes rules that differ from those provided for by law, the rules of international law shall apply.

7. Russian criminal law consists of the Criminal Code of the Russian Federation. Pursuant to article 12, paragraph 3, of the Code, "foreign nationals and stateless persons not permanently residing in the Russian Federation who have committed a crime outside the Russian Federation shall be subject to criminal prosecution under the present Code in cases where the crime is directed against the interests of the Russian Federation or a Russian national or a stateless person permanently residing in the Russian Federation, and in cases provided for by the international treaties to which the Russian Federation is a party, if they have not been convicted in a foreign State and are being tried in the territory of the Russian Federation".

8. The application in the Russian Federation of article 12, paragraph 3, of the Criminal Code is connected with the obligation *aut dedere aut judicare* insofar as the Russian Federation exercises its criminal jurisdiction in accordance with the principle of universality on the basis of an international treaty containing that principle.

Crimes and offences to which the principle of universal jurisdiction in criminal matters is applied in the legislation and practice of the Russian Federation

9. Under article 12, paragraph 3, of the Criminal Code of the Russian Federation, the Russian Federation's universal jurisdiction applies only to those crimes in respect of which the Russian Federation is bound by an international treaty to exercise its criminal jurisdiction. This concerns primarily crimes against the peace and security of mankind (arts. 353–360 of the Criminal Code: the planning, preparation, initiation or waging of a war of aggression; public calls for the initiation of a war of aggression; the development, production, accumulation, acquisition or sale of weapons of mass destruction; the use of prohibited means and methods of waging war; genocide; ecocide; mercenary activities; attacks on internationally protected persons or institutions) and a number of other crimes referred to in conventions (art. 206, "Hostage-taking"; art. 211, "Hijacking of an aircraft, sea vessel or railway train"; art. 227, "Piracy"; and other articles of the Criminal Code).

Does the Russian Federation have authority under its domestic law to extradite persons in cases not covered by a treaty or to extradite persons of its own nationality?

10. The Russian Federation engages in international cooperation on extradition matters not only in accordance with the international treaties to which it is a party but also on the basis of the principle of reciprocity. Pursuant to article 462 of its Code of Criminal Procedure, "the Russian Federation, in accordance with the international treaties to which it is a party or on the basis of the principle of reciprocity, may extradite a foreign national or a stateless person who is present in the territory of the Russian Federation to a foreign State for criminal prosecution or for the enforcement of a sentence for acts which are punishable under the criminal law of the Russian Federation and the laws of the foreign State that has requested the extradition of the person". Article 462, paragraph 2, of the Code specifies that "the extradition of a person on the basis of the principle of reciprocity means that, in accordance with assurances from the foreign State that has requested the extradition, it may be expected that, in a similar situation, extradition will be granted at the request of the Russian Federation".

11. The Constitution of the Russian Federation provides that a Russian national may not be extradited to another State (art. 61, para. 1). Article 13, paragraph 1, of the Russian Criminal Code also provides that "Russian nationals who have committed a crime in the territory of a foreign State shall not be subject to extradition to that State".

12. If the Russian Federation refuses to extradite a person to a foreign State and has criminal jurisdiction in respect of that person (including on the basis of universal jurisdiction), the competent authorities of the Russian Federation propose that the requesting State supply them with the case file so that the person may be prosecuted in the territory of the Russian Federation.

Does the State have authority to assert jurisdiction over crimes occurring in other States that do not involve one of its nationals?

13. The Russian Federation's authority in this regard is provided for in article 12, paragraph 3, of the Criminal Code. As indicated above, the Code provides that the Russian Federation may exercise its criminal jurisdiction in respect of crimes committed outside the Russian Federation by foreign nationals or stateless persons not permanently residing in the territory of the Russian Federation, if the crime is directed against the interests of the Russian Federation or a Russian national or a stateless person permanently residing in the Russian Federation, and in cases provided for by the international treaties to which the Russian Federation is a party, if the foreign nationals or stateless persons not permanently residing in the territory of the Russian Federation have not been convicted in a foreign State.

14. Pursuant to article 460, paragraph 1, of the Code of Criminal Procedure, "the Russian Federation may request a foreign State to extradite a person for criminal prosecution or for the enforcement of a sentence on the basis of an international treaty to which the Russian Federation

and the foreign State are parties or on the basis of a written undertaking by the Procurator-General of the Russian Federation from that point onward to extradite persons to that State on the basis of the principle of reciprocity in accordance with the law of the Russian Federation".

Does the Russian Federation consider the obligation to extradite or prosecute to be an obligation under customary international law and, if so, to what extent?

15. The Russian Federation believes that this question requires further study by the Special Rapporteur and the International Law Commission. However, it considers that the following points should be taken into account.

16. The extradition and prosecution of persons are, as a matter of principle, sovereign rights of the State in whose territory the offender is present. Within its territorial jurisdiction, a State is entitled to decide independently whether extradition or the administration of criminal justice is appropriate. In certain circumstances it may even refrain entirely from prosecuting a person, for example, in exchange for testimony or assistance in the conduct of a criminal investigation.

17. It goes without saying that, when an international treaty containing the obligation *aut dedere aut judicare* is concluded, a State may no longer decide at its sole discretion whether to prosecute or extradite an alleged offender, since it becomes bound by the relevant treaty obligation. Moreover, it is hardly possible, under customary international law, to presume the existence of such an obligation, which significantly restricts the sovereign rights of States in a sensitive area of public law.

18. The Russian Federation does not share the view that the existence of an obligation under customary international law may be inferred from the existence of a large body of international treaties that provide for such an obligation. Otherwise, it could be asserted that the conclusion by States of a large number of extradition treaties testifies to the emergence of a customary rule that obliges States to grant extradition requests. However, in itself the existence of such treaties, even a large number of them, is insufficient proof of the existence of a customary rule of international law. At the same time, it is generally accepted that obligations relating to extradition may arise only from the relevant international instruments.

19. In our view, the existence of a customary rule obliging States to exercise their criminal jurisdiction or to grant extradition requests in respect of a specific type of crime may also not readily be inferred from the existence of a customary rule prohibiting these types of crimes.

20. As the International Court of Justice noted in its Judgment in the case concerning the *Continental Shelf (Libyan Arab Jamahiriya/Malta)*, the material of customary international law is to be looked for primarily in the actual practice and *opinio juris* of States.[1] The Russian Federation *a priori* does not rule out the existence of a rule of customary international law that obliges States to extradite or prosecute persons in respect of certain categories of crime. However, we believe that the existence and scope of application of such a rule may be established only if relevant State practice is identified in the absence of treaty obligations, together with evidence that States act as they do precisely because they consider themselves bound by a rule of law.

21. The latter element here is particularly important, given that in practice it is difficult to determine when a State that extradites or prosecutes a particular person is acting on the basis of the *aut dedere aut judicare* principle. If a State is not bound by a treaty, it may extradite an alleged offender present in its territory not because it considers itself bound by any obligation to another State but simply on the basis of the principle of reciprocity.

22. We believe that significant evidence of *opinio juris* on this issue could come from the judgements of national courts or official declarations of States which state explicitly that the refusal to extradite places an obligation on the requested State to refer the case to the competent national authorities, even in the absence of a relevant treaty obligation. We do not yet see such convincing evidence of the existence of a customary rule *aut dedere aut judicare*.

23. The question of the establishment of an obligation *aut dedere aut judicare* in customary international law with respect to a small number of criminal acts that arouse the concern of the entire international community merits separate analysis. This concerns primarily genocide, war crimes and crimes against humanity.

[1] *Judgment, I.C.J. Reports 1985*, p. 29, para. 27.

PROTECTION OF PERSONS IN THE EVENT OF DISASTERS

[Agenda item 8]

DOCUMENT A/CN.4/598

Preliminary report on the protection of persons in the event of disasters, by Mr. Eduardo Valencia-Ospina, Special Rapporteur

[*Original: Spanish/English*]
[*5 May 2008*]

CONTENTS

Multilateral instruments cited in the present report

	Source
Convention for the Amelioration of the Condition of the Wounded in Armies in the Field (Geneva, 22 August 1864)	ICRC/League of Red Cross Societies, *International Red Cross Handbook*. 12th ed. Geneva, July 1983, p. 19.
Convention (VIII) relative to the laying of automatic submarine contact mines (The Hague, 18 October 1907)	James Brown Scott, ed., *The Hague Conventions and Declarations of 1899 and 1907*. 3rd ed. New York, Oxford University Press, 1918, p. 151.
Convention and Statute establishing an International Relief Union (Geneva, 12 July 1927)	League of Nations, *Treaty Series*, vol. 135, No. 3115, p. 247.

	Source
Convention on the Privileges and Immunities of the United Nations (New York, 13 February 1946)	United Nations, *Treaty Series*, vol. 1, No. 4, p. 15.
Geneva Conventions for the protection of war victims (Geneva, 12 August 1949)	*Ibid.*, vol. 75, Nos. 970–973.
Protocol Additional to the Geneva Conventions of 12 August 1949, and relating to the protection of victims of international armed conflicts (Protocol I) (Geneva, 8 June 1977)	*Ibid.*, vol. 1125, No. 17512, p. 3.
Protocol Additional to the Geneva Conventions of 12 August 1949, and relating to the protection of victims of non-international armed conflicts (Protocol II) (Geneva, 8 June 1977)	*Ibid.*, No. 17513, p. 609.
Convention relating to the Status of Refugees (Geneva, 28 July 1951)	*Ibid.*, vol. 189. No. 2545, p. 137.
Protocol relating to the Status of Refugees (New York, 31 January 1967)	*Ibid.*, vol. 606, No. 8791, p. 267.
International Covenant on Civil and Political Rights (New York, 16 December 1966)	*Ibid.*, vol. 999, No. 14668, p. 171.
International Covenant on Social, Economic and Cultural Rights (New York, 16 December 1966)	*Ibid.*, vol. 993, No. 14531, p. 3.
OAU Convention governing the specific aspects of refugee problems in Africa (Addis Ababa, 10 September 1969)	*Ibid.*, vol. 1001, No. 14691, p. 45.
Convention on the Elimination of All Forms of Discrimination against Women (New York, 18 December 1979)	*Ibid.*, vol. 1249, No. 20378, p. 13.
Cartagena Declaration on Refugees (Cartagena de Indias, 22 November 1984)	*Cartagena Declaration on Refugees.* UNHCR publication, Geneva, October 2006.
African Charter on the Rights and Welfare of the Child (Addis Ababa, 11 July 1990)	*Human Rights: A Compilation of International Instruments*, vol. II, *Regional Instruments* (United Nations publication, Sales No. E.97.XIV.1), sect. C, No. 39.
Inter-American Convention to Facilitate Disaster Assistance (Santiago, 7 June 1991)	*OAS Official Records* (OEA/Ser.A/49 (SEPF) (EEPF), p. 15.
Tampere Convention on the Provision of Telecommunication Resources for Disaster Mitigation and Relief Operations (Tampere, 18 June 1998)	United Nations, *Treaty Series*, vol. 2296, No. 40906, p. 5.
Framework Convention on civil defence assistance (Geneva, 22 May 2000)	*Ibid.*, vol. 2172, No. 38131, p. 213.
ASEAN Agreement on Disaster Management and Emergency Response (Vientiane, 26 July 2005)	*ASEAN Documents Series 2005*, p. 157.
Protocol on the Protection and Assistance of Internally Displaced Persons (Nairobi, 30 November 2006)	International Conference on the Great Lakes Region (https://icglr.org)
Convention on the Rights of Persons with Disabilities (New York, 13 December 2006)	United Nations, *Treaty Series*, vol. 2515, No. 44910, p. 3.

Works cited in the present report

BERRAMDANE, Abelkhaleq

"L'obligation de prévention des catastrophes et risques naturels", *Revue du droit public et de la science politique en France et à l'étranger*, vol. 113, 1997, pp. 1717–1751.

CANÇADO TRINDADE, Antônio Augusto

"International law for humankind—towards a new *jus gentium* (II): general course on public international law", *Collected Courses of The Hague Academy of International Law, 2005.* Leiden, Martinus Nijhoff, 2006. Vol. 317, pp. 9–312

CARON, David D.

"Addressing catastrophes: conflicting images of solidarity and separateness", in David D. Caron and Charles Leben, eds., *The International Aspects of Natural and Industrial Catastrophes.* The Hague, Martinus Nijhoff, 2001, pp. 3–29.

EBERSOLE, Jon M.

"The Mohonk Criteria for Humanitarian Assistance in Complex Emergencies: Task Force on Ethical and Legal Issues in Humanitarian Assistance", *Human Rights Quarterly*, vol. 17, 1995, pp. 192–208.

EL BARADEI, Mohamed and others

Model Rules for Disaster Relief Operations. United Nations publication, Sales No. E.82.XV.PE/8 (Policy and Efficacy Studies No. 8).

FISHER, David

Law and legal issues in international disaster response: a desk study. Geneva, IFRC, 2007. 216 p.

HENCKAERTS, Jean-Marie and Louise DOSWALD-BECK

Customary International Humanitarian Law. Vol. 1: *Rules.* Cambridge, Cambridge University Press, 2005. 628 p.

HOFFMAN, Michael H.

"What is the scope of international disaster response law?", *International Disaster Response Laws, Principles and Practice: Reflections, Prospects and Challenges.* Geneva, IFRC, 2003, pp. 13–20.

IFRC

"International disaster response laws (IDRL): project report 2002–2003" (03/IC/11), document prepared for the 28th International Conference of the Red Cross and Red Crescent, 2–6 December 2003, Geneva, 2003.

INSTITUTE OF INTERNATIONAL LAW

Yearbook, vol. 70, part II. Session of Bruges, 2003: second part. Paris, Pedone.

JAKOVLJEVIĆ, Boško

"International Disaster Relief Law", *Israel Yearbook on Human Rights*, vol. 34 (2004), pp. 251–286.

KALSHOVEN, Frits

"Assistance to the victims of armed conflicts and other disasters", *in* Frits Kalshoven, ed., *Assisting the Victims of Armed Conflict and Other Disasters: Papers delivered at the International Conference on Humanitarian Assistance in Armed Conflict, The Hague, 22–24 June 1988*. Dordrecht, Martinus Nijhoff, 1989, pp. 13–26.

KENT, Randolph C.

Anatomy of Disaster Relief: The International Network in Action. London, Pinter, 1987. 201 p.

MACALISTER-SMITH, P.

"The International Relief Union: reflections on the Convention Establishing an International Relief Union of July 12, 1927", *Legal History Review*, vol. LIV, 1986, pp. 363–374.

PATRNOGIC, Jovica

"Some reflections on humanitarian principles applicable in relief actions", *in* Christophe Swinarski, ed., *Studies and Essays on International Humanitarian Law and Red Cross Principles in Honour of Jean Pictet*. Geneva/The Hague, Martinus Nijhoff, 1984, pp. 925–936.

PROVOST, René

International Human Rights and Humanitarian Law. Cambridge, Cambridge University Press (Cambridge studies in international and comparative law), 2002. 418 p.

ROMANO, Cesare P. R.

"L'obligation de prévention des catastrophes industrielles et naturelles", in David D. Caron and Charles Leben, eds., *The International Aspects of Natural and Industrial Catastrophes*. The Hague, Martinus Nijhoff, 2001, pp. 379–428.

UNITED NATIONS, OFFICE FOR THE COORDINATION OF HUMANITARIAN AFFAIRS

Guidelines on the Use of Foreign Military and Civil Defence Assets in Disaster Relief. Revision 1.1 of November 2007. Geneva, OCHA, 2008.

VATTEL, Emer DE

The Law of Nations, or the Principles of Natural Law Applied to the Conduct and to the Affairs of Nations and of Sovereigns, vol. III, English translation of the edition of 1758, *in* James Brown Scott, ed., *The Classics of International Law*. Washington, D.C., Carnegie Institution, 1916.

Introduction*

A. Inclusion of the topic in the programme of work of the International Law Commission

1. At the fifty-fourth session of the Commission in 2002, its Planning Group established the Working Group on the Long-term Programme of Work, chaired by Mr. Alain Pellet,[1] which was reconstituted at the Commission's fifty-eighth session in 2006.[2] During that quinquennium, the Working Group requested its members, other Commission members and the Secretariat to prepare drafts on a number of topics. A proposal concerning international protection of persons in critical situations had been submitted by Mr. Maurice Kamto in 2004 for the consideration of the Working Group.[3] The Codification Division of the Office of Legal Affairs of the United Nations Secretariat, which serves as the secretariat of the Commission, submitted proposals to the Working Group, under the title "International disaster relief", during the fifty-eighth session of the Commission in 2006.[4] At that session, the Commission expressed its appreciation for the valuable assistance rendered by the Codification Division in the preparation of such proposals. At the same session, the Planning Group recommended, and the Commission endorsed without discussion, the inclusion in its long-term programme of work of the topic "Protection of persons in the event of disasters"[5] and, as the syllabus on that topic, reproduced the Secretariat's proposal as annex C to its report.

2. At its fifty-ninth session in 2007, the Commission decided to include the topic in its current programme of work and appointed Mr. Eduardo Valencia-Ospina as Special Rapporteur.[6]

3. At its sixty-first session, the General Assembly, on the recommendation of its Sixth Committee, adopted resolution 61/34 of 4 December 2006, entitled "Report of the International Law Commission on the work of its fifty-eighth session", by which, *inter alia*, it took note of the decision of the Commission to include five topics in its long-term programme of work.

4. At its sixty-second session, the General Assembly, on the recommendation of the Sixth Committee, adopted resolution 62/66 of 6 December 2007, entitled "Report of the International Law Commission on the work of its fifty-ninth session", by which, *inter alia*, it took note of the decision of the Commission to include the topic "Protection of persons in the event of disasters" in its programme of work.

---

* The Special Rapporteur wishes to express his gratitude for their support and advice to: Mr. Arjen Vermeer, PhD candidate, and the T.M.C. Asser Instituut under the directorship of Mr. Frans Nelissen, The Hague; Ms. Liz Heffernan, lecturer in law at Trinity College, Dublin; Mr. Guglielmo Verdirame, lecturer in international law, Cambridge University, fellow of the Lauterpacht Centre for International Law under the directorship of Mr. James Crawford, Whewell professor of international law, Cambridge University, United Kingdom; Mr. Sebastián Machado, LLM candidate at the International Law Department, Law School, University of Los Andes, Bogotá, under the directorship of Ms. Liliana Obregón; Mr. Christophe Swinarski, former legal adviser at ICRC, Geneva; Mr. Diego Basile, LLM (Groningen), Buenos Aires; and Messrs. Paul Walegur and Vincent Stittelaar, The Hague.

[1] *Yearbook ... 2002*, vol. II (Part Two), p. 102, para. 521.

[2] *Yearbook ... 2006*, vol. II (Part Two), p. 185, para. 256.

[3] ILC(LVI)/WG/LT/INFORMAL/2. Copies are on file with the Codification Division.

[4] *Yearbook ... 2006*, vol. II (Part Two), p. 186, para. 261.

[5] *Ibid.*, p. 185, para. 257.

[6] *Yearbook ... 2007*, vol. II (Part Two), p. 90, para. 375.

5. During the consideration by the Sixth Committee in 2007 of the Commission's report on the work of its fifty-ninth session, a number of representatives welcomed the inclusion of the topic in the Commission's programme of work,[7] while one representative continued to have doubts as to whether the topic was appropriate for the codification or progressive development of international law.[8]

6. Upon his appointment, the Special Rapporteur undertook to establish initial contacts with representatives of interested governmental and non-governmental organizations, including the Representative of the Secretary-General on the human rights of internally displaced persons, the Assistant Secretary-General for Humanitarian Affairs and Deputy Emergency Relief Coordinator, OCHA, and senior officials of the International Disaster Response Laws, Rules and Principles programme of IFRC.

7. For the benefit of the Special Rapporteur, a one-day round-table meeting on the topic "Protection of persons in the event of disasters" was convened at the University of Cambridge by the Lauterpacht Centre for International Law in March 2008. The meeting was presided over by the Director of the Centre, Mr. James Crawford, a former member and Special Rapporteur of the Commission, and was attended by 18 participants who brought to the discussion a variety of relevant expertise.

8. At its fifty-ninth session in 2007, the Commission expressed its appreciation for the valuable assistance of the Codification Division in the preparation of research projects, by providing legal materials and their analysis.[9] At that session, the Commission requested the Secretariat to prepare a background study, initially limited to natural disasters, on the topic, "Protection of persons in the event of disasters".[10] The Special Rapporteur takes this opportunity to express, as did the Commission, his appreciation to the Legal Counsel and, in particular, the Director and members of the Codification Division for their most comprehensive study which will doubtless prove to be an indispensable point of reference in the Commission's future work on the topic. The Special Rapporteur also expresses his thanks to the Division for furnishing him with background material, including bibliographical references. With the benefit of the Secretariat study and keeping in mind the preliminary character of the present report, the Special Rapporteur deems it more economical to refrain as much as possible from duplicating the information provided by the Secretariat in its study.

B. Purpose of the present report

9. The present report is of necessity preliminary in character. It is mainly intended to deal in a general way with the scope of the topic, in order to properly circumscribe it. It is, therefore, an exploratory rather than a definitive study. It will attempt to identify the basic assumptions that should inform the work of codification and progressive development of the topic. To that end, it will raise a number of preliminary questions, some of which were dealt with to a certain extent in the Secretariat's initial proposal for the topic. Whereas that proposal focused on the general principles applicable to the operational mechanisms, the present report places emphasis on the general scope of the subject. Its purpose is to broadly outline the questions that need to be considered at the outset by the Commission in connection with the protection of persons in the event of disasters and the legal problems to which they give rise. The report aims to stimulate discussion in the Commission in order to provide the Special Rapporteur with the requisite guidance as regards the approach to be followed.

10. In including the topic in its long-term programme of work, the Commission gave it the title of "Protection of persons in the event of disasters". However, there are no official records that would throw light on the reasons that might have led the Commission to single out "protection of persons" over "relief" or "assistance", the basic aspect emphasized by the Secretariat in its original proposal. There is, therefore, a need at the preliminary stage clearly to define the topic, elucidating its core principles and concepts.

11. An initial step in the process involves determining the scope of the topic, not only *ratione materiae* but also *ratione personae* and *ratione temporis*. The title agreed to by the Commission—protection of persons in the event of disasters—must have some bearing on its scope. On the face of it, it may imply that the work to be undertaken would not entail an exhaustive analysis of the legal ramifications of disasters but only those that pertain to the protection of persons.

12. The title also imports a distinct perspective, that is, of the individual who is a victim of a disaster, and therefore suggests a definite rights-based approach to treatment of the topic. The essence of a rights-based approach to protection and assistance is the identification of a specific standard of treatment to which the individual, the victim of a disaster, *in casu*, is entitled. To paraphrase the Secretary-General,[11] a rights-based approach deals with situations not simply in terms of human needs, but in terms of society's obligation to respond to the inalienable rights of individuals, empowers them to demand justice as a right, not as a charity, and gives communities a moral basis from which to claim international assistance when needed.

13. The present report first traces the evolution of the protection of persons in the event of disasters. Next, reference is made to the sources and international efforts to codify and develop the law on this topic. The report

[7] See the statements made by Benin (*Official Records of the General Assembly, Sixty-second Session, Sixth Committee*, 18th meeting (A/C.6/62/SR.18), para. 47); Egypt (*ibid.*, para. 71); Guatemala (19th meeting (A/C.6/62/SR.19), para. 12); the United Kingdom of Great Britain and Northern Ireland (*ibid.*, para. 42); Sri Lanka (*ibid.*, para. 55); India (*ibid.*, para. 107); Poland (20th meeting (A/C.6/62/SR.20), para. 1); the United States of America (*ibid.*, para. 23); Hungary (21st meeting (A/C.6/62/SR.21), para. 7); Greece (*ibid.*, para. 53); Romania (*ibid.*, para. 78); Israel (ibid., para. 99), Kenya (*ibid.*, para. 112); Sierra Leone (24th meeting (A/C.6/62/SR.24), para. 100); and New Zealand (25th meeting (A/C.6/62/SR.25), para. 19).

[8] See the statement made by Portugal (*ibid.*, 19th meeting (A/C.6/62/SR.19), para. 77).

[9] *Yearbook ... 2007*, vol. II (Part Two), p. 93, para. 386.

[10] *Ibid.* The study has been issued as document A/CN.4/590 and Add.1–3 and will be published as an addendum to the present volume.

[11] *Official Records of the General Assembly, Fifty-third Session, Supplement No. 1* (A/53/1), para. 174.

then presents in broad outline the various aspects of the general scope with a view to identifying the main legal questions to be covered. Lastly, the Special Rapporteur advances a tentative conclusion without prejudice to the outcome of the discussion that the report aims to trigger in the Commission.

CHAPTER I

Background

A. Evolution of the protection of persons in the event of disasters

14. Disasters have always played an important part in the history of the human species. Examples include the eruption of Vesuvius in A.D. 79, the plague that occurred during the Middle Ages and the tsunami which struck large parts of Asia in 2004. Considerations of humanity have informed the moral appeals to assist victims of disasters and the solidarity in response to disasters. It is worth recalling that orders of chivalry, such as the Knights of Malta, better known as the Order of Saint John, founded in 1080, provided relief to those in need, including those affected by disasters. With the rise of the modern nation State and international law, the Swiss diplomat and lawyer Emer de Vattel wrote in 1758 a passage often quoted:

> [W]hen the occasion arises, every Nation should give its aid to further the advancement of other Nations and save them from disaster and ruin, so far as it can do so without running too great a risk ... if a Nation is suffering from famine, all those who have provisions to spare should assist in its need, without, however, exposing themselves to scarcity ... To give assistance in such dire straits is so instinctive an act of humanity that hardly any civilized Nation is to be found which would refuse absolutely to do so ... Whatever be the calamity affecting a Nation, the same help is due to it.[12]

15. However, 100 years would pass before another Swiss citizen, Henri Dunant, would successfully rally support for international norm-setting to assist victims effectively in the event of armed conflict as a form of disaster. The creation of ICRC and the adoption of the Geneva Convention of 22 August 1864 for the Amelioration of the Condition of the Wounded in Armies in the Field resulted from the concerns expressed over the protection of those wounded in the field during armed conflict. The first arrangements for the protection and assistance to be given to certain groups of persons were thus made in the context of warfare.

16. Equal recognition of the needs of those affected by other disasters began to come about in the second half of the nineteenth century. In accordance with their mandate,[13] national Red Cross and Red Crescent societies provide assistance and relief in disasters which may afflict peoples during peacetime as a condition of their vigorous development and a useful preparation for their wartime work; in peacetime, they devote themselves to humanitarian work that corresponds to their wartime duties, that is, giving relief in case of public calamity which, like war, demands immediate and organized assistance. Nevertheless, the provision of international assistance to victims of disasters other than armed conflict has only positioned itself as a major issue on the agenda of the international community since the beginning of the twentieth century. The importance attached to disaster relief has gained further recognition over the course of the past century as the frequency, intensity and complexity of disasters increased. With the formation of the International Red Cross and Red Crescent Movement and the establishment of the International Relief Union,[14] international disaster relief began to make its way into the realm of international law. Since then, the legal aspects of the subject have increasingly attracted attention at the international level. Whereas mutual self-interest has driven States to conclude instruments concerning their conduct in war, international cooperation in the area of protection and assistance in the event of disasters has taken on a wider dimension. Enhanced international solidarity in the event of disasters has reinforced the need for greater regulation of international law.

17. Protection and assistance activities undertaken in the event of disasters have generally been approached pragmatically. This is reflected in the steady growth of regulatory frameworks, mostly on a bilateral basis but also through the organs of the United Nations and its specialized agencies and entities such as ICRC. International law-making and organizational developments in disaster governance reveal both the recurring need to deal with the protection of persons and the approach of the international community in that regard. These two themes—international legislation and organization—go hand in hand for purposes of providing adequate and effective assistance to those affected by a humanitarian emergency, such as a disaster.[15]

18. In 2001, IFRC undertook to evaluate the dispersed body of existing international and national norms relating to disaster relief by implementing its International Disaster Response Laws (IDRL) project. On the basis of the project's results, the International Red Cross and Red Crescent Movement, consisting of the Red Cross

[12] De Vattel, *The Law of Nations or the Principles of Natural Law Applied to the Conduct and to the Affairs of Nations and of Sovereigns*, book II, chap. I, pp. 114–115.

[13] See resolution 3 of the Second International Red Cross Conference (Berlin, 1869), *Compte rendu des travaux de la Conférence internationale tenue à Berlin du 22 au 27 avril 1869 par les délégués des gouvernements signataires de la Convention de Genève et des Sociétés et Associations de secours aux militaires blessés et malades* (Berlin, J. F. Starcke, 1869), p. 251.

[14] The Convention and Statute establishing an International Relief Union was opened for signature in 1927 and entered into force in 1932; the Union is, however, no longer in operation.

[15] See Kalshoven, "Assistance to the victims of armed conflicts and other disasters", p. 14.

and Red Crescent organs and the States parties to the Geneva Conventions for the protection of war victims, adopted in November 2007 a set of operational guidelines on assistance in the event of disasters. According to IFRC, the legal core of international disaster relief law consists of the laws, rules and principles applicable to the access, facilitation, coordination, quality and accountability of international disaster response activities in times of non-conflict related to disasters, which includes preparedness for imminent disaster and the conduct of rescue and humanitarian assistance activities,[16] and is grounded on the premise that such activities apply in the event of a disaster, regardless of its origin, except in situations of armed conflict which are covered by international humanitarian law. Moreover, the primary focus of IDRL is on the operational side of protection, namely, assistance.

19. An IFRC desk study,[17] and the Secretariat's study both identify a distinct corpus of law relating to international disaster response and relief, and provide detailed inventories of its various sources. There exists a significant number of bilateral treaties dealing with matters of mutual assistance. In addition, IDRL is informed by a considerable amount of soft-law instruments applicable to humanitarian assistance activities in the event of disasters, notably decisions of organs of the United Nations and other international organizations. Not surprisingly, the precepts making up IDRL vary significantly from one another in their material, spatial and temporal dimensions. Therefore, assessing the weight of IDRL and the level of support it garners within the international community is by no means straightforward.

20. On a wider conceptual level, IDRL shares with international humanitarian law a significant number of fundamental principles which will usefully guide its future development.[18] Furthermore, IDRL draws on international human rights law and international law on refugees and internally displaced persons. To that extent, the sources that inform IDRL are largely the same as those that underlie the present, distinct topic, as outlined in section B below. At the same time, IDRL raises questions *vis-à-vis* the topic under consideration by the Commission, including how to classify, as opposed to merely identify, existing law and practice.

B. Sources

21. Three immediate sources of present-day international disaster protection and assistance can be singled out: international humanitarian law, international human rights law and international law on refugees and internally displaced persons. For the purposes of the present report, it suffices to give a brief characterization of each of these three sources from the perspective of the topic under consideration.

1. International humanitarian law and humanitarian assistance

22. As pointed out, the first agreements concluded by States recognizing humanitarian concerns and humanitarian action were limited to a particularly grave emergency situation: armed conflict. Historically, the dynamics of armed conflict have stood out from those of peacetime situations. Based on the principles of humanity, neutrality and impartiality, specific standards of conduct were developed, including those for international assistance. These initial agreements focused, in particular, on protection and assistance given to the military rather than the civilian population. However, owing to the increase in the number of civilian victims suffering the effects of war, the protection of all those hors de combat became a major focus of subsequent agreements concerning the behaviour of parties engaged in armed conflict.

23. The agreements dealing with conduct during armed conflict gradually formed the body of law known today as international humanitarian law,[19] a field of law that has been codified in a fairly comprehensive manner. The application of international humanitarian law is conditioned upon the existence of an armed conflict and upon persons belonging to specific categories. At any rate, the multifaceted layers of protection offered by international humanitarian law envisage the individual as the ultimate beneficiary.[20]

24. The basic rules of providing relief to the civilian population in armed conflict, that is, humanitarian assistance, are embodied in the Geneva Conventions of 12 August 1949 and the Additional Protocols thereto. The rules found in these instruments reflect to a large extent the corresponding customary rules.[21] In addition, rules can be found in agreements between the parties to a conflict or between one or more parties to a conflict and ICRC. Moreover, whether intergovernmental or not, international organizations such as IFRC, the main organs of the United Nations and the specialized agencies, and departments of the United Nations Secretariat such as OCHA, play a major role through their internal rules and decisions on matters of relief in conflict situations, including peacekeeping missions.[22] Consequently, in conflict situations there exists a large body of law dealing with assistance that may not only inspire rules on the protection of persons in the event of disasters, but may even be applied by analogy to the extent that a rule is relevant to disaster situations other than armed conflict.

2. International human rights law as the paradigm for a rights-based approach to protection

25. International human rights law comprises rights and freedoms enjoyed by the individual by virtue of international law. International human rights law bestows upon

[16] IFRC, "International disaster response laws (IDRL): project report 2002–2003" (03/IC/11), p. 15.

[17] Fisher, *Law and Legal Issues in International Disaster Response: A Desk Study*.

[18] See Hoffman, "What is the scope of international disaster response law?".

[19] See *Legality of the Threat or Use of Nuclear Weapons, Advisory Opinion, I.C.J. Reports 1996*, p. 226, paras. 74–87.

[20] See Provost, *International Human Rights and Humanitarian Law*, p. 34.

[21] See Henckaerts and Doswald-Beck, *Customary International Humanitarian Law*.

[22] See Jakovljević, "International disaster relief law", p. 256.

the individual the status of rights holder. States are under permanent and universal obligation to provide protection to those on their territory under the various international human rights instruments and customary international human rights law.

26. In the context of disasters, a number of human rights are of particular importance. Examples of the rights that are pertinent in the event of a disaster include the right to life,[23] the right to food,[24] the right to health and medical services,[25] the right to the supply of water,[26] the right to adequate housing, clothing and sanitation,[27] and the right not to be discriminated against.[28] The link between international human rights law and disasters has not yet been generally reflected in existing hard-law instruments on either subject. To date, only two international human rights instruments are expressly applicable in the event of disasters. The Convention on the Rights of Persons with Disabilities does not refer to a right to protection, the provision being formulated rather as an obligation on the contracting State to ensure protection and safety in the occurrence of a natural disaster.[29] Equally, the African Charter on the Rights and Welfare of the Child explicitly sets forth the obligation to ensure that a child receives appropriate protection and humanitarian assistance.[30] The relevant provisions of both of the aforementioned instruments refer to international human rights law and international humanitarian law as the context in which those obligations should be fulfilled. The nature of these provisions would, thus, seem to set public order standards for States, informed by the principle of humanity rather than that of individual rights. In this connection, it is important to recall that each human right is deemed to entail three levels of obligation on the State: the duty to respect, protect and fulfil.[31] A rights-based approach to protection and assistance in the event of disasters contemplates those obligations as well.

3. International law on refugees and internally displaced persons and disasters

27. Disasters often generate the mass displacement of persons, either across borders (refugees) or within those of a disaster-affected State (internally displaced persons). Refugees and internally displaced persons are generally treated as distinct categories entitled to particular rights by virtue of a situation-specific protection regime.

28. International refugee law has been developed against the background of displacement caused by persecution and destruction during armed conflict, in particular the Second World War, which led to the adoption in 1951 of the Convention relating to the Status of Refugees,[32] the cornerstone document of international refugee law. International refugee law obliges a State to provide protection to persons entitled to the status of refugee in cases in which such persons are not adequately protected in their State of origin because of its unwillingness or inability to do so. The occurrence of a disaster is not envisaged as grounds for granting refugee status. However, it is often in an emergency situation, such as a disaster, where persecution—a legal ground for the granting of refugee status—is likely to take place. In addition, a party to the Convention, under article 23, has the obligation to accord refugees lawfully staying in its territory the same treatment in respect of public relief and assistance as accorded its own nationals.

29. At present, there is no legally binding instrument governing internally displaced persons. An authoritive (non-binding) source of norms guiding the protection of internally displaced persons is the Guiding Principles on Internal Displacement, drawn up by the Representative of the Secretary-General on internally displaced persons (E/CN.4/1998/53/Add.2, annex).[33] The Guiding Principles provide for the protection, *inter alia*, of those displaced by a natural or man-made disaster.[34] In particular, the Guiding Principles expressly state that the primary responsibility for protection and assistance lies with the national authorities and that internally displaced persons have the right to request and to receive protection and assistance from them.[35]

---

[23] International Covenant on Civil and Political Rights, art. 6.

[24] International Covenant on Social, Economic and Cultural Rights, art. 11.

[25] *Ibid.*, art. 12.

[26] Convention on the Elimination of All Forms of Discrimination against Women, art. 14, para. 2 (*h*).

[27] International Covenant on Social, Economic and Cultural Rights, art. 11.

[28] International Covenant on Civil and Political Rights, art. 2.

[29] Convention on the Rights of Persons with Disabilities, Art. 11.

[30] African Charter on the Rights and Welfare of the Child, art. 23, paras. 1 and 4.

[31] See, for example, the comments made by the Human Rights Committee in 1982 concerning article 6 (Right to life) of the International Covenant on Civil and Political Rights, in which the Committee considered that States should take positive measures "to eliminate malnutrition and epidemics" (Report of the Human Rights Committee, *Official Records of the General Assembly, Thirty-seventh Session, Supplement No. 40* (A/37/40), annex V, general comment No. 6, para. 5). These levels of obligation have been more explicitly addressed in the context of the International Covenant on Economic, Social and Cultural Rights. The Committee on Economic, Social and Cultural Rights, in considering in 1999 article 11 of the Covenant (The right to adequate food), commented that (*a*) "States have a core obligation to take the necessary action to mitigate and alleviate hunger … even in times of natural or other disasters" (Report of the Committee on Economic, Social and Cultural Rights, *Official Records of the Economic and Social Council, 2000, Supplement No. 2* (E/2000/22-E/C.12/1999/11 and Corr.1*)*, annex V, general comment No. 12, para. 6); (*b*) "the State has to demonstrate that every effort had been made to use all the resources at its disposal" (*ibid.*, para. 17); and (*c*) that if it was unable to carry out its obligation, it had the burden of proving that this was the case and that it had "unsuccessfully sought to obtain international support" (*ibid.*).

[32] The Convention entered into force on 22 April 1954 and the Protocol relating thereto on 4 October 1967. See also the OAU Convention governing the specific aspects of refugee problems in Africa and the Cartagena Declaration on Refugees, adopted on 22 November 1984 by the Colloquium on the International Protection of Refugees in Central America, Mexico and Panama (UNHCR, Geneva).

[33] See also the Protocol on the Protection and Assistance of Internally Displaced Persons adopted on 30 November 2006 by the International Conference on the Great Lakes Region, in which Member States undertake to adhere to the Guiding Principles on Internal Displacement.

[34] E/CN.4/1998/53/Add.2, annex: "Introduction: scope and purpose", para. 2.

[35] *Ibid.*, principles 3 and 25.

4. Legal instruments specifically applicable to assistance in the event of disasters

30. The three sets of rules described above determine in a general way the legal context in which the protection of persons takes place. However, a vast number of more directly applicable instruments is available, specifically tailored to the operational component of protection (i.e. assistance) in the event of disasters. The Special Rapporteur does not find it useful to repeat here the exhaustive list of instruments identified in the Secretariat study.[36] For the purposes of the present report, it suffices to highlight certain significant legal frameworks and norm-setting trends in the event of disasters.

Multilateral treaties

31. While no universal comprehensive instrument dealing with the general aspects of protection of persons in the event of disasters exists at the multilateral level, a number of instruments, both universal and regional, deal with specific aspects of protection. Moreover, a considerable number of soft-law and non-legal pronouncements has been prepared and adopted, including under the aegis of or in collaboration with the United Nations. Furthermore, the non-governmental community has contributed through the adoption of guidelines or model rules.

32. The first multilateral treaty exclusively concerned with the general aspects of disaster relief was the Convention and Statute establishing an International Relief Union. However, it only contributed to relief on two occasions.[37] Though technically still in force among 17 States, the assets and responsibilities of the Union were transferred to the United Nations by the Economic and Social Council in its resolution 1268 (XLIII) of 4 August 1967. One of the main reasons for the Union becoming inactive was the structure of the Convention. The treaty system was considered weak as it relied on specific rights and duties without taking into account their legal underpinnings and thereby identifying the applicable general rights and duties.[38] It is worth noting that the scope of the Convention covered both armed conflict and peacetime situations.[39]

33. There are at present only two universal treaties in force which contain general rules for the provision of international assistance: (*a*) the Framework Convention on Civil Defence Assistance, adopted in 2000, which deals with cooperation among national civil defence entities; and (*b*) the Tampere Convention on the Provision of Telecommunication Resources for Disaster Mitigation and Relief Operations, adopted in 1998 and which entered into force in 2005. The latter Convention offers a comprehensive legal framework for the provision of telecommunications assistance during disaster relief operations, including the coordination of such assistance and the reduction of regulatory barriers. It deals with an important number of general issues, albeit limited to telecommunications, which could influence more general future codification. It should be noted that the Convention does not contain a statutory limitation to its applicability in armed conflict. Besides, it incorporates non-governmental organizations as assisting actors granted a number of specific facilities. Neither instrument has attracted wide participation and both have suffered from ineffective application in the field.

34. A number of relevant agreements have been adopted at the regional and subregional levels, for example, in Asia, Europe and Latin America. The regional treaties are of particular relevance to the study of this topic in that they tend to be more general in nature, covering a wide range of issues. The most recent such agreement is the ASEAN Agreement on Disaster Management and Emergency Response, adopted on 26 July 2005 following the tsunami of December 2004, which reflects much of contemporary thinking in terms of disaster mitigation and risk reduction and addresses international cooperation in disaster response. Some of the agreements establish regional entities entrusted with mandates to undertake a variety of tasks.

Bilateral treaties

35. The multilateral agreements are, in turn, buttressed by a significant number of bilateral agreements regulating the provision of assistance and cooperation among States, primarily, although not exclusively, in Europe (see A/CN.4/590 and Add.1–3).[40]

Domestic legislation

36. Almost every country in the world has legislation dealing with national calamities or aspects thereof. While some States have put into place legislation that deals specifically with disaster-related matters, such as risk reduction, provision of assistance and civil defence, it is worth bearing in mind that, as pointed out in the study by the Secretariat (A/CN.4/590 and Add.1–3),[41] States regulate different aspects of disaster prevention and response through a variety of domestic laws, such as those on the protection of the environment and conservation, forestry, health, food safety, sanitation, epidemics, security, safety, protection, civil defence, immigration, customs duties and tariffs, search and rescue, emergencies, water, fire safety, prevention of industrial accidents, taxation, meteorology, spatial planning, and earthquake prevention. According to the same study, on a number of issues the national rule is determinative either by way of providing the content for an international norm or by serving to trigger the operation of international cooperation.

Other key instruments

37. The existing body of international treaties and agreements on disaster relief (encompassing both prevention and assistance) is in turn supplemented by a number of non-binding instruments, adopted primarily at the

[36] A/CN.4/590 and Add.1–3 (see footnote 10 above). For a detailed survey of applicable rules and instruments, see also Fisher, *op. cit.*, part II, pp. 33–87.

[37] Macalister-Smith, "The International Relief Union: reflections on the Convention Establishing an International Relief Union of July 12, 1927", p. 370.

[38] *Ibid.*, p. 372.

[39] *Ibid.*, p. 367.

[40] See footnote 10 above.

[41] *Ibid.*

intergovernmental level, but also by private institutions and entities. For example, a survey jointly carried out by the former Office of the United Nations Disaster Relief Co-ordinator and the League of Red Cross Societies resulted in a series of recommendations designed to expedite international relief by facilitating the functioning of relief personnel and the delivery of relief consignments. These measures to expedite international relief[42] were endorsed by the General Assembly in its resolution 32/56 of 8 December 1977.

38. The General Assembly, by its resolution 46/182 of 19 December 1991, established the basic framework within which contemporary disaster relief activities are undertaken. In that resolution, the Assembly recognized as key areas of activity disaster prevention and mitigation, preparedness, improved stand-by capacity and coordination, cooperation and leadership in the provision of disaster assistance, and laid down a number of guiding principles. It also established the linkage among relief, rehabilitation and development.

39. Special mention might also be made of the Principles and Rules for Red Cross and Red Crescent Disaster Relief,[43] the Declaration of Principles for International Humanitarian Relief to the Civilian Population in Disaster Situations,[44] the Council of Europe resolution on precautions against natural and other disasters and the planning and provision of disaster relief,[45] and the Code of Conduct for the International Red Cross and Red Crescent Movement and NGOs in Disaster Relief adopted in 1995.[46] Other significant texts include the draft model agreement on international medical and humanitarian law adopted by the International Law Association in 1980,[47] the Model Rules for Disaster Relief Operations proposed by UNITAR in 1982,[48] which were aimed at closing the lacunae in international humanitarian law regarding assistance to victims of disasters, the Guiding Principles on the Right to Humanitarian Assistance, adopted by the International Institute of Humanitarian Law in 1993,[49] the Mohonk Criteria for Humanitarian Assistance in Complex Emergencies, adopted in 1995,[50] the Guiding Principles on Internal Displacement, adopted in 1999 (E/CN.4/1998/53/Add.2, annex), the Sphere Project,[51] the Guidelines on the Use of Foreign Military and Civil Defence Assets in Disaster Relief (also known as the Oslo Guidelines),[52] and the Operational Guidelines on Human Rights and Natural Disasters adopted by the Inter-Agency Standing Committee in 2006 (A/HRC/4/38/Add.1, annex).

40. Furthermore, in the 1980s a draft convention on expediting the delivery of emergency assistance was drawn up and submitted to the Economic and Social Council for consideration (see A/39/267/Add.2-E/1984/96/Add.2, annex). Although the draft convention was never adopted, its provisions provide a useful reference point for the kinds of provisions that might eventually be included in a legal instrument were one to be adopted.

5. Recent developments

41. The increasing involvement in recent times of the international community in disaster situations has led to recognition of the need to improve regulatory law in the event of disasters to overcome the obstacles to the provision of effective assistance. Current developments attest to the importance attached to this need. They include the substantial number of resolutions related to the topic, which have been adopted by the General Assembly at its recent sessions in connection with many separate but related items of its agenda,[53] the resolution on humanitarian assistance, adopted by the Institute of International Law, at its session held in Bruges, Belgium in 2003,[54] the Hyogo Declaration, adopted by the World Conference on Disaster Reduction in 2005,[55] and the resolution endorsing the Guidelines for the Domestic Facilitation and Regulation of International Disaster Relief and Initial Recovery Assistance, adopted by the Thirtieth International Conference of the Red Cross and Red Crescent in 2007.[56]

6. Customary international law

42. While this topic seems in principle to be the subject of progressive development, the possibility of identifying applicable customary norms should not be excluded. The IFRC desk study concerning the framing of IDRL recognizes that research does not suggest the existence of a system of customary IDRL.[57] It points out, however, that IFRC research might yet produce evidence warranting reconsideration of that point.[58]

---

[42] See the report of the Secretary-General on the Office of the United Nations Disaster Relief Co-ordinator (A/32/64 and Corr.1), annex II, paras. 1–3.

[43] Adopted by the Twenty-first International Conference of the Red Cross (Istanbul, 1969) and revised by the Twenty-second to Twenty-sixth Conferences (Tehran (1973), Bucharest (1977), Manila (1981), Geneva (1986) and Geneva (1995), respectively), reprinted in *International Review of the Red Cross*, vol. 36 (1996), No. 310, annex IV.

[44] Resolution XXVI of the Twenty-first International Conference of the Red Cross, held in Istanbul from 6 to 13 September 1969 (*ibid.*, vol. 9 (1969), No. 104, p. 632).

[45] Resolution (72) 6 adopted by the Committee of Ministers on 18 February 1972 at the 207th meeting of the Ministers' Deputies.

[46] Adopted by the Twenty-sixth International Conference of the Red Cross and Red Crescent held in Geneva, from 3 to 7 December 1995 (*International Review of the Red Cross* (see footnote 43 above), annex VI.

[47] Reproduced in French as "Rapport spécial sur un projet d'accord-type relatif aux actions de secours humanitaires", in *Report of the Fifty-ninth Conference of the International Law Association, Belgrade, 17–23 August 1980*, pp. 520–527.

[48] El Baradei and others, *Model Rules for Disaster Relief Operations*.

[49] Proposed at the seventeenth Round-table Meeting on Current Problems of Humanitarian Law, held in San Remo, Italy, from 2 to 4 September 1992.

[50] See Ebersole, "The Mohonk Criteria for Humanitarian Assistance in Complex Emergencies: Task Force on Ethical and Legal Issues in Humanitarian Assistance".

[51] *The Sphere Project: Humanitarian Charter and Minimum Standards in Disaster Response*, 2nd ed. (Geneva, 2004).

[52] OCHA, *Guidelines on the Use of Foreign Military and Civil Defence Assets in Disaster Relief.*

[53] For a list of relevant General Assembly resolutions, see A/CN.4/590 and Add.1–3 (footnote 10 above).

[54] Institute of International Law, *Yearbook*, vol. 70, part II, p. 263.

[55] See Report of the World Conference on Disaster Reduction, Kobe, Hyogo, Japan, 18–22 January 2005 (A/CONF.206/6 and Corr.1), chap. 1, resolution 1. See also the Hyogo Framework for Action 2005–2015: Building the Resilience of Nations and Communities to Disasters (*ibid.*, resolution 2).

[56] Resolution 4, Introduction to the Guidelines for the Domestic Facilitation and Regulation of International Disaster Relief and Initial Recovery Assistance (Geneva, IFRC, 2008), p. 20.

[57] Hoffman, *loc. cit.*, p. 16.

[58] *Ibid.*, footnote 25.

Chapter II

Scope of the topic

43. At the preliminary stage of work on the topic, the Special Rapporteur requires the Commission's guidance concerning the scope of the topic before he can be in a position to propose the corresponding draft article (or articles). To facilitate the discussion, three aspects of scope are treated below: *ratione materiae*, *ratione personae* and *ratione temporis*. The question of whether the scope should also be defined *ratione loci* is left open.

A. *Ratione materiae*: the concept and classification of disasters

44. The concept and classification of disasters have a significant bearing on the scope of the topic. Although disasters manifest themselves in different forms, they share common elements, the identification of which should assist in achieving a proper understanding of the concept itself.

45. A disaster situation arises from the vulnerability of human beings when exposed to a hazard. The Hyogo Framework for Action 2005–2015 defines a hazard as:

> A potentially damaging physical event, phenomenon or human activity that may cause the loss of life or injury, property damage, social and economic disruption or environmental degradation. Hazards can include latent conditions that may represent future threats and can have different origins: natural (geological, hydrometeorological and biological) or induced by human processes (environmental degradation and technological hazards).[59]

46. The term "disaster", however, is not a legal term. There is no generally accepted legal definition of the term in international law. While some international instruments prefer to omit completely a definition of disaster,[60] others provide an all-encompassing definition. An example of the latter includes the Tampere Convention on the Provision of Telecommunication Resources for Disaster Mitigation and Relief Operations, which defines a disaster as a serious disruption of the functioning of society that poses a significant, widespread threat to human life, health, property or the environment, whether caused by accident, nature or human activity, and whether developing suddenly or as the result of complex, long-term processes.[61]

47. One first aspect that can be singled out is that the concept of disaster does not differentiate between its occurrence in a single State or among multiple States. In other words, an international component (i.e. transboundary effects) is not a prerequisite. Secondly, it should be noted that the threshold is often expressed in terms of the degree of dysfunction of a State, region or society. The third element relates to the inherent suffering or damage that may result from the threat to human life, health, property or the environment. The international significance of the event may then be found in the unwillingness or inability of the affected State, region or society to cope with the disaster by using only its own resources. The abovementioned elements, in which human suffering is a critical factor, typically generate attention and response at the international level. The role of assisting actors may then be qualified as that of agents of humanity,[62] an assertion that carries its own implications for the scope insofar as it relates to protection, as discussed in the section below.

48. It is common for international instruments to differentiate among disasters according to some pre-established criteria. To begin with, disasters can be divided into two categories, according to cause: natural disasters (e.g. earthquakes, tsunamis and volcanic eruptions) and man-made disasters (e.g. oil spills, nuclear accidents and armed conflict). Furthermore, disasters are often classified in terms of their duration as sudden-onset disasters (e.g. hurricanes) and slow-onset, or creeping, disasters (e.g. droughts, food shortages and crop failures). Lastly, a classification may be made according to the context in which the disaster occurs, that is, in a single or complex emergency. A complex emergency is generally defined as "a humanitarian crisis in a country, region, or society in which there is a total or considerable breakdown of authority resulting from internal or external conflict and which requires an international response that goes beyond the mandate or capacity of any single agency and/or the ongoing UN country programme".[63]

49. The Secretariat proposal for the topic suggested that it be limited initially to natural disasters, based on a perceived more immediate need.[64] For his part, the Special Rapporteur is of the view that the title eventually agreed upon by the Commission suggests a broader scope. Such an approach would seem best for achieving the underlying objective codification and progressive development of the topic, namely, fashioning rules for the protection of persons. The need for protection can be said to be equally strong in all disaster situations. The conceptual scope should envisage taking account of all of the aforementioned categories, thus acknowledging the

[59] A/CONF.206/6 and Corr.1 (see footnote 55 above), resolution 2, footnote 2.

[60] For example, the Inter-American Convention to Facilitate Disaster Assistance, which entered into force on 16 October 1996.

[61] See article 1, paragraph 6, of the Convention. See also article 1, paragraph 3, of the ASEAN Agreement on Disaster Management and Emergency Response (not yet in force), which states that "'disaster' means a serious disruption of the functioning of a community or a society causing widespread human, material, economic or environmental losses".

[62] See Caron, "Addressing catastrophes: conflicting images of solidarity and separateness", p. 13.

[63] *Civil-Military Guidelines and Reference for Complex Emergencies*. The concept of complex emergencies should be distinguished from what has been termed "complex disaster", that is "where one disaster agent exposes vulnerabilities which open the way for the impact of other disaster agents" (Kent, *Anatomy of Disaster Relief: The International Network in Action*, p. 6).

[64] *Yearbook ... 2006*, vol. II (Part Two), Annex III, p. 206, para. 2. See, however, the Secretariat's subsequent study where it took a more inclusive approach, noting that while the bulk of the study pertained to disasters emanating from natural phenomena, few of the legal instruments and texts cited maintained a clear distinction between natural and man-made disasters (A/CN.4/590 and Add.1–3, para. 8 (footnote 10 above).

complexities involved in the categorization of disasters according to their cause, duration and context. The categories may overlap. It is not always possible to maintain a clear delineation between causes, as may be the case with desertification and global warming. An apparent natural disaster can be caused or aggravated by human activity, for example, desertification caused by excessive land use and deforestation. Another example would be the occurrence of epidemics, which may not be the direct result of a human agency, but may certainly be aggravated by it due to neglect of hygiene, in particular in camps for refugees or internally displaced persons. The foregoing demonstrates the high degree of arbitrariness in disaster categorization, militating in favour of a more holistic approach. However, armed conflict *per se* will be excluded because there is an applicable, highly developed particular field of law dealing in great detail with such situations of social reality: namely, international humanitarian law. This would accord with the approach taken in the advisory opinion on the legality of the threat or use of nuclear weapons, in which ICJ viewed the law applicable in armed conflict which is designed to regulate the conduct of hostilities as the applicable *lex specialis*.[65]

B. *Ratione materiae*: the concept of protection of persons

50. As the title given to the topic must have a bearing on its scope, the concept of protection of persons calls for further examination. Persons affected by disasters do not constitute a separate legal category. However, because disaster victims face a very distinct factual situation, they do have specific needs that require addressing. The fundamental tenet of international humanitarian law and international human rights law applicable in the event of disasters is the principle of humanity which underpins all humanitarian action.[66]

51. In the first place, the concept of protection raises a general question when contrasted with the concepts of response, relief and assistance: should the concept of protection be seen as distinct, or as encompassing those other concepts? In any disaster situation, three phases can be distinguished: pre-disaster, the disaster proper and post-disaster. The concept of response restricts itself temporally to the disaster phase. Relief is a broader concept which, like assistance, encompasses the pre-disaster stage as well as the stage beyond immediate response. In the present context, assistance can be described as the availability and distribution of the goods, materials and services essential to the survival of the population. The elements of the concept of protection depend largely on the context or area of law in which the concept is employed. Protection can be said to be all-encompassing, covering the more specific concepts of response, relief or assistance with which it is often associated. One should, however, differentiate between protection *sensu lato* and protection *sensu stricto*. This may be conceptualized as follows: there is a general, all-encompassing concept of protection which includes protection in a strict sense, denoting a rights-based approach, and other concepts, in particular assistance.

52. For the purposes of the present topic, protection has been qualified as the protection of persons. The protection of persons concept is not new in international law; it reflects a particular relationship between the qualification of persons as being those affected by disasters, and the rights and obligations attached thereto. As stated above, the regimes of protection of persons are international humanitarian law, international human rights law and international law relating to refugees and internally displaced persons. These regimes may apply simultaneously to the same situation because they essentially complement each other. In addition, "they are guided by a basic identity of purpose: the protection of the human person in all and any circumstances".[67] The three areas of law underscore the essential universality of humanitarian principles. The protection of persons in the event of disasters is also predicated on such principles as humanity, impartiality, neutrality and non-discrimination, as well as sovereignty and non-intervention.

53. While the title of the topic explicitly refers to the protection of persons, a protection regime often extends to protection of property and the environment. In this respect, the Special Rapporteur requires the guidance of the Commission as to whether these elements should also be treated, and with what degree of specificity.

54. It is important to define the rights and obligations that enter into play in disaster situations and the consequences that may flow from such rights and obligations. From the standpoint of the victims of disasters, this is a question not only of international humanitarian law, but also of international human rights law, including the existence or not of a right to humanitarian assistance. The question of the latter right is pertinent as it is presently uncertain whether existing international law takes into account all of the legitimate needs of persons affected by disaster or whether there are gaps in the law in this respect. In international humanitarian law that right has been recognized as a matter of law. In disaster situations, however, it appears that no legal instruments explicitly acknowledge the existence of such a right. At most, it could be said to be implicit in international human rights law. The nature of such a right is, however, unclear. Would it be a human right or just a right of those affected by a disaster? Would it be an individual right or a collective right? Against whom, if at all, would it be enforceable? After all, the criteria to determine the existence and status of a human right are subject to controversy. This raises the more fundamental question of whether international human rights law has developed in that direction. However, it could be argued that formulating and elaborating such a right to assistance in the event of disasters, as a matter of progressive development of the law, would prevent the risk of fragmentation of existing human rights because of the otherwise necessary but arbitrary selection

[65] *I.C.J. Reports 1996* (see footnote 19 above), p. 240, para. 25. Compare this with the position taken in *Legal Consequences of the Construction of a Wall in the Occupied Palestinian Territory, Advisory Opinion, I.C.J. Reports 2004*, p. 178, para. 106.

[66] As far back as 1949, ICJ stated that Convention VIII of 1907 relative to the laying of automatic submarine contact mines, one of the pillars of modern international humanitarian law, contained "certain general and well-recognized principles, namely: elementary considerations of humanity, even more exacting in peace than in war" (*Corfu Channel, Merits, Judgment, I.C.J. Report 1949*, p. 22).

[67] Cançado Trindade, "International law for humankind—towards a new *jus gentium* (II): general course on public international law", p. 150.

of or emphasis accorded these rights.[68] At any rate, such an approach could be taken as constituting a challenge to the principle of the sovereignty of the State and its corollary of non-intervention,[69] according to which the State has primary responsibility to offer protection and assistance to those affected by disasters on its territory.[70] Tension is created between, on the one hand, the principles of the sovereignty of States and of non-intervention and, on the other, international human rights law.[71]

55. Another source of tension is often between the rights and obligations of the assisting actor and those of the State affected by a disaster. In view of the social, economic and political implications of disaster relief and governance, States might be inclined to redefine their sovereignty by means of a constructive use of international law. The traditional State system is currently witnessing the emergence of various concepts related to the responsibility of States. As the Secretariat noted in its proposal for the topic,[72] the protection of persons may be located within contemporary reflection on an emerging principle entailing the responsibility to protect. The latter concept entails the responsibility to prevent, react and rebuild, corresponding, respectively, to the three phases of a disaster situation. However, the appropriateness of extending the concept of responsibility to protect and its relevance to the present topic both require careful consideration. Even if the responsibility to protect were to be recognized in the context of protection and assistance of persons in the event of disasters, its implications would be unclear. For example, to what extent would the responsibility create rights for third parties? What would the contents of those rights be? What would trigger those rights? Would those rights be singular or collective?

C. *Ratione personae*

56. The multiplicity of actors involved in disaster situations is a highly pertinent factor. Work on the topic will clearly need to take account of the role of international organizations, non-governmental organizations and commercial entities in addition to that of State actors. It will require assessing the practice of non-State actors and the weight to be accorded to it in order to place them properly within the framework of protection of persons in the event of disasters. There are pertinent questions to be posed. For example, is there a right of initiative, as is recognized as a matter of law in international humanitarian law instruments? Is a formal offer from or request to an assisting non-State actor necessary? What are the obligations of non-State actors to protect, if at all, as distinct from providing assistance? Does the individual have a right in relation to non-State actors? What is the position of commercial subcontractors? As these questions suggest, the legal consequences may differ, depending on the actor involved.

D. *Ratione temporis*

57. A broad approach appears indicated as concerns the phases which should be included, in order to provide fully fledged legal space. The importance of a coherent framework in terms of rights and obligations becomes apparent when considering the wide range of specific issues to which providing disaster assistance gives rise through successive phases, not only of disaster response but also pre-disaster and post-disaster: prevention and mitigation on the one hand, and rehabilitation on the other. A good example is the potentially controversial question of prevention. It is interesting to note that the concept of responsibility to prevent is also a recognized component in the emerging concept of protection in international humanitarian law. However, the nature and extent of the purported obligation of States to prevent disasters (acting individually or collectively) raises profound questions, which may need to be addressed.[73] In this connection, work carried out by the Commission on the topic of prevention of transboundary harm from hazardous activities[74] would be of relevance.

58. At the other end of the spectrum is the rehabilitation phase. Rehabilitation activities are properly linked to the response phase which addresses the immediate needs of individuals affected by a disaster. This should be distinguished from development activities, which can be described in terms of support to and implementation of autonomous development policies. These phases may not always be easy to separate in reality, but their nature differs considerably *ratione materiae*, *ratione temporis* and *ratione personae*. It is the reason why the Special Rapporteur considers it appropriate not to consider such activities for the purposes of the present topic while treating the legal consequences of the rehabilitation phase carefully[75] so as not to be detrimental to the norms governing development matters.[76]

---

[68] See Patrnogic, "Some reflections on humanitarian principles applicable in relief actions", p. 934.

[69] On sovereignty as a cardinal principle of international law, see the *Corfu Channel case* (footnote 66 above), p. 35. On non-intervention, see *Military and Paramilitary Activities in and against Nicaragua (Nicaragua* v. *United States of America), Merits, Judgment, I.C.J. Report 1986*, pp. 106–108, paras. 202–205 ("The principle of non-intervention involves the right of every sovereign State to conduct its affairs without outside interference; though examples of trespass against this principle are not infrequent, the Court considers that it is part and parcel of customary international law" (para. 202)); and General Assembly resolution 2625 (XXV) of 24 October 1970, annex.

[70] See, for example, General Assembly resolution 46/182, annex, para. 4.

[71] This point has been acknowledged in the Mohonk Criteria, which state that the "principles of non-intervention and sovereignty should not be used as an obstacle to humanitarian assistance", and that the "objective of humanitarian assistance is to save lives and is not intended to challenge the sovereignty of the state on whose territory aid is to be delivered" (Ebersole, *loc. cit.*, p. 198).

[72] *Yearbook ... 2006*, vol. II (Part Two), Annex III, para. 9, p. 207.

[73] See Romano, "L'obligation de prévention des catastrophes industrielles et naturelles", and Berramdane, "L'obligation de prévention des catastrophes et risques naturels."

[74] *Yearbook ... 2001*, vol. II (Part Two), p. 144.

[75] See, for example, *Doğan and Others* v. *Turkey* (Applications Nos. 8803–8811/02, 8813/02 and 8815–8819/02), judgment of 29 June 2004, European Court of Human Rights, *Reports of Judgments and Decisions 2004–VI*, p. 123, para. 154, where the Court discussed the legal consequences of rehabilitation activities after the occurrence of an emergency. The relevant paragraph reads in part: "For the Court, however, the authorities have the primary duty and responsibility to establish conditions, as well as provide the means, which allow the applicants to return voluntarily, in safety and with dignity, to their homes or places of habitual residence, or to resettle voluntarily in another part of the country (see in this respect Principles 18 and 28 of the United Nations Guiding Principles on Internal Displacement, E/CN.4/1998/53/Add.2, dated 11 February 1998)."

[76] See the Declaration on the Right to Development (General Assembly resolution 41/128 of 4 December 1986, annex).

Chapter III

Form of the work

59. Citing the Convention on the Privileges and Immunities of the United Nations as a possible model, the stated objective of the Secretariat's proposal for the topic was the elaboration of a set of provisions which would serve as a legal framework for the conduct of international disaster relief activities.[77] In this connection, some consideration might be given at the outset to the qualitative purpose of the Commission's work on this topic. Is the Commission's task limited to codification of existing law and practice or will it extend beyond *de lege ferenda*? The Secretariat proposal indicated that the work would be primarily limited to the former, with emphasis on progressive development as appropriate. At any rate, the Commission has itself considered that its drafts constitute both codification and progressive development of international law in the sense in which those concepts are defined in the Statute, and has found it impracticable to determine into which category each provision falls. Nevertheless, given the amorphous state of the law relating to international disaster response, striking the appropriate balance between *lex lata* and *lex ferenda* poses a singular challenge.

60. Regarding the form that the final product is to take, the Secretariat's proposal, by stating that the objective is the elaboration of a framework convention, would seem to have placed the emphasis on progressive development, in conformity with article 15 of the Commission's statute,[78] which contemplates the progressive development of international law by means of the preparation of draft conventions. Nevertheless, in practice, the Commission has utilized a variety of other forms in which to couch its final drafts: model rules, principles, guidelines, declarations, codes, etc. Regardless of the final form, the Commission, with few exceptions, embodies the result of its work in draft articles, prepared following its well-established methods of work. That should also be the case as regards the present topic. In conformity with its usual practice, the Commission's decision on the form to be recommended to the General Assembly for its final draft articles may, in principle, await the completion of work on the present topic. Nevertheless, the special characteristics of such a novel undertaking might make it advisable to arrive at an early understanding of what the final form should be, especially if guidelines, rather than a convention, might make the final draft more acceptable to States.

[77] *Yearbook ... 2006*, vol. II (Part Two), Annex III, para. 24, p. 210.

[78] General Assembly resolution 174 (II) of 21 November 1947.

Chapter IV

Conclusions

61. The present, preliminary report is intended to provide a basis for a constructive discussion in the Commission which will facilitate determination of the general scope of the topic on the protection of persons in the event of disasters.

62. Without prejudice to the outcome of the Commission's discussion of the scope, it is the view of the Special Rapporteur that the title chosen for the topic implies a wide perspective. Work on the topic can be undertaken with a rights-based approach that will inform the operational mechanisms of protection.

63. The identification of the underlying principles and the elaboration of the rules derived therefrom need to be reflected in a future set of draft articles as regards each of the two elements of protection (a lesson that can be learned from the experience of the International Relief Union).

64. While the Commission requested the Secretariat to prepare a background study initially limited to natural disasters, the Special Rapporteur is of the view that the Commission could usefully embark, *pari passu*, on work concerning both natural and man-made disasters.

65. Work on the topic will clearly need to take account of the multiplicity of actors in disaster situations.

66. To achieve complete coverage, work on the topic should extend to all three phases of a disaster situation, but it would appear justified to give particular attention to aspects relating to prevention and mitigation of a disaster as well as to provision of assistance in its immediate wake.

IMMUNITY OF STATE OFFICIALS FROM FOREIGN CRIMINAL JURISDICTION

[Agenda item 9]

DOCUMENT A/CN.4/601

Preliminary report on immunity of State officials from foreign criminal jurisdiction, by Roman Anatolevich Kolodkin, Special Rapporteur

[*Original: Russian*]
[*29 May 2008*]

CONTENTS

Multilateral instruments cited in the present report

	Source
Agreement for the prosecution and punishment of the major war criminals of the European Axis (London, 8 August 1945)	United Nations, *Treaty Series*, vol. 82, No. 251, p. 288.
Convention on the privileges and immunities of the United Nations (New York, 13 February 1946)	*Ibid.*, vol. 1, No. 4, p. 15.
Convention on the privileges and immunities of the specialized agencies (New York, 21 November 1947)	*Ibid.*, vol. 33, No. 521, p. 261.
Convention on the prevention and punishment of the crime of genocide (New York, 9 December 1948)	*Ibid.*, vol. 78, No. 1021, p. 277.
Geneva Conventions for the Protection of War Victims (Geneva, 12 August 1949)	*Ibid.*, vol. 75, pp. 31 *et seq.*
Geneva Convention for the Amelioration of the Condition of the Wounded and Sick in Armed Forces in the Field (Geneva, 12 August 1949)	*Ibid.*, vol. 75, No. 970, p. 31.
Geneva Convention for the Amelioration of the Condition of the Wounded, Sick and Shipwrecked Members of the Armed Forces at Sea (Geneva, 12 August 1949)	*Ibid.*, vol. 75, No. 971, p. 85.
Geneva Convention relative to the Treatment of Prisoners of War (Geneva, 12 August 1949)	*Ibid.*, vol. 75, No. 972, p. 135.
Geneva Convention relative to the Protection of Civilian Persons in Time of War (Geneva, 12 August 1949)	*Ibid.*, vol. 75, No. 973, p. 287.
Protocol additional to the Geneva Conventions of 12 August 1949, and relating to the protection of victims of international armed conflicts (Protocol I) (Geneva, 8 June 1977)	*Ibid.*, vol. 1125, No. 17512, p. 3.
Protocol additional to the Geneva Conventions of 12 August 1949, and relating to the protection of victims of non-international armed conflicts (Protocol II) (Geneva, 8 June 1977)	*Ibid.*, No. 17513, p. 609.
General Agreement on Privileges and Immunities of the Council of Europe (Paris, 2 September 1949)	*Ibid.*, vol. 250, No. 3515, p. 14.
Vienna Convention on Diplomatic Relations (Vienna, 18 April 1961)	*Ibid.*, vol. 500, No. 7310, p. 95.
Vienna Convention on Consular Relations (Vienna, 24 April 1963)	*Ibid.*, vol. 596, No. 8638, p. 261.
Vienna Convention on the law of treaties (Vienna, 23 May 1969)	*Ibid.*, vol. 1155, No. 18232, p. 331.
Convention on Special Missions (New York, 8 December 1969)	*Ibid.*, vol. 1400, No. 23431, p. 231.
Convention on the Prevention and Punishment of Crimes against Internationally Protected Persons, including Diplomatic Agents (New York, 14 December 1973)	*Ibid.*, vol. 1035, No. 15410, p. 167.
Vienna Convention on the Representation of States in their Relations with International Organizations of a Universal Character (Vienna, 14 March 1975)	A/CONF.67/16.
Convention against torture and other cruel, inhuman or degrading treatment or punishment (New York, 10 December 1984)	United Nations, *Treaty Series*, vol. 1465, No. 24841, p. 113.
Rome Statute of the International Criminal Court (Rome, 17 July 1998)	*Ibid.*, vol. 2187, No. 38544, p. 3.
United Nations Convention on Jurisdictional Immunities of States and Their Property (New York, 2 December 2004)	*Official Records of the General Assembly, Fifty-ninth Session, Supplement No. 49* (A/59/49), vol. I, resolution 59/38, annex.

Works cited in the present report

AKANDE, Dapo

"International law immunities and the International Criminal Court", AJIL, vol. 98, No. 3, July 2004, pp. 407–433.

ALTMAN, Heidi

"The Future of Head of State Immunity: the Case against Ariel Sharon", April 2002, p. 4.

BANKAS, Ernest K.

The State Immunity Controversy in International Law: Private Suits Against Sovereign States in Domestic Courts. Berlin-Heidelberg, Springer, 2005.

BANTEKAS, Ilias

"Head of State immunity in the light of multiple legal regimes and non-self-contained system theories: theoretical analysis of ICC third party jurisdiction against the background of the 2003 Iraq war", *Journal of Conflict & Security Law*, vol. 10, No. 1, Spring 2005, pp. 21–42.

BARKER, J. Craig

"The future of former Head of State immunity after *ex parte* Pinochet", *International and Comparative Law Quarterly*, vol. 48, part 4, October 1999, pp. 937–948.

BORGHI, Alvaro

L'immunité des dirigeants politiques en droit international. Basel, Helbling & Lichtenhahn, 2003.

BOWETT, Derek William

"Jurisdiction: changing patterns of authority over activities and resources", BYBIL, vol. 53 (1982), No. 1, pp. 1–26.

BRÖHMER, Jürgen

State Immunity and the Violations of Human Rights. The Hague, Kluwer Law International, 1997.

BROWNLIE, Ian

Principles of International Law, 6th ed. New York, Oxford University Press, 2003.

CARTER, Barry E.

"Immunity for Foreign Officials: Possibly Too Much and Confusing as Well", *American Society of International Law Proceedings. New world order or a world in disorder? Testing the limits of international law,* vol. 99, 30 March–2 April, 2005, pp. 230–233.

CASSESE, Antonio

International Law. New York, Oxford University Press, 2001.

"When may senior State officials be tried for international crimes? Some comments on the *Congo v. Belgium* Case", *European Journal of International Law*, vol. 13, No. 4, 2002, pp. 853–875.

International Criminal Law. New York, Oxford University Press, 2003.

CHERNICHENKO, S.V.

"Jurisdiction of the State (or national jurisdiction) as a manifestation of State sovereignty", *Theory of International Law*, vol. 2. Moscow, Independent Institute of International Law, 1999 (in Russian).

CROOK, John R.

"Contemporary practice of the United States relating to international law: U.S. Brief suggests Pope's immunity as a head of State", AJIL, vol. 100, No. 1 (January 2006), p. 219.

DAY, Adam

"Crimes against humanity as a nexus of individual and State responsibility: why the ICJ got *Belgium v. Congo* wrong", *Berkeley Journal of International Law*, vol. 22, No. 3, 2004, pp. 489–512.

DE SMET, Simon

"The immunity of Heads of States in US Courts after the Decision of the International Court of Justice", *Nordic Journal of International Law*, vol. 72, No. 3, 2003, pp. 313–339.

DENZA, Eileen

Diplomatic Law: A Commentary on the Vienna Convention on Diplomatic Relations, 2nd edition, Oxford, Clarendon Press, 1998.

"*Ex Parte Pinochet*: Lacuna or Leap?" *International and Comparative Law Quarterly*, vol. 48, part 4, October 1999, pp. 949–958.

DICKINSON, Andrew, Rae LINDSAY and James P. LOONAM

State Immunity: Selected Materials and Commentary. New York, Oxford University Press, 2004.

DU PLESSIS, Max and Shannon BOSCH

"Immunities and universal jurisdiction—The World Court steps in (or on?)", *South African Yearbook of International Law*, vol. 28, 2003, pp. 246–642.

FONTEYNE, Jean-Pierre

"Acts of State", in *Encyclopedia of Public International Law*, vol. I, Amsterdam, Elsevier, 1992, pp. 17–20.

FORCESE, Craig

"De-immunizing Torture: Reconciling Human Rights and State Immunity", *McGill Law Journal*, vol. 52, No. 1, Spring 2007, pp. 127–169.

FOURNIER, Alain

"Compétence pénale", *Encyclopédie Dalloz. Répertoire de droit international*, 1998, pp. 1–10.

FOX, Hazel

The Law of State immunity, New York, Oxford University Press, 2002.

"International law and restraints on the exercise of jurisdiction by national courts of States", in Malcom D. Evans, (ed.), *International Law*, 2nd ed., Oxford, Oxford University Press, 2006, pp. 361–394.

FRULLI, Michaela

"The question of Charles Taylor's immunity: still in search of balanced application of personal immunities?" *Journal of International Criminal Justice*, vol. 2, No. 4, December 2004, pp. 1118–1129.

GULLY-HART, Paul

"The function of State and diplomatic privileges and immunities in international cooperation in criminal matters: the position in Switzerland", *Fordham International Law Journal*, June 2000, vol. 23, No. 5, p. 1334–1343.

HAMID, Abdul Ghafur, Khin Maung SEIN and Hunud Abia KADOUF

"Immunity versus international crimes: the impact of Pinochet and Arrest Warrant cases", *Indian Journal of International Law*, vol. 46, No. 4, October–December 2006, pp. 495–516.

HIGGINS, Rosalyn

"After Pinochet: developments on head of State and ministerial immunities", The Incorporated Council of Law Reporting Annual Lecture 2006, London pp. 1–18.

INSTITUTE OF INTERNATIONAL LAW

Yearbook, 1889–1892, vol. XI, Hamburg session, September 1892, Brussels, Weissenbruch, 1892, pp. 426–438.

Tableau général des résolutions (1873–1956), Basel, Editions juridiques et sociologiques, 1957, pp. 15 and 16.

Yearbook, vol. 69 (2000–2001), Vancouver session, pp. 680–692. Rapporteur J. Verhoeven.

JENNING, Robert and Arthur WATTS

Oppenheim's International Law, vol. I, *Peace*, parts 2–4, 9th ed., Harlow, Longman, 1992.

KESSEDJIAN, Catherine

"Immunités", *Encyclopédie Dalloz. Répertoire de droit international*, 1998, pp. 1–21.

KHLESTOVA, I.O.

"Immunity of a State implies that it is not subject to the jurisdiction of another State", *Problems of the jurisdictional immunity of a foreign State (legislation and practice)*, Moscow, 2002, p. 9 (in Russian).

KOLLER, David S.

"Immunity of foreign ministers: paragraph 61 of the *Yerodia* judgment as it pertains to the Security Council and International Criminal Court", *American University International Law Review*, vol. 20, No.1, 2004, pp. 7–42.

LOWE, Vaughan

"Jurisdiction", in Malcolm D. Evans (ed.), *International Law*, 2nd ed., Oxford, Oxford University Press, 2006, pp. 335–360.

LUKASHUK, Igor I.

International Law, General section, 3rd ed. Moscow, Wolters Kluwer, 2007.

MALANCZUK, Peter

Akehurst's Modern Introduction to International Law, 7th revised ed. London and New York, Routledge, 1997.

Meagher, J. Patrick

"Act of State and sovereign immunity: the Marcos cases", *Harvard International Law Journal*, vol. 29, No. 1, Winter 1988, pp. 127–134.

Oxman, Bernard H.

"Jurisdiction of States", *Encyclopedia of Public International Law*, vol. III. Amsterdam, Elsevier Sciences Publishers, 1997, pp. 55–60.

Parlett, Kate

"Immunity in civil proceedings for torture: the emerging exception", *European Human Rights Law Review*, No. 1, 2006, pp. 49–66.

Parry, Clive and John Grant

Encyclopaedic Dictionary of International Law, New York, London, Rome, Oceana, 1986.

Parseghian, L.Y.

"Defining the 'public act' requirement in the act of State doctrine", *University of Chicago Law Review*, vol. 58, 1991, pp. 1151–1180.

Pierson, Charles

"Pinochet and the end of immunity: England's House of Lords holds that a former Head of State is not immune for torture", *Temple International & Comparative Law Journal*, vol. 14, No. 2, Fall 2000, pp. 263–326.

Przetacznik, Frank

Protection of Officials of Foreign States according to International Law, The Hague, Martinus Nijhoff, 1983.

"Basic principles of international law concerning the protection of the officials of foreign States", *Revue de Droit International de Sciences Diplomatiques et Politiques*, vol. 69 (1) (January–March 1991), pp. 52 –81.

Rousseau, Charles

Droit international public, vol. IV, Paris, Sirey, 1980, pp. 10 and 11. Salmon, Jean (dir.)

Dictionnaire de droit international public. Brussels, Bruylant, 2001.

Sassoli, Marco

"L'arrêt Yerodia: quelques remarques sur une affaire au point de collision entre les deux couches du droit international", *Revue générale de droit international public*, vol. 106, 2002, pp. 791–818.

Shaw, Malcolm

International Law, 5th ed. Cambridge University Press, 2003, 1288 p.

Simbeye, Yitha

Immunity and International Criminal Law. Aldershot, England/Burlington, Vermont, Ashgate, 2004.

Sinclair, I.

"The law of sovereign immunity: recent developments", *Recueil des cours de l'Académie de droit international de La Haye*, 1980-II, vol. 167, pp. 113–284.

Smis, Stefan and Kim Van der Borght

"Belgian law concerning the punishment of grave breaches of international humanitarian law: a contested law with uncontested objectives". *American Society of International Law Insights*, July 2003.

Steinberger, Helmut

"State immunity", in *Encyclopedia of Public International Law*, vol. 4 Amsterdam, Elsevier, 2000, pp. 615–633.

Stern, Brigitte

"Immunités et doctrine de l'*Act of State*. Différences théoriques et similitudes pratiques de deux modes de protection des chefs d'État devant les juridictions étrangères", *Journal du droit international*, No. 133 (1) (Jan./Feb./March 2006), pp. 63–88.

Strisower, Leo

"L'exterritorialité et ses principales applications", *Recueil des Cours de l'Académie de droit international de la Haye*, vol. I, 1923, pp. 233 *et seq*.

Sucharitkul, Sompong

"Immunities of foreign States before national authorities", *Recueil des cours de l'Académie de droit international de La Haye*, 1976-I, vol. 149, pp. 87–215.

Summers, Mark A.

"Immunity or impunity? The potential effect of prosecutions of State officials for core international crimes in States like the United States that are not parties to the Statute of the International Criminal Court", *Brooklyn Journal of International Law*, vol. 31, No. 2, 2006, pp. 463–493.

"Diplomatic Immunity *Ratione Personae*: Did the International Court of Justice Create a New Customary Rule in *Congo v. Belgium*?" *Michigan State Journal of International Law*, vol. 16, No. 1, (2007), p. 459–473.

Tomonori, Misushima

"The individual as beneficiary of State immunity: problems of the attribution of *ultra vires* conduct", *Denver Journal of International Law and Policy*, vol. 29 (Summer/Fall 2001), pp. 261–288.

Toner, Paul J.

"Competing concepts of immunity: The (R)evolution of the Head of State immunity defense", *Penn State Law Review*, vol. 108, No. 3, Winter 2004, pp. 899–927.

Triffterer, Otto (ed.)

Commentary on the Rome Statute of the International Criminal Court: Observer's Notes, Article by Article, Baden-Baden, Nomos, 1999.

Van Panhuys, H.F.

"In the borderland between the act of state doctrine and questions of jurisdictional immunities", *International Comparative Law Quarterly*, vol. 13, Part 4, October 1964, pp. 1193–1213.

Verhoeven, Joe

"Les immunités de juridiction et d'exécution du chef d'Etat et de gouvernement en droit international", in Institute of International Law, *Yearbook*, vol. 69, 2000–2001, session of Vancouver, 2001, Paris, Pedone.

"Les immunités propres aux organes ou autres agents des sujets du droit international", *Le droit international des immunités: contestation ou consolidation?* Brussels, Larcier, 2004, pp. 61–148.

Watts, Arthur

"The legal position in International Law of Heads of States, Heads of Government and Foreign Ministers", *Recueil des cours de l'Académie de droit international de La Haye*, 1994-III, vol. 247, Dordrecht, Martinus Nijhoff, 1995, pp. 9–130.

Wickremasinghe, Chanaka

"Immunities enjoyed by officials of States and International Organizations", in Malcolm D. Evans (ed.), *International Law*, 2nd ed., Oxford, Oxford University Press, 2006, pp. 395–421.

Wirth, Steffen

"Immunity for core crimes? The I.C.J.'s Judgment in the *Congo v. Belgium* Case", *European Journal of International Law*, vol. 13, No. 4, 2002, pp. 877–893.

Zander, Michael

"The act of state doctrine", AJIL, vol. 53, 1959, pp. 826–852.

Introduction

1. At its fifty-eighth session, in 2006, the International Law Commission, on the recommendation of the Planning Group,[1] endorsed the inclusion in its long-term programme of work of the topic "Immunity of State officials from foreign criminal jurisdiction".[2] A brief outline of the topic, including a select bibliography, was annexed to the report of the Commission on its fifty-eighth session.[3]

[1] The Planning Group in turn based its recommendation on the report submitted to it by the Working Group on Long-term Programme of Work, in which it proposed six new topics, including the present one, for inclusion in the long-term programme of work of the Commission (see A/CN.4/L.704, para. 4).

[2] *Yearbook ... 2006*, vol. II (Part Two), p. 185, para. 257.

[3] *Ibid.*, annex I.

2. During the discussion in the Sixth Committee of the General Assembly of the new topics included in the long-term programme of work of the Commission, there was general support for this topic. In that connection, "the view was expressed that the time seemed ripe to take stock of present practice and to attempt to elaborate general rules on the subject. It was also noted that due priority should be given to the need for State officials to enjoy such immunity, for the sake of stable relations among States" (A/CN.4/577, para. 126). At its fifty-ninth session, the Commission decided to include this topic in its current programme of work.[4] By its resolution 62/66 of 6 December 2007, the General Assembly took note of that decision.

[4] *Yearbook ... 2007*, vol. II (Part Two), p. 90, para. 376.

Chapter I

Purpose of the preliminary report

3. The present preliminary report briefly describes the history of the consideration by the Commission and the Institute of International Law of the question of immunity of State officials from foreign jurisdiction and outlines the range of issues proposed for consideration by the Commission in the preliminary phase of work on the topic. These issues, on which the Commission's views will be important for further consideration of the substance of the topic, include:

(*a*) the issue of the sources of immunity of State officials from foreign criminal jurisdiction;

(*b*) the issue of the content of the concepts of "immunity" and "jurisdiction", "criminal jurisdiction" and "immunity from criminal jurisdiction" and the relationship between immunity and jurisdiction;

(*c*) the issue of the typology of immunity of State officials (immunity *ratione personae* and immunity *ratione materiae*);

(*d*) the issue of the rationale for immunity of State officials and the relationship between immunity of officials and immunity of the State, diplomatic and consular immunity and immunity of members of special missions;

(*e*) the issues to be considered when determining the scope of this topic.

4. The issues in subparagraph (*e*) include:

(*a*) whether all State officials or only some of them (for example, only Heads of State, Heads of Government and ministers for foreign affairs) should be covered by the future draft guiding principles or draft articles that may be prepared by the Commission resulting from its consideration of the topic;

(*b*) the extent of immunity enjoyed by current and former State officials to be covered by the topic under consideration;

(*c*) the waiver of immunity of State officials (and possibly other procedural aspects of immunity).

5. Thus, the purpose of the report is to give a rough outline of two types of issue: (*a*) those which should in principle be analysed by the Commission as part of its consideration of the topic of immunity of State officials from foreign criminal jurisdiction; (*b*) those which should probably be addressed by the Commission in a possible formulation of any instrument resulting from the consideration of this topic—for example, draft guiding principles or draft articles.

Chapter II

History of the consideration of the question of immunity of State officials from foreign jurisdiction by the International Law Commission and the Institute of International Law

A. Work of the Commission

6. The survey of international law prepared by the Secretariat for the Commission before its first session in 1948 contains a section entitled "Jurisdiction over foreign States", which is said to cover "the entire field of jurisdictional immunities of States and their property, of their public vessels, *of their sovereigns**, and of their armed forces" (emphasis added)[5].

[5] *Survey of International Law, in Relation to the Work of Codification of the International Law Commission* (United Nations publication, Sales No. 1948.V.1 (I)), para. 50.

7. The Commission touched on the issue in 1949, when it was preparing the draft Declaration on Rights and Duties of States. Draft article 2 states: "Every State has the right to exercise jurisdiction over its territory and over all persons and things therein, subject to the immunities recognized by international law".[6] The commentary to this draft article notes that "the concluding phrase is a safeguard for protecting such immunities as those of diplomatic officers and officials of international organizations".[7] State officials are thus not directly mentioned as such.

8. The issue was considered during the preparation of the draft Principles of International Law recognized in the Charter of the Nürnberg Tribunal and in the Judgment of the Tribunal, adopted by the Commission in 1950. According to draft principle III, "The fact that a person who committed an act which constitutes a crime under international law acted as Head of State or responsible Government official does not relieve him from responsibility under international law".[8] As noted in the Commission's commentary, this text is based on article 7 of the Charter of the Nürnberg Tribunal.[9] According to the Commission, the same idea was expressed in the following passage of the Tribunal judgment: "He who violates the laws of war cannot obtain immunity while acting in pursuance of the authority of the State if the State in authorizing action moves outside its competence under international law".[10]

9. This subject was also considered by the Commission in its work on the 1954 draft code of crimes against the peace and security of mankind. According to draft article 3 of the Code, which is similar to draft principle III of the Principles of International Law Recognized in the Charter of the Nürnberg Tribunal and in the Judgment of the Tribunal, "The fact that a person acted as Head of State or as responsible government official does not relieve him of responsibility for committing any of the offences defined in this Code".[11]

10. This idea is reflected, in a somewhat different wording, in draft article 7 of the Code of Crimes against the Peace and Security of Mankind, adopted by the Commission in 1996: "The official position of an individual who commits a crime against the peace and security of mankind, even if he acted as head of State or Government, does not relieve him of criminal responsibility or mitigate punishment".[12] In draft article 11 proposed in 1988, which became draft article 7 in the final version of the draft Code, instead of "even if he acted as head of State or Government" the words "and particularly the fact that he acts as head of State or Government" were used.[13] The commentary to this article states, *inter alia*, that the wording contains elements from the corresponding provisions of the Charters of the Nürnberg and Tokyo Tribunals (*Documents on American Foreign Relations*, Princeton University Press, 1948, vol. VIII (July 1945–December 1946), pp. 354), the Nürnberg principles adopted by the Commission in 1950 and the draft Code adopted by the Commission in 1954.[14]

11. It should be noted that both the draft Principles of International Law Recognized in the Charter of the Nürnberg Tribunal and in the judgment of the Tribunal and the draft Code of Crimes against the Peace and Security of Mankind were conceptually related to the idea of an international criminal jurisdiction (although originally the draft Code had been intended for use by both national and international courts). The commentaries to the Nürnberg Principles adopted by the Commission were based mainly on the conclusions of the Nürnberg Tribunal.[15] Regarding the Code of Crimes against the Peace and Security of Mankind, the Commission noted: "As to the implementation of the code, since some members considered that a code unaccompanied by ... a competent criminal jurisdiction would be ineffective, the Commission requested the General Assembly to indicate whether the Commission's mandate extended to the preparation of the statute of a competent international criminal jurisdiction for individuals."[16] When the draft statute for the International Criminal Court, prepared by the Commission at the

---

[6] *The Work of the International Law Commission*, 7th ed., vol. I, New York: United Nations, 2007, p. 262 (United Nations publication, Sales No. E.04.V.6).

[7] *Yearbook ... 1949*, p. 253.

[8] *Yearbook ... 1950*, vol. II, p. 375.

[9] "The official position of defendants, whether Heads of State or responsible officials in Government Departments, shall not be considered as freeing them from responsibility or mitigating punishment." Agreement for the prosecution and punishment of the major war criminals of the European Axis.

[10] *Yearbook ... 1950*, vol. II, p. 375. As noted by Triffterer, the wording of the Principles adopted by the Commission differs slightly from the provisions in the documents of the Nürnberg Tribunal "in wording but not in substance except for the fact that the words 'or mitigating punishment' were no longer included". "Irrelevance of official capacity", *Commentary on the Rome Statute of the International Criminal Court: Observer's Notes, Article by Article*, 1999, p. 503.

[11] *Yearbook ... 1954*, vol. II, p. 152.

[12] *Yearbook ... 1996*, vol. II (Part Two), p. 26.

[13] *Yearbook ... 1988*, vol. II (Part Two) p. 71.

[14] *Ibid*. In addition, the Commission noted: "Although it refers expressly to Heads of State or Government, because they have the greatest power of decision, the words 'the official position of an individual ... and particularly' show that the article also relates to other officials. The real effect of the principle is that the official position of an individual who commits a crime against peace and security can never be invoked as a circumstance absolving him from responsibility or conferring any immunity upon him, even if the official claims that the acts constituting the crime were performed in the exercise of his functions." In the commentary to the final draft of article 7, the Commission noted: "It would be paradoxical to allow the individuals who are, in some respects, the most responsible for the crimes covered by the Code to invoke the sovereignty of the State and to hide behind the immunity that is conferred on them by virtue of their positions ..." (*Yearbook ... 1996*, vol. II (Part Two), p. 26). However, Verhoeven states, on the subject of this provision of the 1996 draft Code, that "... such a provision does not *ipso facto* imply either that immunity should be maintained or that it should be waived: it is simply unrelated to immunity". "Les immunités propres aux organes ou autres agents des sujets du droit international", p. 92.

[15] *Yearbook ... 1950*, vol. II, p. 191, para. 42.

[16] *Yearbook ... 1988*, vol. II (Part Two), p. 55, para. 198. In this regard, a typical statement was made, for example, by the Commission member Mr. McCaffrey when discussing the draft article on the obligation to punish or prosecute. He said, *inter alia*, that he did not believe that universal jurisdiction would be any more acceptable to States than an international criminal court—in fact, it might be less so. Consequently he was not sure that the Commission would be well advised to proceed with the drafting of the article on universal jurisdiction before having at least attempted to draft the statute of an international criminal court. (*Yearbook ... 1988*, vol. I, 2082nd meeting, para. 47, p. 273. See also *Yearbook ... 1989*, vol. II (Part Two), pp. 65 and 66, paras. 211–216.)

request of the General Assembly within the framework of the draft Code of Crimes against the Peace and Security of Mankind,[17] became a separate document, regret was expressed in the Sixth Committee because "the court had originally been envisaged as a legal body in which the Code would be applied".[18] In this regard, the footnote to the commentary to draft article 7 of the 1996 Code is significant. Noting that "[t]he absence of any procedural immunity with respect to prosecution or punishment in appropriate judicial proceedings is an essential corollary of the absence of any substantive immunity or defense", the Commission saw fit to add in a footnote: "Judicial proceedings before an international criminal court would be the quintessential example of appropriate judicial proceedings in which an individual could not invoke any substantive or procedural immunity based on his official position to avoid prosecution and punishment".[19]

12. It should also be borne in mind that, in considering this provision of the draft Code, the Commission took into account the fact that a number of States had raised the related issue of the possible immunity of State officials, including Heads of State or Government. In that connection, the Chairman of the Drafting Committee, introducing the draft Code adopted by it on second reading in the plenary, noted that, in the opinion of the Drafting Committee, the issue of immunity was a matter of implementation of the Code and therefore should not be dealt with in the part of the Code on general principles.[20]

13. The Commission considered the issue of immunity of State officials from foreign jurisdiction when preparing the draft articles on jurisdictional immunities of States and their property. In accordance with article 2, paragraph 1 (*b*) (v), "State" means "representatives of the State acting in that capacity".[21] These representatives include Heads of State or Government, heads of ministerial departments, ambassadors, heads of missions, diplomatic agents and consular officials.[22] The words "in that capacity" at the end of article 2, paragraph 1 (*b*) (v), were intended to clarify that this immunity is accorded to the representative capacity of such persons *ratione materiae*.[23] The draft articles do not cover the immunities *ratione personae* to which, as noted by the Commission, Heads of State and ambassadors "are entitled".[24]

14. It was initially suggested that, in considering this topic, the Commission should consider immunities in various forms and manifestations; for instance, immunities from civil, administrative and criminal jurisdiction. This proposal was contained in a report of the working group established by the Commission to consider the question of future work by the Commission on the topic.[25] The seventh and eighth reports of the Special Rapporteur, Mr. Sucharitkul, contained, *inter alia*, draft article 25 on the immunities *ratione personae* of "personal sovereigns and other heads of State", including immunities from the criminal jurisdiction of another State.[26] This draft article was criticized at the thirty-first session of the Commission, 1979, and was not included in the draft articles submitted to the General Assembly.[27] The draft articles made no further mention of the immunity of Heads of State (or other State representatives) from criminal jurisdiction.

15. The Commission confined itself to the inclusion of a "without prejudice" clause in the draft articles. In accordance with article 3, paragraph 2, the articles are "without prejudice to privileges and immunities accorded under international law to heads of State *ratione personae*". As indicated in the commentary to that paragraph, "[t]he present draft articles do not prejudge the extent of immunities granted by States to foreign sovereigns or other heads of State, their families or household staff which may also, in practice, cover other members of their entourage. Similarly, the present draft articles do not prejudge the extent of immunities granted by States to heads of Government and ministers for foreign affairs. Those persons are, however, not expressly included in paragraph 2, since it would be difficult to prepare an exhaustive list, and any enumeration of such persons would moreover raise the issues of the basis and of the extent of the jurisdictional immunity exercised by such persons. A proposal was made at one stage to add after 'heads of State' in paragraph 2, heads of government and ministers for foreign affairs, but was not accepted by the Commission".[28] Another noteworthy part of the commentary reads: "The reservation of article 3, paragraph 2, therefore refers exclusively to the private acts or personal immunities ... accorded in the practice of States, without any suggestion that their status should in any way be affected by the present articles. The existing customary law is left untouched."[29]

16. The immunity of State officials from the criminal jurisdiction of another State and the status of State officials

[17] By its resolution 44/39 of 4 December 1989, the General Assembly requested the Commission "*when considering* at its forty-second session the *item entitled 'Draft Code of Crimes against the Peace and Security of Mankind'*, to address the question of establishing an international criminal court or other international criminal trial mechanism with *jurisdiction over persons alleged to have committed crimes which may be covered under such a code**". By resolution 46/54 of 9 December 1991, the Assembly invited the Commission "... *within the framework of the draft Code of Crimes against the Peace and Security of Mankind**, to consider further and analyse the issues raised in its report on the work of its forty-second session concerning the question of an international criminal jurisdiction, including proposals for the establishment of an international criminal court or other international criminal mechanism ...".

[18] Topical summary of the discussion of the Sixth Commission of the General Assembly at its fiftieth session, document A/CN.4/472, para. 42. It was also noted that "the Code would be better implemented by an international criminal court than by national courts" (para. 43). The view was also expressed that "the Code and the future court shared a common purpose of enabling *national courts** or an international body to punish particularly abhorrent crimes committed by States or individuals" (para. 45).

[19] *Yearbook ... 1996*, vol. II (Part Two), p. 27.

[20] *Yearbook ... 1995*, vol. I, 2408th meeting, p. 202, para. 36.

[21] *Yearbook ... 1991*, vol. II (Part Two), p. 14.

[22] *Ibid*., p. 18, para. 17. From the commentary to draft article 2 it is clear that this list was not exhaustive. In the opinion of the Commission, all natural persons authorized to represent the State enjoy State immunity.

[23] *Ibid*.

[24] *Ibid*., p. 18, para. 19.

[25] *Yearbook ... 1978*, vol. II (Part Two), p. 154, para. 22.

[26] *Yearbook ... 1985*, vol. II (Part One), document A/CN.4/388, pp. 44 and 45; *Yearbook ... 1986*, vol. II (Part One), document A/CN.4/396, p. 31.

[27] For the Commission's discussion of draft article 25, submitted in the eighth report of the Special Rapporteur, see *Yearbook ... 1986*, vol. I, 1943rd–1945th meetings, pp. 9–28.

[28] *Yearbook ... 1991*, vol. II (Part Two), p. 22, para. (7).

[29] *Ibid*., para. (6).

were issues considered by the Commission when preparing the draft articles on diplomatic and consular relations; on special missions; on the prevention and punishment of crimes against diplomatic agents and other internationally protected persons; and on the representation of States in their relations with international organizations.

17. The draft articles on diplomatic relations, on consular relations, on special missions and on the representation of States in their relations with international organizations made reference to special categories of State officials, including "diplomatic agents", "consular officials", "representatives of the sending State" and "delegates", who are entrusted by a State with performing on its behalf certain functions in its relations with another State or with an international organization. The draft articles provided that those categories of State officials would enjoy immunity from the criminal jurisdiction of the receiving State.[30]

18. An issue of particular interest was the Commission's consideration of the status of the Head of State and other persons of high rank when preparing the draft articles on special missions. The Commission initially considered the possibility of including in the draft articles a section on so-called high-level special missions, which would have included missions led by Heads of State, Heads of Government, ministers for foreign affairs and other ministers.[31] The Special Rapporteur submitted draft provisions on such special missions at the seventeenth session of the Commission in 1965.[32] Those draft provisions ("rules") envisaged complete inviolability and full immunity from the jurisdiction of the receiving State for Heads of State, Heads of Government, ministers for foreign affairs and other ministers leading special missions.[33] The Commission did not discuss the draft articles themselves but considered whether special rules should be laid down for such missions.[34] Taking into account the opinion of States on that issue, the Commission recommended the Special Rapporteur not to prepare draft provisions concerning so-called high-level special missions but to include in the draft articles a provision on the status of the Head of State as head of a special mission, and to consider whether it was desirable to mention the particular situation of such special missions in the provisions dealing with certain immunities.[35] In that connection, the draft articles submitted by the Commission to the General Assembly in 1967 included draft article 21 on the status of the Head of State and persons of high rank, which reads as follows:

> 1. The Head of the sending State, when he leads a special mission, shall enjoy in the receiving State or in a third State, in addition to what is granted by these articles, the facilities, privileges and immunities accorded by international law to Heads of State on an official visit;
>
> 2. The Head of the Government, the Minister for Foreign Affairs and other persons of high rank, when they take part in a special mission of the sending State, shall enjoy in the receiving State or in a third State, in addition to what is granted by these articles, the facilities, privileges and immunities accorded by international law.[36]

19. The commentary to this draft article noted that "in international law ... rank may confer on the person holding it exceptional facilities, privileges and immunities which he retains on becoming a member of a special mission" and that "[t]he Commission did not specify the titles and ranks which these 'other persons' must hold in order to enjoy additional facilities, privileges and immunities, since such titles and ranks would vary from one State to another according to the constitutional law and protocol in force".[37] The Commission thus left it unclear who was included among the persons "of high rank", including in draft article 21, paragraph 2, only two generally accepted examples: the Head of Government and the minister for foreign affairs. The extent of the immunities granted by international law beyond the scope of the draft articles, to Heads of State, Heads of Government, ministers for foreign affairs and other officials "of high rank" also remained unclear.

20. A similar article was included in the draft articles on the representation of States in their relations with international organizations, submitted by the Commission to the General Assembly in 1971.[38] As noted by the Commission in its commentary to the draft article, several States had expressed the view in their written comments that article 50 was on the whole unnecessary, since the persons concerned "would enjoy the facilities, privileges and immunities accorded to them by international law whether the article was included or not in the draft".[39] The

[30] See, in particular: articles 27, 29, 30, 37, 38, 39 and 40 of the draft articles on diplomatic relations and the commentaries thereto (*Yearbook ... 1958*, vol. II, pp. 97–99 and 102–104); articles 41, 43, 45, 53, 54 and 55 of the draft articles on consular relations and the commentaries thereto (*Yearbook ... 1961*, vol. II, pp. 115–119 and 122–123); articles 29, 31, 41, 43 and 44 of the draft articles on special missions and the commentaries thereto (*Yearbook ... 1967*, vol. II, pp. 361, 362, 365 and 366); and articles 28, 30, 31, 37, 38, 59, 61, 62, 68 and 69 of the draft articles on the representation of States in their relations with international organizations and the commentaries thereto (*Yearbook ... 1971*, vol. II (Part One), pp. 302–305, 308, 309, 319–321 and 323).

[31] "At its sixteenth session, the International Law Commission decided to ask its Special Rapporteur to submit at its succeeding session an article dealing with the legal status of the so-called high-level Special Missions, in particular, Special Missions led by Heads of State, Heads of Governments, Ministers of Foreign Affairs and Cabinet Ministers." *Yearbook ... 1967*, vol. II, p. 393.

[32] *Yearbook ... 1965*, vol. II, pp. 143 and 144. In that respect, the Special Rapporteur, Mr. Bartoš, noted: "Despite all his efforts to establish what are the rules specially applicable to missions of this kind, the Special Rapporteur has not succeeded in discovering them either in the practice or in the literature." *Ibid.*, p. 143.

[33] *Ibid.*, pp. 143 and 144, draft rule 2 (*i*) and (*j*); draft rule 3 (*e*) and (*g*); draft rule 4 (*f*) and (*h*); and draft rule 5 (*d*) and (*f*).

[34] *Yearbook ... 1966*, vol. I (Part Two), 881st meeting, pp. 259–261. Summing up the discussion, the Special Rapporteur noted, *inter alia*: "There could be no doubt that for missions led by a Head of State rules of general international law already existed, so that there was no need to lay down any special rules." *Ibid.*, 883rd meeting, p. 261.

[35] *Yearbook ... 1966*, vol. II, p. 277, para. 69.

[36] *Yearbook ... 1967*, vol. II, p. 359.

[37] *Ibid.*

[38] "Article 50. *Status of the Head of State and persons of high rank*

"1. The Head of the sending State, when he leads the delegation, shall enjoy in the host State or in a third State, in addition to what is granted by the present articles, the facilities, privileges and immunities accorded by international law to Heads of State.

"2. The Head of the Government, the Minister for Foreign Affairs and other persons of high rank, when they take part in a delegation of the sending State, shall enjoy in the host State or in a third State, in addition to what is granted by the present articles, the facilities, privileges and immunities accorded by international law to such persons."

Yearbook ... 1971, vol. II (Part One), p. 315.

[39] *Ibid.*

Commission nevertheless decided to retain the draft article, pointing out in the commentary that it reflected "a well-established practice".[40]

21. Also of interest is the Commission's consideration of the definition of the term "internationally protected person" for the purposes of the draft articles on the prevention and punishment of crimes against internationally protected persons. In defining this term for the purposes of the draft articles, the Commission also thereby determined the scope of application of the draft articles, *ratione personae*. In accordance with article 1, paragraph 1, of the draft articles submitted by the Commission to the General Assembly in 1972, for the purposes of the draft articles " 'internationally protected person' means: (*a*) A Head of State or a Head of Government, whenever he is in a foreign State, as well as members of his family who accompany him; (*b*) Any official of either a State or an international organization who is entitled, pursuant to general international law or an international agreement, to special protection for or because of the performance of functions on behalf of his State or international organization, as well as members of his family who are likewise entitled to special protection".[41]

22. As noted in the commentary to the draft article, in subparagraph (*a*) specific mention is made of a Head of State or a Head of Government on account of the exceptional protection which, under international law, attaches to such a status.[42] The Commission emphasized that a Head of State or a Head of Government "is entitled to special protection whenever he is in a foreign State and whatever may be the nature of his visit—official, unofficial or private".[43]

23. A proposal for the text of the draft article to indicate that international protection should also be extended to cabinet members or other persons of similar (high) rank, at all times and in all circumstances when in a foreign State, was rejected. Firstly, the Commission decided that, while there was some support for the principle that such persons were entitled to international protection, "it could not be based upon any broadly accepted rule of international law and consequently should not be proposed".[44] Secondly, the opponents of this proposal pointed out that the Commission had already considered the possibility of using similar wording (for example, "other personality of high rank") in its work on special missions and on the representation of States in their relations with international organizations, but had decided against such wording because its meaning was not sufficiently precise.[45]

24. Unlike Heads of State or Government, the entitlement of the officials mentioned in draft article 1 (*b*) to special protection, in the opinion of the Commission, depends on the performance by them of official functions.[46]

B. Work of the Institute

25. The Institute first considered the issue of the immunity of Heads of State from the jurisdiction of foreign courts in the nineteenth century. Draft international regulations on the competence of courts in proceedings against foreign States, sovereigns or Heads of State were adopted in 1891.[47] The immunity of a Head of State was considered in the context of the immunity of the State. The articles did not single out immunity from foreign criminal jurisdiction and referred to immunity in general terms. In accordance with draft articles 4 to 6, national courts could consider only a very limited number of civil legal actions against Heads of foreign States.[48]

26. The Institute examined the issue of immunity of Heads of State for the second time at the turn of this century, when the topic had begun to attract a great deal of public, political and professional interest.[49] This resulted in the adoption by the Institute in 2001 of a resolution enabled "Immunities from Jurisdiction and Execution of Heads of State and of Government in International Law".[50]

---

[40] *Ibid.*

[41] *Yearbook ... 1972*, vol. II, p. 312.

[42] *Ibid.*

[43] *Ibid.*

[44] *Ibid*, p. 313.

[45] *Yearbook ... 1972*, vol. I, 1191th meeting, p. 237. The last argument, as we know, did not reflect the final outcome of the Commission's work on both the topics mentioned: the draft articles on special missions and on the representation of States in their relations with international organizations included a reference to "other persons of high rank", alongside Heads of State and ministers for foreign affairs.

[46] *Ibid.*, vol. II, pp. 313 and 314. Thus, a diplomatic agent on vacation in a State other than a host or receiving State would not normally be entitled to special protection (*ibid.*, p. 313).

[47] *Yearbook of the Institute of International Law*, 1889–1892, vol. XI, pp. 426–438. For consideration of this subject by the Institute, see also Verhoeven, "Les immunités de juridiction et d'exécution. Rapport provisoire". December 2000. *Yearbook of the Institute of International Law*, vol. 69 (2000–2001), p. 487.

[48] Institute of International Law, *Tableau général des résolutions* (1873–1956), pp. 15 and 16.

"*Article 4*

"The only admissible actions against a foreign State are:

"1. Actions *in rem*, including possessory actions relating to immovable or movable property in the territory;

"2. Actions based on the status of the foreign State as heir or legatee of a national of the territory, or as having an entitlement to a succession opened in the territory;

"3. Actions relating to a commercial or industrial establishment or a railway operated by the foreign State in the territory;

"4. Actions for which the foreign State has expressly recognized the competence of the court ...;

"5. Actions arising from contracts concluded by the foreign State in the territory, if full performance thereof in the same territory may be requested by virtue of an express clause or by virtue of the very nature of the action;

"6. Claims for damages arising as a result of a delict or quasi-delict committed in the territory.

"*Article 5*

"Actions brought as a result of acts of sovereignty, actions arising from a contract of the claimant acting as a State official and actions having regard to debts of the foreign State incurred by public donations shall not be admissible.

"*Article 6*

"Actions brought against foreign sovereigns and Heads of State shall be subject to the rules laid down in articles 4 and 5." Institute of International Law, *Tableau général des résolutions* (1873–1956), Basel, 1957, pp. 15 and 16.

[49] At that time, in particular, the high-profile *Pinochet* case was under consideration in the United Kingdom of Great Britain and Northern Ireland. *Regina v. Bow Street Metropolitan Stipendiary Magistrate*, ex Parte Pinochet Ugarte. *The Law Reports 2000*, Appeal cases, vol. 1, p. 61.

[50] Institute of International Law. *Yearbook*, vol. 69 (2000–2001), pp. 680–692. Rapporteur J. Verhoeven.

The resolution provides for the immunity of a serving Head of State and a serving Head of Government from criminal jurisdiction before the courts of a foreign State, irrespective of the gravity of the offence committed.[51] Under the resolution, former Heads of State and Heads of Government enjoy immunity from foreign criminal jurisdiction only in respect of acts performed in the exercise of official functions. However, this immunity is limited, since they may in any case be subject to criminal prosecution if the acts of which they are accused are crimes under international law, if they are performed exclusively to satisfy personal interests, or if they constitute an illegal appropriation of State property.[52]

[51] *Ibid.*, pp. 687, 691.

"*Article 2*

"In criminal matters, the Head of State shall enjoy immunity from jurisdiction before the courts of a foreign State for any crime he or she may have committed, regardless of its gravity.

...

"*Article 15*

"The Head of Government of a foreign State enjoys ... immunity from jurisdiction ... recognised, in this Resolution, to the Head of the State."

[52] *Ibid.*, pp. 691–692.

"*Article 13*

...

"Nor does he or she enjoy immunity from jurisdiction, in criminal ... proceedings, except in respect of acts which are performed in the exercise of official functions and relate to the exercise thereof. Nevertheless, he or she may be prosecuted and tried when the acts alleged constitute a crime under international law, or when they are performed exclusively to satisfy a personal interest, or when they constitute a misappropriation of the State's assets and resources."

...

"*Article 16*

"Articles 13 and 14 are applicable to former Heads of government."

Chapter III

Preliminary issues

A. Sources

1. International treaties

27. International treaties were adopted on the basis of the draft articles prepared by the Commission: the 1961 Vienna Convention on Diplomatic Relations; the 1963 Vienna Convention on Consular Relations; the 1969 Convention on Special Missions; the 1973 Convention on the Prevention and Punishment of Crimes against Internationally Protected Persons, including Diplomatic Agents; the 1975 Vienna Convention on the Representation of States in Their Relations with International Organizations of a Universal Character;[53] and the 2004 United Nations Convention on Jurisdictional Immunities of States and Their Property.[54] These treaties contain provisions concerning the status of State officials and/or their immunity from foreign jurisdiction, sometimes reproducing verbatim the above-mentioned provisions of the draft articles prepared by the Commission.[55]

28. The subject of immunity of States' representatives is also dealt with in other international treaties. For example, there are corresponding articles in the treaties governing the privileges and immunities of international organizations in the territories of Member States or in the host State. Thus the immunity of representatives of States, including from criminal jurisdiction, is proclaimed in article IV of the 1946 Convention on the privileges and immunities of the United Nations; article V of the 1947 Convention on the privileges and immunities of the Specialized Agencies; part IV of the 1949 General Agreement on Privileges and Immunities of the Council of Europe and others. The immunities of consular officials, including from criminal jurisdiction, are governed by the provisions of bilateral consular conventions.[56]

29. One view held is that the question of immunity of State officials is also covered in certain international treaties which do not deal with immunity. For example, Borghi notes that "several conventions concerning the suppression of international crimes contain provisions precluding immunity of heads of State".[57] These are the treaties aimed at combating international crimes—in particular the 1948 Convention on the prevention and punishment of the crime of genocide and the 1984 Convention against torture and other cruel, inhuman or degrading treatment or punishment. There is, however, another viewpoint. For example, Verhoeven considers that there is to date no treaty explicitly precluding the immunity normally applicable in a national court in cases of crimes under international law, whether for the State or the various State organs.[58] He further notes that there are admittedly conventions which try to organize effective suppression of such crimes. However, it seems that nobody finds in them

[53] Not yet in force.

[54] Not yet in force.

[55] At the concluding stage of work on the 2004 draft Convention on Jurisdictional Immunities of States and Their Property, a final understanding was reached that such immunity did not extend to criminal proceedings. This understanding was subsequently embodied in paragraph 2 of General Assembly resolution 59/38 of 2004, by which this Convention was adopted.

[56] See, for example, section III (Privileges and immunities) of the Consular Convention between the Russian Federation and the Republic of Moldova of 14 June 1994. Text available (in Russian) at www.businesspravo.ru/Docum/DocumShow_DocumID_45519.html (accessed 21 November 2013).

[57] See Borghi, *L'immunité des dirigeants politiques en droit international*, p. 66.

[58] See Verhoeven, "Les immunités propres aux organes ou autres agents des sujets du droit international", p. 123. He states: "It must be ... observed, as has been pointed out, that these conventions (genocide, torture, etc.) contain no provision explicitly precluding it [immunity] and that there is nothing in their *travaux préparatoires* or elsewhere to indicate that this was the implicit wish of the States that negotiated them or became parties to them." *Ibid.*, p. 125.

any wish—implicit but definite—on the part of their signatories to derogate from immunity.[59]

2. Customary international law

30. Existing international treaties regulate important but separate aspects of the issue of immunity of certain categories of State officials from foreign criminal jurisdiction: immunity from the host State's and, in certain cases, the transit State's criminal jurisdiction of State officials performing diplomatic and consular functions (diplomatic agents and consular officials); immunity from the host State's criminal jurisdiction of States' representatives to international organizations; and immunity from the host State's criminal jurisdiction of members of special missions. This shows that the group of persons enjoying immunity from foreign criminal jurisdiction is not limited to Heads of State. However, these treaties do not regulate questions of immunity of State officials from foreign criminal jurisdiction in general or as regards many specific situations or as regards the precise definition of the group of officials enjoying immunity, etc. There is no universal international treaty fully regulating all these issues and related issues of immunity of current and former State officials from foreign criminal jurisdiction. Moreover, not all the international treaties regulating this subject have entered into force,[60] and those which have entered into force are not noted for the broad participation in them of States.[61] It is noteworthy that certain provisions of these treaties actually state that the rules contained therein merely supplement existing international law in that area.[62] They thus confirm the existence here of customary international law. In addition, even though they codify individual aspects of customary international law as regards immunity of State officials from foreign criminal jurisdiction, the above-mentioned international treaties do not preclude the existence of relevant norms of customary international law, which continue to govern the subject under consideration.

31. International custom is the basic source of international law in this sphere. As noted by Fox, "[i]n the absence of any general convention on the status and immunities of a head of State, the rules are provided by customary international law".[63] This is the situation with regard to immunity from foreign criminal jurisdiction not only for Heads of State but also for other State officials.

32. When determining the source of applicable law in the question of the immunity of the Minister for Foreign Affairs of the Democratic Republic of the Congo from the criminal jurisdiction of Belgium in the *Arrest Warrant* case, ICJ noted in its 2002 judgment, regarding the conventions on diplomatic relations, consular relations and special missions, which were among the instruments referred to by the parties: "These conventions provide useful guidance on certain aspects of immunities. They do not, however, contain any provision specifically defining the immunities enjoyed by Ministers for Foreign Affairs. It is consequently on the basis of customary international law that the Court must decide the questions relating to the immunities of such Ministers raised in the present case."[64]

33. The fact that the source of immunity from foreign jurisdiction is customary international law is noted in rulings of national courts.[65] For example, in its 2001 ruling on the so-called "*Qaddafi* case", the French Court of Cassation stated: "In the absence of contrary international provisions binding on the parties concerned, international custom precludes the institution of proceedings against incumbent heads of State before the criminal jurisdictions of a foreign State".[66]

34. States, in the person of their Executive, also refer to custom as the source of international law in this sphere. For example, the parties in *Arrest Warrant* of 11 April 2000 (*the Democratic Republic of the Congo v. Belgium*) largely substantiated their positions on whether the Congolese Minister for Foreign Affairs enjoyed immunity from the criminal jurisdiction of Belgium by references to customary international law.[67] In its "suggestions of immunity" to be submitted to United States courts considering cases involving the immunity of officials of foreign

[59] *Ibid.*, p. 123.

[60] For example, the 1975 Vienna Convention on the Representation of States in Their Relations with International Organizations of a Universal Character and the 2004 United Nations Convention on Jurisdictional Immunities of States and Their Property have not entered into force.

[61] For example, 38 States are parties to the 1969 Convention on Special Missions.

[62] For example, article 21 of the 1969 Convention on Special Missions and article 50 of the 1975 Vienna Convention on the Representation of States in Their Relations with International Organizations of a Universal Character.

[63] Fox, *The Law of State Immunity*, p. 426. See also Watts, "The legal position in international law of Heads of States, Heads of Government and Foreign Ministers", p. 36; Borghi, *op. cit.*, pp. 71–72; Simbeye, *Immunity and International Criminal Law*, p. 94; Summers, "Diplomatic Immunity *Ratione Personae*: Did the International Court of Justice Create a New Customary Rule in Congo v. Belgium?", at p. 466; Altman, "The Future of Head of State Immunity: the Case against Ariel Sharon", April 2002, p. 4.

[64] *Case concerning the Arrest Warrant of 11 April 2000 (Democratic Republic of the Congo v. Belgium)*, Judgment of 14 February 2002, *I.C.J. Reports 2002*, p. 21, para. 52.

[65] As Borghi notes, "... customary law is also established as the source of immunity in many judicial decisions, including in Switzerland, France, the United States and Germany". *Op. cit.*, p. 71. See also *Regina v. Bartle and the Commissioner of Police for the Metropolis and Others Ex Parte Pinochet* ("Pinochet No. 1"), House of Lords, 25 November 1998, reproduced in *International Legal Materials*, vol. 37, p. 1302, at pp. 1309–1311; *Regina v. Bartle and the Commissioner of Police for the Metropolis and Others Ex Parte Pinochet* ("*Pinochet No. 3*"), House of Lords, 24 March 1999, reproduced in *International Legal Materials*, vol. 38, p. 581, at pp. 621, 622, 641 and 644; *Wei Ye, Hao Wang, Does, A, B, C, D, E, F, and others similarly situated v. Jiang Zemin and Falun Gong Control Office*, United States District Court, Northern District of Illinois (2003), p. 5; *Bouzari v. Islamic Republic of Iran*, 2004, CanLII 871 (Court of Appeal for Ontario), paras. [40] and [85] (available at www.canlii.org/en/on/onca/doc/2004/2004canlii871/2004canlii871.pdf, accessed 21 November 2013).

[66] Court of Cassation, Criminal Chamber, 13 March 2001, 00-87.215, published in *Bulletin criminel*, 2001, No. 64, p. 218 (available (in French and in English translation) at http://www.legifrance.gouv fr/rechJuri.do (accessed 21 November 2013)). Reprinted as *Gaddafi*, France, Court of Cassation, Criminal Chamber, 13 March 2001, *ILR*, vol. 125, p. 508, at p. 509.

[67] *I.C.J. Pleadings, Case concerning the Arrest Warrant of 11 April 2000 (Democratic Republic of the Congo v. Belgium)*, Application Instituting Proceedings, 17 October 2000, p.13, Part IV(B) (emphasis in the original): "[t]he *non-recognition* ... of the *immunity of a Minister for Foreign Affairs* in office is contrary to international caselaw ..., to customary law and to international courtesy ...". See also Democratic Republic of the Congo Memorial, paras. 6, 55 and 97(1); Belgian Counter-Memorial, paras. 3.4.6, 3.5.144, etc.

States, the United States Government refers to customary international law as a source of the law on immunity.[68] In his conclusions in the "*Qaddafi* case", the French Advocate General stated that "the principle of the immunity of Heads of State is traditionally regarded as a rule of international custom necessary for the preservation of friendly relations between States".[69]

3. International comity

35. The view has been expressed that immunity from foreign jurisdiction is granted not as a matter of right but as a matter of international comity.[70] However, this theory is difficult to accept. Immunity is above all a question of right, a question of the juridical rights and obligations of States. It is natural for disputes regarding immunity of State officials to be considered by the courts as disputes concerning violation of juridical rights and obligations. In *Jones v. Ministry of Interior Al-Mamlaka Al-Arabiya AS Saudiya (the Kingdom of Saudi Arabia)* in 2006, which considered the questions of the immunity of the State and of its officials, Lord Hoffmann noted: "As Lord Millett said in *Holland v. Lampen-Wolfe* [2000] 1 WLR 1573, 1588, state immunity is not 'self-imposed restriction on the jurisdiction of its courts which the United Kingdom has chosen to adopt' and which it can, as a matter of discretion, relax or abandon. It is imposed by international law without any discrimination between one state and another."[71] In its judgment in *Arrest Warrant*, ICJ found that Belgium had violated an international legal obligation towards the Democratic Republic of the Congo, because the issue of an arrest warrant against Mr. Yerodia Ndombasi and its international circulation had failed to respect the immunity from criminal jurisdiction which the incumbent Minister for Foreign Affairs of the Democratic Republic of the Congo enjoyed under international law.[72] This case involved an obligation under customary international law. It is even more obvious that the immunity of officials from foreign criminal jurisdiction derives from international law in the case of relevant treaty obligations mentioned above.

36. However, firstly, nothing prevents a State from granting to officials of other States, and particularly to high-ranking officials, immunity from jurisdiction on the basis not only of obligations under international law but also of international comity.[73] Secondly, there is another issue involved. In both doctrine and practice, the issue sometimes arises of the immunity from foreign jurisdiction of members of the family or of the immediate entourage of senior officials. As regards this category, there are much more solid grounds for stating that the source of their immunity from foreign jurisdiction is not international law but international comity.[74] Finally, the view exists that, when senior State officials are travelling abroad not in an official but in a private capacity, the host State has no legal obligation to grant them immunity, but may in this case grant immunity out of comity.[75] (This issue will be considered in the section dealing with the extent of immunity.)

[68] For example, in 2001 in its "suggestions of immunity" in *Tachiona v. Mugabe*, the State Department stated: "Under customary rules of international law recognized and applied in the United States, [...] President Mugabe, as the head of a foreign state, is immune from the court's jurisdiction in this case." *AJIL*, vol. 95 (October 2001), p. 874. In 2005, on the subject of the immunity of Pope Benedict XVI, the State Department noted: "The doctrine of head of state immunity is applied in the United States as a matter of customary international law". Crook, "Contemporary practice of the United States relating to international law: US Brief suggests Pope's immunity as a head of State", p. 219. See also paragraph 3 of the "suggestions of immunity" posted on the website of the United States State Department (www.state.gov) in the cases of *Li Weixum v. Bo Xilai* ("further suggestion", cc. 2-8); *Hartmann v. Sheikh Zayed Bin Sultan Al-Nayhan: Gladys M. Lafontant v. Jean-Bertrand Aristide; First American Corporation v. Sheikh Zayed Bin Sultan Al-Nayhan; Josephine Alicog and Spiyani Marian Fernando v. Kingdom of Saudi Arabia, His Royal Highness King Fahd Bin Abdulaziz Al-Saud, Majid Afifi, Salim Afifi; Guardian F. v. Archdiocese of San Antonio*.

[69] *Gaddafi*, Submissions of the Advocate General, *ILR*, vol. 125, p. 500.

[70] This theory is found both in judicial decisions and in doctrine. It is also well known in United States legal proceedings. For example, as long ago as 1812, the United States Supreme Court noted in its decision in *The Schooner Exchange v. McFaddon*: "... as a matter of comity, members of the international community had implicitly agreed to waive the exercise of the jurisdiction over other sovereigns in certain classes of cases, such as those involving foreign ministers or the person of the sovereign". *The Schooner Exchange v. McFaddon*, 11 U.S. 116, 137 (1812). In its decision of 11 March 1998 in *Flatow v. the Islamic Republic of Iran*, the Columbia District Court noted: "Foreign sovereign immunity, both under the common law and now under the FSIA, has always been a matter of grace and comity rather than a matter of right under United States law". 999 F.Supp. 1, United States District Court, District of Columbia. In *Wei Ye, Hao Wang, Does, A, B, C, D, E, F, and others similarly situated v. Ziang Zemin and Falun Gong Control Office*, Counsel for petitioners stated that "immunity is accorded to heads of state as a matter of comity in recognition of the mutual need not to allow courts to interfere with the proper operations of foreign governments by imposing barriers and penalties upon visiting heads of state" (at p. 5).

Judge van Den Wyngaert, in his opinion dissenting from the judgment in the case *Concerning the Arrest Warrant of 11 April 2000*, also notes: "There is no evidence for the proposition that a State is under an obligation to grant immunity from criminal process to an incumbent Foreign Minister under customary international law. By issuing and circulating the warrant, Belgium may have acted contrary to international comity. It has not, however, acted in violation of an international obligation." *I.C.J. Reports 2002*, p. 139, para. 1. However, it will be recalled that the overwhelming majority of judges supported the opposite view in this matter.

As stated in *Oppenheim's International Law*, "the basis for the special treatment accorded to Heads of States is variously ascribed, *inter alia*, to the dictates of international comity and courtesy". Jenning and Watts, *Oppenheim's International Law*, 1992, p. 1034. Caplan writes: "Two leading rationales explain the legal source of the doctrine [of foreign state immunity]. One asserts that state immunity is a fundamental state right by virtue of the principle of sovereign equality. The other views state immunity as evolving from an exception to the principle of state jurisdiction, i.e., when the forum state suspends its right of adjudicatory jurisdiction as a practical courtesy to facilitate interstate relations." "State immunity, human rights, and *jus cogens*: a critique of the normative hierarchy theory", at p. 748. It should be noted that a number of the cited opinions concerning comity speak of it not as a source but as one of the rationales for immunity.

[71] *Jones v. Ministry of Interior Al-Mamlaka Al-Arabiya AS Saudiya (the Kingdom of Saudi Arabia)*, House of Lords, Appellate Committee, 14 June 2006 ("Jones No. 2"), [2006] UKHL 26, para. 101.

[72] *I.C.J. Reports 2002*, p. 33.

[73] "Whether conventional or customary, the obligation [to grant immunity] does not preclude national authorities granting to a foreign head of State a treatment more favourable than that imposed by international law ...". Verhoeven, "Les immunités de juridiction et d'exécution. Rapport provisoire", p. 509.

[74] See para. 128 below.

[75] According to Cassese, "[w]hen they [senior State officials] are on a private visit and are not travelling incognito, the host State is bound to afford them special protection; it may also grant them privileges and immunities out of comity, that is, politeness and good will; however, it is under no obligation to do so". *International Law*, p. 96.

4. Role of international and domestic law

37. The question of the immunity of officials of foreign States is covered in the legislation of certain States. This basically concerns Heads of State. In the laws on the immunity of a foreign State adopted, for example, in the United Kingdom, Singapore, Pakistan, South Africa, Canada and Australia, the Head of a foreign State acting in an official capacity is, as is the case in the 2004 Convention on Jurisdictional Immunities of States and their Property, included in the concept of a State.[76] In this connection, under United Kingdom legislation, the Head of a foreign State acting in an official capacity enjoys the same immunity as the head of a diplomatic mission.[77] In accordance with article 36, paragraph 1, of the Foreign States Immunities Act of Australia, "[s]ubject to the succeeding provisions of this section, the Diplomatic Privileges and Immunities Act 1967 extends, with such modifications as are necessary, in relation to the person who is for the time being—(*a*) the head of a foreign State; or (*b*) a spouse of the head of a foreign State".[78]

38. The legislation of the Russian Federation contains provisions on the immunity of all officials of foreign States. In accordance with article 3, paragraph 2, of the Russian Code of Criminal Procedure, criminal proceedings against a foreign official enjoying immunity from such proceedings in accordance with the generally recognized rules of international law or with international treaties concluded by the Russian Federation may be instituted with the agreement of the foreign State whom the person is or was serving. In this connection, information as to whether the person concerned enjoys immunity from such criminal proceedings and on the extent of such immunity is provided to the relevant Russian court or law enforcement agency by the Ministry of Foreign Affairs of the Russian Federation.[79] In this case, it is noteworthy that it follows from domestic law that, as regards immunity of foreign officials from Russian criminal jurisdiction, international law prevails.

39. In connection with the appearance in certain States' legal systems of the institution of universal jurisdiction, provisions have started to appear in their legislation which can be interpreted as refusing immunity to foreign officials over whom the State in question exercises universal criminal jurisdiction. For example, the Belgian Law of 1993 concerning the criminal prosecution of grave violations of the 1949 Geneva Conventions on the protection of war victims was amended in 1999 to include a provision preventing the use of immunity as protection from criminal prosecution: "The immunity conferred by a person's official capacity does not prevent application of this Law."[80] This allowed criminal proceedings to be brought against the Minister for Foreign Affairs of the Democratic Republic of the Congo. However, after ICJ issued its judgment in the *Arrest Warrant* case, this Law was amended[81] in 2003 to read "... by setting aside immunities only as far as international law permits".[82] Thus the extent of immunity of foreign officials from criminal jurisdiction for war crimes under Belgian law in essence began to be determined on the basis of international law.

40. The respective roles played by international and domestic law in the consideration by national courts and other national law enforcement agencies of the question of immunity of officials of a foreign State mainly depend on the place occupied by international law in the legal system of the State concerned, on the legal culture there and on law and enforcement traditions. It is well known that national courts widely apply international law (combined, naturally, with domestic law) when considering questions of immunity of foreign officials and that national courts make practically no reference to international law when considering cases of this kind.

41. The question of immunity of State officials from foreign criminal jurisdiction, as well as the question of jurisdictional immunity of States, are matters concerning inter-State relations. For this reason, the basic primary source of law in this matter is international law. Ideally, therefore, international law on this matter should either determine the content of the domestic law applicable by national courts and other law enforcement agencies or be applied by them directly when they consider questions of immunity.[83] Ideally, domestic law should in this sphere

---

[76] See, for example, art. 14 of the State Immunity Act 1978, United Kingdom; art. 16 of the State Immunity Act 1979, Singapore; art. 15 of the State Immunity Ordinance 1981, Pakistan; art. 1 of the Foreign Sovereign Immunity Act 1981, South Africa; art. 2 of the State Immunity Act 1982, Canada; art. 3 of the Foreign States Immunities Act 1985, Australia. The relevant provisions of these acts are cited in Bankas, *The State Immunity Controversy in International Law: Private Suits Against Sovereign States in Domestic Courts*, pp. 431–459; and in Dickinson, Lindsay and Loonam, *State Immunity: Selected Materials and Commentary*, pp. 469–523.

[77] Article 20 of the State Immunity Act of the United Kingdom contains a reference to the *Diplomatic Privileges Act* of 1964. Bankas, *op. cit.*, p. 440.

[78] Dickinson, Lindsay and Loonam, *op. cit.*, at p. 483.

[79] See Federal Act No. 26 of 4 March 2008 on amendments to article 3 of the Code of Criminal Procedure of the Russian Federation. Available (in Russian) at http://document.kremlin.ru/page.aspx?1108302 (accessed 20 March 2014).

[80] Law of 16 June 1993, Art 5, § 3, as amended by the Law of 10 February 1999 concerning the punishment of grave violations of international humanitarian law, *dossier numéro*: 1993-06-16/36, available (in Flemish and French) at http://www.ejustice.just.fgov.be/loi/loi.htm (accessed 20 November 2013).

[81] Law of 5 August 2003 pertaining to serious violations of international humanitarian law, *dossier numéro*: 2003-08-05/32, available (in Flemish and French) at http://www.ejustice.just.fgov.be/loi/loi.htm (accessed 20 November 2013).

"*Article 13*

The following article 1 *bis* is inserted in chapter I of the Preliminary Title of the Code of Criminal Procedure:

'*Article 1* bis. § 1. In accordance with international law, proceedings may not be brought against:

—Heads of State, Heads of Government and ministers for foreign affairs while in office, and other persons with immunity recognized by international law;

—persons who enjoy full or partial immunity on the basis of a treaty binding on Belgium.

'§ 2. In accordance with international law, no restraining measure related to the institution of public proceedings may be imposed during their stay on any persons officially invited to stay in the territory of the Kingdom by the Belgian authorities or by an international organization based in Belgium with which Belgium has concluded a headquarters agreement."

[82] Smis and Van der Borght, "Belgian law concerning the punishment of grave breaches of international humanitarian law: a contested law with uncontested objectives".

[83] Mention may be made, in this connection, of the situation in France described by R. Abraham, the Agent of the French Republic, during the hearings in the International Court on the case *Certain Criminal Proceedings in France (Republic of the Congo v. France)*: "In conformity with international law, French law embodies the principle of the

play a subsidiary role, allowing implementation of the provisions of international law regulating the question of immunity.[84] Since national courts often have difficulty determining the content of the customary rules of international law that should be applied, codification of international law in this matter would be most useful.

5. Material to be used

42. In research on the topic under consideration and in the possible formulation of relevant draft normative provisions, it would be advisable to use the following material: State practice, including domestic legislation, national court rulings, particularly those issued at the turn of the century, reflecting current understanding of the topic; presentations of the Executive in national and international judicial organs, statements by representatives of States on this issue; international treaties relating to the topic; judgments and other documents of the International Court, particularly in the *Arrest Warrant* case and the current cases *Certain Criminal Proceedings in France (Republic of the Congo v. France)* and *Certain Questions of Mutual Assistance in Criminal Matters (Djibouti v. France)*; relevant decisions of international criminal tribunals; material of the Commission, as mentioned above, and also other material on the topic; material on the consideration of the question of immunity of Heads of State and Heads of Government by the Institute of International Law in the period 1997–2001; academic research in this area; and other material on the topic.[85]

B. Immunity and jurisdiction

1. Jurisdiction

43. The very title of the topic under consideration presupposes that there are similarities and differences between the concepts of "immunity" and "jurisdiction". As noted in a joint separate opinion by Judges Higgins, Kooijmans and Buergenthal in the *Arrest Warrant* case, " 'Immunity' is the common shorthand phrase for 'immunity from jurisdiction'."[86] Jurisdiction precedes immunity. If there is no jurisdiction, there is no reason to raise or consider the question of immunity from jurisdiction.[87] In the judgment in *Arrest Warrant*, ICJ states that "it is only where a State has jurisdiction under international law in relation to a particular matter that there can be any question of immunities in regard to the exercise of that jurisdiction".[88]

44. The topic under consideration concerns national and not international jurisdiction, i.e. the jurisdiction of a State and not the jurisdiction of international organs. According to M. Shaw, "jurisdiction concerns the power of the state to affect people, property and circumstances and reflects the basic principles of state sovereignty, equality of states and non-interference in domestic affairs".[89] Jurisdiction is often described as the authority or competence of a State.[90] Jurisdiction is a manifestation of the sovereignty of the State[91] and of its authoritative prerogatives, especially in the territory over which that State exercises sovereignty. Lukashuk noted that jurisdiction "means the authority of the State to prescribe behaviour and to ensure that its prescriptions are carried out using all lawful means at its disposal".[92] Brownlie notes that "at least as a presumption, jurisdiction is territorial".[93] However, jurisdiction may also be exercised on other grounds (such as citizenship[94]) and may be extraterritorial.

45. Jurisdiction is exercised through the actions of the branches of government—legislative, executive and judicial. Usually a distinction is drawn between legislative, executive and judicial jurisdiction.[95] Legislative or prescriptive (law-making) jurisdiction consists of the promulgation by government authorities of laws and other legal prescriptions. Executive jurisdiction consists of actions by the State, its executive authorities and officials in

immunity of foreign Heads of State. There are no written rules deriving from any legislation relating to the immunities of State and their representatives. It is the jurisprudence of the French courts which, referring to customary international law and applying it directly, have asserted clearly and forcefully the principle of these immunities." Document CR 2003/21 (translation), Monday 28 April 2003 at 4 p.m., para. 32.

[84] As Verhoeven notes, "There would seem to be no doubt that immunity primarily raises a question of international law and that it is therefore international law which should regulate the problems raised by immunity. And it is domestic law which should determine how this rule is actually respected in each internal legal order, in the knowledge that, as in other areas, the international responsibility of the State is incurred in the event of any shortcomings." "Les immunités propres aux organes ou autres agents des sujets de droit international".

[85] For example, INTERPOL appeals to States to circulate international arrest warrants for foreign officials.

[86] *I.C.J. Reports 2002*, p. 64, para. 3.

[87] As Brohmer notes, "the question of jurisdiction logically precedes that of sovereign immunity, because if there is no jurisdiction the question of immunity cannot arise." *State Immunity and the Violations of Human Rights*, p. 34. "Before one can analyze whether or not immunity is a viable defense, the establishment of jurisdiction … is necessary. Jurisdiction must be established first because, by definition, immunity is shorthand for immunity from jurisdiction." Toner, "Competing concepts of immunity: revolution of the Head of State immunity defense", p. 903.

[88] *I.C.J. Reports 2002*, p. 19, para. 46. The same idea was expressed by the then President, Judge G. Guillaume: "... a court's jurisdiction is a question which it must decide before considering the immunity of those before it. In other words, there can only be immunity from jurisdiction where there is jurisdiction." *Ibid.*, p. 35, para. 1. This view is also shared by Judges Higgins, Kooijmans and Buergenthal in their joint separate opinion: "If there is no jurisdiction *en principe*, then the question of an immunity from a jurisdiction which would otherwise exist simply does not arise." *Ibid.*, p. 64, para. 3.

[89] Shaw, *International Law*, p. 572.

[90] "*Jurisdiction*"—"Term referring to the concept of power, used in a series of expressions such as competence and another set of relative expressions such as power to judge". Salmon (dir.), *Dictionnaire de droit international public*, p. 624. According to Lowe, " 'jurisdiction' is the term that describes the limits of the legal competence of a State or other regulatory authority (such as the European Community) to make, apply and enforce rules of conduct upon persons." "Jurisdiction", in Evans (ed.), *International Law*, 2nd ed., p. 335. Oxman is of the view that "in its broadest sense, the jurisdiction of a State refers to its lawful power to act and hence to its power to decide whether and, if so, how to act. While lawyers frequently use the term 'jurisdiction' more narrowly to refer to the lawful power to make and enforce rules, it is useful to bear in mind the broadest meaning". "Jurisdiction of States", p. 55.

[91] Bowett, "Jurisdiction: changing patterns of authority over activities and resources", "Jurisdiction of the State (or national jurisdiction) as a manifestation of State sovereignty", Chernichenko, *Theory of International Law*, p. 126.

[92] Lukashuk, *International law. General section*, pp. 330 and 331.

[93] Brownlie, *Principles of International Law*, p. 297. As Lukashuk points out, the basic principle of jurisdiction is territorial. However, the scope of jurisdiction may be both territorial and extraterritorial. *Op. cit.*

[94] Shaw, *op. cit.*, p. 572.

[95] *Ibid.*, pp. 576–578; Lukashuk, *op. cit.*

execution of and enforcement of its laws and other legal prescriptions. Judicial jurisdiction consists of the activity of its judicial authorities, primarily in consideration of cases. Executive and judicial jurisdiction have common features: both involve the application and enforcement of the law. This is why some authors mention the existence of only two types of jurisdiction—legislative (prescriptive) and executive.[96]

46. In his second report on the jurisdictional immunities of States and their property, the Special Rapporteur, S. Sucharitkul, proposed the following definition of jurisdiction: " 'Jurisdiction' means the competence or power of a territorial State to entertain legal proceedings, to settle disputes, or to adjudicate litigations, as well as the power to administer justice in all its aspects" (draft article 2, paragraph 1 (*g*)). This definition was amplified by the draft interpretative provisions clarifying the elements in the concept of "jurisdiction":

Article 3. Interpretative provisions

1. In the context of the present articles, unless otherwise provided,

...

(*b*) the expression "jurisdiction", as defined in article 2, paragraph 1 (*g*), ... includes:

(i) the power to adjudicate,

(ii) the power to determine questions of law and of fact,

(iii) the power to administer justice and to take appropriate measures at all stages of legal proceedings, and

(iv) such other administrative and executive powers as are normally exercised by the judicial or administrative and police authorities of the territorial State.[97]

47. Two conclusions may be drawn from this definition and from the interpretative provisions. Firstly, for the purpose of the draft articles on jurisdictional immunities of States, the Special Rapporteur thought it advisable to consider jurisdiction only in its executive and judicial aspect. Legislative (prescriptive) jurisdiction is not covered by this definition. Secondly, for the purpose of the articles, the concept of jurisdiction covers the entire spectrum of procedural actions.[98]

2. Criminal jurisdiction

48. Jurisdiction can be divided into civil, administrative and criminal jurisdiction, depending on the substance of the laws (orders) issued by the authorities, the acts performed by the authorities, and the questions or cases governed by the orders or under consideration by the authorities. Criminal jurisdiction involves the adoption of laws and other orders that criminalize the acts of individuals and establish and enforce their responsibility for those acts, and the activity of government bodies in implementing the laws and orders.[99] It is noteworthy that judicial bodies, some executive bodies and some bodies which are not part of the executive or the judiciary may be responsible for applying and enforcing criminal law—that is, they exercise the executive or executive and judicial criminal jurisdiction of the State. The legal system of the State determines which government and judicial authorities are involved in the exercise of criminal jurisdiction.[100] The rules of domestic law that criminalize specific acts of individuals and establish responsibility for such acts are the substantive criminal law rules. The rules establishing the practice and procedures for implementation of the substantive rules of criminal law are the rules of procedural criminal law. In general, the activity of the government authorities, governed by the rules of criminal procedural law, to apply or enforce the rules of substantive criminal law relates to criminal proceedings and is included in the concept of criminal procedure.

49. As mentioned above, jurisdiction is basically territorial, but may be exterritorial, especially in the case of criminal jurisdiction. A State may extend its criminal jurisdiction beyond the borders of its own territory in a number of cases: (*a*) in relation to acts which are criminal under its law and are committed abroad by one of its citizens; (*b*) in relation to acts committed abroad which are criminal under its law and injure one of its citizens; (*c*) in relation to acts committed abroad which are criminal under its law and injure the State; and (*d*) in relation to acts committed abroad which are crimes under international law. Example (*a*) refers to the "active personality" principle of exterritorial criminal jurisdiction; (*b*) refers to the "passive personality" principle (sometimes these two forms are combined into one form of exterritorial criminal jurisdiction referred to as "personal jurisdiction"); (*c*) refers to the "protective" principle; and (*d*) refers to the "universal" principle.[101]

50. The question of immunity of an official may arise during the exercise by a foreign State of territorial criminal jurisdiction or of passive personality, protective or universal exterritorial criminal jurisdiction. The question of immunity may also arise in a case where several States try to exercise criminal jurisdiction in relation to the same individual.

3. Criminal jurisdiction and civil jurisdiction

51. In contrast to civil executive jurisdiction and civil procedure, criminal executive jurisdiction and criminal procedure may begin long before the actual trial phase. Criminal prosecution includes a substantial pre-trial

[96] See, for example, Chernichenko, *op. cit.*, pp. 112–117.

[97] *Yearbook ... 1980*, vol. II (Part One), document A/CN.4/331 and Add.1, pp. 206 and 211.

[98] As the Special Rapporteur himself noted, explaining the draft definition, for the purpose of the draft articles the concept of jurisdiction "covers the entire judicial process, from the initiation or institution of proceedings, service of writs, investigation, examination, trial, orders which can constitute provisional or interim measures, to decisions rendering various instances of judgements and execution of the judgements thus rendered, or their suspension and further exemption". *Ibid.*, p. 206.

[99] "State criminal jurisdiction broadly can be defined as much as the jurisdiction of the applicable substantive criminal law, which criminalizes and punishes, as the determination of the jurisdictional repressive enforcement of criminal statutes." A. Fournier, "Compétence pénale", p. 1.

[100] In the Russian Federation, for example, the courts and internal affairs authorities are responsible for law enforcement, but some of these functions are performed by the Procurator's offices, which are not part of the Executive.

[101] See notes 22 to 26 of the memorandum by the Secretariat on the immunity of State officials from foreign criminal jurisdiction (A/CN.4/596).

phase. A significant number of criminal procedure actions take place after law enforcement agencies receive a report of the (alleged) crime and before the case goes to trial. The actions of the police and other law enforcement agencies in the preliminary investigation, such as drafting reports on the inspection of the crime scene, collection of material evidence, interrogation of witnesses, institution of criminal proceedings and so on, do not require or at least in many countries may not require judicial decisions. Such actions may affect a foreign official. Accordingly, the exercise of criminal jurisdiction may already raise the question of immunity from it in this pre-trial phase. This is important for defining the boundaries of the topic under consideration and the extent of immunity.

52. Civil jurisdiction may be exercised both in relation to individuals and in relation to a State. Yet according to the 2004 Convention on Jurisdictional Immunities of States and Their Property, for instance, institution of a civil suit against a State representative who is acting in that capacity constitutes institution of a suit against the State.[102] Accordingly, consideration of such a suit by the court amounts to exercise of civil jurisdiction over a State.

53. Criminal jurisdiction is exercised only over individuals and not over the State. A State, unlike an individual, does not incur criminal responsibility. As noted by Lord Bingham of Cornhill in the 2006 decision on *Jones v. Ministry of Interior Al-Mamlaka Al-Arabiya AS Saudiya (the Kingdom of Saudi Arabia)*, indicating the difference between criminal and civil jurisdictions, "a state is not criminally responsible in international or English law, and therefore cannot be directly impleaded in criminal prosecution".[103] An important element of this opinion is the word "directly". It is clear that the exercise of criminal jurisdiction over a State official, even indirectly, affects the State which that official serves. This is particularly clear in the case of a criminal prosecution of high-ranking State officials, especially a Head of State or Government, minister for foreign affairs or other members of a government who represent the State in international affairs and/or perform critical functions for the State in connection with ensuring its sovereignty and security. It is also apparent in a situation where the criminal prosecution of a State official at any level is connected with acts performed by him in an official capacity. As noted in a 2004 decision in *Ronald Grant Jones and others v. The Ministry of the Interior Al-Mamlaka Al-Arabiya AS Saudiya (The Kingdom of Saudi Arabia) & Anor.*, "criminal proceedings against an alleged torturer may be said indirectly to implead the foreign state. It is not easy to see why civil proceedings against an alleged individual torturer should be regarded as involving any greater interference in or a more objectionable form of adjudication upon the internal affairs of a foreign state".[104] Moreover, it is highly likely that a State conducting a criminal investigation of an official of a foreign State will gain access to information relating to the sovereignty and security of the State served by the official. In these situations, although legally this concerns criminal prosecution of physical persons, it essentially concerns the exercise of sovereign prerogatives of one State in relation to another. At the same time, the sovereign interests of the other State are affected. In the exercise of criminal jurisdiction, which often involves extremely intrusive actions of investigation, these sovereign interests may be affected to a much greater degree than in the exercise of civil jurisdiction. As noted in the decision of the Federal Court of Switzerland in *Adamov*, "In accordance with the general principles of international law a domestic criminal justice system should avoid intervening in the affairs of other states."[105]

54. Finally, there are some situations where criminal jurisdiction and civil jurisdiction are not so easily distinguished. In some legal systems, for instance, a civil action may be initiated in the context of a criminal proceeding.[106]

55. On the whole, although at first glance there seems to be a clear distinction between exercising criminal and civil jurisdiction over officials of a foreign State, they do have enough features in common for consideration of the topic to take into account existing practice in relation to immunity of State officials and of the State itself from foreign civil jurisdiction.

4. Immunity

56. A State is entitled to exercise jurisdiction, including criminal jurisdiction, over all individuals in its territory, except when the individual in question enjoys immunity.[107] There are no definitions of the concept of immunity, at least not in universal international agreements, although they often employ the term. Immunity is usually understood to be the exception or exclusion of the entity, individual, or property enjoying it from the jurisdiction of the State; an obstacle to the exercise of jurisdiction; limitation of jurisdiction; a defence used to prevent the exercise of jurisdiction over the entity, individual or property; and, finally, the right for jurisdiction not to be exercised over the entity, individual or property, that is, the right not to be subject to jurisdiction.[108]

---

[102] This follows from the definition of the term "State" for the purposes of the Convention. According to article 2, para. 1(*b*) (iv), of the Convention, the meaning of "State" includes "representatives of the State acting in that capacity" and according to article 6, para. 2(*b*), "a proceeding before a court of a State shall be considered to have been instituted against another State if that other State ... is not named as a party to the proceeding but the proceeding in effect seeks to affect the property, rights, interest or activities of that other State".

[103] Jones No. 2 (see note 71 above), para. 31.

[104] *Jones v. Ministry of Interior Al-Mamlaka Al-Arabiya AS Saudiya* (*the Kingdom of Saudi Arabia*), Court of Appeal, 28 October 2004 ("Jones No. 1"), [2004] EWCA Civ 1394, para. 75.

[105] *Evgeny Adamov v. Federal Office of Justice*, Federal Tribunal, Switzerland, Judgment of 22 December 2005, ATF 132 II 81, para. 3.4.3.

[106] In accordance with the Code of Criminal Procedure of the Russian Federation, art. 44, para. 2, "a civil claim may be presented after the institution of criminal proceedings and before the completion of the investigation in court, when the criminal case is tried by a court of first instance".

[107] See paragraph 7 above in connection with article 2 of the draft Declaration on Rights and Duties of States prepared by the Commission.

[108] For example, Stefko understood immunity to mean "exemption from the jurisdiction of local authorities". *Diplomatic Exemption from Civil Jurisdiction*, p. 30 (in Polish), cited in Przetacznik, *Protection of Officials of Foreign States according to International Law*, p. 10. The *Dictionnaire de droit international public*, gives the following definition of immunity: "Exemption faisant échapper les personnes, les engins ou les biens qui en bénéficient (Etats, chefs d'Etats, agents diplomatiques, fonctionnaires consulaires, organisations internationales et leurs agents, forces militaires étrangères, navires et aéronefs d'Etat, et jadis les étrangers en pays de capitulation) à des procédures

57. In the second report on the jurisdictional immunities of States and their property, the Special Rapporteur suggested the following definitions of the terms "immunity" and "jurisdictional immunities" in draft article 2, paragraph 1: "(*a*) 'immunity' means the privilege of exemption from, or suspension of, or non-amenability to, the exercise of jurisdiction by the competent authorities of a territorial State; (*b*) 'jurisdictional immunities' means immunities from the jurisdiction of the judicial or administrative authorities of a territorial State."[109] As the Special Rapporteur noted in his introduction to the draft articles: " 'Immunity' is a legal concept which can be expressed in terms of jural relationship"; " 'immunity' to which a person ... or State is entitled is correlated to 'no power' on the part of the corresponding authority"; "the expression 'immunity' connotes the non-existence of power or non-amenability to the jurisdiction of the national authorities of a territorial State."[110]

58. It is very clear from this definition of "immunity" and from the commentary of Sucharitkul that, although he defines immunity as a jural relationship, the right of the person entitled to immunity in this jural relationship does not correspond to any duty of the foreign State (the only element corresponding to the right is non-amenability to jurisdiction). Yet in a jural relationship the right of one individual corresponds to the duty of another or of others. Immunity in this sense is no exception. If immunity from jurisdiction is considered as a rule of law (together with the jural relationship corresponding to this rule) which establishes a right and a corresponding duty, as seems to be the case, then on the one hand there is a right for the State's jurisdiction not to be exercised over the person enjoying immunity, while on the other hand there is a duty of the State that has jurisdiction not to exercise it over the person enjoying immunity.[111]

59. There is another view of immunity. It is also seen as a derogation from the jurisdiction of the host State for the foreign official. This concept of immunity emphasizes not the right of the individual enjoying immunity and the corresponding duty of the State that has jurisdiction, but the agreement or willingness of the State that has territorial jurisdiction, out of respect for the other State and accordingly for its representatives, not to exercise this jurisdiction in relation to the other State. In essence, this understanding of immunity is based not on international law but on international comity.[112] If this concept is applied in its pure form, immunity becomes not a question of right but a question of the discretionary powers of the State with jurisdiction. However, in practice this concept is not applied in this distilled sense. Rather, it is understood as being complementary to the interpretation and rationale of immunity international law. As noted by Shaw, "[a]lthough constituting a derogation from the host State's jurisdiction, in that, for example, the UK cannot exercise jurisdiction over foreign ambassadors within its territory, it is to be construed nevertheless as an essential part of the recognition of the sovereignty of foreign states, as well as an aspect of the legal equality of all states".[113]

60. Neither the draft articles adopted by the Commission nor the 2004 Convention on Jurisdictional Immunities of States and Their Property contain definitions of the terms "immunity" and "jurisdiction" and corresponding interpretative provisions. Yet they do to a large extent reflect generally accepted ideas about the content of the concepts of "immunity" and "jurisdiction". An attempt should perhaps be made to develop a definition of the terms "immunity" and/or "immunity from criminal jurisdiction" in the context of the topic under consideration, if normative provisions are to be drafted.

61. Despite the interrelationship of immunity and jurisdiction and the fact that the development of the institution of exterritorial and, in particular, universal jurisdiction has had a significant influence on thinking on immunity, the issue of immunity may be considered and studied without consideration of the substance of the question of jurisdiction as such, and vice versa. As indicated by ICJ in the judgment in *Arrest Warrant*, "the rules governing the jurisdiction of national courts must be carefully distinguished from those governing jurisdictional immunities: jurisdiction does not imply absence of immunity, while absence of immunity does not imply jurisdiction. Thus, although various international conventions on the prevention and punishment of certain serious crimes impose on States obligations of prosecution or extradition, thereby requiring them to extend their criminal jurisdiction, such extension of jurisdiction in no way affects immunities under customary international law ... These remain opposable before the courts of a foreign State, even where those courts exercise such a jurisdiction under these conventions".[114]

62. In their joint separate opinion in the judgment in *Arrest Warrant*, Judges Higgins, Kooijmans and Buergenthal noted that "immunity" and "jurisdiction" were inextricably linked and that whether there was immunity

ou à des obligations relevant du droit commun". Salmon (dir.), *op. cit.*, p. 558. Immunity from jurisdiction, as defined in this dictionary, is an "exemption qui permet à certaines entités et personnes (Etats, chefs d'Etats, agents diplomatiques, fonctionnaires consulaires, organisations internationales et leurs agents, forces militaires étrangères, etc.) d'échapper à l'action des juridictions de l'Etat de séjour ou d'Etat tiers." *Ibid.*, p. 559. As noted by Kessedjian, the concept of immunity from jurisdiction consists of "empêcher qu'un Etat ou une organisation internationale soient poursuivis devant une juridiction d'un autre Etat". "Immunités", p. 5. According to Steinberger, "In the context of public international law the law of State immunity means the legal principles and rules under which a foreign State may claim exemption from, suspension of, or non-amenability to the jurisdiction of another State". ("State immunity", p. 615). Wirth considers that "state immunity is the right not to be submitted to the exercise of foreign jurisdiction". ("Immunity for core crimes? The I.C.J.'s Judgment in the Congo v. Belgium Case", p. 882). According to Khlestova, "immunity of a State implies that it is not subject to the jurisdiction of another State". (*Problems of the jurisdictional immunity of a foreign State (legislation and practice)*, p. 9).

[109] *Yearbook ... 1980*, vol. II (Part One), document A/CN.4/331 and Add.1, para. 33.

[110] *Ibid.*, para. 17.

[111] According to Sinclair, "immunity can be defined jurisprudentially as the correlative of a duty imposed upon the territorial State to refrain from exercising its jurisdiction over a foreign State". "The law of sovereign immunity: recent developments", p. 199.

[112] See paras. 35 and 36 above.

[113] Shaw, *op. cit.*, p. 621. S. Sucharitkul also writes: "Reciprocity of treatment, comity of nations and *courtoisie internationale* are very closely allied notions, which may be said to have afforded a subsidiary or additional basis for the doctrine of sovereign immunity." "Immunities of foreign States before national authorities", p. 119.

[114] *I.C.J. Reports 2002*, pp. 24 and 25, para. 59.

in any given instance depended not only on the status of the individual but on the type of jurisdiction and on what basis the State authorities sought to assert it.[115] They also noted that "while the notion of 'immunity' depends, conceptually, upon a pre-existing jurisdiction, there is a distinct corpus of law that applies to each" and that the Court, in bypassing the issue of jurisdiction, "has encouraged a regrettable current tendency … to conflate the two issues".[116]

63. In the context of this topic, there will be a need to consider the issue of the immunity of State officials from foreign criminal jurisdiction and perhaps to formulate draft articles or guiding principles on this issue. The Special Rapporteur did not consider it appropriate in this connection to consider further the substance of the issue of jurisdiction *per se*, or the issue of exterritorial and universal criminal jurisdiction in particular. There thus seems to be no need to formulate any draft provisions concerning jurisdiction in the context of this topic. At the same time, the issue of jurisdiction will clearly have to be taken up when considering the question of the extent of immunity, including whether there are any exemptions from or exceptions to the rule on immunity.

5. Immunity from criminal jurisdiction and its procedural nature

64. The above views on immunity and jurisdiction are also relevant to the consideration, in the context of this topic, of the concept "immunity from criminal jurisdiction". It is important that immunity from jurisdiction, and particularly immunity from criminal jurisdiction, does not remove the individual who enjoys it from the legislative (prescriptive) jurisdiction of the State. It is noteworthy that the definition of immunity from jurisdiction proposed by Sucharitkul spoke of immunity from the jurisdiction only of judicial and administrative authorities. In view of the above-mentioned draft definition of the concept of "jurisdiction" for the articles on jurisdictional immunities of States and their property, it is clear that the reference was to immunity only from the executive and judicial jurisdiction and not from the legislative (prescriptive) jurisdiction of the State, i.e. immunity from process, from procedural actions.[117] Thus the person enjoying immunity is not exempt from the law established by the State possessing jurisdiction (the law applicable in the territory of that State).[118] However, the State possessing jurisdiction cannot guarantee that its law will be applied to the person enjoying immunity. For the person who enjoys it, immunity provides protection from the law enforcement process in the State from whose jurisdiction immunity exists but not from the law of that State. This view is widely supported by doctrine.[119] It is noteworthy that the conventions on diplomatic and consular relations and on special missions, while granting to a specific category of individuals immunity from the jurisdiction of the host State, at the same time establish the obligation of such individuals to respect the laws of that State.[120]

65. It should be noted that there is also another viewpoint regarding the nature of immunity. Reference is sometimes made not only to procedural but also to substantive or material immunity, whereby a person enjoying immunity may not be subject to the laws and thus to the legislative jurisdiction of a State.[121] However, this view is not shared by the majority of authors writing on this question.

66. This is especially important as regards the scope of criminal jurisdiction. In particular, an individual enjoying immunity from criminal jurisdiction is not exempt from the rules of substantive law criminalizing a particular act and establishing the punishment for it. Immunity from foreign criminal jurisdiction protects that individual only from criminal process and criminal procedure actions by judicial and law enforcement agencies of the foreign State possessing jurisdiction. (It might be more accurate to speak not of immunity of State officials from foreign criminal jurisdiction or criminal process

[115] *I.C.J. Reports 2002*, p. 64, para. 3.

[116] *Ibid.*, para. 4.

[117] Sucharitkul wrote: "The immunities under consideration [immunities of foreign States before national authorities] are mainly from jurisdiction or from the exercise of local power or territorial authority, and not immunities from substantive law or essential legal provisions. They are immunities from the procedural laws, or at best from legal process or from suit, but not from local laws. When State immunity is invoked, local jurisdiction may be suspended. But the same immunity can at any time be waived in many different ways, whereby enabling the legal process to proceed with complete resumption of the operation of substantive local law." *Loc. cit.*, p. 96.

[118] "Immunity from jurisdiction does not amount to an exemption from the legal order of the territorial State. The question may arise as a prejudicial matter in proceedings in which the foreign State is not engaged, or before the courts of third State who by their rules regarding conflict of laws may have to apply the substantive law of the (first) territorial State, e.g. the *lex loci delicti commissi*." Steinberger, *loc. cit.*, p. 616.

[119] For example, "The term immunity is employed primarily to denote exemption from legal process. As such, an immunity does not imply or involve non-amenability to or non-liability *ratione materiae*, as must be clear when it is appreciated that an immunity may be invariably waived" (Parry and Grant, *Encyclopaedic Dictionary of International Law*, p. 165); "… immunity from jurisdiction does not mean exemption from the legal system of the territorial state in question" (Shaw, *op. cit.*, p. 623); "The plea [of immunity] is one of immunity from suit, not of exemption from law. Hence if immunity is waived the case can be decided by the application of the law in the ordinary way. The underlying liability or State responsibility of the defendant State is unaffected though, as will be seen where no remedy is available in a court of the defendant State, the immunity from the suit may enable liability to be avoided" (Fox, "International law and restraints on the exercise of jurisdiction by national courts of States", p. 370); "State immunity under international law is no more than immunity from legal proceedings before domestic courts, and it does not make states immune either from their own legal proceedings or from any sort of responsibility. In other words, to grant state immunity prescribed by international law does not mean the end of the rule of law" (Tomonori, "The individual as beneficiary of State immunity: problems of the attribution of ultra vires conduct", p. 274).

[120] Article 41 of the 1961 Vienna Convention on Diplomatic Relations, article 55 of the 1963 Vienna Convention on Consular Relations, and article 47 of the 1969 Convention on Special Missions. The preamble to the 2001 resolution of the Institute of International Law (see footnote 50 above) also mentions that "immunities afforded to a Head of State or Head of Government in no way imply that he or she is not under obligation to respect the law in force on the territory of the forum".

[121] See, for example, Stern, "Immunités et doctrine de l'Act of State: Différences théoriques et similitudes pratiques de deux modes de protection des chefs d'État devant les juridictions étrangères", p. 64. "In international law state immunity refers to the legal rules and principles determining the conditions under which a foreign state may claim freedom from the jurisdiction (the legislative, judicial and administrative powers) of another state (often called the 'forum state')." Malanczuk, *Akehurst's Modern Introduction to International Law*, p. 118; Khlestova, *op. cit.*, p. 9.

but of immunity from certain measures of criminal procedure and from criminal proceedings by the foreign State. However, this question cannot be answered until the question of the extent of immunity has been considered.) Thus immunity from foreign criminal jurisdiction falls within the area of procedural and not substantive law and is procedural in nature.[122] Accordingly, the person enjoying immunity is in principle not exonerated from criminal responsibility; it is simply that it is more difficult to invoke such responsibility. As the International Court emphasized in its judgment in the *Arrest Warrant* case, "the *immunity* from jurisdiction enjoyed by incumbent Ministers for Foreign Affairs does not mean that they enjoy *impunity* in respect of any crimes they might have committed... Immunity from criminal jurisdiction and individual criminal responsibility are quite separate concepts. While jurisdictional immunity is procedural in nature, criminal responsibility is a question of substantive law. Jurisdictional immunity may well bar prosecution for a certain period or for certain offences; it cannot exonerate the person to whom it applies from all criminal responsibility."[123]

67. The question of the immunity of an official may arise already at an early stage of the criminal process, even before the criminal case has been transmitted to the court for substantive consideration. For example, in the *Case concerning certain criminal proceedings in France (Republic of the Congo v. France)*, currently under consideration by ICJ, the Congo is disputing (and referring, *inter alia*, to the immunity of the Head of State from foreign criminal jurisdiction) the legality of certain criminal procedure measures against a number of Congolese officials, including the Head of State, taken by France at the preliminary stage of the investigation and criminal proceedings relating to crimes allegedly committed in the Congo.[124] The legality of similar measures taken by France against certain Djibouti officials, including the Head of State, is also disputed in the other case currently being considered by the Court, *Certain Questions of Mutual Assistance in Criminal Matters (Djibouti v. France)*.[125] In the *Pinochet* case, the question of immunity of a former Head of State from the criminal jurisdiction of the United Kingdom arose in connection with the consideration of Spain's request for his extradition.[126] In the *Adamov* case, the question of immunity from foreign criminal jurisdiction of the former Minister for Atomic Energy of the Russian Federation also arose in the context of the consideration of the question of his extradition to a third State.[127]

68. When a national court begins to try a criminal case, the question of immunity is considered as a preliminary issue, before the court considers the case on its merits.[128] As ICJ stated in its advisory opinion in the case *Difference relating to immunity from legal process of a Special Rapporteur of the Commission on Human Rights*, national courts must consider the question of immunity from jurisdictional process "as a preliminary issue to be expeditiously decided *in limine litis*".[129]

69. In addition, the State served by the official concerned often raises a general objection both to consideration of the question of immunity in a foreign court and to other non-judicial criminal procedure measures that the foreign State tries to apply or applies to the official. In such cases, the State served by the official usually makes diplomatic approaches to the foreign State that is applying criminal procedure measures, pointing to the need to respect the immunity of its official, or even raises the issue of the responsibility of that foreign State for violation of obligations arising from the rules of international law on immunity. This is because, as has already been remarked, the question of immunity of State officials from foreign criminal jurisdiction is a question of inter-State relations and the right to immunity and the corresponding duty to respect immunity and to refrain from exercising jurisdiction over the person enjoying immunity are derived primarily from the rules of international law.

70. The exercise of criminal jurisdiction also includes the adoption of interim measures of protection or measures of execution. Some international legal instruments concerning questions of immunity contain various provisions relating to immunity from jurisdiction and to immunity from measures of execution or interim measures of protection (for example: article 31, paragraphs 1 and 3, of the 1961 Vienna Convention on Diplomatic Relations; article 31, paragraphs 1 and 4, of the 1969 Convention on Special Missions; and article 30, paragraphs 1 and 2, of the 1975 Vienna Convention on the Representation of States in Their Relations with International Organizations of a Universal Character). However, there is no such provision in the 1963 Vienna Convention on Consular Relations (article 43 of the Convention refers simply to immunity from jurisdiction). At this stage at least, it seems advisable simply to address immunity of State officials from foreign criminal jurisdiction, without dealing with the question of immunity from interim measures of protection or measures of execution.

---

[122] In the Russian Federation, for example, a provision on immunity of officials of a foreign State from measures of criminal procedure is contained in the Code of Criminal Procedure, which governs the criminal process, and not in the Criminal Code, which contains rules of substantive criminal law.

[123] *I.C.J. Reports 2002*, p. 25, para. 60.

[124] *Certain Criminal Proceedings in France (Republic of the Congo v. France)*, provisional measures, *I.C.J. Reports 2004*, p. 62.

[125] *Certain Questions of Mutual Assistance in Criminal Matters, (Djibouti v. France)*, Judgment, *I.C.J. Reports 2008*, p. 177.

[126] In October-November 1998, after the Supreme Court of Spain had ruled that the Spanish courts had jurisdiction in respect of Augusto Pinochet, the Spanish judicial authorities issued an international arrest warrant for the Senator and requested his extradition to Spain. In accordance with these orders and the 1989 Extradition Act, on 16 and 23 October 1998 the Metropolitan Stipendiary Magistrate issued two preliminary arrest warrants for the former Chilean dictator. See *ILM*, vol. 37 (1998), pp. 1302 and 1303 and vol. 38 (1999), p. 432.

[127] In May 2005, the former Minister for Atomic Energy of the Russian Federation, E. Adamov, was arrested in Bern at the request of the United States and placed in preventive detention with a view to his subsequent extradition to the United States. The American authorities accused him of a series of financial crimes, including the large-scale misappropriation and use for personal ends of money allocated for Russian nuclear energy projects. The Russian Federation also requested Switzerland to extradite Adamov so that it could institute criminal proceedings against him.

[128] As Shaw notes, "the question of sovereign immunity is a procedural one and one to be taken as a preliminary issue". *Op. cit.*, pp. 623 and 624. "English law treats the immunity as a procedural issue to be taken account of at the earliest stage of the proceedings; international law seems so to require." Fox, *The Law of State immunity*, p. 13.

[129] *Difference relating to immunity from legal process of a Special Rapporteur of the Commission on Human Rights*, advisory opinion of 20 April 1999, *I.C.J. Reports 1999*, para. 67.

6. Immunity, the non-justiciability doctrine and the act of State doctrine

71. In addition to immunity, there are also other limitations on State jurisdiction. These are the non-justiciability and act of State doctrines. Both were developed in the Anglo-Saxon legal system and are mainly used in the courts of common law States. However, as Stern notes, similar approaches are also found in civil law countries.[130]

72. No precise definition exists of the two doctrines. As Fox notes, "non-justiciability is a doctrine of uncertain scope. It may be raised as a plea in proceedings whether or not a foreign State is itself made a party to them, and may arise as preliminary plea or in the course of determination of the substantive law".[131] Wickremasinghe writes that in essence the non-justiciability doctrine means that "the subject matter of the claim is in fact governed by international law (or, possibly foreign public law) and so falls outside the competence of national courts to determine".[132] Referring to the non-justiciability doctrine, a domestic court may decide that it cannot consider, for example, a question pertaining to the realm of inter-State relations.[133]

73. Sinclair has noted that a distinction must be drawn between the concept of immunity and the concept of non-justiciability.[134] "Immunity, expressed in the maxim par *in parem non habet imperium*, is a principle concerned with the status of sovereign equality enjoyed by all independent States. This principle will be satisfied if the State waives its immunity, since the consent to the exercise of jurisdiction by the local courts upholds the status of sovereign equality. Non-justiciability, or lack of jurisdiction in the local courts by reason of the subject-matter, is a concept which, although it may be related, is distinct. Thus, a court may refuse to pronounce upon the validity of a law of a foreign State applying to matters within its own territory, on the ground that to do so would amount to an assertion of jurisdiction over the internal affairs of that State."[135]

74. The act of State doctrine also essentially limits the exercise of jurisdiction over a foreign State. Its application is closely connected with the consideration by courts of questions of prejudice to the right to property located in the foreign State caused by acts performed by that State which affect this right.[136] In such proceedings, the validity of acts (normative or enforcing) performed by the foreign State may be disputed. Fox writes that "act of State is a defence to the substantive law requiring the forum court to exercise restraint in the adjudication of disputes relating to legislative or other governmental acts which a foreign State has performed within its territorial limits".[137] Usually the result of application of the non-judiciability doctrine is that the court recognizes the validity of the act of the foreign State. This approach is based on the principle of respect for State sovereignty, for the sovereign equality of States. Because what is involved is an act of another sovereign State, the national court refrains from considering the question of its validity and limits itself to formally acknowledging the act.

75. At least in this form, the act of State doctrine seems narrower than the non-justiciability doctrine. By applying the act of State doctrine in this way, the court (albeit to a limited extent) does consider the substance of the question whether the act of the foreign State is valid. When it applies the non-justiciability doctrine in a similar situation, the court does not consider the substance of the question at all.[138] However, the two doctrines can be viewed as being quite similar, especially if, applying the act of State doctrine, the court declines outright to rule on the validity of the act of the foreign State, as do United States courts, for example. For instance, in the 1962 ruling in *Banco Nacional de Cuba v. Sabbatino*, Judge Waterman noted: "The Act of State Doctrine, briefly stated, holds that American Courts will not pass on the validity of the acts of foreign governments performed in their capacities as sovereigns within their own territories. ... This doctrine is one of the conflict of law rules applied by American Courts; it is not itself a rule of international law. ... The act of state doctrine stems from the concept of the immunity of the sovereign because 'the sovereign can do no wrong'."[139]

76. In the latter ruling, it is noteworthy that direct reference is made to the link between the act of State concept and the concept of immunity.[140] The similarity between the two concepts is particularly striking when one considers the question of immunity of State officials from foreign criminal jurisdiction in respect of acts performed by them in an official capacity. However, there are also significant differences between immunity and the act of State doctrine. "The law of sovereign immunity goes to the jurisdiction of the court. The act of state doctrine is

[130] *Loc. cit.*, p. 64.

[131] *Loc. cit.*, p. 384.

[132] "Immunities enjoyed by officials of States and International Organizations", p. 398.

[133] "Non-justiciability bars a national court from adjudicating certain issues, particularly international relations between States, by reason of them lacking any judicial or manageable standards by which to determine them," Fox, *loc. cit.*, p. 364.

[134] *Loc. cit.*, p. 198.

[135] *Ibid.*, pp. 198 and 199.

[136] "The Act of State doctrine has been applied in the United States primarily in the context of foreign expropriations in which a governmental act is alleged to have violated the applicable norms of international law." Fonteyne, "Acts of State", p. 17.

[137] *Loc. cit.*, p. 364.

[138] As Lord Wilberforce noted in the case *Buttes Gas & Oil Co. v. Hammer* [1982], "there exists in English law a more general principle that the courts will not adjudicate upon the transactions of foreign sovereign States. Though I would prefer to avoid argument on terminology, it seems desirable to consider this principle, if existing, not as a variety of 'act of state' but one for judicial restraint or abstention". ILR, vol. 64, p. 331, at p. 344.

[139] *Banco Nacional de Cuba v. Sabbatino,* U.S. Court of Appeals, 2nd Circuit, 6 July 1962, 307 F 2d 845, reproduced in *AJIL*, vol. 56 (1962), p. 1085, at pp. 1090 and 1091. As Denza notes, "the terms 'act of state' and 'non-justiciability' might more appropriately be replaced by a modern 'doctrine of a proper court'—parallel to the doctrine of *forum non conveniens* in private international law". "*Ex Parte Pinochet*: Lacuna or Leap?", p. 949, at pp. 957–958.

[140] The similarity of the two concepts is noted, for example, in the ruling of the Court of Appeals in the case *International Association of Machinists and Aerospace Workers v. Organization of Petroleum Exporting Countries (OPEC) et al.*: "The doctrine of sovereign immunity is similar to the act of state doctrine in that it also represents the need to respect the sovereignty of foreign states". U.S. Court of Appeals, Ninth Circuit, 6 July 1981 (amended 24 August 1981), 649 F 2nd 1354, 1359; reproduced in ILR, vol. 66, p. 413, at p. 418.

not jurisdictional. ... Rather it is a prudential doctrine designed to avoid judicial action in sensitive areas. Sovereign immunity is a principle of international law, recognized in the US by statute. It is the states themselves, as defendants, who may claim sovereign immunity. The act of state doctrine is a domestic legal principle, arising from a peculiar role of American courts. It recognizes not only the sovereignty of foreign states, but also the spheres of power of the co-equal branches of our government."[141]

77. It is also noteworthy that the act of State and non-justiciability doctrines, unlike the immunity of State officials from foreign criminal jurisdiction, apply only in court and therefore may limit only the judicial and not the executive jurisdiction of the foreign State. They are not used as a defence from the criminal jurisdiction of a foreign State (from criminal procedure actions) in the pre-trial phase.[142]

7. Immunity of officials *ratione personae* and immunity of officials *ratione materiae*

78. A distinction is usually drawn between two types of immunity of State officials: immunity *ratione personae* and immunity *ratione materiae*.[143] Immunity *ratione personae* or personal immunity is derived from the official's status and the post occupied by him in government service and from the State functions which the official is required to perform in that post. This type of immunity from foreign criminal jurisdiction is enjoyed by officials occupying senior or high-level government posts[144] and by diplomatic agents accredited to the host State (in accordance with customary international law and with article 31, paragraph 1, of the 1961 Vienna Convention on Diplomatic Relations).[145] It would seem that immunity *ratione personae* is the oldest form of immunity. It was enjoyed and is still enjoyed to this day by Heads of State. A Head of State was considered to be invested with sovereignty and was identified with and personified the State itself. This was the source of the absolute immunity of the Head of State, which also extended to the State. Over time, the immunity of the State and the immunity of the Head of State started to be considered separately, but the immunity *ratione personae* of the Head of State is still generally recognized today.

79. Immunity *ratione personae* extends to acts performed by a State official in both an official and a private capacity, both before and while occupying his post. Since it is connected with the post occupied by the official in government service, it is temporary in character, becomes effective when the official takes up his post and ceases when he leaves his post.

80. State officials enjoy immunity *ratione materiae* regardless of the level of their post, by virtue of the fact that they are performing official State functions. Immunity *ratione materiae* is sometimes also called functional immunity. This type of immunity extends only to acts performed by State officials acting in an official capacity, i.e. performed in fulfilment of functions of the State. Accordingly, it does not extend to acts performed in a private capacity. When the official leaves government service, he continues to enjoy immunity *ratione materiae* with regard to acts performed while he was serving in an official capacity.[146]

81. If this categorization of immunity is used, it follows that certain State officials (exactly which ones is not clear) enjoy both immunity *ratione personae* and immunity *ratione materiae* from foreign jurisdiction and that all State officials enjoy immunity *ratione materiae*.[147]

---

[141] *Ibid.* In this sense, the act of State doctrine seems close to the non-justiciability doctrine and to the political question doctrine. The latter is mentioned in the ruling quoted above: "The act of state doctrine is similar to the political question doctrine in domestic law. It requires that the courts defer to the legislative and executive branches when those branches are better equipped to resolve a politically sensitive question." *Ibid.*, p. 417.

[142] For details on the similarity and differences between immunity and the act of State and non-justiciability doctrines, see, for example, Brownlie, *op. cit.*, 2003, pp. 320 and 321; Fox, *op. cit.*, pp. 477–502; Meagher, "Act of State and sovereign immunity: the *Marcos* cases", pp. 127–134; Van Panhuys, "In the borderland between the act of state doctrine and questions of jurisdictional immunities", pp. 1193–1213; Parseghian, "Defining the 'public act' requirement in the act of state doctrine", pp. 1151–1180; Stern, *op. cit*, pp. 63–87; Zander, "The act of state doctrine".

[143] These two types of immunity are dealt with in detail, for example, in the *Pinochet No. 3* case, *International Legal Materials*, vol. 38 (1999), p. 581, at pp. 600, 601, 605, 606, 644, 645, etc. The existence of these two types of immunity of officials was also recognized by France and Djibouti during ICJ oral pleadings in the case *Certain Questions of Mutual Legal Assistance in Criminal Matters (Djibouti v. France)*: I.C.J., document CR 2008/3, p. 15, para. 23 and CR 2008/5, pp. 50 and 51, paras. 75–77. These two types of immunity are mentioned in the commentaries of the ILC to article 2, paragraph 1 (*b*) (v), of the draft articles on jurisdictional immunities of States and their property: *Yearbook ... 1991*, vol. II (Part Two), pp. 18 and 19. See also, for example, Cassese, *International Criminal Law*, pp. 265–273; Day, "Crimes against humanity as a nexus of individual and State responsibility: why the ICJ got Belgium v. Congo wrong", p. 489, at p. 493; Frulli, "The question of Charles Taylor's immunity: still in search of balanced application of personal immunities?", pp. 1118–1129 at pp. 1125 and 1128; Wirth, *loc. cit.*, pp. 877–893, at pp. 882 and 883; Summers, "Immunity or impunity? The potential effect of prosecutions of State officials for core international crimes in States like the United States that are not parties to the Statute of the International Criminal Court", *loc. cit.*, pp. 463–493, at p. 464; Toner, *loc. cit.*, p. 902; Borghi, *op. cit.*, pp. 53–56; Barker, "The future of former Head of State immunity after *ex parte Pinochet*", pp. 937–949, at pp. 938–945; Simbeye, *op. cit.*, pp. 109–111, 123; Hamida, Sein and Kadouf, "Immunity versus international crimes: the impact of *Pinochet* and *Arrest Warrant* cases", pp. 495–516, at pp. 510 and 511.

[144] The question whether it is possible (and, if it is possible, how) to single out those high-ranking officials who, unlike other high-ranking officials, enjoy personal immunity will be considered in the section concerning the group of officials covered by this topic.

[145] Other State officials—for example, representatives of the sending State in a special mission (in accordance with article 31, paragraph 1, of the 1969 Convention on Special Missions)—may also enjoy such immunity under international treaties.

[146] Of course, the question is which acts should be considered as having been performed "in an official capacity". The answer to this question is of paramount importance for determining the extent and limits of immunity. The question will be considered in the section concerning the extent of immunity.

[147] Sometimes immunity *ratione personae* is called procedural immunity and immunity *ratione materiae* is called substantive immunity. For example, Cassese considers that immunity *ratione materiae* "relates to substantive law, that is, it is a substantive defence" and immunity *ratione personae* "relates to procedural law, that is, it renders the State official immune from civil or criminal jurisdiction (it is a procedural defence)". *International Criminal Law*, p. 266. However, he admits that "if the State official acting abroad has breached criminal rules of the foreign State, he may incur criminal liability and be liable under foreign criminal jurisdiction". *Ibid.*, footnote 6. Koller holds a

(*Continued on next page.*)

82. The distinction between these two types of immunity of State officials is minor, in the case of serving officials occupying high-level posts in government service. The immunity *ratione personae* of a Head of State, Head of Government, minister for foreign affairs and some other high-ranking officials essentially encompasses immunity *ratione materiae*. For this reason, in order to distinguish more precisely the two types of immunity in the case of high-ranking officials, it is sometimes said that immunity *ratione personae* extends only to acts performed by them in a private capacity (acts of high-ranking officials in an official capacity are covered by immunity *ratione materiae*, regardless of whether the official is occupying the post or has already left it).[148]

83. The separation of immunity of officials into immunity *ratione personae* and immunity *ratione materiae* and the use of these terms are appropriate for analytical purposes for the study of this question and for the process of demonstrating the immunity of State officials.[149] The question arises, however, how necessary this is for the legal regulation of the subject of immunity of State officials from foreign criminal jurisdiction. In the wording of its judgment in the *Arrest Warrant* case, the International Court did not use this categorization of immunity or, as a result, the terms "immunity *ratione personae*" and "immunity *ratione materiae*". The Court decided whether the Minister for Foreign Affairs enjoyed immunity from foreign criminal jurisdiction on the basis of whether the acts were performed by him while in office or after he had already left office and whether the acts had been performed by him in an official capacity or in a private capacity.[150] This categorization was also not used in the conventions on diplomatic and consular relations, on special missions and on the representation of States in their relations with international organizations of a universal character. The concepts of immunity *ratione personae* and immunity *ratione materiae* were not used in the Resolution of the Institute.[151]

8. Rationale for the immunity of State officials from foreign criminal jurisdiction

84. The rationale for the immunity of State officials may determine which officials enjoy immunity and the extent of their immunity. The preambles to the 1961 Vienna Convention on Diplomatic Relations, the 1963 Vienna Convention on Consular Relations and the 1969 Vienna Convention on Special Missions contain provisions explaining why immunity is granted to the individuals concerned.[152]

85. The preamble to the 1961 Vienna Convention states, *inter alia*: "... the purpose of ... privileges and immunities is not to benefit individuals but to ensure the efficient performance of the functions of diplomatic missions as representing States". Similar provisions are contained in the preambles to the 1963 Vienna Convention and the Convention on Special Missions.[153] In the judgment of ICJ in the *Arrest Warrant* case, the granting of immunities to the Minister for Foreign Affairs is explained in almost the same terms: "In customary international law, the immunities accorded to Ministers for Foreign Affairs are not granted for their personal benefit, but to ensure the effective performance of their functions on behalf of their respective States."[154]

86. Regarding this provision in the Court judgment, commentators usually emphasize that the Court justified the immunity of the Minister for Foreign Affairs by reference to functional necessity.[155] However, no attention

(*Footnote 147 continued.*)

similar opinion; cf. "Immunity of foreign ministers: paragraph 61 of the Yerodia judgment as it pertains to the Security Council and International Criminal Court", p. 7–42, at pp. 25 and 26. See also, for example, Day, *op. cit.*, p. 490; Frulli, *loc. cit.*, pp. 1125 and 1126. The same views were advanced by the plaintiff in the case *Wei Ye, Hao Wang, Does A, B, C, D, E, F, and others similarly situated v. Jiang Zemin and Falun Gong Control Office, a/k/a Office 610*, Supreme Court of the United States, Petition for a writ of *certiorari*, p. 7. However, it seems that, for the reasons stated above, immunity in any case is procedural in nature. An additional argument is provided by the opinion of the Appeals Chamber of the Special Court for Sierra Leone: "The question of sovereign immunity is a procedural question", *Prosecutor v. Charles Ghankay Taylor*, Decision on Immunity from Jurisdiction, 31 May 2004, para. 27.

[148] See, for example, the commentaries to the Commission's draft articles on jurisdictional immunities of States and their property: "Apart from immunities *ratione materiae* by reason of the activities or the official functions of representatives, personal sovereigns and ambassadors are entitled, to some extent in their own right, to immunities *ratione personae* in respect of their persons or activities that are personal to them and unconnected with official functions." *Yearbook ... 1991*, vol. II (Part Two), p. 18.

[149] For the purpose of substantiating the existence or absence of immunity, this categorization was used, for example, in the cases *Pinochet No. 1* and *No. 3* (see footnote 65 above) and *Jones No. 1* (footnote 104) and *No. 2* (footnote 71).

[150] See, *inter alia*, paragraphs 54, 55 and 61 of the judgment.

[151] In the 2004 Convention on Jurisdictional Immunities of States and their Property, this categorization of immunity is used, partly explicitly and partly implicitly: article 3, paragraph 2, states that the Convention is without prejudice to the immunities of a Head of State *ratione personae*. Immunity *ratione materiae* is not mentioned directly but it appears from article 1 (on the application of the Convention to the immunity of a State) and from article 2, paragraph 1 (*b*) (iv) (from which it follows that "State" includes representatives of the State acting in that capacity), that it is indeed governed by the Convention.

[152] A provision explaining why special treatment must be given to Heads of State and Heads of Government and why they must be granted immunity from foreign jurisdiction is also contained in the preamble to the resolution of the Institute of International Law: "... special treatment is to be given to a Head of State or Head of Government, as a representative of that State and not in his or her personal interest, because this is necessary for the exercise of his or her functions and the fulfillment of his or her responsibilities in an independent and effective manner, in the well-conceived interest of both the State or the Government of which he or she is the Head and the international community as a whole." *Yearbook of the Institute of International Law*, vol. 69 (2000–2001), p. 743.

[153] The fifth preambular paragraph of the 1963 Vienna Convention states that "the purpose of ... privileges and immunities is not to benefit individuals but to ensure the efficient performance of functions by consular posts on behalf of their respective States". The seventh preambular paragraph of the 1969 Convention on Special Missions states: "... the purpose of privileges and immunities relating to special missions is not to benefit individuals but to ensure the efficient performance of the functions of special missions as missions representing the State."

[154] *I.C.J. Reports 2002*, p. 21, para. 53.

[155] According to Cassese, the Court "... logically inferred from the rationale behind the rules on personal immunities of senior state officials, such as heads of state or government or diplomatic agents, that such immunities must perforce prevent any prejudice to the 'effective performance' of their functions". "When may senior State officials be tried for international crimes? Some comments on *Congo v. Belgium* Case", p. 855. As Koller notes, "[t]he Court contended these functions make it necessary that the foreign minister receive absolute immunity from the jurisdiction of foreign state courts, even when visiting such states on private visits". *Loc. cit.*, p. 11. Sassoli writes: "[t]he Court states ... the functions of a minister of foreign affairs in international

is paid to the part of the Court's justification where it states that immunities are granted to ministers for foreign affairs in order to ensure the effective performance of functions "on behalf of their respective States". As noted above, the rationale for the immunity of ministers for foreign affairs given by the Court is similar to the rationale for the immunities in the above-mentioned conventions. However, in these convention rationales for immunity, the words "as representing States", "on behalf of their respective States" and "representing the State" are included deliberately in order to emphasize that immunity is granted not only in order to ensure the performance of the actual functions of diplomatic and consular agents and members of special missions, but because the functions are performed by diplomatic missions, consular services and special missions, as the case may be, as representatives of the State, acting on its behalf.[156] It appears that this is also how the words "on behalf of their respective States" in the above-mentioned passage from the judgment of ICJ should be taken into account and interpreted.

87. These convention formulations of the rationale for immunities reflect the two basic theories explaining the reasons for granting to State officials immunity from foreign jurisdiction: the "functional necessity" theory and the "representative character" theory.[157] As noted in the Commission's commentaries to the draft articles on diplomatic relations, the "representative" theory gave as the rationale for diplomatic immunity the idea that the diplomatic mission personifies the sending State and the "functional" theory gave as the rationale the fact that immunity is necessary to enable the diplomatic mission to perform its functions. In addition, the Commission noted that it was guided by the "functional necessity" theory "in solving problems on which practice gave no clear pointers, while also bearing in mind the representative character of the head of the mission and of the mission itself".[158] Thus traces of both these theoretical approaches can be found in the rationale for immunity granted in accordance with the rules of international law codified in the above-mentioned Conventions. Neither approach has been used exclusively. In the light of the foregoing, this is also true of the judgment in the *Arrest Warrant* case.[159]

88. As the Commission noted in the commentaries to article 2, paragraph 1 (*b*) (v), of the draft articles on jurisdictional immunities of States and their property, immunity *ratione materiae* is granted "by reason of the activities or the official functions of [State] representatives".[160] Officials of a State acting in an official capacity are performing acts of the State. In other words, the State is acting through its representatives, when they are acting in this capacity. In this connection, the Commission noted: "Actions against ... representatives or agents of a foreign Government in respect of their official acts are essentially proceedings against the State they represent. The foreign State, acting through its representatives, is immune *ratione materiae*. Such immunities characterized as *ratione materiae* are accorded for the benefit of the State ..."[161] Just as acts performed in an official capacity by officials of the State are in fact acts of the State itself, so the immunity which they enjoy in respect of such acts is in fact immunity of the State. Immunity in respect of acts performed in an official capacity remains in effect after the official has left the service of the State because it is in fact immunity of the State. Indeed, "State immunity survives the termination of the mission or the office of the representative concerned. This is so because the immunity in question not only belongs to the State, but is also based on the sovereign nature or official character of the activities, being immunity *ratione materiae*."[162] It seems that this is true of immunity both from civil and from criminal jurisdiction.[163]

89. Does the attribution to the State of illegal and criminally punishable conduct by a State official (i.e. an individual) mean that this conduct cannot also be attributed to the individual himself? It would seem not. The conduct of a State official, acting in an official capacity, is not

relations, and then concludes that, for the duration of his term of office, he enjoys immunity from criminal jurisdiction and total inviolability abroad". "Les immunités internationales", in "L'arrêt Yerodia: quelques remarques sur une affaire au point de collision entre les deux couches du droit international", p. 797.

[156] See, for example, Denza, *Diplomatic Law: A Commentary on the Vienna Convention on Diplomatic Relations*, pp. 11 and 12.

[157] A third basic theory on this subject—the theory of exterritoriality, according to which the premises of the sovereign, ambassador or diplomatic mission in the host State represents a sort of extension of the territory of the sending State to the place where they are located in the host State—has long ceased to exist and be used. For more details regarding the theory, see Strisower, "L'exterritorialité et ses principales applications".

[158] *Yearbook ... 1958*, vol. II, p. 95. For further details regarding theories explaining the immunity of officials, see Borghi, *op. cit.*, pp. 42–57 and Sucharitkul, *loc. cit.*, pp. 115–121.

[159] If, when the functional theory is applied, it is argued that immunity is necessary for the official to perform not simply functions, but specifically functions in order to represent the State or functions on behalf of the State, no difference between the two theories is discernible.

[160] *Yearbook ... 1991*, vol. II (Part Two), p. 18.

[161] *Ibid.*

[162] *Ibid.*

[163] Among recent examples of this rationale for immunity of State officials from foreign criminal jurisdiction, mention may be made of the discussion between the Counsel for Djibouti, L. Condorelli, and the Counsel for France, A. Pellet, during oral pleadings in ICJ on the case *Certain Questions of Mutual Legal Assistance in Criminal Matters (Djibouti v. France)*. L. Condorelli thus described the immunity of the State Prosecutor and Head of National Security of Djibouti: "What Djibouti requests of the Court is to acknowledge that a State cannot regard a person enjoying the status of an organ of another State as individually criminally liable for acts carried out in that official capacity, that is to say in the performance of his duties. Such acts, indeed, are to be regarded in international law as attributable to the State on behalf of which the organ acted and not to the individual acting as that organ [para. 24]. The Respondent cannot overlook the fact that if one consults the writings of reputed experts who have analysed the subject, one is struck by the conclusion that the vast majority of them have the same point of view. From Kelsen and Fox to Morelli and Quadri, Dahm, Bothe, Akehurst, Cassese and still many more [footnotes omitted], all are convinced of the existence of a principle of international law stipulating that organs of a State benefit from immunity from the jurisdiction of foreign States for acts carried out in the performance of that function." Document CR 2008/3 (translation), 22 January 2008 at 3 p.m., pp. 9 and 10, paras. 23 and 24. A. Pellet did not object to the principle stated by L. Condorelli. He noted, "when they act in an official capacity, the organs of the State do not engage their own responsibility, but that of the State; consequently their acts enjoy the immunities of the State." Document CR 2008/5 (translation), 25 January at 10 a.m., p. 42, paras. 74 and 75. The Counsel for France did not agree with his opponent on how to put this principle into practice. Ibid., p. 43, paras. 76 and 77.

exclusively attributed to the State itself.[164] If the illegal conduct of an official in an official capacity were attributed only to the State which the official is serving, the question of the criminal liability of the official could never arise. However, this is not the case. If the State waives the immunity enjoyed by the official, that official will incur criminal liability for those acts which are his (of course, waiver of immunity is not in itself sufficient to create liability, but it makes it possible for foreign criminal jurisdiction to be exercised over the official to the full extent, including criminalization). The immunity *ratione materiae* enjoyed by an official is derived from the fact that his conduct is official and is attributed to the State on behalf of which he is acting but it does not preclude this conduct also being attributed to the official himself.[165] Immunity does not change anything as regards the substantive conditions which must exist in order for the individual enjoying immunity to incur criminal liability. This, incidentally, seems to provide further evidence that immunity *ratione materiae* is procedural and not substantive in nature.

90. Immunity *ratione personae* also has a mixed functional/representative rationale.[166] As has been noted, immunity *ratione personae* is enjoyed only by persons occupying senior or high-level posts in the government and is directly related to those posts. Authors describing the functional rationale for immunity *ratione personae* usually state that this immunity is granted to persons who occupy not only senior or high-level posts but also posts that are directly connected with the performance of functions of representation of the State in international relations.[167] Here, however, a question arises: can the sole rationale for personal immunity be the need to perform functions of representation of the State in international relations? Supposing the Defence Minister is the official concerned? He usually has functions of representation of the State in international relations. However, he mainly performs functions inside the country. Yet they are directly concerned with ensuring the sovereignty and security of his State. In this connection, is not another logical rationale for immunity *ratione personae* the fact that the official concerned occupies a senior or high-level government post, in which he performs functions that are extremely important for ensuring the sovereignty of the State?

91. Despite the popularity of the functional necessity theory, the immunity of the Head of State, for example, is frequently justified by reference to the fact that the Head of State personifies the State itself, i.e., the representation theory. This rationale for the immunity of the Head of State became particularly clear during the consideration of the *Pinochet* case.[168] However, court rulings also provide examples of a "more functional" rationale for the immunity of the Head of State. United States court rulings, for example, have drawn attention to the fact that Heads of State need immunity in order to be able to freely perform their State duties (see *In re Grand Jury Proceedings* and *Lafontant v. Aristide*).[169]

[164] In the *Blaškić* case, the International Tribunal for the Former Yugoslavia stated that "officials are mere instruments of a State and their official act can only be attributed to the State". *Prosecutor v. Blaškić*, Appeals Chamber, Judgment on the request of the Republic of Croatia for review of the Decision of Trial Chamber II of 18 July 1997, 29 October 1997, para. 38. This assertion seems to be contradicted by the theory advanced in the text. However, later in the judgment, the Court affirms that "each State is entitled to claim that acts or transactions performed by one of its organs in its official capacity be attributed to the State, so that individual organ may not be held accountable for those acts or transactions". *Ibid.*, para. 41. Thus in fact the Court seems to be saying that the State is entitled to request that acts performed by its official in an official capacity should be considered as acts of the State itself but does not preclude the possibility of such acts being attributed not only to the State but also to the official, unless the State concerned insists that they should not.

[165] As Verhoeven notes, "[q]u'un acte soit imputable à l'Etat au sens du droit international n'implique pas de soi que la personne à l'intermédiaire de laquelle cet acte a été nécessairement accompli ne puisse pas être tenue d'en rendre compte devant une autorité étrangère et sur la base de droit national. C'est précisement la raison pour laquelle certains 'organes' bénéficient d'immunités". "Les immunités propres aux organes ou autres agents des sujets du droit international", p. 68. Although this is not the subject covered by the topic, it is also noteworthy that waiver of immunity enjoyed by an official does not alter the situation as regards attribution of acts performed by that official to the State waiving immunity. These continue to be attributed not only to the individual who performed them but also to the State. Thus, in the event of waiver of immunity by a State, the liability of the official, the individual, still exists, as does the basis for raising the issue of the liability for these acts of the State itself.

[166] As the Court noted in the *Tachiona v. Mugabe* case, "... any form of legal compulsion asserted directly against a foreign state leader or diplomat not only serve to create hindrances to the performance of the foreign official's functions, but constitute affronts to both the person and dignity of the ruler and to the sending foreign state". United States District Court, Southern District of New York, 30 October 2001. Compare also: "Customary public international law grants such privileges *ratione personae* to Heads of State as much to take account of their functions and symbolic embodiment of sovereignty as by reason of their representative character in inter-State relations." *Marcos and Marcos v. Federal Department of Police*, Swiss Federal Tribunal, 2 November 1989, reproduced in *ILR*, vol. 102, p. 198, at p. 201.

[167] "... les fonctions qui doivent être prises en considération sont celles qui sont internationales par nature, c'est-à-dire qui impliquent nécessairement une relation avec un ou plusieurs autres Etats (sujets de droit international)." Verhoeven, "Les immunités propres aux organes ou autres agents des sujets du droit international", p. 89.

[168] See Pinochet No. 3, *ILM*, vol. 38 (1999), p. 580. *Lord Millet*: "[t]he immunity of the serving head of state is enjoyed by reason of his special status as the holder of his state's highest office. He is regarded as the personal embodiment of the state itself. It would be an affront to the dignity and the sovereignty of the state which he personifies and a denial of the equality of the sovereign states to subject him to the jurisdiction of the municipal courts of another state, whether in respect of his public acts or private affairs" (at p. 644); *Lord Brown-Wilkinson*: "It is a basic principle of international law that one sovereign state (the forum state) does not adjudicate on the conduct of a foreign state. The foreign state is entitled to procedural immunity from the processes of the forum state. This immunity extends to both criminal and civil liability. State immunity probably grew from the historical immunity of the person of the monarch. In any event, such personal immunity of the head of state persists to the present day: the head of state is entitled to the same immunity as the state itself. ... This immunity enjoyed by a head of state in power [...] is a complete immunity attaching to the person of the head of state ... and rendering him immune from all actions and prosecutions whether or not they relate to matters done for the benefit of the state. Such immunity is said to be granted *ratione personae*" (at p. 592); *Lord Goff of Chieveley*: "The principle of state immunity is expressed in the Latin maxim *par in parem non habet imperium*, the effect of which is that one sovereign does not adjudicate on the conduct of another. This principle applies as between states, and the head of a state is entitled to the same immunity as the state itself ..." (at p. 598).

[169] "Like the related doctrine of sovereign immunity, the rationale of head-of-state immunity is to promote comity among nations by ensuring that leaders can perform their duties without being subject to detention, arrest or embarrassment in a foreign country's legal system." *In re Grand Jury Proceedings*, Doe No. 700, United States Court of Appeals, Fourth Circuit, 5 May 1987, reproduced in *ILR*, vol. 81, p. 599 at p. 601. (See also *United States v. Noriega and Others*, United States District Court, Southern District of Florida, 8 June 1990, reproduced in *ILR*, vol. 99, p. 143 at p. 161). In the *Lafontant v. Aristide* case, the District Court stated: "Heads of state must be able to freely perform

92. The primarily functional rationale for the immunity of ministers for foreign affairs, cited by the International Court in the *Arrest Warrant* case, is also extrapolated to other individuals who enjoy immunities *ratione personae*.[170] The Court itself provided the grounds for this in paragraph 51 of its judgment by placing ministers for foreign affairs on the same level as some other high-ranking State officials, such as the Head of State and the Head of Government.[171] The immunity enjoyed by high-ranking officials, such as Heads of State, Heads of Government and ministers for foreign affairs, protects them from foreign jurisdiction, not only in connection with their official actions, but also in connection with actions performed by them in a personal capacity. The latter may not be directly attributed to the State. It is sometimes said that immunity *ratione personae*, i.e. personal immunity, is enjoyed by the relevant officials "to some extent in their own right".[172] If that assertion is true, then it only appears to be so because of the words "to some extent". It is no coincidence that almost immediately following this phrase the Commission, in its commentary to article 2, paragraph 1 (*b*)(v), of the draft articles on jurisdictional immunities of States and their property, noted: "Indeed, even such immunities inure not to the personal benefit of sovereigns and ambassadors but to the benefit of the States they represent, to enable them to fulfil their representative functions or for the effective performance of their official duties."[173]

93. Even when there is a functional rationale for the immunity *ratione personae* of the relevant officials, as expressed by ICJ and the International Law Commission, the connection between such immunity and the State served by such officials appears to be obvious. The immunity that they enjoy, even in respect of acts performed in a personal capacity (including acts performed prior to taking office), protects them only because it is necessary in order to ensure that their activities in senior or high-level government positions are free from foreign interference, i.e. only because it is necessary in the interest of the State they are serving. This immunity is granted only because the duties performed by the individual in the State are so important for the sovereign and independent functioning of the State. In this sense, immunity *ratione personae* can only conditionally be called "personal".

94. The State stands behind both the immunity *ratione personae* of its officials from foreign jurisdiction and their immunity *ratione materiae*.[174] It is the State that is entitled to waive the immunity enjoyed by an official, whether it is *ratione personae* or *ratione materiae* (in the case of a serving high-ranking official) or only *ratione materiae* (in the case of any official who has left government service).[175] In the final analysis, the immunity of State officials from foreign jurisdiction belongs to the State itself, so that it alone is entitled to waive such immunity.

95. The functional, representative or functional/representative rationale for the immunity of State officials is, so to speak, a direct rationale. One State, in exercising its criminal jurisdiction over officials of another State, may not hamper the performance by those officials of their government functions, interfere with activities related to the performance of those functions, or create obstacles to the activities of persons representing the other State in its international relations, because in essence they are activities of another sovereign State. As was also the case many years ago, the underlying principles of inter-State relations are the reason behind the functional, representative or mixed rationale. Alongside international comity, the principles of full equality and absolute interdependence of sovereigns and sovereign States,[176] referred to in connection with the exercise of national jurisdiction

their duties at home and abroad without the threat of civil and criminal liability in a foreign legal system." United States District Court, Eastern District of New York, 27 January 1994, reproduced in *ILR*, vol. 103, p. 581 at p. 585.

[170] According to Akande: "Since heads of states, diplomats, and other officials accorded immunity *ratione personae* will be hindered in the exercise of their functions if they are arrested and detained while in a foreign state, these officials are absolutely immune from the criminal jurisdiction of the foreign state." "International law immunities and the International Criminal Court", p. 407, at pp. 409 and 410. Wirth notes that "... according to the Court, the rationale of the immunity available for Heads of State and Ministers of Foreign Affairs is their ability to discharge their *functions*." *Loc. cit.*, p. 879. As De Smet notes: "The rationale for the concept of personal immunity is based on the need to guarantee the unhindered exercise of official functions." "The immunity of Heads of States in US Courts after the Decision of the International Court of Justice".

[171] One can only conjecture what the rationale for immunity would have been had this case concerned the Head of State rather than the Minister for Foreign Affairs. In this connection, it is worth noting the rationale for the immunity of the Head of State cited by Rosalyn Higgins, President of ICJ: "The situation regarding sitting Heads of State is clear under general international law. The Head of State is seen as personifying the sovereign State and the immunity to which he was entitled is predicated on status." "After Pinochet: developments on Head of State and ministerial immunities", p. 12.

[172] *Yearbook ... 1991*, vol. II (Part Two), p. 18.

[173] *Ibid.*, pp. 18 and 19. It should be noted that this wording is very similar to the wording cited in paragraph 85 above, contained in paragraph 53 of the judgment of ICJ in the *Arrest Warrant* case.

[174] In the words of Lord Saville of Newdigate concerning the *Pinochet* case: "These immunities [immunities *ratione personae* and *ratione materiae*] belong not to the individual but to the state in question". Pinochet No. 3, *ILM*, vol. 38 (1999), p. 580 at p. 642.

[175] As noted in the judgment of ICJ in the *Arrest Warrant* case, State officials "will cease to enjoy immunity from foreign jurisdiction if the State which they represent or have represented decides to waive that immunity". *Arrest Warrant* case (Judgment), para. 61. Regarding the fact that only the State served by the official is entitled to waive the immunity enjoyed by that official, see, for example, Brownlie, *op. cit.*, p. 335; and Wirth, *loc. cit.*, p. 882. The fact that the State is entitled to waive the immunity of diplomatic agents, consular officials and members of special missions was established, respectively, in the 1961 Vienna Convention on Diplomatic Relations (article 32), the 1963 Vienna Convention on Consular Relations (article 45) and the 1969 Convention on Special Missions (article 41).

[176] In the *Parlement Belge* case, Lord Justice Brett said: "The principle to be deduced from all these cases is that, as a consequence of the absolute independence of every sovereign authority, and of the international comity which induces every sovereign state to respect the independence and dignity of every other foreign state, each and every one declines to exercise by means of its courts any of its territorial jurisdiction over the person of any sovereign". Court of Appeal (United Kingdom), 27 February 1880, *The Law Reports. Probate Division*, vol. 5, p. 203 at p. 214. In *The Schooner Exchange v. McFaddon*, C. J. Marshall said: "The world being composed of distinct sovereignties, possessing equal rights and equal independence, whose mutual benefit is promoted by intercourse with each other, and by an interchange of those good offices which humanity dictates and its wants require, all sovereigns have consented to a relaxation, in practice, in cases under certain peculiar circumstances, of that absolute and complete jurisdiction within their respective territories which sovereignty confers." Supreme Court of the United States, 1812, 7 Cranch, 116, at p. 136.

in the maxim *par in parem non habet imperium*, were already cited in the judgments in the *Schooner Exchange v. McFaddon* (1812) and *Parlement Belge* (1880) cases as the rationale for immunity, including the immunity of the State, the Head of State and the diplomatic representatives of the State. In contemporary international law these principles, transformed into the principles of sovereign equality of States and non-interference in internal affairs, continue to serve as the legal basis for the immunity of State officials from foreign criminal jurisdiction.[177] The principles of sovereign equality of States and *par in parem non habet imperium* were referred to as the rationale for the immunity of the Head of State in the *Pinochet* case.[178] The International Tribunal for the Former Yugoslavia referred to these very principles in the *Blaškić* case when considering whether it could address subpoenas to State officials: "The general rule under discussion is well established in international law and is based on the sovereign equality of States (*par in parem non habet imperium*)."[179] In the judgment in the *Adamov* case, in the context of the issue of the immunity of a former member of the Government of the Russian Federation—the former Minister for Atomic Energy—the Federal Tribunal of Switzerland ruled that, under international law, immunity was designed to prevent one State from narrowing the immunity of another State and from exercising jurisdiction in respect of its sovereign acts and bodies.[180] These principles, which have been confirmed as the basis for immunity in numerous other court rulings[181] and cited as the rationale for the immunity of officials by States themselves, including in their submissions to the courts,[182] are widely supported in doctrine.[183]

96. The international law rationale given for the immunity of State officials from foreign criminal jurisdiction is, in turn, based on political considerations that are fundamental for States and the international community. Recognition of the immunity required for the normal functioning of States and their representation in international relations, based on the principles of sovereign equality of States and non-interference in internal affairs, is predicated on the need to ensure stability and predictability in inter-State relations.[184] The need to ensure stability in relations between States is frequently cited, alongside these principles of international law as the rationale for immunity, in court rulings, positions of States and doctrine. The need to support normal inter-State relations as the rationale for immunity was already referred to by the courts in the aforementioned rulings in the *Schooner Exchange v. McFaddon* and *Parlement Belge* cases.[185] As was noted in the *Adamov* case, the main purpose of immunity for sitting members of Government from criminal jurisdiction and from enforcement and executive proceedings is to maintain political stability. Immunity from criminal prosecution is designed to prevent the formal business of officials from becoming paralysed as a result of politically motivated charges being

---

[177] "The substantive foundations of State immunity in international law as evidenced in the usages and practice of States may be expressed in terms of the sovereignty, independence, equality and dignity of States. All these notions seem to coalesce and together they constitute a firm international legal basis for sovereign immunity. As the term suggests, either 'State' or 'sovereign' immunity is derived from the principle of sovereignty … It has become an established rule that between two equals, one cannot exercise sovereign will or power over the other, *par in parem non habet imperium*." Sucharitkul, *loc. cit.*, p. 117.

[178] See, for example, footnote 168 above.

[179] *Prosecutor v. Blaškić*, Appeals Chamber, Judgment on the request of the Republic of Croatia for review of the Decision of Trial Chamber II of 18 July 1997, 29 October 1997, para. 41.

[180] Federal Tribunal, *Evgeny Adamov v. Federal Office of Justice*, Judgment of 22 December 2005, ATF 132 II 81, para. 3.4.2.

[181] For example, in the ruling in the *Charles Taylor* case, the Appeals Chamber of the Special Court for Sierra Leone ruled that the principle of State immunity derives from the equality of sovereign States and therefore one State may not adjudicate on the conduct of another State. Appeals Chamber, *The Prosecutor v. Charles Ghankay Taylor*, Decision on Immunity from Jurisdiction, Case No. SCSL-2003-01-I, 31 May 2004, para 51. The European Court of Human Rights has repeatedly stated that "sovereign immunity of States is a concept of international law, developed out of the principle *par in parem non habet imperium*, by virtue of which one State shall not be subject to the jurisdiction of another State" (decision of 12 December 2002 on the inadmissibility of *Kalogeropoulou and Others v. Greece and Germany, Reports of Judgments and Decisions 2002-X*, Application No. 59021/00). See also the three rulings adopted by the European Court on 21 November 2001 with respect to *Al-Adsani v. the United Kingdom* (Application No. 35763/97), *McElhinney v. Ireland* (Application No. 31253/96, *ibid.*) and *Fogarty v. the United Kingdom* (Application No. 37112/97, *ibid.*). According to United States judicial practice: "Head-of-state immunity is founded on the need for comity among nations and respect for the sovereignty of other nations." *In re Grand Jury Proceedings*, John Doe No. 700, 817 F.2d 1108, 1110, Judgment of 5 May 1987, reproduced in *ILR*, vol. 81, p. 599 at pp. 601 and 602.

[182] The Democratic Republic of the Congo, in its Memorial to the International Court in the *Arrest Warrant* case, complained of harm done to its sovereignty in the person of a member of its Government and expressed its intention to uphold a principle essential to the existence of well-ordered relations between civilized States, namely respect for the immunity of the persons responsible for conducting those relations (*I.C.J. Pleadings*). According to the Memorial of Djibouti to the International Court in *Certain Questions of Mutual Legal Assistance in Criminal Matters* (*Djibouti v. France*), the actions of France towards President Ismaël Omar Guelleh could be perceived as an attack on the integrity and honour of the Head of State of Djibouti and on the sovereignty of Djibouti (para. 41).

[183] As noted by Rousseau, "[l]a justification de l'exception de la juridiction étrangère est habituellement présentée en fonction du principe de l'indépendance de l'Etat … Mais on peut aussi y voir une conséquence du principe de l'égalité des Etats …: du moment que toutes les compétences d'Etat sont juridiquement égales, aucune d'elles ne peut entreprendre sur les autres, au moins que son action ne repose sur un titre conventionnel dérogatoire au droit commun", *Droit international public*, pp. 10 and 11. According to Cassese, personal immunity "is predicated on the notion that any activity of a head of state or government, or diplomatic agent or foreign minister, must be immune from foreign jurisdiction to avoid foreign states either infringing sovereign prerogatives of states or interfering with the official functions of foreign state agent[s] under the pretext of dealing with an exclusively private act". *Loc. cit.*, p. 862. Toner notes that "[t]he importance of safeguarding states from foreign interference is the policy foundation of immunities *ratione personae* and *ratione materiae*". *Loc. cit.*, p. 902. See also Bantekas, "In its more general form, immunity safeguards the political independence of the state concerned." "Head of State immunity in the light of multiple legal regimes and non-self-contained system theories: theoretical analysis of ICC third party jurisdiction against the background of the 2003 Iraq war", p. 32.

[184] As Pierson notes: "Head of state immunity logically derives from state immunity that, in turn, derives from the equal and independent status of the nation state. Immunity is a concomitant of state sovereignty. Sovereignty's essence is that there be no authority higher than the state (*par in parem non habet imperium*). For one state to be compelled to submit to the jurisdiction of another is offensive to the 'dignity' of that state. Apart from these theoretical considerations, the practical justification for state immunity is that immunity promotes respect among states and helps preserve the smooth functioning of international relations. Reciprocity is key. The forum state grants immunity to other states so that they in turn will respect the immunity of the forum state." "Pinochet and the end of immunity: England's House of Lords holds that a former Head of State is not immune for torture", at pp. 269–270.

[185] See paragraph 95 above.

brought against them.[186] Furthermore, in the 2001 ruling in the *Tachiona v. Mugabe* case, the United States District Court noted: "The potential for harm to diplomatic relations between the affected sovereign states is especially strong in cases ... that essentially entail branding a foreign ruler with the ignominy of answering personal accusations of heinous crimes."[187] The foreign policy rationale for the need to ensure immunity is generally found in submissions of the United States Department of State to United States courts, for example, when considering cases concerning immunity of foreign officials.[188]

97. Accordingly, the rationales given for the immunity of State officials from foreign criminal jurisdiction may be said to be complementary and interrelated. At least, in many cases this is how they are applied by the courts, used by the executive branches of States and cited in doctrine.

9. Immunity of State officials; diplomatic and consular immunities

98. Diplomatic agents, consular officials, members of special missions and representatives of States in and to international organizations are State officials. They also possess special status and perform special functions—representation of the State in relations with other States and with international organizations. This special status and the role of these officials in organizing relations between States became the basis for the formulation of the special rules governing immunity of this category of officials from the jurisdiction of the host State. The immunities of these officials are generally called diplomatic and consular immunities, although—strictly speaking—the immunity of each of the above-mentioned four categories of officials is governed by rules contained in various sources. The immunity of diplomatic agents is governed by the rules of customary international law and the provisions of the 1961 Vienna Convention on Diplomatic Relations; the immunity of consular officials is governed by the rules of customary international law, the provisions of the 1963 Vienna Convention on Consular Relations and the provisions of bilateral consular conventions; the immunity of members of special missions is governed by the provisions of the 1969 Convention on Special Missions.[189] Lastly, immunity of representatives of States to international organizations is governed by the provisions of the conventions on the privileges and immunities of the relevant organizations or their headquarters agreements. The immunities of various categories of State officials that are embodied in international treaties undoubtedly carry much more weight than the immunity of other State officials.

99. Obviously, State officials who are diplomatic agents, consular officials, members of special missions or representatives of States to international organizations can be said to enjoy both the immunities common to all officials and the special immunities granted by international law to these special categories of officials. Usually, these officials enjoy the corresponding special immunities. However, there may be situations in which these officials enjoy not special immunities but the usual immunities of a State official from foreign criminal jurisdiction. For example, there are cases in which a diplomatic agent accredited to one State is sent by the accrediting State to attend events in the territory of a third State. In this case, this person enjoys not diplomatic immunity but the usual immunity of an official from the jurisdiction of that third State.[190]

100. Often the immunity of a Head of State is equated to diplomatic immunity. Thus the question of the immunity of the Head of a foreign State is sometimes decided by reference to national legislation.[191] In other cases, the authorities of the State exercising jurisdiction draw an analogy between the immunity of the Head of a foreign State and diplomatic immunity.[192]

---

[186] See footnote 180 above.

[187] United States District Court for the Southern District of New York, *Tachiona v. Mugabe*, 30 October 2001, No. 00 CIV. 6666 (VM), p. 291.

[188] The decision of the United States District Court in the case concerning the former Director of the Israeli General Security Service, Avraham Dichter, contains a reference to the Statement of Interest of the United States Government: "[P]arting with this international consensus would threaten serious harm to U.S. interests, by inviting reciprocation in foreign jurisdictions. Given the global leadership responsibilities of the United States, its officials are at special risk of being made the targets of politically driven lawsuits abroad—including damages suits arising from alleged war crimes. The immunity defense is a vital means of deflecting these suits and averting the nuisance and diplomatic tensions that would ensue were they to proceed. It is therefore of critical importance that American courts recognize the same immunity defense for foreign officials, as any refusal to do so could easily lead foreign jurisdictions to refuse such protection for American officials in turn." United States District Court for the Southern District of New York, *Ra'ed Mohamad Ibrahim Matar, et al. v. Avraham Dichter, former Director of Israel's General Security Service*, 2 May 2007, 500 F. Supp. 2d 284. The text of the Statement of Interest of the United States Government is available on the website of the United States Department of State at http://www.state.gov/documents/organization/98806.pdf; the text of the ruling is available at http://www.cja.org/downloads/Matar_DIchter_2nd_circuit_decision_1.pdf (accessed 21 November 2013).

[189] Further study is required to determine whether there exist customary rules of international law governing the status of members of special missions. As has already been noted, there are very few parties to this Convention. In addition, in order for members of special missions to enjoy the immunity granted by this Convention, a number of conditions specified therein must be met.

[190] As Wirth notes, "[d]iplomats and consular agents are state officials and therefore are protected not only by diplomatic immunity but also by state immunity (*ratione materiae*). This protection is necessary with regard to third states which are not bound by the regulations of diplomatic or consular immunity". *Loc. cit*, pp. 883 and 884.

[191] For the legislation of the United Kingdom and Australia on this subject, see para. 37 above.

[192] For example, in its decision in the *Tachiona v. Mugabe* case, the District Court in New York noted: "... scope of protection would extend to heads-of-state a level of immunity from territorial jurisdiction at minimum commensurate with that accorded by treaties and widely accepted customary international law to diplomatic and consular officials... As one court observed, it would be anomalous for states to confer upon their foreign envoys abroad diplomatic privileges and immunities extending farther than the immunity they recognize for heads-of-state." United States District Court, Southern District of New York, 30 October 2001. There are also examples of how the question of immunity of other senior officials is resolved by granting diplomatic immunity and by applying the 1961 Vienna Convention. Higgins, in particular, describes the following situation: "Turning... to the immunity of *all kinds* of senior officials, a recent ministerial order of the Schweizererische Bundesanwaltschaft is of some interest. The Order of 8 May 2003 refused to allow the 'Association for solidarity with victims of the war against Iraq' to bring a suit against George W. Bush, Dick Cheney, Donald Rumsfeld, Colin Powell, Condoleezza Rice, Bill Clinton, Tony Blair, Jack Straw and others for crimes against humanity, genocide and war crimes. The Order stated, *inter alia*, that in the absence of a warrant from an international court or tribunal, President Bush had absolute immunity. The Order then went to the Vienna Convention on Diplomatic Relations of [1961] and used article 31 (1) to grant immunity to ministers and high-ranking persons, noting that international law is not precise about the situation of high-ranking persons and the jurisprudence is evolving." *Loc. cit.*, p. 4.

101. The functional/representative rationale for diplomatic and consular immunity has been discussed above.[193] On the subject of the international law and political rationale for these immunities, Shaw notes "[t]he special privileges and immunities related to diplomatic personnel of various kinds grew up partly as a consequence of sovereign immunity and the independence and equality of states, and partly as an essential requirement of an international system. States must negotiate and consult with each other and with international organizations and in order to do so need diplomatic staffs. Since these persons represent their states in various ways, they thus benefit from the legal principle of state sovereignty".[194] Thus diplomatic and consular immunities have the same basis as the immunity of State officials.[195]

C. Summary

102. To sum up chapters I–III of this preliminary report, the following points, *inter alia*, may be made:

(*a*) The basic source of the immunity of State officials from foreign criminal jurisdiction is international law, and particularly customary international law;

(*b*) Jurisdiction and immunity are related but different. In the context of the topic under discussion, the consideration of immunity should be limited and should not consider the substance of the question of jurisdiction as such;

(*c*) The criminal jurisdiction of a State, like the entire jurisdiction of the State, is exercised in the form of legislative, executive and judicial jurisdiction (or in the form of legislative and executive jurisdiction, if this is understood to include both executive and judicial jurisdiction);

(*d*) Executive (or executive and judicial) criminal jurisdiction has features in common with civil jurisdiction but differs from it because many criminal procedure measures are adopted in the pre-trial phase of the juridical process. Thus the question of immunity of State officials from foreign criminal jurisdiction is more important in the pre-trial phase;

(*e*) Immunity of officials from foreign jurisdiction is a rule of international law and the corresponding juridical relations, in which the juridical right of the person enjoying immunity not to be subject to foreign jurisdiction reflects the juridical obligation of the foreign State not to exercise jurisdiction over the person concerned;

(*f*) Immunity from criminal jurisdiction means immunity only from executive and judicial jurisdiction (or only from executive jurisdiction, if this is understood to include both executive and judicial jurisdiction). It is thus immunity from criminal process or from criminal procedure measures and not from the substantive law of the foreign State;

(*g*) Immunity of State officials from foreign criminal jurisdiction is procedural and not substantive in nature. It is an obstacle to criminal liability but does not in principle preclude it;

(*h*) Actions performed by an official in an official capacity are attributed to the State. The official is therefore protected from the criminal jurisdiction of a foreign State by immunity *ratione materiae*. However, this does not preclude attribution of these actions also to the person who performed them;

(*i*) Ultimately the State, which alone is entitled to waive an official's immunity, stands behind the immunity of an official, whether this is immunity *ratione personae* or immunity *ratione materiae*, and behind those who enjoy immunity;

(*j*) Immunity of an official from foreign criminal jurisdiction has some complementary and interrelated components: functional and representative components; principles of international law concerning sovereign equality of States and non-interference in internal affairs; and the need to ensure the stability of international relations and the independent performance of their activities by States.

[193] See paras. 86 and 87 above.

[194] *Op. cit.*, pp. 668 and 669.

[195] Ultimately, the immunity of the State itself is behind all the immunities of all State officials from foreign jurisdiction. The International Law Commission drew attention to this in the commentaries to the draft articles on jurisdictional immunities of States and their property: "The fact that the immunities enjoyed by representatives of government, whatever their specialized qualifications, diplomatic or consular or otherwise, are in the ultimate analysis State immunities has never been doubted. Rather, it has been unduly overlooked." *Yearbook ... 1991*, vol. II (Part Two), p. 18, footnote 44.

Chapter IV

Issues to be considered when defining the scope of the topic

A. Boundaries of the topic

103. The following points should be considered when defining the boundaries of the topic. Firstly, it concerns only the immunity of State officials from *foreign criminal* jurisdiction. This means that the subject under consideration here is not immunity from international criminal jurisdiction or immunity from national civil or national administrative jurisdiction *per se*. Immunity from international criminal jurisdiction appears to be fundamentally different from immunity from national criminal jurisdiction. International criminal jurisdiction is of a different legal nature, as it is exercised by international courts and tribunals. These courts and tribunals are established and therefore have and exercise their jurisdiction on the basis of an international agreement or decision of a competent international organization. This means that they have a mandate from the States themselves, or, as noted in the decision of the Special Court for Sierra Leone in *Prosecutor v. Charles Ghankay Taylor*, from the international

community.[196] The principle of sovereign equality of States, expressed in the formula *par in parem non habet imperium*, which is the fundamental international law rationale for the immunity of State officials from foreign jurisdiction, cannot be the rationale for immunity from international jurisdiction.[197] The absence of immunity of State officials from international criminal jurisdiction in the international law instruments on which the exercise of such jurisdiction is based cannot be invoked to claim that State officials therefore also do not have immunity from national jurisdiction, or as proof that they do not have such immunity. As for the immunity of State officials from other forms of national jurisdiction—civil and administrative—although such immunity is not *per se* a subject for consideration here, examples of their analysis in the practice of States and in doctrine are entirely relevant for the present topic, as the international law rationale for immunities of State officials from the various forms of foreign jurisdiction is one and the same.

104. Secondly, the topic is concerned with immunity of State officials, which is based on *international* law. Immunity may also be granted to officials of another State on the basis of national law. However, the granting of immunity under national law is of interest in the context of this topic only because the corresponding provisions of national law may be considered as one indication of the existence of rules of customary international law in this sphere.

105. Thirdly, the topic is concerned with immunity of officials of one State from the jurisdiction of another State. This means that there is no intention to consider immunity of officials from the jurisdiction of their own State *per se*.

B. Persons covered

1. All officials; definition of the concept of "State official"

106. There are many different definitions of the group of persons whose immunities should be considered in the context of this topic and who would be covered by the draft guiding principles or draft articles which may be prepared as a result of this review. More specifically, a first definition covers only the three officials directly referred to in the judgment of ICJ in *Arrest Warrant* and in the 1969 Convention on Special Missions—that is, Heads of State, Heads of Government and ministers of foreign affairs; a second definition includes all high-ranking State officials who enjoy immunity because of their post; a third definition includes all incumbent and former State officials. The last definition seems entirely appropriate and preferable for this topic.

107. In the practice of States, especially in national court rulings and in doctrine, it is generally recognized that all State officials enjoy immunity from foreign criminal jurisdiction in respect of acts performed by them in their official capacity, or immunity *ratione materiae*. As noted by Lord Browne-Wilkinson in the *Pinochet No. 3* case, "[i]mmunity *ratione materiae* applies not only to ex-heads of state and ex-ambassadors but to all state officials who have been involved in carrying out the functions of the state. Such immunity is necessary in order to prevent state immunity being circumvented by prosecuting or suing the official who, for example, actually carried out the torture when a claim against the head of state would be precluded by the doctrine of immunity".[198] State officials enjoy such immunity regardless of the level of their post. For instance, in 2006 in *Belhas et al. v. Moshe Ya'alon* the United States District Court for the District of Columbia recognized the immunity of M. Ya'alon,[199] who

[196] Appeals Chamber, *Prosecutor v. Charles Ghankay Taylor*, Decision on Immunity from Jurisdiction, Case No. SCSL-2003-01-1, 31 May 2004, para. 51.

[197] "A reason for the distinction, in this regard, between national courts and international courts, though not immediately evident, would appear due to the fact that the principle that one sovereign state does not adjudicate on the conduct of another state; the principle of state immunity derives from the equality of sovereign states and therefore has no relevance to international criminal tribunals which are not organs of a state but derive their mandate from the international community." *Ibid.* This clearly refers to those cases when, in accordance with the constituent documents of the corresponding international court or tribunal, the State has international law obligations that deprive its officials of the right to immunity from the jurisdiction of that court or tribunal. At the same time, the principle of sovereign equality may in some cases also be the rationale for immunity from international criminal jurisdiction, for example, in a situation where the official of a State that is not a party to the Statute of the International Criminal Court is in the territory of a State party to the Statute and there is a request for the surrender of that official to the Court. As noted by Fox, "State immunity may serve as a bar to proceedings before an international tribunal—for example, the Rome Statute… provides that a State may not be under an obligation to surrender to the ICC for trial an individual present in its territory who, as a representative of another State, enjoys diplomatic immunity; but its main significance relates to its effect upon the jurisdiction of a national court". "International law and restraints on exercise of jurisdiction by national courts of States", p. 363.

[198] Pinochet No. 3, *ILM*, vol. 38 (1999), p. 580, at p. 594. A similar rationale for the need to extend immunity *ratione materiae* to all State officials was given by an English court in *Propend Finance Pty Ltd.* v. Sing: "The protection afforded by the Act of 1978 to States would be undermined if employees, officers (or, as one authority puts it, 'functionaries') could be sued as individuals for matters of State conduct in respect of which the State they were serving had immunity. Section 14(1) must be read as affording to individual employees or officers of a foreign State protection under the same cloak as protects the State itself." High Court, Queen's Bench Division, 14 March 1996, reproduced in *ILR*, vol. 11, p. 611. In *Jones No. 1*, Lord Philipps noted: "The dignity of a state may also be affronted if those who are or were its officials are impleaded in relation to the conduct of its affairs before the courts of another state. In those circumstances the state can normally extend the cloak of its own immunity over those officials. It can be said that to implead those officials amounts, indirectly, to impleading the state" (para. 105). Lastly, in *Jones No. 2* (see footnote 71 above), Lord Bingham of Cornhill noted that there was "a wealth of authority to show that in such case the foreign state is entitled to claim immunity for its servants as it could if sued itself. The foreign state's right to immunity cannot be circumvented by suing its servants or agents" (para. 10).

According to Wickremasinghe, "[i]t appears that under the doctrine of State immunity, other State officials [other than heads of State, heads of government and ministers for foreign relations] enjoy immunity *ratione materiae* for their official acts from the jurisdiction of the courts of other States, where the effect of proceedings would be to undermine or render nugatory the immunity of the employer" ("Immunities enjoyed by officials of States and international organizations", pp 409–410). See also Forcese, "De-immunizing Torture: Reconciling Human Rights and State Immunity", pp. 138 and 139.

[199] United States District Court for the District of Colombia, *Belhas et Others v. Moshe Ya'alon*, 14 December 2006, 466 F. Supp. 2d 127. The judge determined that it was "undisputed" that M. Ya'alon at the time of the attack was acting in his official capacity and that his actions were conditioned by the need to defend the interests of the Israeli State. The basis for this conclusion was mainly a letter from the Ambassador of Israel in the United States to the United States Department of State Under-Secretary for Political Affairs. The letter, in particular, stated that anything that M. Ya'alon had done was in the course of his official duties and that his actions were "sovereign actions of the State of Israel, approved by the Government of Israel in defense of its citizens

(*Continued on next page.*)

had been the head of Israeli army intelligence at the time of the events underlying the case brought against him, while the French Court of Cassation in 2004 recognized the immunity from criminal jurisdiction of the head of the Malta Ship Registry in connection with acts performed by him in his official capacity.[200]

108. The term "State official" is widely used in practice, including in judicial rulings and doctrine. Yet there is no definition of the concept of "State official" in international law, at least not in universal international agreements. As for doctrine, there is, for instance, the definition given by F. Przetacznik: "An official of a foreign State is a person who either, under its law, is invested with legal authority to act as its official representative (a head of State, a Head of government, or a Minister of Foreign Affairs) and is authorized by the sending State to act in the capacity of its representative (a diplomatic agent or a diplomatic member of a special mission), or to act officially on its behalf (a consular officer, a diplomatic member of a permanent mission to an international organization, or a diplomatic member of a delegation to a international conference) in the receiving state."[201] In this definition, the category of State officials is, in essence, limited to those persons who represent the State in international relations. At the same time, the official functions in respect of which State officials enjoy immunity are not limited to such representation. In this connection, the above-mentioned author has also stated: "The basic element of the notion 'an official of foreign State' is that he must either represent that State or officially act on its behalf or both."[202] Officials perform acts on behalf of the State not only in the area of foreign relations, but in all areas in which the State exercises its sovereign prerogatives. They are given full powers by the State in order to represent the State or otherwise act on its behalf in accordance with the State's law or practice. In addition to the term "State official", the terms "State representative",[203] "State agent",[204] "State organ"[205] are used. The last term is used in the articles on responsibility of States for internationally wrongful acts and includes, according to article 4, paragraph 2, "any person or entity which has that status in accordance with the internal law of the State".[206] In the commentary to this article, the Commission notes that the reference to a "State organ" is "not limited to the organs of central government, to officials at a high level or to persons with responsibility for the external relations of the State, [but also] organs of government of whatever kind or classification, exercising whatever functions, and at whatever level in the hierarchy".[207] As the term "State organ" includes, but is not limited to, individual officials, its use seems appropriate for the purposes of this topic. At this stage at least, the terms "State official" may continue to be used. If the Commission in the future finds it appropriate to define this term or in some other way to indicate its meaning, the approach that it used for the drafting of article 4, paragraph 2, on State responsibility (*Yearbook ... 2001*, vol. II (Part Two), p. 26) could also be useful *mutatis mutandis* for the present topic.

2. Officials enjoying immunity *ratione personae*

109. As already mentioned, all State officials enjoy immunity *ratione materiae* from foreign criminal jurisdiction and only some officials enjoy immunity *ratione personae*. It has not yet been possible to define this category of officials. It is appropriate to recall the difficulties experienced by the Commission in this connection when working on the draft articles on special missions, on representation of States in their relations with international organizations and on the prevention and punishment of crimes against internationally protected persons.[208]

110. First of all, the category of persons enjoying personal immunity naturally includes Heads of State. Their personal immunity from foreign criminal jurisdiction has the broadest possible confirmation in practice and in doctrine.[209] However, Heads of State are not the only category

(*Footnote 199 continued.*)

against terrorist attacks" and also that "to allow a suit against [the former official] is to allow a suit against Israel itself". Having established that Ya'alon acted in an official capacity, the judge considered that his actions could be seen as the actions of a State body/institution in the sense of the above-mentioned Foreign Sovereign Immunities Act.

[200] According to the French court of cassation, "... la coutume internationale qui s'oppose à la poursuite des Etats devant les juridictions pénales d'un Etat étranger s'étend aux organes et entités qui constituent l'émanation de l'Etat ainsi qu'à leurs agents en raison d'actes qui, comme en l'espèce, relèvent de la souveraineté de l'Etat concerné". *Arrêt de la Cour de Cassation, chambre criminelle*, 23 November 2004, published in *Bulletin Criminel* 2004, No. 292, p. 1096. The text of the ruling is available (in French and in English translation) at http://www.legifrance.gouv.fr/initRechJuri.Judi.do (accessed 21 November 2013).

[201] "Basic principles of international law concerning the protection of the officials of foreign states", p. 52.

[202] *Ibid.*

[203] See, for example, article 2, paragraph 1 (*b*) (iv) of the Convention on Jurisdictional Immunities of States and Their Property. In the commentary to this provision (contained in the section on paragraph 1 (*b*) (v) of draft article 2), the Commission noted that the category of representatives of the State acting in that capacity encompassed "all the natural persons who are authorized to represent the State in all its manifestations". *Yearbook ... 1991*, vol. II (Part Two), p. 18.

[204] See, for example, Verhoeven, "Les immunités propres aux organes ou autres agents des sujets du droit international", *Op. cit.*, p. 64. Borghi uses the term "les dirigeants politiques", including as the title of a book (*op. cit.*).

[205] The term "organ of State" was used, for example, by parties in the *Case concerning Certain Questions of Mutual Assistance in Criminal Matters* relation to the State Prosecutor and the Head of National Security of Djibouti. The Counsel for France, A. Pellet, during the oral pleadings agreed with the Counsel for Djibouti, L. Condorelli, that "when they act in an official capacity, the organs of the State do not engage their own responsibility, but that of the State". However, in his opinion, "outside certain organs or categories of organs that can be counted on the fingers of one hand (head of State, minister for foreign affairs, head of government and diplomats—to varying extents moreover), it is totally excluded 'that it can be claimed that persons enjoying the status of an organ of State, even of a high rank, benefit from personal immunity (also known as *ratione personae*) in any way comparable to that which international law accords to the highest organs of States!'." *ICJ*, document CR2008/5, oral argument, 25 January 2008, para. 75.

[206] *Yearbook ... 2001*, vol. II (Part Two), p. 40.

[207] *Ibid.*, para. (6).

[208] See paras. 18–20 and 23 above.

[209] "Heads of States ... enjoy absolute jurisdictional immunity in all foreign States for all acts which would ordinarily be subject to the jurisdiction of those States, whatever the connection in which those acts were committed." *Marcos and Marcos v. Federal Department of Police*, Swiss Federal Tribunal, 2 November 1989, reproduced in *ILR*, vol. 102, p. 198, at p. 203. "A head-of-state recognized by the United States government is absolutely immune from personal jurisdiction in United States courts unless that immunity has been waived by statute or by the foreign government recognized by the United States." *Lafontant v. Aristide*, United States District Court, Eastern District of New York, 27 January 1994, reproduced in *ILR*, vol. 103, p. 581, at pp. 584–585. "Grounded in customary international law, the doctrine of head of state

of persons considered. Although previously it was only the Head of State (and ambassadors) who enjoyed personal immunity, the category of officials enjoying such immunity has started to expand.[210] There are objective reasons for this.[211] The nature and structure of administration of the State have changed. The functions of administering a contemporary State and ensuring its sovereignty and representation in international relations used to be concentrated in the person of the Head of State, but now belong to a significant degree to the Head of Government, members of the Government and, in particular, ministers for foreign affairs. In many countries, the Head of Government plays a larger role than the Head of State in the administration of the State. Hence the need to ensure the maximum independence and maximum security from interference by other States in the activity not only of the Head of State but also of some other officials who are very significant for the State, thereby protecting the sovereignty of the State itself in its relations with other States. Above all, the category of officials enjoying personal immunity started to be expanded to include Heads of Government and ministers for foreign affairs in addition to Heads of State.

111. Heads of State, Heads of Governments and ministers for foreign affairs constitute, in a manner of speaking, the basic threesome of State officials who enjoy personal immunity. Under international law, only these three categories of officials are considered to be representatives of the State in international relations by virtue of their functions and consequently of their posts. Only these officials, for instance, can sign international treaties on behalf of their State without the need to produce full powers (article 7, paragraph 2, of the Vienna Convention on the Law of Treaties). The special status and, accordingly, the special nature of immunity of Heads of Government and ministers for foreign affairs, together with the special status and immunity of Heads of State, is confirmed in article 21 of the 1969 Convention on Special Missions, in article 1, paragraph 1 (*a*), of the 1973 Convention for the Prevention and Punishment of Crimes against Internationally Protected Persons, including Diplomatic Agents and in article 50 of the 1975 Vienna Convention on the Representation of States in Their Relations with International Organizations of a Universal Character. These officials, together with Heads of State, are also mentioned by ICJ in its judgment in the *Arrest Warrant* case among the high-ranking State officials who enjoy immunity from foreign jurisdiction. It will be recalled that, in paragraph 51 of the judgment, the Court indicated that "in international law it is firmly established that, as also diplomatic and consular agents, certain holders of high-ranking office in a State, such as the Head of State, Head of Government and Minister for Foreign Affairs, enjoy immunities from jurisdiction in other States, both civil and criminal".[212]

112. There are also examples of recognition of the immunity of a Head of Government from foreign jurisdiction in rulings of national courts. In 1988, in *Saltany and Others v. Reagan and Others*, the United States District Court recognized the immunity from jurisdiction of the Prime Minister of the United Kingdom, Margaret Thatcher, agreeing with the opinion of the United States Department of State on that issue.[213] In 2003, the Belgian Court of Cassation noted in *A. Sharon* that "la coutume internationale s'oppose à ce que les chefs d'Etat et de gouvernement en exercice puissent, en l'absence de dispositions internationales contraires s'imposant aux Etats concernés, faire l'objet de poursuites devant les juridictions pénales d'un Etat étranger".[214] The Belgian Court thus confirmed, after ICJ had done so, that immunity not only of the Head of State but also of the Head of Government from foreign criminal jurisdiction is based on customary international law.

113. There is a well-known instance in the Russian Federation of recognition of the immunity of the Head of a foreign Government in the pre-trial phase of criminal proceedings. In 2005, a visit to the Russian Federation was planned for the Prime Minister of Ukraine, Yulia Timoshenko, against whom a criminal case had been brought in the Russian Federation prior to her appointment to that position. The day before the visit, the General Procurator of the Russian Federation announced that the Prime Minister of Ukraine would not have any problems if she wished to travel to the Russian Federation, as senior

immunity provides that a head of state is not subject to the jurisdiction of foreign courts, at least as to official acts taken during the ruler's term of office." *United States v. Noriega and Others*, United States District Court, Southern District of Florida, 8 June 1990, reproduced in *ILR*, vol. 9, p.143, at p. 161. "Attendu que la coutume internationale s'oppose à ce que les chefs d'Etat en exercice puissent, en l'absence de dispositions internationales contraires s'imposant aux parties concernées, faire l'objet de poursuites devant les juridictions pénales d'un Etat étranger" *Kaddafi* case, judgment by the Court of Cassation, criminal chamber, 13 March 2001, published in *Bulletin criminel* 2001 No. 64, p. 218. "Whilst international law evolves over a period of time international customary law which is embodied in our Common Law currently provides absolute immunity to any Head of State." *Mugabe*, Bow Street, 14 January 2004, reproduced in *International and Comparative Law Quarterly*, vol. 53 (July 2004), p. 770.

According to Watts, "[s]o far as concerns criminal proceedings, a Head of State's immunity is generally accepted as being absolute ...". *Loc.. cit.*, p. 54. Simbeye also notes that "[a] sitting head of state, as the holder of the highest office and the representative of his state, is immune from legal suit in a foreign court". *Op. cit.*, p. 94. As Verhoeven states, "Quelles que soient les incertitudes entourant la responsabilité pénale des agents de l'Etat, il n'est pas contesté que le chef d'Etat bénéficie d'une immunité pénale absolute devant les juridictions d'un Etat étranger. Le caractère absolu de l'immunité exclut qu'il puisse lui être apporté aucune exception, tenant par exemple à la nature de l'infraction qui lui est reprochée ou à la date à laquelle elle a été commise." "Les immunités de juridiction et d'exécution", p. 516. See also Higgins, *loc. cit.*, pp. 12–13.

[210] "There is a tendency to extend to 'High-ranking personalities', in the words of the Convention... on Special Missions, the benefit of special protection, including, where applicable immunities." Verhoeven, "Les immunités propres aux organes ou autres agents des sujets du droit international", p. 65.

[211] As noted by Toner, "[t]he modern political realities under which nation-states operate no longer allow for a strict differentiation of the powers and responsibilities of governmental ministers. The offices of foreign minister, and many other prominent ministerial positions, currently represent a state in the same way as a Head of State. Thus, to a greater extent than previously recognized, the rationale for immunizing a Head of State can be extended to other ministers". *Loc. cit*, pp. 912 and 913.

[212] *I.C.J. Reports*, 2002, pp. 20 and 21, para. 51.

[213] *Saltany and Others v. Reagan and Others*, United States District Court, District of Columbia, 23 December 1988, reproduced in *ILR*, vol. 80, pp. 19–24.

[214] *H.S.A. et al. v. S.A. et al.*, Decision related to the indictment of Ariel Sharon, Amos Yaron and others, Belgian Court of Cassation, No. P.02.1139.f, 12 February 2003, reproduced in *International Law Materials*, vol. 42, 2003, pp. 596–605.

State leaders, including Heads of Government, enjoy immunity.[215]

114. Apart from the *Arrest Warrant* case, there is hardly any information on cases in which the question of immunity of ministers for foreign affairs was considered. We do know that, in 1963, a United States court declined to consider a lawsuit against the Minister for Foreign Affairs of the Republic of Korea, following the "suggestion of immunity" of the United States Government. It is noteworthy, however, that the State Department's "suggestion", in addition to stating that ministers for foreign affairs enjoy immunity from the jurisdiction of the United States courts in accordance with customary international law, also mentioned recognition of the diplomatic status of the Minister for Foreign Affairs of the Republic of Korea, because in that instance he was on an official visit to the United States.[216] In 2001, a United States District Court agreed with the "suggestion of immunity" submitted by the Government with regard to the Minister for Foreign Affairs of Zimbabwe in the *Tachiona v. Mugabe* case.[217]

115. The paucity of information on practice, including court rulings on the question of immunity of ministers for foreign affairs, led Judge Van den Wyngaert to state, in his dissenting opinion in the *Arrest Warrant* case, that "There is no evidence for the proposition that a State is under an obligation to grant immunity from criminal process to an incumbent Foreign Minister under customary international law. By issuing and circulating the warrant, Belgium may have acted contrary to international comity. It has not, however, acted in violation of an international legal obligation".[218] The view that ministers for foreign affairs do not possess personal immunity has also been stated in the doctrine, even after the judgment in *Arrest Warrant*.[219] At the same time, the opinion of ICJ set forth in this judgment, for which the overwhelming majority of the judges voted, is shared by a number of authors.[220]

116. The above-mentioned judgment of ICJ concerning the immunity of the Minister for Foreign Affairs was referred to by the Republic of the Congo in its submission to the Court in the case *Certain Criminal Proceedings in France* and by Djibouti and France in the case *Certain Questions of Mutual Assistance in Criminal Matters*. Here the parties agreed with the view of the Court.[221]

117. As has already been noted, article 21 of the 1969 Convention on Special Missions and article 50 of the 1975 Vienna Convention on the Representation of States in Their Relations with International Organizations of a Universal Character single out, in addition to Heads of State, Heads of Government and ministers for foreign affairs, yet another category of persons possessing special status under international law: "persons of high rank". The fact that there are other high-ranking officials—apart from Heads of State, Heads of Government and ministers for foreign affairs—who under customary international law enjoy personal immunity from foreign criminal jurisdiction was confirmed in paragraph 51 of the judgment of ICJ in the *Arrest Warrant* case, mentioned in paragraph 11 above. It is obvious that, although the Court also did not say precisely which high-ranking officials—apart from Heads of State, Heads of Government and ministers for foreign affairs—enjoy immunity from foreign jurisdiction, it clearly confirmed that the category of such officials is not limited to the three mentioned.

118. This interpretation of the *Arrest Warrant* judgment was confirmed in at least two rulings of British courts. The 2004 ruling of the District Judge in the case of General Shaul Mofaz (then Defence Minister of Israel) notes "the use of the words 'such as' the Head of State, Head of Government and Minister for Foreign Affairs indicates to me that other categories could be included. In other words, those categories are not exclusive".[222] Thus distancing itself from the ICJ judgment, the British court declined to issue an arrest warrant for the Defence Minister of Israel and recognized his immunity, giving a functional rationale similar to that which the Court gave for the immunity of a minister of foreign affairs.[223] With similar reference to the above-mentioned judgment of the Court, the immunity of Bo Xilai, Minister for Commerce

[215] The text of this statement is available (in Russian) at http://www.newsru.com/russia/15feb2005/timoshenko.html (accessed 21 November 2013).

[216] *Chong Boon Kim v. Kim Yong Shik and David Kim*, Circuit Court of the First Circuit, State of Hawaii, 9 September 1963, reproduced in *ILR*, vol. 81, pp. 604 and 605. The "suggestion of immunity" in this case spoke of immunity under customary law not only of a foreign minister for foreign affairs but also of a foreign Head of State.

It should also be noted that, in the wording existing at that time, the 1962 Restatement of Foreign Relations Law of the United States announced that Heads of Government and ministers for foreign affairs of States enjoyed, in respect of official and personal acts, the same immunity as Heads of State. *Restatement (Second) of Foreign Relations Law of the United States*, St. Paul, American Law Institute, 1962, paras. 66, 200 and 202.

[217] District Court for the Southern District of New York, *Tachiona v. Mugabe*, Judgment of 30 October 2001, 169 F.Supp.2d 259, Judgment of 30 October 2001, p. 297.

[218] *I.C.J. Reports 2002*, p. 139, para. 1.

[219] See, for example, Koller, *loc. cit.*, p. 16: "The most comprehensive study of foreign minister immunity reveals that the rationale for according immunity to foreign ministers on private visits is much weaker than for Heads of State and is derived primarily from comity, not law. The necessity of immunity on private visits is a tough empirical question to which the Court's cursory handling—and the lack of available state practice—does not give due treatment. By simply blurring the distinctions between foreign ministers, Heads of State, and diplomats, the Court has created conceptual confusion."

[220] According to Cassese, "[t]he Court must be commended for elucidating and spelling out an obscure issue of existing law. In so doing it has considerably expanded the protection afforded by international law to foreign ministers". *Loc. cit.*, p. 855. See also, for example, Wirth, *loc. cit*, p. 889: "... it seems very plausible that the position of a Minister of Foreign Affairs is important enough to accord him or her the same immunities as a Head of State: a Minister of Foreign Affairs maintains the foreign relations of a state and thus plays a crucial role in the management of inter-state conflicts; in this respect, he or she is even more important than an ambassador, who—at least in the receiving state—enjoys immunity *ratione personae*."

[221] See, *inter alia*, the application by the Republic of the Congo dated 9 December 2002 instituting proceedings against France (p. 11) and the Memorial of Djibouti dated 15 March 2007 in the case *Certain Questions of Mutual Assistance in Criminal Matters (Djibouti v. France)* (p. 51).

[222] District Court (Bow Street), *Re General Shaul Mofaz*, Judgment of 12 February 2004, reproduced in *International and Comparative Law Quarterly*, vol. 53 (2004), at p. 773.

[223] The British court stated, *inter alia*: "Although travel [in case of a Defense Minister] will not be on the same level as that of a Foreign Minister, it is a fact that many States maintain troops overseas and there are many United Nations missions to visit in which military issues do play a prominent role between certain States, it strikes me that the roles of defense and foreign policy are very much intertwined, in particular in the Middle East." *Ibid.*

and International Trade of China, was recognized in a case of the same name in 2005. The senior District Judge declined to issue an arrest warrant for the Minister, stating that "under the customary international law rules Mr. Bo has immunity from prosecution as he would not be able to perform his functions unless he is able to travel freely".[224]

119. The doctrine is careful to recognize that, in addition to the "basic threesome", there are other high-ranking State officials enjoying immunity from foreign jurisdiction.[225] In the case *Certain Questions of Mutual Assistance in Criminal Matters*, the parties also recognize in principle that the same immunity as is enjoyed by ministers for foreign affairs may also be enjoyed by certain other high-ranking State officials. However, they agreed that those concerned in *Certain Questions of Mutual Assistance in Criminal Matters (Djibouti v. France)*—the State Prosecutor of Djibouti and the Head of National Security of Djibouti—were not among their number.[226] Mention may be made of examples of other State officials who enjoy or may enjoy immunity *ratione personae* (for instance, ministers of defence, ministers of foreign trade). However, the Special Rapporteur is not aware that an exhaustive list of such officials exists anywhere. As has been noted earlier, no list has been drawn up of other high-ranking officials enjoying special status and immunity and, in its work on the draft articles on special missions, the Commission quite rightly considered that the specific officials or posts are determined by the domestic law of the State.[227]

120. It seems that which other high-ranking officials enjoy personal immunity from foreign criminal jurisdiction can be determined, albeit in general terms, only if it is possible to determine the criterion or criteria to be met by these officials in order to enjoy such immunity. In the rulings of national courts cited above which recognized the immunity of the Minister of Defence and the Minister of Foreign Trade, the courts reasoned that the functions of these officials are to a large extent comparable to the functions of a minister for foreign affairs and that they consequently need immunity in order to perform precisely this type of function. It is interesting that, according to this reasoning, in the case of General Shaul Mofaz, the judge stated that he considered it highly unlikely that "ministerial appointments such as Home Secretary, Employment Minister, Environment Minister, Culture Media and Sports Minister would automatically acquire a label of State immunity".[228] The fact that immunity *ratione personae* may be enjoyed only by those other high-ranking State officials for whom representation of the State in international relations is an indispensable and primary part of their functions was mentioned by the Counsel of France, Pellet, during the oral pleadings in the *case Certain Questions of Mutual Assistance in Criminal Matters*.[229] According to Parlett, "immunity *ratione personae* is conferred on offices whose function is so important to the maintenance of international relations that they require a broad conferral of immunity".[230] Some other authors also mention the performance of functions of ensuring participation of the State in international relations as the rationale for possibly granting personal immunity to other members of the government in addition to the minister for foreign affairs.[231]

121. Admittedly, however, ensuring that the State participates or is represented in international relations is hardly a basic function of, say, the minister of defence or other members of the Government apart from the minister for foreign affairs (although, in today's globalized world, almost all cabinet members participate to varying degrees in international affairs, representing their country in specialized areas of international relations). At the same time, for the basic functions of a minister of defence, as for certain other high-ranking officials, there is usually special involvement in the solution of the most important issues affecting the sovereignty of the State. The exercise by a foreign State of criminal jurisdiction over serving officials of this type would be an obstacle to their independent activity in their posts and consequently to the exercise by the State which they are serving of the prerogatives inherent in its sovereignty. Because of the importance for the State of the functions performed by such high-ranking officials, the exercise of foreign criminal jurisdiction over them would quite likely involve interference by the State exercising jurisdiction in matters which are basically within the competence of the State served by these officials. In this connection, the question is whether the importance

[224] *Re Bo Xilai*, England, Bow Street Magistrates' Court, 8 November 2005, reproduced in *ILR*, vol. 128, p. 714. It should be noted that the judge also referred to Mr. Bo's immunity as a member of a special mission. *Ibid.*, p. 715.

[225] As Verhoeven notes, "[l]a solution est plus incertaine lorsque sont en cause d'autres membres du gouvernement. Elle pourrait se revendiquer d'une logique incontestable lorsque ces autres ministres exercent des fonctions internationales, qu'il s'agisse par exemple de négocier des accords ou de représenter l'État à l'étranger. Il s'en faut de beaucoup néanmoins qu'elle soit à ce jour confirmée sans ambiguïté par la pratique internationale". "Les immunités propres aux organes ou autres agents des sujets du droit international", p. 65. Cassese also notes that immunity *ratione personae* protects "only some categories of state officials, namely diplomatic agents, heads of state, heads of government, perhaps (in any case under the doctrine set out by the Court) foreign ministers and possibly even other senior members of cabinet". *Loc. cit.*, at p. 864. This opinion is also shared by Carter: "In the United States today, head of State immunity would seem to be available to a foreign state's head, foreign minister, and possibly their families and maybe other high-ranking officials. ... In part because of its basis in case law, the doctrine is unclear regarding exactly who might be covered". "Immunity for foreign officials: possibly too much and confusing as well", p. 230.

[226] As the Counsel of Djibouti, L. Condorelli, stated during the oral pleadings in The Hague on 22 January 2008, "Nobody here asks the Court to acknowledge that, like a Head of State or a diplomatic agent, the Public Prosecutor and the Head of National Security should benefit for the duration of their appointments from immunity from jurisdiction and complete inviolability abroad, extending to their private acts." *ICJ*, document CR 2008/3, 22 January 2008, p. 9, para. 23.

[227] See para. 19 above.

[228] District Court (Bow Street), *Re General Shaul Mofaz*, Judgment of 12 February 2004, reproduced in *International and Comparative Law Quarterly*, vol. 53 (2004), at p. 773.

[229] According to Pellet, "immunities are not granted to officials of the State simply because, in the exercise of their functions, they may, fairly occasionally, or even regularly, have to make trips abroad. This only applies if such immunities are indispensable to those missions being carried out and provided they are inherent to the functions concerned". *ICJ*, document CR 2008/5, 25 January 2008, p. 38, para. 63.

[230] "Immunity in civil proceedings for torture: the emerging exception", p. 59. The author consequently suggests that the other senior officials enjoying such immunity could include ministers of defence or permanent under-secretaries for foreign affairs. *Ibid.*

[231] See, for example, Toner, *loc. cit.*, pp. 912 and 913; Forcese, *loc. cit.*, p. 137; Du Plessis and Bosch, "Immunities and universal jurisdiction—The World Court steps in (or on?)", p. 246; and Wickremasinghe, *loc. cit.*, p. 401.

of the functions performed by high-ranking officials for ensuring the State's sovereignty is an additional criterion—in addition to ensuring the State's participation in international relations—for including the official among those enjoying immunity *ratione personae*.

3. The question of recognition in the context of this topic

122. Generally the question of immunity is considered with reference to recognized States and officials of such States, and recognized Heads of State and Heads of Government. However, there may be situations in which it is necessary to consider the question of immunity of a State that is not recognized by the State exercising jurisdiction or the question of immunity of an official of an unrecognized State or the question of the immunity of a person who is not recognized as the Head of State or Head of Government (in this case, the State itself is recognized but the Head of State or Head of Government is not). In these situations, the question of recognition becomes relevant to the consideration of the subject of immunity. As Watts notes, "the question of recognition ... will, in particular, usually be critical whenever any question of immunity arises".[232] This is confirmed, in particular, by a number of rulings by United States courts. For example, in the 1995 *Kadic v. Karadzic* case, the Court of Appeals for the Second Circuit noted that "recognized States enjoy certain privileges and immunities relevant to judicial proceedings".[233] Because the Government of the United States did not recognize Radovan Karadzic as the Head of State, the Court also did not recognize his immunity as Head of State. In 1990, in the case *United States v. Noriega and Others*, the District Court noted that "in order to assert Head of state immunity, a government official must be recognized as Panama's Head of State either under the Panamanian Constitution or by the United States".[234] Because the United States Government did not recognize Noriega as a Head of State, the Court declined to recognize that he enjoyed diplomatic immunity in that capacity. In the 1994 case *Lafontant v. Aristide*, on the other hand, the United States District Court agreed with the Executive's "suggestion of immunity" and recognized the Head-of-State immunity of Jean-Bertrand Aristide because the United States Government had recognized Mr. Aristide, who was living in exile in the United States, as the lawful Head of State of Haiti.[235]

123. The question of the immunity of officials of unrecognized States and unrecognized Heads of State and Heads of Government may arise in various contexts. One situation, for example, is when the entity served by the official whose immunity is under discussion is not recognized as an independent State by anyone, including by the State exercising jurisdiction. From the viewpoint of international law, immunity of a State official is based on the principle of the sovereign equality of States. This principle does not govern relations between the State exercising jurisdiction and an entity which is not recognized as a State. For this reason, it is difficult to speak of the right of officials of that entity to immunity or of the obligation, corresponding to that right, of the State exercising jurisdiction not to grant immunity. The situation is more complicated in the case of immunity of an official of a State that has been recognized by a significant segment of the international community but not by the State whose authorities are considering the question of immunity. The comment made above concerning the question of recognition in the context of the subject of immunity of officials of an unrecognized State is also applicable to the question of recognition in the context of the subject of immunity of unrecognized Heads of State and Heads of Government.

124. Any consideration of the role of recognition in the context of this topic must obviously include consideration of the substance of the question of recognition, including for instance the question of the declarative or constitutional character of recognition. This is not really part of the Commission's mandate on this topic. In this connection, the question is whether issues of recognition should in future be included within the framework of the topic under consideration and, moreover, whether any kind of provisions should be drafted on the role of recognition as related to the question of immunity of officials. It should be noted that the resolution of the Institute of International Law limits itself in this regard to a provision stating that the resolution "is without prejudice to the effect of recognition or non-recognition of a foreign state or government on application of its provisions".[236]

4. Family members

125. In practice, the question sometimes arises of the immunity of the members of the family of a Head of State (naturally this immunity can be only personal in nature). In 1991, in the case *Marcos et Marcos c. Office fédéral de la police*, the Swiss Federal Tribunal recognized the immunity of Imelda Marcos, the wife of the former President of the Philippines: "Customary international law has always granted to Heads of State, as well as to the members of their family and their household visiting a foreign State, the privileges of personal inviolability and immunity from criminal jurisdiction ... This jurisdictional immunity is also granted to a Head of State who is visiting a foreign State in a private capacity and also extends, in such circumstances, to the closest accompanying family members as well as to the senior members of his household staff."[237] Similarly, but this

[232] "The Legal Position in International Law of Heads of State, Heads of Government and Foreign Ministers", p. 34.

[233] *Kadic v. Karadzic*, Court of Appeals for the Second Circuit, Judgment of 13 October 1995, 70 F.3d 232, 64 USLW 2231, p. 244.

[234] *United States v. Noriega and Others*, United States District Court, Southern District of Florida, 8 June 1990, reproduced in *ILR*, vol. 99, pp. 143–183.

[235] *Lafontant v. Aristide*, United States District Court, Eastern District of New York, 27 January 1994, reproduced in *ILR*, vol. 103, pp. 581–593. It should be noted that, in the question of recognition in particular, in the context of the consideration of the question of immunity, the American and British courts rely on the opinion of the Executive. For example, in the judgment of the British Court of Appeal in the case *Sayce v. Ameer Ruler Sadig Mohammad Abbasi Bahawalpur State*, Judge Somervell noted: "Our State cannot speak with two voices on such a matter, the judiciary saying one thing, the executive another. Our sovereign has to decide whom he will recognize as a fellow sovereign in the family of States; and the relations of the foreign States with ours in the matter of State immunities must flow from that decision alone." *Sayce v. Ameer Ruler Sadig Mohammad Abbasi Bahawalpur State*, Court of Appeal, England, 20 May 1952, reproduced in *ILR*, vol. 19, p. 215.

[236] *Annuaire de l'Institut de droit international*, vol. 69 (2000–2001), pp. 680–692, article 12, at p. 685.

[237] *Marcos et Marcos c. Office fédéral de la police, Revue suisse de droit international et européen*, 1991, p. 535 (English version in *ILR*, vol. 102, p. 201).

time in a civil case, the immunity of the wife of the President of Mexico was recognized by a United States court in 1988 in *Kline v. Kaneko*. The court stated that "[u]nder general principles of international law, heads of State and immediate members of their families are immune from suit".[238] In 1978, another United States court recognized the immunity from jurisdiction of the son of the Queen of England, Prince Charles, in the case *Kilroy v. Windsor (Prince Charles, the Prince of Wales) and Others*.[239]

126. However, there are also instances in which the immunity of the members of the family of a Head of State was not recognized by the courts. This was the case in *Mobutu v. SA Cotoni*.[240] In 1988, the ruling in this case of the Belgian Civil Court noted, *inter alia*, that the children of the President of Zaire had already attained their majority and thus were "distinct from their father and cannot in any case benefit from the same immunity as he is entitled to benefit from".[241] Similarly, in 2001 in the case *W. v. Prince of Liechtenstein*, the Austrian Supreme Court did not recognize the immunity of the sister and two brothers of the Head of State of Liechtenstein, because they were not close members of the family of the Head of State forming part of his household and entitled to immunity under customary international law.[242]

127. It should first be noted that, in the two cases mentioned in which the courts declined to recognize the immunity of members of the family of the Head of State, the rulings were based on the fact that the persons concerned were not among the immediate family of the Head of State and were not dependent on him. Perhaps the courts would have recognized the immunity of these persons if they had been family members more closely connected with the Head of State and forming part of his household. This is clearly indicated by the passage from the ruling of the Austrian court quoted above. Secondly, in three of the five rulings mentioned, the courts noted that immunity is granted to members of the family of a Head of State on the basis of customary international law. In the few cases on record where national legislation establishes the immunity of a Head of State (United Kingdom, Australia), it also establishes the immunity of family members forming part of his household[243] and of his spouse.[244] It will also be recalled that the immunity from the jurisdiction of the receiving State of members of the family of a diplomatic agent forming part of his household, of members of the family of a consular officer forming part of his household, of members of the family of a representative of the sending State in a special mission and of members of the family of a representative of a State to an international organization forming part of his household is established, respectively, in article 37, paragraph 1, of the 1961 Vienna Convention on Diplomatic Relations, in article 53, paragraph 2, of the 1963 Vienna Convention on Consular Relations, in article 39, paragraph 1, of the Convention on Special Missions and in article 36, paragraph 1, of the 1975 Vienna Convention on the Representation of States in Their Relations with International Organizations of a Universal Character.

128. The doctrine reflects the various viewpoints. It is noted in *Oppenheim's International Law* that a comparison of the status of members of the family of a Head of State with the position of the family of a diplomatic agent indicates that members of the family of a Head of State forming part of his household enjoy immunity from the jurisdiction of the host State.[245] The fact that members of the family of a Head of State and Head of Government are protected by immunity is also acknowledged by P. Gully-Hart.[246] In the view of A. Watts, the immediate family of a Head of State may enjoy immunity, but on the basis of comity and not of international law.[247] This view is endorsed by S. Sucharitkul.[248] The view that, if the members of the family of a Head of State are also granted immunity, it is on the basis only of international comity and not of international law was supported in the resolution of the Institute of International Law.[249]

129. Does the Commission need to consider the subject of immunity of members of the family of a Head of State (and possibly of other individuals enjoying personal immunity) under the topic? The Special Rapporteur has doubts on this score, because—strictly speaking—the subject of immunity of the members of the family of officials is outside the scope of this topic.

C. Summary

130. The contents of this chapter of this preliminary report can be summarized in the following statements:

(*a*) This topic covers only immunity of officials of one State from national (and not international) criminal (and not civil) jurisdiction of another State (and not of the State served by the official);

(*b*) It is suggested that the topic should cover all State officials;

(*c*) An attempt may be made to define the concept "State official" for this topic or to define which officials are covered by this concept for the purposes of this topic;

[238] Supreme Court (New York County), *Kline v. Kaneko*, Judgment of 31 October 1988, 141 Misc.2d 787, p. 788.

[239] United States District Court for the Northern District of Ohio, Eastern Division, 7 December 1978, *ILR*, vol. 81, pp. 605–607.

[240] Civil Court of Brussels (Attachment Judgment), 29 December 1988, reproduced in *ILR*, vol. 91, pp. 259–263.

[241] *Ibid.*

[242] Supreme Court, Judgment of 14 February 2001, 7 Ob 316/00x, para. 11.

[243] Section 20 (1) of the British State Immunity Act of 20 July 1978, reproduced in *ILM*, vol. 17, 1978, p. 1123.

[244] Section 36 (1) (*b*) of the Australian Foreign States Immunities Act of 1985, reproduced in A. Dickinson, R. Lindsay and J. P. Loonam (eds.), *op. cit.*, p. 483.

[245] Jenning and Watts, *op. cit.*, pp. 1039 and 1040.

[246] "The function of State and diplomatic privileges and immunities in international cooperation in criminal matters: the position in Switzerland", p. 1335.

[247] Watts mentions the difference between members of the family of a Head of State and members of the family of a Head of Government and of a minister for foreign affairs, and between the status of such persons, depending on whether they are present in the host State on an official or a private visit. *Loc. cit.*, pp. 75–80 and 110–112.

[248] *Yearbook ... 1989*, vol. II (Part Two), pp. 102–103, paras. 446–450.

[249] *Annuaire de l'Institut de droit international*, vol. 69 (2000–2001), pp. 680–692, article 5, at p. 682.

(*d*) The high-ranking officials who enjoy personal immunity by virtue of their post include primarily Heads of State, Heads of Government and ministers for foreign affairs;

(*e*) An attempt may be made to determine which other high-ranking officials, in addition to the threesome mentioned, enjoy immunity *ratione personae*. It will be possible to single out such officials from among all high-ranking officials, if the criterion or criteria justifying special status for this category of high-ranking officials can be defined;

(*f*) It is doubtful whether it will be advisable to give further consideration within the framework of this topic to the question of recognition and the question of immunity of members of the family of high-ranking officials.

CHECKLIST OF DOCUMENTS OF THE SIXTIETH SESSION

Document	*Title*	*Observations and references*
A/CN.4/587	Provisional agenda for the sixtieth session	Mimeographed. For agenda as adopted, see *Yearbook ... 2008*, vol. II (Part Two).
A/CN.4/588	Topical summary of the discussion held in the Sixth Committee of the General Assembly during its sixty-second session, prepared by the Secretariat	Mimeographed.
A/CN.4/589 [and Corr.1]	Fourth report on the effects of armed conflicts on treaties, by Mr. Ian Brownlie, Special Rapporteur	Reproduced in the present volume.
A/CN.4/590 and Add.1–3	Protection of persons in the event of disasters: Memorandum by the Secretariat	Mimeographed.
A/CN.4/591	Fifth report on shared natural resources: transboundary groundwaters, by Mr. Chusei Yamada, Special Rapporteur	Reproduced in the present volume.
A/CN.4/592 and Add.1	Effects of armed conflicts on treaties: Comments and observations received from international organizations	*Idem.*
A/CN.4/593 and Add.1	Responsibility of international organizations: Comments and observations received from international organizations	*Idem.*
A/CN.4/594	Fourth report on the expulsion of aliens, by Mr. Maurice Kamto, Special Rapporteur	*Idem.*
A/CN.4/595 and Add.1	Shared natural resources: comments and observations by Governments on the draft articles on the law of transboundary aquifers	*Idem.*
A/CN.4/596	Immunity of State officials from foreign criminal jurisdiction: Memorandum by the Secretariat	Mimeographed.
A/CN.4/597	Sixth report on responsibility of international organizations, by Mr. Giorgio Gaja, Special Rapporteur	Reproduced in the present volume.
A/CN.4/598	Preliminary report on the protection of persons in the event of disasters, by Mr. Eduardo Valencia-Ospina, Special Rapporteur	*Idem.*
A/CN.4/599	The obligation to extradite or prosecute (*aut dedere aut judicare*): Comments and observations received from Governments	*Idem.*
A/CN.4/600	Thirteenth report on reservations to treaties, by Mr. Alain Pellet, Special Rapporteur	*Idem.*
A/CN.4/601	Preliminary report on immunity of State officials from foreign criminal jurisdiction, by Mr. Roman Anatolevich Kolodkin, Special Rapporteur	*Idem.*
A/CN.4/602 and Add.1	Filling of casual vacancies in the Commission: Note by the Secretariat	A/CN.4/602 reproduced in the present volume. A/CN.4/602/ Add.1 mimeographed.
A/CN.4/603	Third report on the obligation to extradite or prosecute (*aut dedere aut judicare*) by Zdzislaw Galicki, Special Rapporteur	Reproduced in the present volume.
A/CN.4/L.721	Note by the Chairperson of the Working Group on effects of armed conflicts on treaties: Draft article 8	*Idem.*
A/CN.4/L.722	Shared natural resources: Note on a preamble by the Special Rapporteur	Mimeographed.
A/CN.4/L.723 [and Corr.1–3]	Reservations to Treaties: Titles and Texts of the Draft Guidelines adopted by the Drafting Committee on 7, 9, 13, 14, 16 and 28 May 2008	*Idem.*

Document	*Title*	*Observations and references*
A/CN.4/L.724	The law of transboundary aquifers: Title and texts of the preamble and draft articles 1 to 19 on the law of transboundary aquifers adopted, on second reading, by the Drafting Committee	*Idem.*
A/CN.4/L.725 and Add.1	Responsibility of international organizations: Titles and texts of articles 46, 47, 48, 49 [48], 50 [49], 51 [50], 52 [51] and 53, provisionally adopted by the Drafting Committee on 21, 22, 28, 29 and 30 May 2008	*Idem.*
A/CN.4/L.726	Effects of armed conflicts on treaties: report of the Working Group	*Idem.*
A/CN.4/L.727/Rev.1 and Add.1	Effects of armed conflicts on treaties: Texts of draft articles 1, 2, 3, 4, 5, 6 [5 *bis*], 7 [5], 8, 9 [8 *bis*], 10 [8 *ter*], 11 [8 *quater*], 12 [9], 13 [10], 14 [11], 15, 16 [12], 17 [13], 18 [14] provisionally adopted on first reading by the Drafting Committee on 4 June 2008	*Idem.*
A/CN.4/L.728	Draft Report of the International Law Commission on the Work of its Sixtieth Session: chapter I (Introduction)	*Idem.* For the adopted text, see *Official Records of the General Assembly, Sixty-third Session, Supplement No. 10* (A/63/10). The final text appears in *Yearbook ... 2008*, vol. II (Part Two).
A/CN.4/L.729	*Idem*: Chapter II (Summary of the work of the Commission at its sixtieth session)	*Idem.*
A/CN.4/L.730	*Idem*: Chapter III (Specific issues on which comments would be of particular interest to the Commission)	*Idem.*
A/CN.4/L.731 and Add.1–2	*Idem*: Chapter IV (Shared natural resources)	*Idem.*
A/CN.4/L.732 and Add.1–2 [and Add.2/Corr.1]	*Idem*: Chapter V (Effects of armed conflicts on treaties)	*Idem.*
A/CN.4/L.733 and Add.1–5 [and Corr.1, Add.3/Corr.1, Add.4/Corr.1 and Add.5/Corr.1]	*Idem*: Chapter VI (Reservations to treaties)	*Idem.*
A/CN.4/L.734/Rev.1, A/CN.4/L.734/Add.1, A/CN.4/L.734/Add.2 and A/CN.4/L.734/Add.2/Corr.1	*Idem*: Chapter VII (Responsibility of international organizations)	*Idem.*
A/CN.4/L.735 and Add.1	*Idem*: Chapter VIII (Expulsion of aliens)	*Idem.*
A/CN.4/L.736	*Idem*: Chapter IX (Protection of persons in the event of disasters)	*Idem.*
A/CN.4/L.737 and Add.1	*Idem*: Chapter X (Immunity of State officials from foreign criminal jurisdiction)	*Idem.*
A/CN.4/L.738 and Add.1	*Idem*: Chapter XI (The obligation to extradite or prosecute (*aut dedere aut judicare*))	*Idem.*
A/CN.4/L.739 [and Corr.1]	Reservations to Treaties: Text of draft guidelines 2.6.5, 2.6.11, 2.6.12 and 2.8 provisionally adopted by the Drafting Committee on 5 June 2008	Mimeographed.
A/CN.4/L.740	Reservations to Treaties: Text of draft guidelines 2.8.1, 2.8.2, 2.8.3, 2.8.4, 2.8.5, 2.8.6, 2.8.7, 2.8.8, 2.8.9, 2.8.10, 2.8.11 and 2.8.12 provisionally adopted by the Drafting Committee on 7, 8, 9, 10, 16 and 22 July 2008	*Idem.*
A/CN.4/L.741	Draft Report of the International Law Commission on the Work of its Sixtieth Session: chapter XII (Other decisions and conclusions of the Commission)	*Idem.* For the adopted text, see *Official Records of the General Assembly, Sixty-third Session, Supplement No. 10* (A/63/10). The final text appears in *Yearbook ... 2008*, vol. II (Part Two).
A/CN.4/L.742	Report of the Planning Group	Mimeographed.
A/CN.4/SR.2956–A/CN.4/SR.2997	Provisional summary records of the 2956th to 2997th meetings	*Idem.* The final text appears in *Yearbook ... 2008*, vol. I.